*German Language
and Literature:
Seven Essays*

German Language and Literature:
Seven Essays

Edited by
Karl S. Weimar
Chairman, German Department
Brown University

PRENTICE-HALL, INC., *Englewood Cliffs, New Jersey*

Library of Congress Cataloging in Publication Data

WEIMAR, KARL SIEGFRIED, *date.*
    German language and literature.

    Includes bibliographies.
      1. German literature—Addresses, essays, lectures.
2. German language—Addresses, essays, lectures.
I. Title.
PT91.W4   830'.9   73-20078
ISBN   0-13-354084-7
ISBN   0-13-354076-6 (pbk.)

Printed in the United States of America

10 9 8 7 6 5 4 3 2 1

PRENTICE-HALL INTERNATIONAL, INC., *London*
PRENTICE-HALL OF AUSTRALIA, PTY. LTD., *Sydney*
PRENTICE-HALL OF CANADA, LTD., *Toronto*
PRENTICE-HALL OF INDIA PRIVATE LIMITED, *New Delhi*
PRENTICE-HALL OF JAPAN, INC., *Tokyo*

ACKNOWLEDGMENTS

Nationale Forschungs- und Gedenkstätten der klassischen deutschen Literatur, Weimar, German Democratic Republic, for Goethe's library at Weimar (p. xiv) and the Büchner wanted-poster (p. 222).

Landesbibliothek Kassel, Federal Republic of Germany, for the manuscript page from *Hildebrandslied* (p. 64).

Historia-Photo, Bad Sachsa, Federal Republic of Germany, for the *Laokoon* title page and manuscript page (p. 124).

Emil Vollmer Verlag, Wiesbaden, Federal Republic of Germany, for the E. T. A. Hoffmann self-portrait (p. 184).

Insel Verlag, Wiesbaden, Federal Republic of Germany, for the manuscript page from Rilke's *Sonette an Orpheus* (p. 308).

Contents

PREFACE, *xi*

THE GERMAN LANGUAGE, *1*
William G. Moulton

Introduction, *1*

Sounds and Spelling, *7*

Grammar, *14*

History, *34*

GERMAN LITERATURE TO GOETHE, *65*
George Schulz-Behrend

Old High German Literature, *65*

The Post-Carolingian Era. Cluny, *69*

The Age of Courtly Literature ca. 1150–ca. 1250, *72*

The Late Middle Ages 1250–1550, *85*

Humanism and the Reformation 1400–1624, *90*

The Age of the Baroque: Counterreformation, Absolutism
1600–1720, *95*

The Age of Enlightenment 1720–1750,   *104*

THE AGE OF GOETHE,   *125*
Wolfgang Leppmann

Johann Joachim Winckelmann,   *128*

Gotthold Ephraim Lessing,   *131*

Johann Gottfried Herder,   *136*

Friedrich Gottlieb Klopstock,   *138*

Christoph Martin Wieland,   *139*

Johann Wolfgang Goethe 1749–1788,   *141*

Johann Wolfgang Goethe 1788–1832,   *150*

Faust,   *154*

Friedrich Schiller,   *158*

Heinrich von Kleist,   *165*

BETWEEN THE 18th AND 19th CENTURIES: HÖLDERLIN,   *175*
Michael Hamburger

THE ROMANTICS,   *185*
Karl S. Weimar

The Brothers Schlegel,   *185*

Novalis,   *190*

Clemens Brentano,   *194*

E. T. A. Hoffmann,   *204*

Ludwig Tieck,   *208*

Josef Freiherr von Eichendorff,   *211*

Louis Charles Adelaide Chamisso,   *214*

GERMAN LITERATURE IN THE AGE OF EUROPEAN REALISM, 223

J. P. Stern

Franz Grillparzer, *225*

Friedrich Hebbel, *228*

Johann Nestroy, *234*

Georg Büchner, *236*

Heinrich Heine, *245*

Eduard Mörike, *257*

Adalbert Stifter, *264*

Gottfried Keller, *269*

Theodor Fontane, *276*

Stories of Charisma and Fate, *286*

Friedrich Wilhelm Nietzsche, *289*

MODERN GERMAN LITERATURE 1900–1966, *309*

Adolf D. Klarmann

GENERAL BIBLIOGRAPHY, *355*

INDEX, *361*

Preface

Like the anthology, the collection of essays on a single grand subject is as indispensable as it is invariably unsatisfactory. There is always justification for a new attempt to present a fresh view reflecting revaluations and shifts in emphasis, to offer the possibility of different approaches and to suggest reinterpretations and reorientations. This collection of essays—and there have been surprisingly few attempts to survey in a manner more critical than merely historical the language and literature of the German area—is intended to guide and stimulate the student whether his field is German, or European or Comparative studies, or whether he is inside or outside the university, and to provide that more advanced student who considers himself already to be a specialist with a more extensive background and a wider perspective with which to focus anew his attention on his own field. It is a formidable undertaking to survey the vast and complex panorama of language and literature that stretches over one thousand six hundred years from the earliest document in the Gothic language, now on display in the library at Uppsala, to the poetess and the novelist who are the most recent German Nobel Prize winners (1966 and 1972).

The seven contributors have approached their fields differently: the responsibility for the divisions and demarcations is the editor's alone. Professor Moulton outlines the grammar, history, dialectology, phonology, orthography, and morphology of German with a bounty of contrastive examples and representative samples. Professors Schulz-Behrend and Klarmann proceed somewhat encyclopedically in accord with their times, the former working with a period of fourteen hundred years and the latter with a literature so recent and so much a part of us that any greater degree of selectivity and exclusion would seem too willfully arbitrary. Professor Leppmann has a thematic center, the incomparable figure of Goethe, around which he views the age. Mr. Hamburger considers only Hölderlin, but Hölderlin represents a critical marginal phenomenon between that which is no longer tenable and that which is not yet not possible. The Romantics have something uniquely in common, with both a determinable genesis and decline, which permits treatment apart. Professor Stern has chosen to look at a particular period and its European ambience by selecting only certain major representative figures. It is clear and inevitable that some omissions will occasion complaint, but it is hoped that a reasonable balance of critical and historical exposition has been maintained.

Two particular features should prove to be especially useful and attractive: many samples of text have been quoted to illustrate the style and the flavor of a work, or of a writer and his work, and in many cases new and original translations are offered. The selective bibliographies, which the contributors were invited to provide with some critical comment, are intended to provoke further exploration. Accountability for the general capsule bibliography, the selection of illustrations, and the index is the editor's.

KARL S. WEIMAR

*German Language
and Literature:
Seven Essays*

Goethe's library at Weimar.

The German Language

WILLIAM G. MOULTON
Princeton University

INTRODUCTION

German is one of the half dozen or so major world languages of literature and science. It is spoken throughout a large area in central Europe; from here it has been carried by migration to many other parts of the world. It is the official language of Germany, with some 70 million speakers; the official language of Austria, with some 7 million speakers; one of the two official languages (beside French) of the Grand Duchy of Luxembourg; and one of the four national languages of Switzerland, with some 3.5 million speakers. (The other national languages of Switzerland are French, ca. one million; Italian, ca. 300,000; and Romansh, ca. 50,000.) As part of this central area there are also some 1.7 million speakers of German in eastern France (in Alsace and Lorraine), and some 200,000 speakers in northern Italy (in Southern Tyrol). Up to the end of World War II this central area extended considerably farther to the east into what is now part of Poland (which still has an estimated 1.4 million speakers of German) and into Czechoslovakia. There were also—and

William G. Moulton received his A. B. from Princeton and his Ph. D. from Yale. He taught for ten years at Yale, for thirteen years at Cornell, and has been at Princeton since 1960. He received a Fulbright Research Award to The Netherlands in 1953–54, an ACLS Award for dialect research in Switzerland in 1958–59, and returned again to Switzerland in 1964–65 as a Guggenheim Fellow. Past President of the Linguistic Society, he is author of *The Sounds of English and German* (Chicago, 1962), *A Linguistic Guide to Language Learning* (New York: The MLA, 1966), as well as articles in linguistic journals.

to some extent still are—German "speech islands" in eastern Europe: in the former Baltic nations, and in Hungary, Yugoslavia, Rumania, and Russia. Outside of Europe there are German speech communities in many parts of the world, notably in Canada, the United States, Brazil, South Africa, and Australia.

As a written language (called in German the *Schriftsprache*), German is everywhere almost completely uniform. If we read a German book, it is often not possible to tell whether it was written by a German, an Austrian, or a Swiss. Occasionally, however, we find clues as to where the author comes from. If he refers to the month of January as *Jänner* rather than *Januar*, he is almost certainly an Austrian; and if for "interruption" he writes *der Unterbruch* rather than *die Unterbrechung*, he is almost certainly a Swiss. Very rarely there are also slight differences in spelling. If a word like that for "street" is spelled *Strasse* (with double *ss*) rather than *Straße* (with the special letter *ß*), the book was probably published in Switzerland—though some Swiss printers use *ß* just as the Germans and Austrians do. But these are all very minor differences; they are no greater than the differences that we find in English books written in the United States and in Great Britain. Here also we can often read for many pages without knowing whether the author is an American or an Englishman— though we will guess that he is an Englishman if he refers to the *bonnet* of an automobile (rather than the *hood*), or if he uses the spelling *favour* (rather than *favor*).

Though German as a written language is everywhere highly uniform, as a spoken language it exists in far more varieties than does the English of the United States. At one extreme is Standard German, called in German the *Hochsprache*. This is the variety that is used—or is supposed to be used—in radio and television, on stage and screen, in public lectures, and in schools and universities. It is based on the *Schriftsprache*, and rules for its pronunciation are carefully described in a book customarily called the *Siebs*, after its first editor, Theodor Siebs. In theory, at least, the *Siebs* gives the ideal form of Standard German as it "ought" to be pronounced; in practice, relatively few speakers attain this ideal since most of them show by their accents the general areas from which they come. Many speakers—including many of the highly educated— do not really *want* to use this "ideal" type of pronunciation, but prefer to speak a local variety of Standard German. Two outstanding examples are the first President of the German Federal Republic (after World War II), Theodor Heuss, and the first Chancellor, Konrad Adenauer. Both of them used a standard grammatical form of German; but Heuss spoke with a rich Swabian accent (he was born and raised in Württemberg), and Adenauer spoke with a rich Rhenish accent (he was born and raised in Cologne on the Rhine).

In some respects these regional differences in the pronunciation of Standard German are comparable to the regional differences that we find in the pronunciation of English in the United States. Three of our post-war presidents offer good examples. To anyone who had been around the country a bit, it was clear in the 1950's and 1960's that President Eisenhower came from the Midwest, President Kennedy from Boston, and President Johnson from Texas: each of them showed, by his accent, the general area in which he had been born and raised. In one respect, however, there is a sharp difference between Standard German and the English of the United States. For German there is a single, universally recognized standard of pronunciation—that of the *Siebs*—with a specific number of vowels and consonants, even though people do not pronounce them all in the same way. For the English of the United States, on the other hand, there simply *is* no single, universally recognized standard of pronunciation. Should the *o* of such words as *sorry, forest, borrow* be pronounced like the vowel of *far* or the vowel of *for*? Many millions of Americans use the one vowel, other millions the other—and both pronunciations are equally "standard." Should words like *cot, tot, pot* rhyme with words like *caught, taught, bought*? Many millions use the same vowel in both sets, others use different vowels—and both pronunciations are again equally "standard." This presence of a clear standard in German and the absence of it in American English is nicely reflected in the way pronunciation is indicated in the *Siebs* on the one hand and in most American dictionaries on the other. Most American dictionaries never tell the reader *directly* how to pronounce a given vowel or consonant; instead, they give him a number of key words illustrating the various vowels and consonants, and then they tell him to pronounce other words with the sounds he uses in these key words. The *Siebs*, in contrast, carefully describes the pronunciation of each Standard German vowel and consonant; and it lists all sorts of local pronunciations which are to be avoided.

If Standard German—the *Hochsprache*—represents one end of the scale, the other end is represented by a multitude of local dialects (*Dialekte*, or *Mundarten*). Though we are accustomed to using the term "dialect" in the United States, the meaning we give to it is very different from what it means in the German-speaking area. By and large, in the United States we seldom think that we ourselves speak a "dialect"; a "dialect" is usually thought of as a variety of speech spoken by people in some other part of the country, or in some other social class—particularly a lower social class. In the German-speaking area, on the other hand, there are many millions of people who willingly—even proudly—acknowledge that they speak a "dialect"; and the differences among dialects are so strong that in some parts of the area people who live perhaps no more than fifty miles apart cannot really understand each other if each speaks his local dialect. Furthermore, many of these millions can readily engage in what is called "code switching": they talk local dialect to a fellow-townsman, switch to Standard German (perhaps in a locally colored variety) in order to speak with an outsider, and then switch back to dialect again when the outsider has left. This sort of "code switching" exists in the United States (it has been observed, for example, in some Southern politicians), but it is quite rare. All of us can speak various *styles* of English—from the most formal to the most informal—but very few of us can switch back and forth between dialect and standard.

The Central European area in which German is spoken is shown on Map 1. Though this map looks simple enough, it needs a good deal of interpreting. First of all, the map seems to indicate that German is spoken in northern Belgium and most of Holland. Can this be correct? The answer we give will depend on whether we are referring to local dialects or to the standard language. If we are speaking of the standard language, then "German" stops abruptly at the western border of Germany. (Or almost. German is also used—beside French— as a standard language in Luxembourg.) The standard language on the other side of the border is not German but Netherlandic. (This is usually called "Flemish" in northern Belgium and "Dutch" in Holland; but these are merely two different names for one and the same standard language.) If, on the other hand, we are referring to local dialects, then it is entirely correct to say that one and the same language is spoken on both sides of the Dutch/German border. Indeed, if we consider only local dialects, we can start way down south in the Alps of Austria, northern Italy, and Switzerland, travel from village to village up through Germany to the North Sea coast of Holland, Belgium, and bit of adjacent France, and never find a point where the local language suddenly changes. The only way we will know that we have crossed the border from Germany into Holland, for example, is that the local people will suddenly start quoting prices in guilders and cents rather than in marks and pfennigs. We will of course find a sharp change in the local language if we wander off into the French-speaking part of Belgium or the Frisian-speaking part of Holland; but there is no sharp break at all at the actual political borders. Curiously enough, there is no generally accepted name for this single language which, at the level of local dialects, extends from the Alps of Switzerland, northern Italy, and Austria to the North Sea coast of France, Belgium, Holland, and Germany—though scholars sometimes refer to it as "Netherlandic-German."

Even if we disregard Holland and northern Belgium, the remaining "German" language area shown on Map 1 still needs a good deal of interpretation because of the many different relationships between, and attitudes toward, the standard language and local dialects. Within this area, the local dialects are customarily divided into two main types: "Low German" (*Niederdeutsch*, also popularly called *Plattdeutsch*), originally called "low" because it is spoken in the lowlands of the north; and "High German" (*Hochdeutsch*), originally called "high" because it is spoken in the highlands of the south. The standard language is clearly of the "High German" variety; and because of this the word "high" has gradually changed from a geographical term to a value term. That is to say, since a "higher" value is placed on the standard language, the term *Hochdeutsch* in popular usage now generally means simply "Standard German." Thus one can hear a farmer from southern Switzerland—whose local dialect is about as

North Sea

Baltic Sea

DENMARK

LOW GERMAN

POLAND

NETHERLANDS

(WEST)   (EAST)

GERMANY

BELGIUM

LUXEM-
BOURG

CZECHOSLOVAKIA

HIGH GERMAN

FRANCE

SWITZERLAND

AUSTRIA

HUNGARY

YUGOSLAVIA

ITALY

·················· BOUNDARY OF THE GERMAN LANGUAGE AREA
– – – – – – – NATIONAL BOUNDARIES

0   50   100   150   200 miles
0   50   100   200   300 kilometers

MAP 1

"high" as one can get—apologize for the fact that he is not very good at speaking *Hochdeutsch*, by which he means Standard German.

In northern Germany there are many millions of people who practice "code switching": they speak a Low German dialect with family and friends and local people, but Standard German with outsiders and on formal occasions. There are also many millions of the better educated who speak no dialect at all but *only* a local variety of Standard German. In the south, on the other hand, nearly everyone learns the local dialect as a child. In some areas, where the local dialect is close to Standard German, it is often not easy to draw a sharp line between local dialect and regional standard: speakers fall along a continuous scale between the two. In other areas, where the local dialect and the standard language are farther apart, code switching is very common. In southwestern Germany, for example, a Swabian is never in doubt as to whether he is speaking Swabian or Standard German; and he can speak the standard language in both formal and informal styles. When he *does* speak the standard, like President Heuss he makes no effort to rid his speech of all local Swabian features. Indeed, to get rid of all such features would—in his eyes—make him sound like a "Prussian"; and this he wants to avoid at all costs. So, too, does a Bavarian and, perhaps even more, an Austrian. Even in these areas, however, it is not always easy to draw a sharp line between dialect and local standard. There are perhaps millions—the better educated—who speak a southern variety of the standard language with complete ease, and many of them are no longer truly at home in the local dialect—though they all spoke it fluently as children. Other millions—the less well educated and those in rural areas—do not really handle Standard German very well and are at home only in the local dialect.

The language situation is very different when we come to the German-speaking areas of eastern France, in Alsace and part of Lorraine. Here all natives of the region speak a local dialect of German in daily life, but it is French that serves as their standard language. The respective spheres of the two languages are quite clearly marked out. Local dialect suffices for all normal daily needs; but as soon as one wants to talk about learned topics—history, philosophy, science, and the like—one can do so only in French. Local dialect is simply not considered suitable for such purposes; to try to use it in this way would seem ridiculous.

The language situation is also different in the German-speaking area of Switzerland. Here local dialects exist in great profusion, and they are used by all classes of the population for all purposes. There is no kind of topic—from the most humble to the most learned—that cannot be talked about in local dialect. Everyone is taught Standard German—often a very "Swiss"-sounding Standard German—in school, and the better educated can handle it with relative ease. But they do not like it; and even the best educated can generally speak only *formal* Standard German, seldom *informal* Standard German. In speaking to a foreigner—a German just as well as an American—they may try to make a joke in Standard German; but somehow it never sounds very funny. One can *really* make jokes only in local dialect.

Nevertheless, Standard German plays a very important role in the linguistic life of this part of the area. First and foremost, nearly all types of writing—personal letters, newspapers, books of all sorts, official publications—are written in Standard German. The only exceptions are captions on cartoons, a few humorous publications, and a bit of dialect literature (which very few people read). *Spoken* Standard German, on the other hand, is limited to a very few types of clearly defined formal situations. Church services and university lectures are always given in Standard German; but if a Swiss goes up to talk with the minister or the professor afterwards, he would not dream of talking anything but local dialect. Radio news broadcasts are given in Standard German; but informal programs for the housewife are often given in dialect. As for meetings of the cantonal parliaments, customs vary: in most cantons Standard German is used, but even here some cantons use dialect.

The language situation within this "German"-speaking area of central Europe is very complicated. How does it affect the poor foreigner who has "learned German?" Let us assume that he has *really* learned Standard German, as it is taught in most American schools and colleges, and not some sort of pseudo American-German. If he goes to eastern France, his German will do him little good; he will get along better if he speaks French—or even English. Elsewhere, however, he will have little trouble. By and large, he will find it easier to understand people in northern Germany, somewhat harder to understand speakers in southern Germany, Austria, and Switzerland; and he will find it easier to understand speakers in cities, harder to understand speakers in rural areas. Almost everywhere, however, people will understand *him*—provided he has really learned to speak good Standard German.

SOUNDS AND SPELLING

The relationship between a writing system and the sound system which it symbolizes is customarily called the *fit* of the writing system. If there is a one-to-one correspondence between the units of the sound system (the *phonemes* of the language) and the units of the writing system (the *letters* of the alphabet used), so that each letter always represents the same phoneme and each phoneme is always written with the same letter, the fit is 100 per cent. Though the fit of the German writing system is remarkably good (much better than that of our often whimsical English writing system), it is still far from perfect. In discussing the sounds of German we therefore need to supplement the regular writing system with a phonemic spelling that has perfect fit. Where the two might be confused, we shall write the phonemic spelling between slant lines (/ /), the regular spelling in italics.

Vowels

Standard German, as described in the *Siebs*, has the following 18 vowel phonemes (monophthongs and diphthongs), plus a nineteenth vowel (of marginal status) that is described below:

Checked	Free	Free	
Lax, short	Tense, long	Diphthongal	Unstressed
i ü u	ī ǖ ū		
e ö o	ē ȫ ō	oi	ə
a	ā	ai au	

The first seven vowels are *checked* (they occur only before consonants); they are also *lax* (pronounced with relatively little muscular tension); and they are *short*. The next seven vowels are *free* (they can occur before consonants, before vowels, and word-finally); they are also *tense* (pronounced with relatively great muscular tension); and (at least in stressed syllables) they are *long*. The next three vowels are *diphthongs* (they are not "steady state" sounds but glide from one vowel position to another); they are also *free*. All of these vowels can occur in both stressed and unstressed syllables. The 18th vowel /ə/ occurs only in unstressed syllables.

PHONETIC CLASSIFICATION

According to the position of the tongue in the mouth when they are pronounced, the vowels /i e a o u/ and /ī ē ā ō ū/ can be diagrammed as follows:

	Front Spread		Back Rounded
High	ī i		ū u
Mid	ē e		ō o
Low		a ā	

Front vowels are pronounced with the tongue humped toward the front of the mouth; *back* vowels are pronounced with the tongue humped toward the back of the mouth. *High* vowels are pronounced with the hump relatively high in the mouth; *low* vowels are pronounced with little or no hump in the tongue; *mid* vowels occupy a midway position. Front vowels are pronounced with *spread* lips; back vowels are pronounced with *rounded* lips.

The vowels /ū ü ȫ ö/ are often called *mixed*:

/ū/ has the front tongue position of /ī/, the rounded lips of /ū/
/ü/ has the front tongue position of /i/, the rounded lips of /u/
/ȫ/ has the front tongue position of /ē/, the rounded lips of /ō/
/ö/ has the front tongue position of /e/, the rounded lips of /o/

COMPARISON WITH ENGLISH

The following comparisons are only approximate, since the vowel phonemes of English are pronounced in different ways in different localities:

The checked vowels /i e a o u/ of German *mit, Bett, hat, Gott, Busch* /'mit 'bet 'hat 'got 'buš/ "with, bed, has, god, bush" are much like the vowels of English *mitt, bet, hut, caught, bush*. (The symbol /'/ is used to mark the beginning of a stressed syllable.)

The free vowels /ī ē ā ō ū/ of German *sie, See, sah, so, Schuh* /'zī 'zē 'zā 'zō 'šū/ "she, sea, saw, so, shoe" are much like the vowels of English *see, say, spa, so, shoe*. But the vowels of German *sie, Schuh, See, so* are "steady state" vowels (monophthongal), whereas the vowels of English *see, shoe*, and especially *say, so*, tend to be more or less strongly diphthongal.

The diphthongs /ai oi au/ of German *bei, Heu, Bau* /'bai 'hoi 'bau/ "by, hay, building" are much like the diphthongs of English *by, boy, bough*.

The unstressed /ə/ of German *beginnen, redet* /bə'ginən 'rēdət/ "begin, speaks" is much like the unstressed vowel of English *begin, raided*.

The German vowels /ū ü ȫ ö/, as in *fühle, fülle, Höhle, Hölle* /'fūlə 'fülə 'hȫlə 'hölə/ "(I) feel, (I) fill, cave, hell" do not correspond to any vowels of English.

VOWEL ALTERNATIONS

Short /u o a/, long /ū ō ā/, and diphthongal /au/ often alternate with short /ü ö e/, long /ū ȫ ē/, and diphthongal /oi/, respectively. This alternation is customarily called "umlaut."

EXAMPLES

Short			Long			Diphthongal		
singular	plural		singular	plural		singular	plural	
Mutter	*Mütter*	mother(s)	*Bruder*	*Brüder*	brother(s)	*Braut*	*Bräute*	bride(s)
Tochter	*Töchter*	daughter(s)	*Sohn*	*Söhne*	son(s)			
Mann	*Männer*	man, men	*Vater*	*Väter*	father(s)			

Note the special "umlaut" spellings *ä* (*Männer*), *ä* (*Väter*), *äu* (*Bräute*) for /e ē oi/. Where *ä* stands for a short vowel, as in *Männer* /'menər/, it always represents the regular short vowel /e/; but where *ä* stands for a long vowel, as in *Väter*, the *Siebs* prescribes the special long vowel /ɛ̄/: /'fɛ̄tər/, with the quality of short /e/ but long. However, many speakers of German usually pronounce it as regular long /ē/: /'fētər/. They use the special /ɛ̄/ only as the name of the letter *ä*, to distinguish such pairs of words as *sie geben* /'gēbən/ "they give" vs. *sie gäben* /'gɛ̄bən/ "they would give," and in a few exclamations such as *ätsch*! /'ɛ̄tš/ "shame!"

SPELLINGS

The German alphabet has only seven (or eight) vowel letters (*i, e, a, o, u, ü, ö*, plus *ä*) for the task of symbolizing 14 (or 15) vowel phonemes (short /i e a o u ü ö/, long /ī ē ā ō ū ǖ ȫ/, plus /ɛ̄/). It accomplishes this task rather successfully by using the following devices:

1. A vowel is *short* if it is followed by a double consonant letter; it is *long* if it is followed by a single consonant letter:

Short		Long		Short		Long	
still	silent	*Stil*	style	*Stille*	silence	*Stile*	styles
wenn	if	*wen*	whom	*Betten*	beds	*beten*	to pray
Kamm	comb	*kam*	came	*schaffe*	(I) work	*Schafe*	sheep
Stoff	material	*Hof*	court	*offen*	open	*Ofen*	stove
dumm	dumb	*Hut*	hat	*Busse*	buses	*Buße*	atonement
dünn	thin	*schwül*	sultry	*Hütte*	hut	*Hüte*	hats
Böll	(name)	*Öl*	oil	*öffnen*	to open	*Öfen*	stoves

In this respect, *ck* counts as the doubled form of *k*: short *Hacken* "heels," long *Haken* "hook"; *tz* as the doubled form of *z*: short *putzen* "to clean," long *duzen* "to call someone *du*"; and *ss* as the doubled form of *ß*: short *Masse* "mass," long *Maße* "measurements." By exception, a number of very common words have a short vowel followed by only a single consonant letter: *in* "in," *es* "it," *das* "that," *ob* "whether," *um* "around." Because there is no doubled form of *ch*, the difference between short and long vowels before this consonant is often not clearly symbolized: *Dach, noch, Bruch* "roof, still, fracture" have short vowels; *nach, hoch, Buch* "after, high, book" have long vowels.

2. A vowel is *long* when it has an (unpronounced!) *h* written after it. Contrast long *ihnen, stehlen, Kahn, wohnen, Ruhm* "to them, to steal, boat, to live, fame," vs. short *innen, stellen, kann, Wonne, dumm* "inside, to place, can, bliss, dumb."

3. A vowel is *long* when it is written double. Contrast long *Beet, Staat, Boot* "flower bed, state, boat," vs. short *Bett, statt, Gott* "bed (for sleeping), instead, god." In this respect, *ie* counts as the doubled form of *i*: contrast long *Miete* "rent" vs. short *Mitte* "middle."

4. A vowel (except unstressed *e*) is *long* when it stands at the end of a word:

Schi, je, ja, so, zu "ski, ever, yes, so, to," and also *Nazi, Sofa, Otto, Zulu* "Nazi, sofa, Otto, Zulu."

The diphthong /ai/ is usually spelled *ei: bei* "by," *nein* "no," *Seite* "side"; but sometimes *ai: Saite* "string (of an instrument)," *Kaiser* "kaiser." The diphthong /au/ is spelled *au: Haus* "house," *Maus* "mouse." The diphthong /oi/ is spelled *eu: Heu* "hay," *heute* "today"; but *äu* when it is the umlaut of /au/: *Häuser* "houses," *Mäuse* "mice."

Unstressed /ə/ is spelled *e: beginnen* /bə'ginən/ "to begin," *wartete* /'vartətə/ "waited."

German Consonants

	Labial	Apical	Palatal	Velar
Stops	p, b	t, d		k, g
Fricatives	f, v		[ç ~ x]	
Sibilants		s, z	š, ž	
Nasals	m	n		ŋ
Other		l r j h		

Note the six pairs of consonants separated by a comma: /p t k f s š/ are FORTIS (pronounced with strong muscular tension) and VOICELESS (pronounced without simultaneous vibration of the vocal cords); /b d g v z ž/ are LENIS (pronounced with weak muscular tension) and usually VOICED (pronounced with simultaneous vibration of the vocal cords). (The *Siebs* prescribes that the lenis consonants should always be voiced; but most south German, Austrian, and Swiss speakers pronounce them as voiceless.)

COMPARISON WITH ENGLISH

Most of the consonants are pronounced like those of English. /š/ and /ž/ correspond to English *sh* and *z* in *ash* and *azure*, though the German sounds are pronounced with more lip rounding than in English; German /ž/ is rare and occurs only in foreign words, for example, *Garage* /ga'rāžə/ "garage." /ŋ/ corresponds to English *ng* in *sing*; note that a German word like *Finger* /'fiŋər/ "finger" has only /ŋ/, and not the /ŋ/ + /g/ of English "finger." /j/ corresponds to English *y* in "yes," cf. German *ja* /'jā/ "yes."

The sound [ç] is a voiceless palatal fricative, produced by forcing breath through a narrow opening between the middle of the tongue and the hard palate; the sound [x] is a voiceless velar fricative, produced by forcing breath through a narrow opening between the back of the tongue and the soft palate (the "velum"). [ç] and [x] function as a unit in German, and are therefore both spelled *ch*. [x] occurs only after the vowels /a o u ā ō ū au/; [ç] occurs after all other vowels, after the consonants /n/, /l/, /r/, and initially:

[x]			[ç]			[ç]		
/a/	*Dach*	roof	/e/	*Dächer*	roofs	/n/	*manch*	many a
/o/	*Loch*	hole	/ö/	*Löcher*	holes	/l/	*solch*	such
/u/	*Bruch*	fracture	/ü/	*Brüche*	fractures	/r/	*durch*	through
/ā/	*nach*	after	/ē̜/	*nächst-*	next	(initial)	*China*	China
/ō/	*hoch*	high	/ȫ/	*höchst-*	highest		*Chemie*	chemistry
/ū/	*Buch*	book	/ū/	*Bücher*	books	(but South German /k-/ in
/au/	*Brauch*	custom	/oi/	*Bräuche*	customs		*China*	/ˈkīnā/,
							Chemie	/kēˈmī/, etc.)

[ç] is also used in the diminutive suffix *-chen*, regardless of what precedes: *Mädchen* /ˈmēt-çən/ "girl," *Frauchen* /ˈfrau-çən/ "(dog's) mistress," *bißchen* /ˈbis-çən/ "(a) bit."

German /l/ is always a "clear" *l*, with the tongue flat, in contrast to the typical "dark" *l* of American English in which the back of the tongue is humped up toward the velum (giving what is called technically a "velarized *l*").

German /r/ is quite unlike the usual *r* of American English. The *Siebs* prescribes that /r/ be pronounced in all positions as a tongue-tip trill or flap, or a uvular trill or fricative. (A tongue-tip trill is like the *rrr* we sometimes use to imitate a telephone bell or a policeman's whistle; a tongue-tip flap is like the very quick *t* most Americans pronounce in such a word as *city*. A uvular trill or fricative is made in the back of the mouth, by the back of the tongue and the uvula opposite it; it is the kind of *r* also generally used in French and many other languages.) Most speakers, however, use this full pronunciation of /r/ only when it is followed by a vowel: *rund*, "round," *Tiere* "animals," *lehren* "to teach," *bessere* "better ones." When it is not followed by a vowel, they use a sound much like the *a* of English *sofa*. This "vocalized *r*" therefore occurs in such words as *Tier* "animal," *lehrt* "teaches," *besser* "better."

CONSONANT ALTERNATIONS

The voiced stops and fricatives /b d g v z/ occur freely in the middle of words before vowels, but they are unvoiced to /p t k f s/ in three positions: (1) at the end of a word, (2) before *s*, and (3) before *t*:

Medially	(1) Finally	(2) Before s	(3) Before t
/b/ in *Gräber*	but /p/ in *das Grab*	*des Grabs*	
geben	*gab*	*du gibst*	*er gibt*
/d/ in *Räder*	but /t/ in *das Rad*	*des Rads*	
laden	*lud*	*du lädst*	*er lädt*
/g/ in *Tage*	but /k/ in *der Tag*	*des Tags*	
biegen	*bog*	*du biegst*	*er biegt*
/v/ in *Detektive*	but /f/ in *der Detektiv*	*des Detektivs*	
versklaven		*du versklavst*	*er versklavt*
/z/ in *Gase*	but /s/ in *das Gas*		
lesen	*las*		*er liest*

Though the *Siebs* prescribes the unvoicing of /g/ to /k/ in most positions, as above, in the suffix -*ig* it prescribes unvoicing to [ç]:

/g/ in *Könige*	but [ç] in *der Königs*	*des Königs*	
reinigen		*du reinigst*	*er reinigt*

This double treatment of /g/ represents a compromise between common usage in the north and the south. Many north Germans unvoice /g/ in all positions to [ç~x]: not only in *der König* /'kȫniç/, *er reinigt* /'rainiçt/, but also in *der Tag* /'tāx/, *er biegt* /'bīçt/. And most south Germans, Austrians, and Swiss unvoice /g/ in all positions to /k/: not only in *der Tag* /'tāk/, *er biegt* /'bīkt/, but also in *der König* /'kȫnik/, *er reinigt* /'rainikt/.

SPELLINGS

S is the most overworked letter in the German alphabet. It is the only symbol German has for /z/: *sehen* /'zēən/ "to see," *lesen* "to read," though at the end of a word and before *t* it of course stands for /s/: *er las* "he read," *er liest* "he reads." (The letter *z*, on the other hand, never stands for /z/ but always for /ts/: *zu* /'tsū/ "to," *zwei* /'tsvai/ "two," etc.) The spellings *sp*, *st* stand for /sp/, /st/ in the middle or at the end of a word stem: *Wespe* "wasp," *Nest* "nest"; but for /šp/, /št/ at the beginning of a word stem: *sprechen* /'špreçən/ "to speak," *besprechen* /bə'špreçən/ "to discuss," *stehen* /'štēən/ "to stand," *verstehen* /fər'štēən/ "to understand." Otherwise, however, /š/ is spelled *sch*: *Schiff* "ship," *waschen* "to wash," *Fisch* "fish." Double *ss* is used to symbolize fortis /s/ after a short vowel: *hassen* /'hasən/ "to hate," *Küsse* /'küsə/ "kisses"; after a long vowel or diphthong the special letter *ß* is used: *beißen* /'baisən/ "to bite," *Füße* /'fūsə/ "feet." But double *ss* is written only if a vowel also follows; before *t*, or at the end of a word, it is replaced by *ß*: *er haßt* /'hast/ "he hates" spelled like *er beißt* /'baist/ "he bites"; *der Kuß* /'kus/ "kiss" spelled like *der Fuß* /'fūs/ "foot."

The letter *v* stands in native German words for /f/: *Vater* /'fātər/ "father"; in foreign words it usually stands for /v/: *Vase* /'vāzə/ "vase." The spelling for /v/ in native German words is *w*: *Wasser* /'vasər/ "water."

Sentence Stress

Like English, German uses stress to place a particular word at the center of attention within a sentence. There is no symbol for this in the regular spelling; in the following examples it is symbolized by a raised circle:

(*Wer wohnt hier?*)	°*Hans wohnt hier.* (Who lives here?)	°Hans lives here.
(*Was macht Hans hier?*)	*Hans* °*wohnt hier.* (What does Hans do here?)	Hans °lives here.
(*Wo wohnt Hans?*)	*Hans wohnt* °*hier.* (Where does Hans live?)	Hans lives °here.

Word Stress

Again like English, German uses stress as part of the structure of words. The spelling system has no symbols for the three degrees of word stress; we shall here write /'/ in front of syllables with primary stress, write /ˌ/ in front of syllables with secondary stress, and leave weak stress unmarked.

Native German words are generally stressed on the first syllable:

'Arbeit work   *'arbeitslos* unemployed   *'Arbeitslosigkeit* unemployment

Regular prefixes are unstressed:

'arbeiten, 'arbeitete, ge'arbeitet to work (present, past, past participle)
be'obachten, be'obachtete, be'obachtet to observe (present, past, past participle)

Separable prefixes are stressed:

'aufˌstehen, 'stand . . . 'auf, 'aufgeˌstanden to stand up (pres., past, past part.)

Compound words generally have primary stress on the first element, secondary stress on all other elements:

'Flugˌzeug airplane   *'Kampfˌflugˌzeug*   bomber airplane
'Düsenˌkampfˌflugˌzeug jet bomber airplane

But some compound words have secondary stress on the first element, primary stress on the second:

ˌNord'western* northwest   ˌaller'dings* to be sure   ˌApfel'sine* orange

Foreign words are in general stressed on some syllable other than the first:

Demo'krat democrat   *Demokra'tie* democracy
demokrati'sieren to democratize
e'lektrisch electric   *Elektrizi'tät* electricity   *Elektrifi'zierung* electrification

The noninitial position of the stress, and the full vowels of the unstressed syllables, mark words like these as very un-German and foreign.

GRAMMAR

Major Word Classes

The major word classes of German are *Verbs, Nouns,* and *Adjectives.* These classes are "major" in three senses: (a) they are huge in size (there are many thousands of verbs, nouns, and adjectives); (b) they are open classes (new verbs, nouns, and adjectives are constantly being made up); and (c) the words in these classes have full semantic content (and are therefore often called "content words").

1. **Verbs** function as the one indispensable element in the predicate of a full sentence. To show their elaborate inflection, we give here a sample weak verb *sagen* "to say" (weak verbs form their past tense and past participle by adding -(*e*)*te* and -(*e*)*t* to the stem), a sample strong verb *sprechen* "to speak" (strong verbs form their past tense by stem vowel change, their past participle by adding -*en* to the stem, with or without stem vowel change); plus the verbs *haben* "to have," *sein* "to be," and *werden* "to become," which function both as full verbs and as auxiliary verbs (see below).

Present Indicative

ich	sage	spreche	habe	bin	werde
du	sagst	sprichst	hast	bist	wirst
er	sagt	spricht	hat	ist	wird
wir	sagen	sprechen	haben	sind	werden
ihr	sagt	sprecht	habt	seid	werdet
sie, Sie	sagen	sprechen	haben	sind	werden

Past Indicative

ich	sagte	sprach	hatte	war	wurde
du	sagtest	sprachst	hattest	warst	wurdest
er	sagte	sprach	hatte	war	wurde
wir	sagten	sprachen	hatten	waren	wurden
ihr	sagtet	spracht	hattet	wart	wurdet
sie, Sie	sagten	sprachen	hatten	waren	wurden

Subjunctive I

ich	——	——	——	sei	——
du	sagest	sprechest	habest	seiest	werdest
er	sage	spreche	habe	sei	werde
wir	——	——	——	seien	——
ihr	saget	sprechet	habet	seiet	werdet
sie, Sie	——	——	——	seien	——

Subjunctive II

ich	sagte	spräche	hätte	wäre	würde
du	sagtest	sprächest	hättest	wärest	würdest
er	sagte	spräche	hätte	wäre	würde
wir	sagten	sprächen	hätten	wären	würden
ihr	sagtet	sprächet	hättet	wäret	würdet
sie, Sie	sagten	sprächen	hätten	wären	würden

Imperative

du	*sag(e)*	*sprich*	*hab(e)*	*sei*	*werde*
ihr	*sagt*	*sprecht*	*habt*	*seid*	*werdet*
Sie	*sagen Sie*	*sprechen Sie*	*haben Sie*	*seien Sie*	*werden Sie*
wir	*sagen wir*	*sprechen wir*	———	*seien wir*	———

Infinitive

sagen   *sprechen*   *haben*   *sein*   *werden*

Past Participle

gesagt   *gesprochen*   *gehabt*   *gewesen*   *geworden*

Present Participle

sagend   *sprechend*   *habend*   *seiend*   *werdend*

Present, Past, Subjunctive I, Subjunctive II, and Imperative are called *finite verb forms*; Infinitive, Past Participle, and Present Participle are called *nonfinite verb forms*. One Finite Verb form occurs in every normal sentence. The Infinitive is used in the Future: *er wird sprechen* "he will speak," and in various types of embedding (see below). The Past Participle is used in the Perfect: *gesprochen haben* "to have spoken," *gekommen sein* "to have come," in the Passive: *gesagt werden* "to be said," and as an adjective: *gesprochenes Deutsch* "spoken German." The Present Participle is used as an adjective: *kochendes Wasser* "boiling water."

2. **Nouns** function chiefly as the subject of a sentence: *der Mann arbeitet* "the man is working"; as a predicate nominative: *ein Mann sein* "to be a man"; as the object of a verb: *den Mann kennen* "to know the man"; and as the object of a preposition: *mit dem Mann* "with the man." Every noun has an inherent *gender*: Masculine *der Mann, der Löffel* "the man, the spoon"; Feminine *die Frau, die Gabel* "the woman, the fork"; Neuter *das Kind, das Messer* "the child, the knife." Nouns are inflected for *number* (Singular, Plural) and *case* (Nominative, Accusative, Dative, Genitive). A few examples (N = nominative, A = accusative, D = dative, G = genitive; brackets link forms not differentiated by inflection):

	Masculine				Neuter			Feminine	
	son	father	name	boy	house	hotel	heart	mother	aunt
SINGULAR									
N	*Sohn*	*Vater*	*Name*	*Junge*	*Haus*	*Hotel*	*Herz*	*Mutter*	*Tante*
A	*Sohn*	*Vater*	*Namen*	*Jungen*	*Haus*	*Hotel*	*Herz*	*Mutter*	*Tante*
D	*Sohn(e)*	*Vater*	*Namen*	*Jungen*	*Haus(e)*	*Hotel*	*Herzen*	*Mutter*	*Tante*
G	*Sohn(e)s*	*Vaters*	*Namens*	*Jungen*	*Hauses*	*Hotels*	*Herzens*	*Mutter*	*Tante*
PLURAL									
NAG	*Söhne*	*Väter*	*Namen*	*Jungen*	*Häuser*	*Hotels*	*Herzen*	*Mütter*	*Tanten*
D	*Söhnen*	*Vätern*	*Namen*	*Jungen*	*Häusern*	*Hotels*	*Herzen*	*Müttern*	*Tanten*

In the singular, Nominative and Accusative are always identical except for so-called "weak" masculine nouns (*Name, Junge*); one-syllable masculine and neuter nouns add an optional *-e* in the Dative (*Sohn(e), Haus(e)*); feminine nouns are uninflected. In the plural, Nominative, Accusative, and Genitive are always identical in shape; the Dative adds -*n* unless it already ends in -*n* (*Namen, Jungen, Herzen, Tanten*) or ends in -*s* (*Hotels*). Not included in this table are nouns which take adjective endings (see below): *der Deutsche* "the German (man)," *ein Deutscher* "a German (man)," *die Deutsche* "the German (woman)," *eine Deutsche* "a German (woman)," *zwei Deutsche* "two Germans," *die zwei Deutschen* "the two Germans."

3. **Adjectives** function as verbal complements (predicate adjectives): *intelligent sein* "to be intelligent"; as noun modifiers: *ein intelligenter Mann* "an intelligent man"; and as adverbial expressions of manner: *intelligent arbeiten* "to work intelligently." Adjectives can be compared: *intelligent, intelligenter, intelligentest-* "intelligent, more intelligent, most intelligent," *arm, ärmer, ärmst-* "poor, poorer, poorest." Adjectives are inflected for *gender, number,* and *case* to agree with the gender, number, and case of the noun they modify. They then take the following two sets of endings:

| STRONG ENDINGS | | | | | WEAK ENDINGS | | | |
| SINGULAR | | | | | SINGULAR | | | |
	Masc.	*Neut.*	*Fem.*	*Plural*		*Masc.*	*Neut.*	*Fem.*	*Plural*
N	-er	-es	-e	-e	N	-e	-e	-e	-en
A	-en	-es	-e	-e	A	-en	-e	-e	-en
D	-em	-em	-er	-en	D	-en	-en	-en	-en
G	-en	-er	-er	-er	G	-en	-en	-en	-en

Notice that this 4 x 4 system (4 cases x Masc., Neut., Fem., Plural) gives 16 slots, but that there are only five different strong endings (-*e*, -*em*, -*en*, -*er*, -*es*) and only two different weak endings (-*e*, -*en*). Strong endings are used if the adjective is preceded by an uninflected Determiner: *ein heißer Tag* "a hot day," *kein kaltes Bier* "no cold beer," or by no Determiner: *heißer Kaffee* "hot coffee," *kaltes Bier* "cold beer," *liebe Freunde* "dear friends"; weak endings are used if the adjective is preceded by an inflected Determiner: *der heiße Kaffee,* "the hot coffee," *dieses kalte Bier* "this cold beer," *meine lieben Freunde* "my dear friends."

Minor Word Classes

These include all other words. These classes are "minor" in three senses: (a) they are small in size (some contain only a handful of words); (b) they are closed classes (new members cannot readily be made up); and (c) the words in these classes often have little or no semantic content but serve primarily to perform various grammatical functions (and they are therefore often called "function words," "grammatical words," or "structure words").

1. **Auxiliary Verbs** are used to form the Perfect, Passive, and Future. The Perfect auxiliaries are *haben* and *sein*. *Haben* is used with most verbs, including

all transitive verbs: *gewartet haben* "to have waited," *den Mann gesehen haben* "to have seen the man"; *sein* is used with intransitive verbs meaning change of position ("go, come, get up," etc.) or change of condition ("become, grow, go to sleep," etc.), as well as with *bleiben* (*geblieben sein* "to have stayed") and with *sein* itself (*gewesen sein* "to have been"). The Passive auxiliary is *werden*: plain *getan werden* "to be done," perfect *getan worden sein* "to have been done." (Note that in this use the past participle of *werden* is *worden*, not *geworden*.) The Future auxiliary is also *werden*: plain future *er wird es sehen* "he will see it," *er wird kommen* "he will come," *es wird getan werden* "it will be done"; perfect future *er wird es gesehen haben* "he will have seen it," *er wird gekommen sein* "he will have come," *es wird getan worden sein* "it will have been done." (The Future is often used to express probability—plain future for present probability: *er wird wohl hier sein* "he is probably here"; perfect future for past probability: *er wird wohl hier gewesen sein* "he was probably here.") For the six *modal auxiliaries*, see page 31.

2. **Pronouns** function, in general, as noun substitutes. (See word classes (8) and (9), page 20.) The following occur:

DEFINITE PRONOUNS

	1ST PERSON		2ND PERSON		3RD PERSON			
	I	we	you	you	*Masc.*	*Neut.*	*Fem.*	*Plural*
N	*ich*	*wir*	*du*	*ihr*	*er*	*es*	*sie*	*sie*
A	*mich*	*uns*	*dich*	*euch*	*ihn*	*es*	*sie*	*sie*
D	*mir*	*uns*	*dir*	*euch*	*ihm*	*ihm*	*ihr*	*ihnen*
G	*meiner*	*unser*	*deiner*	*euer*	*seiner*	*seiner*	*ihrer*	*ihrer*

Singular *du* and plural *ihr* are the familiar words for "you"; the normal polite word is *Sie* (singular/plural) which has the same forms as *sie* "they" but is capitalized in spelling: *Sie, Sie, Ihnen, Ihrer*. Uninflected are: *sich* (3rd person reflexive, accusative and dative, singular and plural); and *einander* "one another, each other" (3rd person reciprocal, accusative and dative plural).

INDEFINITE PRONOUNS (all 3rd person singular)

	who?	what?	one, a person	someone	no one
N	*wer*	*was*	*man, einer*	*jemand*	*niemand*
A	*wen*	*was*	*einen*	*jemand(en)*	*niemand(en)*
D	*wem*	*(was)*	*einem*	*jemand(em)*	*niemand(em)*
G	*wessen*	———	———	*jemandes*	*niemandes*

Uninflected: *etwas* "something," *nichts* "nothing."

3. **Determiners** function as noun modifiers and, in part, as pronouns. The following three declensional types occur:

	Masc.	Neut.	Fem.	Pl.		Masc.	Neut.	Fem.	Pl.		Masc.	Neut.	Fem.	Pl.
N	der	das	die	die		dieser	dieses	diese	diese		ein(er)	ein(es)	eine	keine
A	den	das	die	die		diesen	dieses	diese˘	diese		einen	ein(es)	eine	keine
D	dem	dem	der	den(en)		diesem	diesem	dieser	diesen		einem	einem	einer	keinen
G	des(sen)	des(sen)	der(en)	der(en)		dieses	dieses	dieser	dieser		eines	eines	einer	keiner

The word *der* functions in two ways as a noun modifier: unstressed as the definite article, *der 'Mann* "the man"; stressed as a demonstrative, *'der 'Mann* "that man." It also functions in two ways as a pronoun: as a demonstrative, *Wer ist der?* "Who is he?," *Wer ist die?* "Who is she?," *Wer sind die?* "Who are they?," *Wer ist das?* "Who is that?," *Was ist das?* "What is that," *Was sind die?* "What are those things?"; and as a relative pronoun, *(der Mann) der hier wohnt* "(the man) who lives here," *(der Mann) den ich kenne* "(the man) whom I know," *(der Mann) mit dem ich arbeite* "(the man) with whom I work," etc. When used as a pronoun, *der* takes the longer parenthesized endings: *dessen Frau* "that man's wife," *(die Leute) mit denen ich arbeite* "the people with whom I work."

Like *dieser* "this" are inflected *jener* "that" (but the ordinary word for "that" is stressed *der*), *jeder* "each, every," *welcher?* "which?," and (usually in the plural only) *alle* "all," *beide* "both," *mehrere* "several."

Like *ein* (unstressed) "a, an," (stressed) "one" are inflected *kein* "no, not a, not any" and the possessives *mein* "my," *dein* "your," *sein* "his, its," *ihr* "her," *unser* "our," *euer* "your," *ihr* "their," *Ihr* "your" (polite, singular/plural). When used as pronouns, these take the longer parenthesized endings: *Das ist Ihr Hut, aber wo ist meiner?* "That's your hat, but where is mine?"

Numerals other than *ein* are uninflected: *zwei* "two," *drei* "three," etc.; also uninflected is *ein paar* "a few."

4. **Prepositions** take nominal objects (nouns, pronouns, determiners) in a specific case: *wegen des Wetters* "on account of the weather" (genitive), *mit mir* "with me" (dative), *für den* "for him" (accusative). The prepositions *durch, für, gegen, ohne, um* (and a few others) govern the accusative; the prepositions *aus, bei, mit, nach, seit, von, zu* (and several others) govern the dative; the prepositions *trotz, während, wegen, (an)statt, innerhalb, außerhalb, oberhalb, unterhalb, diesseits, jenseits*, and many others govern the genitive (the first three are also used with the dative); the prepositions *an, auf, hinter, in, neben, über, unter, vor, zwischen* govern the accusative when meaning "place to which" (*in den Garten* "into the garden") but the dative when meaning "place where" (*in dem Garten* "in the garden"). A few prepositions also take adverbs as objects: *von hier* "from here," *seit gestern* "since yesterday."

5. **Coordinating Conjunctions** serve to join sentences together in co-ordinate structure (see page 28). They include: *und* "and," *aber* "but (never-

theless)," *sondern* "but (on the contrary, after a negative)," *oder* "or," *denn* "for, because," *doch* "yet" (also an adverb), *allein* "but".

6. **Subordinating Conjunctions** serve to join sentences together in subordinate structure (see page 28). They include: *daß* "that," *ob* "whether," *als* "when (once)," *wenn* "when (every time), whenever, if," *als ob* "as if," *bis* "until," *bevor* and *ehe* "before," *nachdem* "after," *während* "while," *seit(dem)* "since (time)," *da* "since, because," *weil* "because," *obwohl* "although," *damit* "in order that," and a good many others.

7. **Adverbs** are a kind of grab bag class customarily set up for all other words. They include such varied items as *ja* "yes," *nein* "no," *sehr* "every," *nur* "only," *schon* "already," *selbst* "even," etc. (Sometimes a special class of Interjections is set up for such words as *ach*! "oh!")

8. **Question Words** and 9. **Substitute Words** belong to the above classes but have the special functions of asking for or substituting for expressions with full semantic content. Examples:

	QUESTION WORD	FULL EXPRESSION	SUBSTITUTE WORD
PERSONAL:	**Wer** *kommt?*	**Der Postbote** *kommt.*	**Er** *kommt.*
IMPERSONAL:	**Was** *kommt?*	**Der Zug** *kommt.*	**Er** *kommt.*
PERSONAL:	**Wen** *sehen Sie?*	*Ich sehe* **den Postboten.**	*Ich sehe* **ihn.**
IMPERSONAL:	**Was** *sehen Sie?*	*Ich sehe* **den Zug.**	*Ich sehe* **ihn.**
PERSONAL:	**Auf wen** *warten Sie?*	*Ich warte* **auf den Postboten.**	*Ich warte* **auf ihn.**
IMPERSONAL:	**Worauf** *warten Sie?*	*Ich warte* **auf den Zug.**	*Ich warte* **darauf.**
PRED. NOMIN.:	**Was** *sind Sie?*	*Ich bin* **Amerikaner.**	*Ich bin* **es** *auch.*
PRED. ADJEC.:	**Wie** *ist Ihnen?*	*Ich bin* **müde.**	*Ich bin* **es** *auch.*
DEFINITE:	**welcher** *Hut?*	**der graue** *Hut*	**der** *Hut,* **dieser** *Hut*
INDEFINITE:	**was für ein** *Hut?*	**ein grauer** *Hut*	**ein solcher** *Hut,* **so ein** *Hut*
MANNER:	**Wie** *macht man das?*	*Mach es* **mit dem Hammer**!	*Mach es* **so**!
PLACE WHERE:	**Wo** *wohnen Sie?*	*Ich wohne* **in Hamburg.**	*Ich wohne* **hier/dort/da.**
PLACE TO WHICH:	**Wohin** *fahren Sie?*	*Ich fahre* **nach Hamburg.**	*Ich fahre* **dahin/dorthin.**
PLACE FROM WHICH:	**Woher** *kommen Sie?*	*Ich komme* **aus Hamburg.**	*Ich komme* **daher/dorther.**
TIME:	**Wann** *kommt er?*	*Er kommt* **heute nachmittag.**	*Er kommt* **jetzt/dann.**
CAUSE:	**Warum/Weshalb** *kommt er?*	*Er kommt,* **weil** . . .	*Er kommt* **darum/deshalb.**

Sentence Types

There are four basic types of simple sentences in German:

1. STATEMENT. The Finite Verb is in **2nd position**:

    Hans **kommt** *morgen.*   Hans is coming tomorrow.
    Morgen **kommt** *Hans.*   Tomorrow Hans is coming.

2. GENERAL QUESTION. The Finite Verb is in **1st position**:

Kommt *Hans morgen?*	Is Hans coming tomorrow?
Kommt *morgen Hans?*	Is it Hans who is coming tomorrow?

3. SPECIFIC QUESTION. A Question Word is in **1st position**, the Finite Verb is in **2nd position**:

Wer kommt *morgen?*	Who is coming tomorrow?
Wann kommt *Hans?*	When is Hans coming?

4. COMMAND. The Finite Verb is in the **Imperative**, and the subject (if expressed) follows it:

(du) **Komm** *morgen*!	Come tomorrow.
(ihr) **Kommt** *morgen*	Come tomorrow.
(Sie) **Kommen Sie** *morgen*!	Come tomorrow.
(wir) **Gehen wir** *ins Kino*!	Let's go to the movies.

UNDERLYING STRUCTURE

Despite their obvious surface differences, all four of these basic sentence types show the same underlying structure: they all consist of (1) a *nominal expression* (noun, pronoun, noun with modifier) which functions as the *subject* of the sentence; and (2) a *verbal expression* (a main verb with or without one or more auxiliary verbs, and with or without one or more complements) which functions as the *predicate* of the sentence. The predicate may also, optionally, contain one or more *adverbial expressions* such as expressions of time, place, manner, cause, etc.

THE PASSIVE

The sentences illustrated thus far are all *active*; the same basic structure also underlies *passive* sentences, except that the underlying nominal expression is often unstated. Compare the following:

Nominal Expression	*Verbal Expression*
a. *der Junge* the boy	*den Brief schreiben* to write the letter
b. [UNSTATED]	*den Mann verhaften* to arrest the man
c. *der Lehrer* the teacher	*dem Schüler helfen* to help the pupil
d. [UNSTATED]	*jetzt arbeiten* to work now

Active Statements:

a. *Der Junge schreibt den Brief.*	The boy writes the letter.
b. [JEMAND] *verhaftet den Mann.*	[SOMEONE] arrests the man.
c. *Der Lehrer hilft dem Schüler.*	The teacher helps the pupil.
d. [JEMAND] *arbeitet jetzt.*	[SOMEONE] is working now.
Or: *Jetzt arbeitet* [JEMAND].	Or: Now [SOMEONE] is working.

Passive Statements:

a. *Der Brief wird von dem Jungen geschrieben.*   The letter is written by the boy.

b. *Der Mann wird verhaftet.*   The man gets arrested.

c. *Dem Schüler wird von dem Lehrer geholfen.*   The pupil is helped by the teacher.

d. *Es wird jetzt gearbeitet.*
Or: *Jetzt wird gearbeitet.*   (Something like:) Work is being done now; Now we/they will work.

In (a), the subject of the active sentence (*der Junge*) becomes the agent of the passive sentence (*von dem Jungen*); and the direct object of the active sentence (accusative *den Brief*) becomes the subject of the passive sentence (nominative *der Brief*). In (*b*), the subject of the (theoretical) active sentence is unstated, and hence there can be no agent in the passive sentence; the direct object of the active sentence (accusative *den Mann*) again becomes the subject of the passive sentence (nominative *der Mann*). Thus far, German and English passive sentences are quite comparable.

The English version of (c) is similar to (a): the object of the active (help *the pupil*) becomes the subject of the passive (*the pupil* is helped). But the German version of (c) is quite different from (a): since there is no direct object in the active (*helfen* "to help" takes a dative object, not an accusative object), there can be no subject in the passive. The active subject *der Lehrer* becomes the passive agent *von dem Lehrer*; but the dative object *dem Schüler* remains unchanged. The result is a passive sentence with no subject—a construction that is quite impossible in English, but quite ordinary in German.

In (d) there is no object of any kind in the active. There can therefore be no corresponding passive sentence in English, since there is nothing to function as subject. But there *can* be a corresponding passive sentence in German, since German passive sentences do not have to have subjects. (The *es* in the first version of (d) is not the subject but merely a dummy filler of 1st position— needed so that the finite verb *wird* can occur in 2nd position, as it must in a statement. In the second version of (d), 1st position is filled by *jetzt* and the dummy *es* is not needed—and cannot be used.)

Fixed Word Order

There are five types of sentence elements whose position in any given sentence is fixed: (1) the Finite Verb and (2) any Question Word, as described above; in addition, any (3) Separable Prefix (like the *auf* of *aufziehen* "to wind up"), (4) Infinitive, or (5) Past Participle.

The fixed positions of these elements in a Statement can be most simply described if we assume that such a sentence is constructed in two steps. (1)

Choose a Nominal Expression, a Verbal Expression, and a Tense. Then: (2a) if the Tense is Present or Past, shift the last word of the Verbal Expression (it will be either the main verb or an auxiliary) to 2nd position and convert it to the proper finite form; or (2b) if the Tense is Future, leave the Verbal Expression as it is but insert the proper finite form of *werden* in 2nd position. Examples, with fixed position elements in **bold face**:

ACTIVE:

der Mann the man + (Plain) *die Uhr aufziehen* to wind up the clock

+ Present = *Der Mann* **zieht** *die Uhr* **auf.**	The man winds up the clock.
+ Past = *Der Mann* **zog** *die Uhr* **auf.**	The man wound up the clock.
+ Future = *Der Mann* **wird** *die Uhr* **aufziehen.**	The man will wind up the clock.

der Mann the man + (Perfect) *die Uhr aufgezogen haben* to have wound up the clock

+ Present = *Der Mann* **hat** *die Uhr* **aufgezogen.**	The man has wound up the clock.
+ Past = *Der Mann* **hatte** *die Uhr* **aufgezogen.**	The man had wound up the clock.
+ Future = *Der Mann* **wird** *die Uhr* **aufgezogen haben.**	The man will have wound up the clock, probably wound up the clock.

PASSIVE:

die Uhr the clock + (Plain) *aufgezogen werden* to be wound up

+ Present = *Die Uhr* **wird aufgezogen.**	The clock is wound up.
+ Past = *Die Uhr* **wurde aufgezogen.**	The clock was wound up.
+ Future = *Die Uhr* **wird aufgezogen werden.**	The clock will be wound up.

die Uhr the clock + (Perfect) *aufgezogen worden sein* to have been wound up

+ Present = *Die Uhr* **ist aufgezogen worden.**	The clock has been wound up.
+ Past = *Die Uhr* **war aufgezogen worden.**	The clock had been wound up.
+ Future = *Die Uhr* **wird aufgezogen worden sein.**	The clock will have been wound up, has probably been wound up.

General Questions also require two steps. Step (1) is the same as for Statements; step (2) differs only in that the Finite Verb is inserted in 1st position rather than in 2nd position.

Specific Questions require three steps: (1) choose a Nominal Expression and a Verbal Expression (one of these must contain a Question Word) plus a Tense; (2) insert the Finite Verb in 1st position, as for a General Question; and then (3) shift the QuestionWord to 1st position, in front of the Finite Verb. Examples:

ACTIVE:

der Mann the man + (Plain) *was aufziehen?* to wind up what?

+ Present = (2) *zieht der Mann was auf*
     (3) **Was zieht** *der Mann* **auf**?   What does the man wind up?

+ Past = (2) *zog der Mann was auf*
     (3) **Was zog** *der Mann* **auf**?   What did the man wind up?

+ Future = (2) *wird der Mann was aufziehen*
     (3) **Was wird** *der Mann* **aufziehen**?   What will the man wind up?

Similarly for the remaining three active forms (perfect) and for the six passive forms (three plain, three perfect). The "step (2)" described above never occurs as an actual sentence type; but it is useful to assume it as a hypothetical intermediate step between the underlying structure and the actually occurring sentence shapes.

 Commands follow steps (1) and (2) as for General Questions, except that the Verb must be in the Imperative (never Present, Past, or Future, and never Perfect). Then, usually, the subjects *du* and *ihr* are deleted:

du/ihr/Sie/wir + *die Uhr aufziehen*   to wind up the clock

(*du*): **Zieh** (**du**) *die Uhr* **auf**!   Wind up the clock. (familiar singular)
(*ihr*): **Zieht** (**ihr**) *die Uhr* **auf**!   Wind up the clock. (familiar plural)
(*Sie*): **Ziehen Sie** *die Uhr* **auf**!   Wind up the clock. (polite singular/plural)
(*wir*): **Ziehen wir** *die Uhr* **auf**!   Let's wind up the clock.

The subjects *du* and *ihr* are kept only for contrastive emphasis: *Geh du in die Stadt, ich bleibe hier* "*You* go down town, *I'll* stay here."

Variable Word Order

 Within the framework provided by the elements with fixed word order, the order of other elements can be varied to convey different shades of meaning. Consider such a statement as: *Ein Abkommen wurde Ende Mai in London von den Außenministern unterzeichnet* "An agreement was signed the end of May in London by the foreign ministers." In terms of fixed and variable word order, such a sentence can be diagrammed as follows:

| Topic | C | o | m | m | e | n | t |

The elements with fixed word order are clear: *wurde* must be in 2nd position because it is the Finite Verb of a Statement; and *unterzeichnet* must be in last position because it is a Past Participle. The remaining elements are the Subject *ein Abkommen*, the Time expression *Ende Mai*, the Place expression *in London*, and the Agent expression *von den Außenministern*. Their positions are freely variable; let us look at some of the possibilities.

1a. *Ein Abkommen* ‖ **wurde** | *Ende Mai* | *in London* | VON DEN AUßENMINI-STERN | **unterzeichnet.**

1b. *Ein Abkommen* ‖ **wurde** | *von den Außenministern* | *Ende Mai* | IN LON-DON | **unterzeichnet.**

1c. *Ein Abkommen* ‖ **wurde** | *in London* | *von den Außenministern* | ENDE MAI | **unterzeichnet.**

In these three sentences *ein Abkommen* is the *topic* and the meaning is something like: "I'm talking about an agreement; now this is what happened" (and then follows the *comment*). The newsworthy part of the Comment varies: in (1a) it is the fact that the signing was done *by the foreign ministers*; in (1b) it is the fact that the signing took place *in London*; and in (1c) it is the fact that the signing took place *the end of May.*

2a. *Ende Mai* ‖ **wurde** | *ein Abkommen* | *in London* | VON DEN AUßENMINI-STERN | **unterzeichnet.**

2b. *Ende Mai* ‖ **wurde** | *ein Abkommen* | *von den Außenministern* | IN LON-DON | **unterzeichnet.**

2c. *Ende Mai* ‖ **wurde** | *in London* | *von den Außenministern* | EIN ABKOM-MEN | **unterzeichnet.**

In these three sentences *Ende Mai* is the *topic*: "I'm talking about the end of May; now this is what happened." The newsworthy part of the Comment again varies: in (2a) it is the fact that the signing was done *by the foreign ministers;* in (2b) it is the fact that the signing took place *in London*; and in (2c) it is the fact that the signing involved *an agreement.*

Similar sentences are possible in which the Topic is *in London*, or even *von den Außenministern*. (The latter would be rather unusual. If one wanted to make "the foreign ministers" the Topic, one would probably say the sentence in the active: *Die Außenminister unterzeichneten Ende Mai in London ein Abkommen.*)

The principle of using 1st position for the Topic can go so far as to produce a mild violation of fixed word order:

Unterzeichnet ‖ **wurde** │ *das Abkommen* │ *erst Ende Mai* │ IN LONDON.

Here the meaning is something like: "As for the official signing of the agreement, this did not take place until the end of May in London."

The position of the Finite verb *wurde*, on the other hand, is absolutely fixed: in a Statement it must be in 2nd position. To put it in 1st position would give a General Question: *Wurde ein Abkommen . . . unterzeichnet?* "Was an agreement signed . . . ?" To put it in last position would give a Dependent Clause (see below): *(daß) ein Abkommen . . . unterzeichnet wurde* "(that) an agreement was signed . . ." And to put it anywhere else would be simply ungrammatical.

Types of Verbal Expressions

The Nominal Expressions which function as the Subject of a simple sentence are always of the same general type: a Noun (with or without modifiers), a Pronoun, or a Determiner. The Verbal Expressions which function as the Predicate of a simple sentence, on the other hand, may be of many different types, depending on the complement(s) (if any) required by the verb. Such complements may be Adjectival Expressions, Nominal Expressions (in various cases), Prepositional Phrases (of various types), or Adverbial Expressions (of various types), or combinations of these. Examples:

1. Verb without complement. Example: *brennen* to burn.
   Das Feuer brennt.   The fire is burning.

2. Verb + predicate adjective. Example: *(adjective) sein* to be (adjective)
   Mein Bruder ist krank.   My brother is sick.

3. Verb + predicate nominative. Example: *(noun in nominative) sein* to be (noun)
   Mein Bruder ist Student.   My brother is a student.

4. Verb + accusative object. Example: *etwas schreiben* to write something
   Der Junge schreibt einen Brief.   The boy is writing a letter.

5. Verb + dative object. Example: *jemandem helfen* to help someone.
   Der Lehrer hilft dem Schüler.   The teacher helps the pupil.

6. Verb + genitive object (rare). Example: *eines Menschen gedenken* to be mindful of a person
   Wir gedenken der Toten.   We remember the dead.

7. Verb + prepositional phrase. Example: *an etwas denken* to think of something
   Er denkt nie an die Zukunft.   He never thinks of the future.

8. Verb + adverbial expression of place. Example: *irgendwo wohnen* to live somewhere
   Sein Vetter wohnt in Hamburg.   His cousin lives in Hamburg.

9. Verb + adverbial expression of measure. Example: *etwas kosten* to cost something
   Der Kugelschreiber kostet einen Dollar.
   The ball point pen costs a dollar.

10. Verb + dative object + accusative object. Example: *jemandem etwas geben* to give someone something
    Der Postbote gibt dem Mann den Brief.
    The mailman gives the man the letter.

11. Verb + accusative object + genitive object. Example: *jemanden eines Dinges versichern* to assure someone of something
    Der Kanzler versicherte den Minister seines vollen Vertrauens.
    The chancellor assured the minister of his full confidence.

12. Verb + accusative object + prepositional phrase. Example: *jemanden an etwas erinnern* to remind someone of something
    Der Richter erinnerte den Mann an seine Pflicht.
    The judge reminded the man of his duty.

13. Verb + dative object + prepositional phrase. Example: *jemandem zu etwas raten* to advise someone to (do) something
    Der Arzt riet dem Mann zu einer Reise.
    The doctor advised the man to (take) a trip.

14. Verb + prepositional phrase + prepositional phrase. Example: *mit jemandem über etwas sprechen* to speak with someone about something
    Der Kanzler sprach mit seinem Kabinett über die Finanzlage.
    The chancellor spoke with his cabinet about the financial situation.

In addition to the verb and its complement(s) (if any), the Predicate may also contain optional adverbial expressions of time, place, manner, cause, etc.

Recursive Devices

In German, as in every other language, it is theoretically possible to construct an infinite number of sentences, and there is theoretically no such thing as a "longest sentence." This is because the grammars of all human languages contain *recursive devices*: devices for joining one sentence structure to another, over and over again, theoretically without end. These recursive devices are of two basic types: *coordinate joining*, in which one sentence structure is *added* to another ("Mary told Jane, and Jane told Sue, and Sue told Sally, and . . ."");

and *subordinate joining*, in which one sentence structure is *embedded* inside another ("This is the cat that killed the rat that ate the malt that . . .").

COORDINATE JOINING

Two (or more) sentences can be joined together by means of coordinating conjunctions:

> *Hans ging ins Kino* + *Paul blieb zu Hause*
> ⇒ *Hans ging ins Kino,* **aber** *Paul blieb zu Hause.*
>   Hans went to the movies, but Paul stayed home.

Identical parts of sentences joined in this way are generally not repeated:

> *Hans ging ins Kino* + *Paul ging ins Kino*
> ⇒ *Hans* **und** *Paul gingen ins Kino.*   Hans and Paul went to the movies.

Here the *gingen ins Kino* of the derived sentence represents the *ging ins Kino* that is common to both of the underlying simple sentences.

SUBORDINATE JOINING

Subordinate joining takes many forms in German. We shall discuss the following types: (1) *subordinate clauses*, in which the verb of the embedded sentence is finite; (2) *infinitive clauses*, in which the verb of the embedded sentence is nonfinite; and (3) *infinitive phrases*, in which the verb of the embedded sentence is nonfinite and the subject is deleted.

   1. **Subordinate clauses.** Statements, General Questions, and Specific Questions can be embedded as Indirect Statements, Indirect General Questions, and Indirect Specific Questions. They then fill a nominal slot in the matrix sentence. (The "matrix sentence" is the sentence in which another sentence is embedded.) In the following examples they function as the direct object of the verb of the matrix sentence:

> *Ich glaube* [OBJECT] + STATEMENT *Hans kommt morgen*
> ⇒ *Ich glaube,* **daß** *Hans morgen* **kommt.**
>   I think that Hans is coming tomorrow.
>
> *Wissen Sie* [OBJECT] + GENERAL QUESTION *Kommt Hans morgen?*
> ⇒ *Wissen Sie,* **ob** *Hans morgen* **kommt?**
>   Do you know whether Hans is coming tomorrow?
>
> *Ich weiß* [OBJECT] *nicht* + SPECIFIC QUESTION *Wer kommt morgen?*
> *Wann kommt Hans?*
> ⇒ *Ich weiß nicht,* **wer** *morgen* **kommt.**
>   I don't know who is coming tomorrow.
> ⇒ *Ich weiß nicht,* **wann** *Hans* **kommt.**
>   I don't know when Hans is coming.

Note that Indirect Statements are introduced by *daß*, that Indirect General Questions are introduced by *ob*, that Indirect Specific Questions are introduced by a Question Word; and that (as in all subordinate clauses) the Finite Verb stands last. (But *daß* can optionally be deleted, and the finite verb of the embedded statement is then in the usual position: *Ich glaube, Hans kommt morgen* "I think Hans is coming tomorrow.") German has no special type of Indirect Command; instead, it uses a *daß* clause with the subjunctive of *sollen*. Command: *Komm morgen!* "Come tomorrow"; subordinate clause: *Er sagte, daß ich morgen kommen sollte* "He told me to come tomorrow," literally "He said that I should come tomorrow."

Adjectival subordinate clauses, which modify nouns, are customarily called *relative clauses*. They are introduced by the proper form of *der*, which is then said to function as a *relative pronoun*. They are always derived from Statements. Examples:

> *Das ist der Mann + Der Mann wohnt nebenan*
> ⇒ *Das ist der Mann,* **der** *nebenan* **wohnt**.
> That's the man who lives next door.

> *Das ist der Mann + Wir haben den Mann gestern gesehen*
> ⇒ *Das ist der Mann,* **den** *wir gestern gesehen* **haben**.
> That's the man we saw yesterday.

> *Das ist der Mann + Ich arbeite mit dem Mann*
> ⇒ *Das ist der Mann,* **mit dem** *ich* **arbeite**. That's the man I work with.

> *Das ist der Mann + Ich wohne in dem Haus des Mannes*
> ⇒ *Das ist der Mann,* **in dessen Haus** *ich* **wohne**.
> That's the man whose house I live in.

Instead of *der*, a proper form of *welcher* is less commonly used to introduce relative clauses. But *was* is generally used to refer back to indefinite pronouns or adjectives, or to whole sentences: *alles, was er tat* "everything that he did," *das Beste, was wir haben* "the best that we have," *Er trat auf die Bremse, was sicher falsch war* "He stepped on the brake, which was surely wrong."

All other subordinate clauses fill adverbial slots of various sorts. They are introduced by Subordinating Conjunctions; they are always derived from Statements. A few examples:

> *Ich sah ihn* [TIME] + *Ich war in Frankfurt*
> ⇒ *Ich sah ihn,* **als** *ich in Frankfurt* **war**.
> I saw him when I was in Frankfurt.

> *Wir blieben* [CAUSE] *zu Hause + Es regnete stark*
> ⇒ *Wir blieben zu Hause,* **weil** *es stark* **regnete**.
> We stayed at home because it was raining hard.

> *Ich werde ihn* [CONDITION] *anrufen* + *Ich habe Zeit*
> ⇒ *Ich werde ihn anrufen,* **wenn** *ich Zeit* **habe.**
> I'll call him up if I have time.

Since a subordinate clause is truly "embedded" in its matrix sentence, it can occupy 1st position in that sentence. The Finite Verb of the matrix sentence (if it is a statement) must then follow immediately so as to be in 2nd position:

> $\underline{\text{Wenn ich Zeit habe,}}$ $\underline{\text{werde}}$ *ich ihn anrufen.*   If I have time, I'll call him up.
> $\qquad\quad$ 1 $\qquad\qquad\quad$ 2

2. **Infinitive clauses.** These occur when a sentence is embedded as the complement of the verbs *lassen* "to let, to have (somebody do something, something done)" or *heißen* "to order (somebody to do something, something to be done)." Examples:

> *Er läßt* [COMPLEMENT] + *Der Schneider kommt.* The tailor comes.
> ⇒ *Er läßt den Schneider kommen.*   He lets/has the tailor come.
> *Er läßt* [COMPLEMENT] + *Der Schneider bügelt den Anzug.* The tailor presses the suit.
> ⇒ *Er läßt den Schneider den Anzug bügeln.*
> He lets/has the tailor press the suit.
> *Er läßt* [COMPLEMENT] + *Der Anzug wird vom Schneider gebügelt.* The suit is pressed by the tailor.
> ⇒ *Er läßt den Anzug vom Schneider bügeln.*
> He has the suit pressed by the tailor.
> *Er läßt* [COMPLEMENT] + *Der Anzug wird gebügelt.* The suit is pressed.
> ⇒ *Er läßt den Anzug bügeln.*   He has the suit pressed.

Active sentences can also be embedded as the object of such "sensory" verbs as *sehen, hören, fühlen* "to see, hear, feel":

> *Er sah den Wagen* He saw the car + *Der Wagen hielt vor der Tür* The car stopped in front of the door.
> ⇒ *Er sah den Wagen vor der Tür halten.*
> He saw the car stop in front of the door.

Notice how, in the derived sentence, *den Wagen* functions simultaneously as the object of *sehen* "to see" and as the subject of *vor der Tür halten* "to stop in front of the door."

3. **Infinitive phrases.** These occur when a Statement is restructured so that its Predicate can fill nominal slots of various types. In many uses the infinitive must be preceded by *zu.*

a. Subject of sentence. The subject of the embedded sentence is indefinite. Example:

[SUBJECT] *ist schwer* + [MAN] *wird Vater*, [MAN] *ist Vater*
⇒ *Vater werden ist nicht schwer, Vater sein dagegen sehr.*
To become a father is not hard, to be a father on the other hand [is] very [hard]. (A famous couplet by Wilhelm Busch.)

b. Object of preposition. The subject of the matrix sentence and the (deleted) subject of the embedded sentence must be identical. Example:

Er tut es [PURPOSE] + *Er verdient Geld*
⇒ *Er tut es, um Geld zu verdienen.* He does it (in order) to earn money.

Two other prepositions also take infinitive phrases as objects: *ohne Geld zu verdienen* "without earning money," *(an)statt Geld zu verdienen* "instead of earning money."

c. Complement of verb. This is the most frequent use of infinitive phrases. Many verbs take an infinitive phrase with *zu* as complement. A few examples:

Er vergaß [OBJECT] + *Er ruft mich an*
⇒ *Er vergaß, mich anzurufen.* He forgot to call me up.

Er hat uns [OBJECT] *versprochen* + *Er kommt nächstes Jahr wieder*
⇒ *Er hat uns versprochen, nächstes Jahr wiederzukommen.*
He promised us to come next year.

Ich habe ihn [UM ETWAS] *gebeten* + *Er gibt mir das Geld*
⇒ *Ich habe ihn gebeten, mir das Geld zu geben.*
I asked him to give me the money.

Six verbs, in particular, take an infinitive phrase without *zu* as complement. These are the so-called *modal auxiliaries*: *dürfen* "may, to be permitted to," *können* "can, to be able to," *mögen* "may (perhaps), to like to," *müssen* "must, to have to," *sollen* "to be supposed to," *wollen* "to want to." The subject of the matrix sentence and the (deleted) subject of the embedded sentence must be identical. Examples:

Sie dürfen [COMPLEMENT] *nicht* + *Sie tun das*
⇒ *Sie dürfen das nicht tun.*
"You are not permitted to do that, mustn't do that."

Mein Bruder kann [COMPLEMENT] + *Mein Bruder läuft gut Schi*
⇒ *Mein Bruder kam gut schilaufen.* My brother can ski well.

Ich mag [COMPLEMENT] *gern* + *Ich spiele Schach*
⇒ *Ich mag gern Schach spielen.* I like to play chess.

Das Auto muß [COMPLEMENT] + *Das Auto wird repariert*
⇒ *Das Auto muß repariert werden.* The auto must be repaired.

Jeder soll [COMPLEMENT] + *Jeder kann schwimmen*
⇒ *Jeder soll schwimmen können.* Everyone is supposed to be able to swim.

Er hat [COMPLEMENT] *nicht wollen* + *Er sagt es*
⇒ *Er hat es nicht sagen wollen.* He didn't want to say it.

The inflections and the meanings of the modals are irregular in many respects.

Uses of the Subjunctive

The Subjunctive occurs infrequently in simple sentences. An example, contrasting it with the Indicative:

INDICATIVE: *Man* **nimmt** *zwei Pfund Zucker.* One takes 2 pounds of sugar.
SUBJUNCTIVE I: *Man* **nehme** *zwei Pfund Zucker.* Take 2 pounds of sugar.

This second example is typical of recipes in cookbooks.

Far more commonly, the Subjunctive occurs in complex sentences that involve embedding. The two principle uses are: (1) in UNREAL (CONTRARY TO FACT) CONDITIONS; and (2) in INDIRECT DISCOURSE.

1. **Unreal conditions.** The structure of "unreal conditions" is most clearly shown by contrasting them with the corresponding "real conditions":

REAL CONDITION, PRESENT OR FUTURE TIME (INDICATIVE)

Wenn ich Zeit **habe,**　　　　If, when(ever) I have time,
　gehe *ich ins Theater.*　　　　I go to the theater.

Wenn ich Zeit **habe,**　　　　If, when(ever) I have time,
　werde *ich ins Theater* **gehen.**　I'll go to the theater.

UNREAL CONDITION, PRESENT TIME (SUBJUNCTIVE)

Wenn ich Zeit **hätte,**　　　　If I had time,
{ **würde** *ich ins Theater* **gehen.**
{ **ginge** *ich ins Theater.*　　　I would go to the theater.

REAL CONDITION, PAST TIME (INDICATIVE)

Wenn ich Zeit **hatte,**　　　　If, when(ever) I had time,
　ging *ich ins Theater.*　　　　I went to the theater.

UNREAL CONDITION, PAST TIME (SUBJUNCTIVE)

Wenn ich Zeit gehabt hätte,　　If I had had time,
{ **würde** *ich ins Theater* **gegangen sein.**　　　　　　I would have gone to the theater.
{ **wäre** *ich ins Theater* **gegangen.**

In an unreal condition, present time, the verb of the *if*-clause is in Subjunctive II (*hätte*), the verb of the conclusion is either *würde* + the main verb (*würde . . . gehen*) or Subjunctive II of the main verb (*ginge*). In an unreal condition, past time, the verb of the *if*-clause is in Perfect Subjunctive II (*gehabt hätte*), the verb of the conclusion is either *würde* + the perfect of the main verb (*würde . . . gegangen sein*) or Perfect Subjunctive II of the main verb (*wäre . . . gegangen*).

Very commonly, either the *if*-clause or the conclusion is omitted, giving such elliptical sentences as *Wenn ich nur mehr Zeit hätte!* "If only I had more time!" (with a missing conclusion), *Ich wäre auch ins Theater gegangen* "I would have gone to the theater, too" (with a missing *if*-clause). In a few uses, this omission has become so common that the sentences are not really felt to be parts of unreal conditions at all: *Ich möchte gern eine Tasse Kaffee haben* "I'd like to have a cup of coffee" (grammatically, *möchte* is Subjunctive II of *mögen*); *Könnten Sie mir bitte Feuer geben?* "Could you please give me a light?" (grammatically, *könnte* is Subjunctive II of *können*); *Würden Sie mir bitte das Salz reichen?* "Would you please pass me the salt?" (grammatically, *würden* is Subjunctive II of *werden*); *Er sollte es tun* "He ought to do it," *Er hätte es tun sollen* "He ought to have done it" (grammatically, *sollte* is the Plain Subjunctive II of *sollen*, and *hätte . . . sollen* is the Perfect Subjunctive II of *sollen*).

2. **Indirect discourse.**

DIRECT DISCOURSE	INDIRECT DISCOURSE
a. *Ich* **bin** *krank.*	*Er sagte, daß er krank* **wäre** (**sei**). He said that he was sick.
b. *Ich* **sah** *es.* *Ich* **habe** *es* **gesehen.** *Ich* **hatte** *es* **gesehen.**	*Er sagte, daß er es* **gesehen hätte** (**habe**). He said that he had seen it.
c. *Ich* **werde kommen.**	*Er sagte, daß er* **kommen würde** (**werde**). He said that he would come.

If the verb of direct discourse is Present, as in (a), the corresponding verb of indirect discourse is normally in Subjunctive II (*wäre*). If the verb of direct discourse is Past, Perfect, or Past Perfect, as in (b), the corresponding verb of indirect discourse is normally in Perfect Subjunctive II (*gesehen hätte*). If the verb of direct discourse is Future, as in (c), the corresponding verb of indirect discourse is normally Subjunctive II *würde* + infinitive (*kommen würde*). More formally, instead of Subjunctive II, Subjunctive I can be used: (a) *sei*, (b) *gesehen habe*, (c) *kommen werde*.

The use of the Subjunctive in indirect discourse often implies an air of doubt: "He *said* this, but I'm not entirely sure." The Subjunctive is generally not used if the verb of the matrix sentence is in the Present: *Er sagt, daß er krank ist* "He says that he is sick"; *Er sagt, daß er es gesehen hat* "He says that he has seen it"; *Er sagt, daß er kommen wird* "He says that he will come."

HISTORY

If we compare a few words from modern English, Dutch, and German, the resemblances are very striking:

English	Dutch	German		English	Dutch	German
1. one	een	eins	6.	father	vader	Vater
2. two	twee	zwei	7.	mother	moeder	Mutter
3. three	drie	drei	8.	brother	broer	Bruder
4. ten	tien	zehn	9.	foot	voet	Fuß
5. hundred	honderd	hundert	10.	heart	hart	Herz

We would find similar resemblances if we should list the corresponding words in modern Frisian, Icelandic, Norwegian, Danish, and Swedish.

Resemblances like these (and we could give many hundreds of others) can be accounted for in only one plausible way: English, Dutch, and German (as well as Frisian and the Scandinavian languages) must be different modern developments of some single earlier language. This line of reasoning becomes even more convincing when we note that the sound correspondences among the modern languages are not haphazard, put are highly regular and consistent. Consider the following sets of words:

English	Dutch	German		English	Dutch	German
/t-/	/t-/	/ts-/		/ī/	/ā/	/ā/
1. tongue	tong	Zunge	1.	deed	daad	Tat
2. toll	tol	Zoll	2.	sheep	schaap	Schaf
3. tame	tam	zahm	3.	year	jaar	Jahr
4. to	toe	zu	4.	eel	aal	Aal
/d-/	/d-/	/t-/		/ō/	/ē/	/ai/
5. day	dag	Tag	5.	soap	zeep	Seife
6. dead	dood	tot	6.	stone	steen	Stein
7. deaf	doof	taub	7.	most	meest	meist
8. deep	diep	tief	8.	whole	heel	heil
/þ-/	/d-/	/d-/		/ī/	/ō/	/au/
9. thing	ding	Ding	9.	heap	hoop	Haufen
10. thief	dief	Dieb	10.	leap	lopen	laufen
11. thin	dun	dünn	11.	reek	roken	rauchen
12. thank	danken	danken	12.	beam	boom	Baum

The columns to the left show three consistent sets of consonant correspondences: in 1 to 4 the set English *t-*, Dutch *t-*, German *z-* (/ts-/); in 5 to 8 the set English *d-*, Dutch *d-*, German *t-*; and in 9 to 12 the set English *þ-*, Dutch *d-*, German *d-*. We can now attempt to reconstruct a bit of the proto-language (as the assumed parent language is called) from which the modern languages are descended. To account for the three different sets of correspondences in the modern languages we can assume three different consonant phonemes in the proto-language: **t-* for 1-4, **d-* for 5-8, **þ-* for 9-12. (It is customary to use an asterisk to show that such phonemes are hypothetical and not actually attested.) In English they seem to have remained unchanged, giving *t-*, *d-*, *þ-*, as in *tongue, day, thing*. In Dutch, **þ-* has merged with **d-*, giving *t-*, *d-*, *d-*, as in *tong, dag, ding*. In German, **t-* has become *z-* (/ts-/), **d-* has become *t-*, and **þ-* has become *d-*, giving *z-*, *t-*, *d-*, as in *Zunge, Tag, Ding*. In the development of these consonants English has been very conservative, German very radical, while Dutch occupies a middle position.

The columns to the right show three consistent sets of vowel correspondences: in 1 to 4 the set English /ī/, Dutch /ā/, German /ā/; in 5 to 8 the set English /ō/, Dutch /ē/, German /ai/; and in 9 to 12 the set English /ī/, Dutch /ō/, German /au/. To account for these three sets of vowel correspondences in the modern languages we can assume three different vowel phonemes in the proto-language. This time their phonetic nature is a good deal less obvious. For various reasons we believe that the vowel of 1-4 was something like **ǣ*, the vowel of 5-8 approximately **ai*, and the vowel of 9-12 approximately **au*. In English these three vowels have become /ī/, /ō/, /ī/, as in *deed, soap, heap*. In Dutch they have become /ā/, /ē/, /ō/, as in *daad, zeep, hoop*. In German they seem to have remained more or less unchanged, giving /ā/, /ai/, /au/, as in *Tat, Seife, Haufen*. In the development of these vowels English has been very radical, German quite conservative, while Dutch again occupies a middle position.

The procedure that we have been using in the preceding paragraphs is known as "the comparative method of reconstruction." It was developed and elaborated by many scholars during the nineteenth century, and it is our only known way of demonstrating that two or more languages are *related*, that is, that they are descended from a single earlier common source. Note how the method works: we first collect sets of words with similar meanings and consistent correspondences in sound; we then try to set up the phonemes of the proto-language in such a way that we can derive the phonemes of each daughter language by assuming only regular sound changes. These sound changes may be quite different in the different daughter languages; but between the proto-language and each daughter language they must be entirely regular. We cannot permit ourselves the luxury of assuming haphazard sound changes, since this would allow us to derive any modern form from any proto-form and hence to show that any language is related to any other language. This would render the concept "related" quite meaningless.

The assumption that sound change is regular has another advantage. Because it does not permit us to classify any unusual correspondences as simply "irregular exceptions," it leads us to the discovery of further regular sound changes that we might otherwise have overlooked. Consider the following sets:

	English	Dutch	German		English	Dutch	German
1.	toe	teen	Zehe	7.	sit	zitten	sitzen
2.	to	toe	zu	8.	cat	kat	Katze
3.	malt	mout	Malz	9.	water	water	Wasser
4.	salt	zout	Salz	10.	hot	heet	heiß
5.	heart	hart	Herz	11.	east	oosten	Osten
6.	smart	smarten	schmerzen	12.	west	westen	Westen

The English and Dutch examples suggest that all of these words contained a *t in the proto-language. In 1 and 2 it occurred initially; in 3 and 4 it occurred after *l; in 5 and 6 it occurred after *r; in 7-10 it occurred after vowel; and in 11 and 12 it occurred after *s. As for German, examples 1-8 show the development with which we are already familiar: the *t of the proto-language has become /ts/. But in 9 and 10 it seems to have becomes /s/; and in 11 and 12 it seems to have remained t. How can we account for these apparent discrepancies without assuming haphazard sound change? If we disregard 7 and 8 for the moment, we can make the following observations: (a) initially (1, 2), after *l (3, 4), and after *r (5, 6), *t has become /ts/; (b) after vowels (9, 10) it has become /s/; and (c) after *s (11, 12) it has remained t. But what of 7 and 8? We note that the Dutch word for "sit" has double tt: zitten; the plural of "cat" also has double tt: katten. And if we look back into Old English, we find that there also these words had double tt: sittan "to sit," catte "cat." Hence we conclude that both words had double *tt in the proto-language. Now we are able to describe the three-way but completely regular development of *t in German: (a) it has become /ts/ initially, after *l, after *r, and when doubled; (b) it has become /s/ after vowels; and (c) it has remained t after s.

The preceding example has shown the value of looking back at the oldest recorded forms of the languages we are comparing. Let us now look at a wider selection of languages, choosing in each case the oldest form preserved to us. The following list gives our original ten words from the earliest records of: Gothic (fourth century, no modern descendants); English (Old English, seventh century and later); Frisian (Old Frisian, thirteenth century and later); Low

German (Old Low German, usually called Old Saxon, ninth century and later);
and High German (Old High German, eighth century and later):

	Gothic	Old Norse	Old English	Old Frisian	Old Low German	Old High German
1.	ains	einn	ān	ān	ên	ein
2.	twai	tveir	twā	twā	twê	zwei
3.	þreis	þrīr	þrī	thrē	thria	thrī
4.	taihun	tīu	tīen	tiān	tehan	zehan
5.	hund	hund	hund	hund	hund	hunt
6.	fadar	faþir	fæder	feder	fadar	fater
7.	(aiþei)	mōþir	mōdor	mōder	mōdar	muoter
8.	brōþar	brōþir	brōþor	brōther	brōthar	bruoder
9.	fōtus	fōtr	fōt	fōt	fōt	fuoz
10.	hairtō	hjarta	heorte	herte	herta	herza

The resemblances are again very striking, and they suggest that all of these
Germanic languages can be derived by regular sound changes from a single
earlier common source, *Proto-Germanic*. We cannot attempt to give a full demonstration here, since this is a task that would require many pages; but we have
already shown the method (the comparative method of reconstruction) by
which such a demonstration is possible.

The Gothic word *aiþei* "mother" is parenthesized, since it is clearly not *cognate* with the other Germanic words for "mother," that is, it cannot be derived
by regular sound change from the same common source. (The word "cognate"
is from Latin *co-gnātus* "born together with.") The usual Gothic word for
"father" is *atta*, a baby-talk word comparable to English "papa," and this is
also not cognate with the other Germanic words for "father." But here we are
lucky: the word *fadar*, clearly cognate with the others, happens to occur in our
Gothic manuscripts just once.

If we apply the comparative method of reconstruction to the above ten
sets of correspondences (and to hundreds of others), it becomes clear that some
of the Germanic languages are more closely related than others. In the above
list, it is fairly clear (a) that Old English and Old Frisian are more closely related
to each other than to the others; (b) that Low and High German are more closely
related to each other than to the others; and (c) that English-Frisian and Low-
High German, as a group, are more closely related to each other than to Gothic
and Norse. This led nineteenth century scholars to set up the following *family
tree* (German *Stammbaum*) diagram for the Germanic languages:

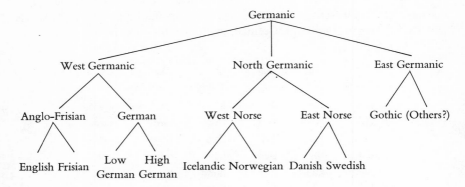

Though there is much truth in this diagram, it is surely not the whole truth. Later on we shall try to improve on it by using a different type of approach.

Let us assume that we have made at least a partial reconstruction of Proto-Germanic. Can we now demonstrate that Germanic is related to other languages or language families? For a partial answer to this question, compare the following ten sets of correspondences in which we place our original ten words from three Germanic languages beside words from three non-Germanic languages:

	Sanskrit	Greek	Latin	Gothic	Old Norse	Old English
1.	énas	oiné	ūnus	ains	einn	ān
2.	dváu	dúō	duō	twai	tveir	twā
3.	tráyas	treîs	trēs	þreis	þrīr	þrī
4.	dáśa	déka	decem	taihun	tíu	tíen
5.	śatám	hekatón	centum	hund	hund	hund
6.	pitár-	patḗr	pater	fadar	faþir	fæder
7.	mātár-	mḗtēr	māter	————	mōþir	mōdor
8.	bhrátar-	phrátēr	frāter	brōþar	brōþir	brōþor
9.	pát, padás	poús, podós	pēs, pedis	fōtus	fōtr	fōt
10.	śrad-	kardía	cor, cordis	hairtō	hjarta	heorte

Correspondences among the three non-Germanic languages are obvious, for example Sanskrit *p*, Greek *p*, Latin *p* in 6, 9; Sanskrit *t*, Greek *t*, Latin *t* in 3, 5, 6, 7, 8; Sanskrit *ś*, Greek *k* (the *he-* of *hekatón* is a prefix), Latin /k/ (spelled *c*) in 4, 5, 10. Presumably these three sets of correspondences are derived from **p, *t, *k* in the proto-language, called *Proto-Indo-European* because its modern descendants extend geographically from India in the east to Europe in the west. (Indo-European includes not only the Indo-Iranian languages [ancient Sanskrit and Persian, and modern descendants], Greek, Italic [Latin and its modern descendants, the Romance languages], but also Celtic, Slavic, Baltic, Albanian, Armenian, and a few extinct languages.)

Can we establish systematic, regular correspondences between Germanic and Indo-European? That is to say, can we demonstrate that the Germanic languages are also descendants of Proto-Indo-European? Since any possible relationship of Germanic to Indo-European must lie farther back in time than the relationships of the Germanic languages to one another, we can expect any systematic correspondences to be less obvious. The only really obvious correspondences seem rather tenuous: Indo-European *n and Germanic *n in 1; Indo-European *r and Germanic *r in 3, 6, 7, 8, 10; Indo-European *d and Germanic *t in 2, 4, 9, 10. More convincing because less obvious yet quite regular are some further correspondences:

Indo-European *p, Germanic *f in 6, 9;

Indo-European *t, Germanic *$þ$ in 3, 8;

Indo-European *k, Germanic *h in 4 (Gothic), 5, 10.

If we assume that Indo-European *k first gave Germanic *x (like German *ch*), only later *h (there is further good evidence for this), these sound changes from Indo-European to Germanic would be highly systematic. They would mean that the Indo-European voiceless stops: labial *p, dental *t, velar *k, changed in Germanic to the corresponding voiceless fricatives: labial *f, dental *p, velar *x.

The task of uncovering these and many other systematic correspondences between Indo-European and Germanic occupied scholars during much of the nineteenth century. The results eventually became completely convincing: the Germanic languages unquestionably *can* be derived from the same source as Sanskrit, Greek, and Latin; and therefore the Germanic languages unquestionably *do* belong to the great Indo-European family of languages, which includes all the languages of Europe except Finnish, Estonian, Hungarian, and Basque.

The most striking differences between Germanic and the other Indo-European languages involve the so-called "Germanic Consonant Shift," of which the above consonant correspondences are a part. This set of changes, often called "Grimm's Law" after the German scholar Jacob Grimm who first formulated them systematically, resulted in a complete restructuring of the Indo-European consonant system:

Indo-European	p	t	k	k^w	b	d	g	g^w	bh	dh	gh	g^{w}h	s
	↓	↓	↓	↓	↓	↓	↓	↓	↓	↓	↓	↓	↓
Germanic	f	þ	x	x^w	p	t	k	k^w	ƀ	ð	ǥ	ǥ^w	s

The IE voiceless stops *p *t *k *k^w became the Germanic voiceless fricatives *f *$þ$ *x *x^w; the IE voiced stops *b *d *g *g^w became the Germanic voiceless stops *p *t *k *kʷ; and the IE voiced aspirate stops *bh *dh *gh *gʷh became the Germanic voiced fricatives *ƀ *ð *g *gʷ.

There are two sets of so-called "exceptions" to the Germanic Consonant Shift: different, but completely regular, developments of the above consonants in certain positions. First, IE *p *t *k *kʷ remained unshifted after *s, cf. Latin speciō "to look," stō "to stand," scabō "to scratch," German spähen, stehen, schaben (earlier scaban). Second, under certain accentual conditions IE *p *t *k *kʷ were first shifted to *f *þ *x *xʷ and then voiced to *ƀ *ð *g *gʷ; and *s was voiced to *z. This second "exception" was first described in 1876 by the Danish linguist Karl Verner, and it is customarily called "Verner's Law." An example is the different development of IE *t in the Germanic words for "brother" and "father": in "brother" the *t followed an accented syllable (Sanskrit bhrátar-, Greek phrátēr) and gave Germanic *þ, Old English þ (brōþar), Old High German d (bruoder); but in "father" the *t followed an unaccented syllable (Sanskrit pitár-, Greek patḗr) and gave Germanic *ð, Old English d (fæder), Old High German t (fater). These different developments still survive in modern German Bruder with d but Vater with t. (The modern English th in father is the result of a later change.) Verner's Law also accounts for some striking consonant alternations in the Germanic strong verb: IE *⊥t- vs. *-t⊥ giving Germanic *-þ- vs. *-ð-, modern German -d- vs. -t- in schneiden, geschnitten; IE *⊥k- vs. *-k⊥ giving Germanic *-x- vs. *-g-, modern German -h- vs. -g- in ziehen, gezogen; IE *⊥s- vs. *-s⊥ giving Germanic *-s- vs. *-z-, modern English s vs. r in was, were (with change of *z to r).

The Germanic Consonant Shift was only one of many changes between Indo-European and Germanic. The vowel system of Indo-European was also drastically changed, though the striking vowel alternations called "ablaut" still survive especially in the Germanic strong verbs: English ride rode ridden, drink drank drunk, German reiten ritt geritten, trinken trank getrunken, etc. Other important changes were: (1) the shift from a free accent (cf. Greek phratēr accented on the first syllable, patēr accented on the second syllable) to a fixed accent (English brother, father, German Bruder, Vater, all accented on the first syllable); (2) the development of a new type of verb inflection, the so-called "weak" verbs of Germanic, for example, English wait waited waited, German warten wartete gewartet; and (3) the development of two types of adjective inflections, "strong" and "weak," now lost in English but still preserved in German heißer Kaffee "hot coffee" vs. der heiße Kaffee "the hot coffee," etc.

In the absence of written records we can know nothing directly about the early history of the Germanic languages and their speakers. Nevertheless, by piecing together bits of linguistic and nonlinguistic evidence, scholars have been able to deduce the following general picture. The "homeland" seems to have been southern Scandinavia and adjacent northern Germany. Though this area had been inhabited since the end of the last glacier (roughly 10,000 B.C.), archaeologists tell us that a new people, bearers of the "battle-axe culture," entered it around 2000 B.C.; it seems to have been their language which eventually became "Germanic." By 800 B.C. they had spread east and west in northern Germany, covering an area roughly from the Ems to the Vistula; and during the following centuries they spread westward to the Rhine and southward up the Elbe and Vistula rivers.

Germanic recorded history begins with the first contact with the Romans, starting in the first century B.C.; this Roman period also gives us our first bits of linguistic information. Roman writers (Caesar, Pliny, Tacitus) cite a few clearly Germanic words: *urus* "bison" (cr. German *Auerochs*), *alces* "elk," *sapo* "cosmetics" (cf. *soap*), *glesum* "amber" (cf. *glass*), *barditus* "war song" (cf. *bard*), plus the names of various places, rivers, tribes, etc. Far more important for the history of German are the great numbers of Latin words that entered Germanic during this period. (In any contact between a higher and a lower culture, it is typical that most of the word borrowings are from the higher to the lower culture rather than vice versa.) These include such diverse items as Latin *campus* "(battle) field" (English *camp*, German *Kampf*); Latin *caupō* "huckster" (E. (*cheap, chapman*, German *kaufen*); Latin *catillus* "small bowl" (E. *kettle*, G. *Kessel*); Latin *coquus* "a cook" (E. *cook*, G. *Koch*); Latin *mīlia* (*passuum*) "a thousand (paces)" (E. *mile*, G. *Meile*); Latin *piper* "pepper" (E. *pepper*, G. *Pfeffer*); Latin (*dua lībra*) *pondō* "(two pounds) in weight" (E. *pound*, G. *Pfund*); Latin *saccus* "sack" (E. *sack*, G. *Sack*); Latin (*via*) *strāta* "paved (road)" (E. *street*, G. *Straße*); Latin *tegula* "tile" (E. *tile*, G. *Ziegel*); Latin *vīnum* "wine" (E. *wine*, G. *Wein*); and many others. Though the German forms of these borrowings show the High German Consonant Shift (to be described in a moment), it is worth noting that neither the English nor the German forms show the effects of the Germanic Consonant Shift (described above). This means that the Germanic Consonant Shift must have been completed well before this first contact with the Romans, though we do not know just when.

The "Proto-Germanic" that we reconstruct on the basis of the recorded Germanic languages implies that, at some time, there was a relatively uniform "Germanic language." By the beginning of the Christian era, however, it seems clear that five general dialect areas had developed: (1) North Germanic, which gives the modern Scandinavian languages; (2) East Germanic, which gave Gothic and probably a few other extinct languages; (3) North Sea Germanic, which gives especially English and Frisian, plus elements of Dutch and Low German; (4) Weser-Rhine Germanic, which gives elements of modern Dutch, Low German, and High German; and (5) Elbe Germanic, which forms the primary basis of modern High German. This belief is based on features that are shared by one or more of the oldest recorded Germanic languages in various groupings. We can diagram these groupings as follows, and thus supplement the old "family tree" diagram of the relationships among the

Germanic languages:

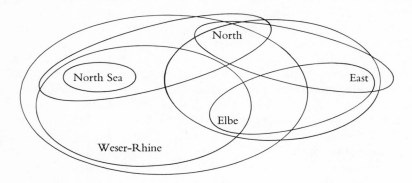

Some features are shared by North and East Germanic, for example, the change
of *ww* to *ggw* (Proto-Germanic **treww-*, English *true*, German *treu*, but Gothic
triggw-, Old Norse *tryggv-*). Some are shared by North Germanic and the so-
called "West Germanic" group North Sea, Weser-Rhine, and Elbe Germanic,
for example, the change of *z* to *r* (PGmc. **maiz-*, Gothic *maiza*, but Old Norse
meir-, English *more*, German *mehr*). Some are shared by the West Germanic
group, for example, the doubling of *t* before *j* (PGmc. **satjan*, Gothic *satjan*,
Old Norse *setja*, but Old English *settan*, modern English *set*, German *setzen*);
or the loss of final unstressed *-z* (PGmc. **dagaz*, Gothic *dags*, Old Norse *dagr*,
but English *day*, German *Tag*). Some are shared by North and North Sea
Germanic, for example, the loss of *n* before *s* (PGmc. **uns*, Gothic *uns*, German
uns, but Old Norse *oss*, English *us*). Some occur only in North Sea Germanic,
for example, the loss of final *-z* in pronouns (PGmc. **wĭz*, Gothic *weis*, Old
Norse *vēr*, German *wir*, but English *we*). Some are shared by East, North, and
Elbe Germanic, for example, the extension of the pronoun ending *-at* to strong
adjectives (PGmc. **hailan*, English *whole*, but Gothic *hailata*, Old Norse *heilt*,
German *heiles*). And some are shared by East and Elbe Germanic, for example,
the pronoun **iz* (PGmc. **hě* in English *he*, Old Saxon *hē*, cf. also Old Norse
hann; but PGmc. **iz* in Gothic *is*, German *er*).

During the early centuries A.D. groups of East Germanic speakers, notably
the Goths, moved farther south up the Vistula and beyond, until they reached
the Black Sea. (Later, as Ostrogoths, Visigoths, and Vandals, they would mi-
grate further to Italy, Spain, and North Africa.) Then, in the late fourth century,
began those vast tribal migrations known in German as the *Völkerwanderung*.
Groups of North Sea Germanic speakers (the later English) migrated across
the channel to England; groups of Weser-Rhine Germanic speakers (the later
Franks) moved south and west into northern France; and groups of Elbe Germanic speakers (the later Alemannians, Bavarians, and Langobards) moved
south. The result was a vast expansion of Germanic speaking territory, notably

to the west (England), southwest (northern France), and south (southern Germany, Austria, northern Italy); but at the same time the territory east of the Elbe and Saale rivers was largely vacated, and Slavic speakers moved in.

Written records of High (south) German do not begin until about 750. During the intervening centuries a number of changes had taken place in the language. The most striking of these is the so-called High German Consonant Shift. We can illustrate it by citing cognate forms from English (which shows the older consonantism) and Old High German (which shows the results of the shift):

	Engl.	*OHG*		*Engl.*	*OHG*		*Engl.*	*OHG*
p-	path	pfad	t-	tongue	zunga	k-	calf	chalb
pp	apple	apful	tt	set	setzen	kk	lick	lecchōn
mp	stamp	stampfōn	nt	plant	pflanzōn	nk	drink	trinchan
lp	help	helpfan	lt	salt	salz	lk	folk	folch
rp	harp	harpfa	rt	heart	herza	rk	stark	starch
Vp	open	offan	Vt	water	wazzar	Vk	make	mahhōn
Vp	sheep	scāf	Vt	hot	heiz	Vk	book	buoh

The High German Consonant Shift affected the Germanic voiceless stops *p, *t, *k. (1) Initially, when doubled, and after nasal, l, r, they became the corresponding affricates (stop plus fricative): pf (modern *Pfad, Apfel, stampfen* and with later change of pf to f, *helfen, Harfe*); ts (modern *Zunge, setzen, pflanzen, Salz, Herz*); and kx (in modern dialects only; the standard language has k in *Kalb, lecken, trinken, Volk, stark*). (2) After vowels they became the corresponding long fortis fricatives: ff (modern /f/ in *offen, Schaf*); zz (modern /s/ in *Wasser, heiß*); and xx (modern /x/ in *machen, Buch*). The sibilant fricative of OHG *wazzar, heiz* seems to have been pronounced much like modern /s/; it was in any case different from the long fortis ss of OHG *giwisso* "gewiß," *eis* "Eis," which seems to have been more similar to (though not identical with) modern /š/.

We do not know just when the High German Consonant Shift took place. One bit of evidence is the name of the king of the Huns, *Attila*, who died in 453: since his name appears in medieval German writings as *Etzel*, with tt shifted to tz, the consonant shift could not have been completed at that time; but apparently it was completed not long afterwards. We also do not know the area in which the shift first arose, though it was most likely southern Bavaria and Austria. From here it spread rapidly to the north and west; the situation at the end of the nineteenth century is indicated on Map 2.

The various numbered lines on this map are customarily used to subdivide the modern dialects of German. Line 2, *maken/machen*, is the customary boundary between *Low German* to the north (with unshifted *maken*) and *High*

NETHERLANDIC — LOW GERMAN

1, 2, 3, 4, 6

EAST MIDDLE

1
2
WEST MIDDLE
3
4
1, 2, 3, 4
6
5
HIGH GERMAN
5
6

UPPER

BOUNDARY OF THE GERMAN LANGUAGE AREA
NATIONAL BOUNDARIES

0   50   100   150   200 miles
0   50   100   200   300 kilometers

MAP 2

German to the south (with shifted *machen*); that is to say, shifted forms eventually spread this far. The line is typical for the shift of *p, t, k* after vowel (*open/ offen, Water/Wasser, maken/machen*), of initial *t-* (*Tunge/Zunge*), and of double *tt* (*sitten/sitzen*). Lines 1, 3, 4 are famous exceptions which spread out in the west to form what is called the "Rhenish fan." Line 1 is *ik/ich* "I," in which shifted *k* after vowel has spread unusually far. Line 3 is *Dorp/Dorf* "village" (cf. archaic English *thorp*), typical of the limited spread of shifted *p* after *r* and *l*. And line 4 is *dat/das* "that," showing the even more limited spread of shifted *t* in this and a few similar words (*wat/was* "what," *it/es* "it," *dit/dies* "this").

Line 5 is *Appel/Apfel*, representing the very limited spread of shifted double *pp*; it is customarily used to subdivide High German dialects into *Middle German* (with unshifted *Appel*) vs. *Upper German* (with shifted *Apfel*). Line 6, finally, is the *Pund/Pfund* "pound" line, showing the limited spread of shifted initial *p-*; it is customarily used to subdivide Middle German into *West Middle German* (with unshifted *Pund*) vs. *East Middle German* (with shifted *Pfund*).

Just as it was Irish missionaries who taught our English-speaking ancestors to read and write, so it was Irish and, later, English missionaries who taught our High German-speaking ancestors to read and write—and thus to produce the first written records of High German around 750 A.D. (Low German records do not begin until about a century later.) All the manuscripts we have from the Old High German period (750–1050) were apparently written by monks, and most of them are connected directly or indirectly with the religious work of the monasteries. The language of the period is perhaps best described as a collection of monastery dialects; there is no indication of any supra-dialectal standard language in process of development.

The special fascination of Old High German is the fact that it *does* show us a collection of local dialects, and that it shows them over a period of three centuries. It permits us to see a number of important linguistic changes unfolding right before our eyes. The change of Germanic *þ* to *d* (cf. English *that*, German *das*) appears earliest in the southeast, in the Bavarian area, and then spreads west and northwest into the Alemannic and Franconian areas; we see it in the gradual replacement of the spelling *thaz* (or *dhaz*) by *daz*. (This change eventually spread throughout the entire Netherlandic-German dialect area, cf. modern Dutch *dat* "that," *dief* "thief," etc.) A change that spreads in the opposite direction is the diphthongization of long *ē, ō* to *ie, uo*: the word for "here" is variously spelled *hēr, hear, hiar, hier*; the word for "good" is variously spelled *gōt, goat, guat, guot*; the new spellings appear first in the west central area, the old spellings survive longest in the southeast.

In order to show what written Old High German looked like—and hence also what spoken Old High German may have sounded like—we give below two versions of the Lord's Prayer, with word-for-word translations into modern German. The first version was written around 830 by an unknown monk at the monastery of Fulda (it is part of the so-called *Tatian*, a translation of much of the gospels from Latin); long marks on vowels have been added. The second was written around 1000 by a monk named Notker (or one of his pupils) at the monastery of St. Gall in modern Switzerland; the monk himself wrote a circumflex accent mark over long vowels—fairly consistently on stressed long vowels, quite inconsistently (no examples appear here) on unstressed long vowels.

TATIAN, ca. 830

fater unser, thū thār bist in	Vater unser, Du der bist in
himile, sī giheilagōt thīn namo,	Himmel, sei geheiligt Dein Name,
queme thīn rīhhi, sī thīn uuillo,	komme Dein Reich, sei Dein Wille,
sō her in himile ist, sō sī her	so er in Himmel ist, so sei er
in erdu, unsar brōt tagalīhhaz	in Erde, unser Brot tägliches
gib uns hiutu, inti furlāz	gib uns heute, und vergib ("verlasse")
uns unsara sculdi, sō uuir	uns unsere Schulden, so wir vergeben
furlāzamēs unsarēn sculdigōn,	("verlassen") unseren Schuldigern,
inti ni gileitēst unsih in costunga,	und nicht geleitest uns in Versuchung,
ūzouh arlōsi unsih fon ubile.	sondern erlöse uns von Übel.

NOTKER, ca. 1000

Fater unser, dû in himele bist.	Vater unser, Du in Himmel bist.
Dín namo uuerde geheiligot. Dín	Dein Name werde geheiligt. Dein
ríche chome. Dín uuillo gescehe	Reich komme. Dein Wille geschehe
in erdo fone menniscon also	in Erde von Menschen also (=ebenso wie)
in himele fone angelis. Vnser tage-	in Himmel von Engeln. Unser täg-
licha brôt kib uns hiuto. Vnde	liches Brot gib uns heute. Und
unsere sculde belâz uns	unsere Schulden vergib ("belasse") uns
also ouh uuir belazen	also (=ebenso wie) auch wir vergeben
unseren sculdigen. Vnde in	unseren Schuldigern. Und in
chorunga ne leitest dû unsih.	Versuchung nicht leitest Du uns.
Nube lôse unsih vone ubele.	Sondern (er)löse uns von Übel.

In the earlier Tatian, Germanic þ is still written th initially: thū "thou," thīn "thine," though it is already written d in other positions: erdu "earth," sculdi "debts"; the later Notker has only d: dû, dín, erdo, sculde. In the more northern Tatian the word for "he" or "it (masculine)" is her, a mixture of northern hē (as in Low German and English) and southern er (as in modern standard German); the more southern Notker has only er (no examples appear in this passage). Note, in both versions, the distinction between dative uns and accusative unsih.

To modern eyes, a striking feature of Old High German is the occurrence of full vowels in unstressed syllables. Note, in the Tatian, final -i, -e, -a, -o, -u in *arlōsi, queme, costunga, namo, erdu*, plus the long *ē* and *ō* of *unsarēn sculdigōn*, where modern German has either its uniform /ə/ or no vowel at all: *erlöse, komme, (Versuch)ung, Name, Erde, unseren, schuldigen*. Yet as early as 830 there is already some uncertainty in the handling of unstressed vowels: note that the word "our" is spelled first *unser* (*fater unser*), but later *unsar* (*unsara sculdi, unsarēn sculdigōn*). This is a foreboding of things to come.

In Notker, some 200 years later, this so-called "weakening" of unstressed vowels has progressed markedly, though as yet they have by no means all become /ə/. We can distinguish three degrees of weakening. (1) The five long vowels *ī, ē, ā, ō, ū* are still not (in general) confused, and sometimes they are even marked as long with a circumflex accent (no examples occur in our passage). (2) Word-finally the five unstressed short vowels of the ninth century have been reduced to three, since *-i* has become *-e* and *-u* has become *-o*, giving only *-e, -a, -o*. (3) Elsewhere the five unstressed short vowels have been weakened to one; this is usually written *e*, though it is also written *i* especially before *g* and *h* or *ch*. This progressive weakening of unstressed vowels can be shown by comparing the following pairs of forms from Tatian and Notker:

	Tatian	Notker		Tatian	Notker		Tatian	Notker
ī	tagalīhhaz	tagelicha	-i	rīhhi	rīche	-i-	himile	himele
				sculdi	sculde		giheilagōt	geheiligot
ē	unsarēn	unseren	-e	queme	chome	-e-	fater	fater
	gileitēst	leitest		ubile	ubele			
ā	(no examples)		-a	costunga	chorunga	-a-	tagalīhhaz	tagelicha
					tagelicha			
ō	giheilagōt	geheiligot	-o	namo	namo	-o-	(no examples)	
		menniscon		uuillo	uuillo			
ū	(no examples)		-u	erdu	erdo	-u-	(costunga)	(chorunga)
				hiutu	hiuto		(-u- kept before ng)	

Since the time of Notker we can assume the existence of a general unstressed vowel /ə/, written *e* in the last column to the right. But especially before *g* and *h* (*ch*) it is also written *i*: *sculdigen, geheiligot, unsih*.

Another two centuries later, in the many documents that we have from around the year 1200, the "weakening" of unstressed vowels has been completed: except for the ending *-iu* as in *guotiu* "good" (nominative singular feminine, nominative-accusative plural neuter), all of the old unstressed vowels —short and long, word-finally or not—are usually written *e*, though the spelling *i* is also used especially before *g, ch, sch*. This is the modern German system: *e* in *löse, Himmel, Name, Erde*, but *i* in *heilig, täglich, englisch*, etc. We can diagram this gradual weaking of unstressed vowels as follows:

	800			1000		1200
	Long	Short	Short	Long	Short	Short
	ī	-i	-i-	ī		
	ē	-e	-e-	ē	-e	
	ā	-a	-a-	ā	-a	-e-(-i-) e(i)
	ō	-o	-o-	ō	-o	
	ū	-u	-u-	ū		

Another vowel change, known as "umlaut," which took place during the Old High German period, was the fronting and raising of stressed vowels before a following unstressed *i, ī, j*. In part, this type of change was very old. Early Old High German had inherited from Proto-Germanic such alternations as:

	Helfen			*Ziehen*	
i	vs.	e	iu	vs.	eo
ih hilfu		wir helfamēs	ih ziuhu		wir zeohamēs
du hilfis(t)		ir helfet	du ziuhis(t)		ir zeohet
er hilfit		sie helfant	er ziuhit		sie zeohant

Here the high vowels *i, iu* appear before the unstressed high vowels *i, u*; but the mid vowels *e, eo* (later *io*) appear before the unstressed nonhigh vowels *e, a*.

Umlaut in the narrower sense seems to have taken place during the Old High German period; it produced the following drastic change in the vowel system:

Before Umlaut									*After Umlaut*								
i	u	ī	ū	iu	io	ie	uo		i	ü	u	ī	iu	ū	ie	üe	uo
e	o	ē	ō			ei	ou		é ö / e ö	o	ē	œ	ō		ei	öu	ou
	a		ā						ä	a	æ	ā					

The system of sixteen vowel phonemes to the left is that of Old High German (750–1050); the system of twenty-three vowel phonemes to the right is that of Middle High German (1050–1350). There was one decrease in the number of vowels, since OHG *io* and *ie* merged to give MHG *ie*. But this was far outweighed by the addition of nine umlaut vowels: *é, ä, ö, ü, æ, ǣ, iu, üe, öu*. (The new umlaut *iu*, phonemically /ū/, was not strictly an addition, since old *iu* had also become /ū/ though its spelling remained unchanged.) Examples:

OHG	*MHG*	*Modern*
slag, *early* slagi, *then* slegi	slac, slége	Schlag, Schläge
maht, mahti	maht, mähte	Macht, Mächte
holz, holzir	holz, hölzer	Holz, Hölzer
zug, zugi	zuc, züge	Zug, Züge
tāt, tāti	tāt, tǣte	Tat, Taten
nōt, nōti	nōt, nœte	Not, Nöte
hūt, hūti, *late* hiute	hūt, hiute	Haut, Häute
guot, guoti	guot, güete	gut, Güte
loufan, loufit	loufen, löufet	laufen, er läuft

The one umlaut that is consistently written in all but earliest OHG is that of *a* to *e*: *slag, slegi,* apparently because it merged with the already existing *e* of *weg* "Weg," etc. But then the continued presence of the following unstressed *-i* seems to have caused it to become still higher, giving MHG *slége* "Schläge," with a vowel higher than that of *wege* "Wege." (Before certain consonants and consonant clusters, however, *a* was umlauted no further than to *ä*, cf. OHG *maht, mahti,* MHG *maht, mähte.*) One other umlaut vowel is consistently written in late Old High German: that of *hūt, hiute* "Haut, Häute." Apparently the old *iu* of *hiutu* "heute" had also become /ū/, and this provided a convenient spelling for the new /ū/ that resulted from umlaut. Note, then, that the MHG spelling *iu* means /ū/: *hiute* /'hūtə/ "Häute," pronounced just like *hiute* /'hūtə/ "heute."

A minor consonantal change of late OHG was that of medial *-nt-* to *-nd-*: earlier *bintan* "to bind," etc. (with *-nt-* as opposed to the *-nd-* of *findan* "to find," etc.), but later *binden* (like *finden*). This explains why the Germanic *d* of English *bind, send, wonder,* etc., is now again *d* in modern German *binden, senden, Wunder,* etc.

It is customary to date Middle High German as beginning about the year 1050. Obviously the language did not suddenly change on January 1, 1050; but a number of changes which occurred around this time make 1050 a convenient date for beginning a new period in the history of the language. First, by about this time the various "full" unstressed long and short vowels (discussed above) had merged as /ə/, usually spelled *e*; by this time also the various umlaut vowels had become established. Second, by about this time the German-speaking Franks in northern France and Langobards in northern Italy had become Romanized, and the modern western and southern borders of the German speech area were more or less stabilized. Third, by about this time the spread of German east beyond the Elbe and Saale rivers into Slavic territory had begun —a process that was to continue for many centuries via migration and colonization, to be reversed only by the massive resettlement of populations following World War II. Finally, by about this time writing had become independent of the monasteries and had begun to spread to wider segments of the population. The numbers of manuscripts written and preserved to us soon increased enormously, and permit us to enjoy the magnificent literature produced especially during the classical period of Middle High German, ca. 1170–1230.

It is during this classical MHG period that we see the first tendency toward the development of a standard language. It was not broadly based, being limited to courtly circles; and it did not survive, but disappeared along with the courtly culture that produced it. We find this tendency in the grammar: poets consciously tried to avoid, especially in rhyme, forms too closely identified with any one dialect; and we find it in the vocabulary: they also tried to avoid words that were felt to be "uncourtly." To a certain extent we find it also in the spelling; though this is still hopelessly irregular when viewed from our modern point of view, it does not vary as much as did the many monastery spelling systems of the earlier period.

A consonant change that appears in the spellings of MHG documents is that of word-final lenis *-b, -d, -g* to fortis *-p, -t, -c.* Compare *-b-, -d-, -g-* in the infinitives *graben, laden, tragen,* but *-p, -t, -c* in the past tense forms *group, luot, truoc.* (Modern German, of course, has exactly this same alternation, though the spelling no longer shows it: *graben grub, laden lud, tragen trug.*)

Another consonant change of the MHG period was that of earlier *sc, sk* (= /sk/) to long fortis *sch* (= /šš/), as in OHG *wascan* but MHG *waschen* "to wash," or OHG *fisc* but MHG *fisch* "fish." This change seems to have "overloaded" the consonant structure, giving a system with three lenis stops: /b d g/, three fortis stops: /p t k/, three lenis fricatives: /f s h/, but now no less than five fortis fricatives: /ff zz ss šš xx/. Examples of the fricatives:

Lenis:	*f, v*		*s*			*h*	
	ofen, oven 'Ofen'		lesen 'lesen'			sehen 'sehen'	
Fortis:	*ff, f*	*zz, z*	*ss, s*		*sch*	*ch, h*	
	offen 'offen'	wazzer 'Wasser'	gewisser 'gewisser'	waschen 'waschen'		machen 'machen'	
	hof 'Hof'	waz 'was'	gewis 'gewiß'	fisch 'Fisch'		noh 'noch'	

Apparently fortis *zz, z* sounded much like modern /s/, fortis *sch* much like modern /š/, whereas fortis *ss, s* lay more or less between these two.

This "overloading" of the system of fortis fricatives seems to have led to a further change: the elimination in sound (though not in spelling) of fortis *ss, s.* Misspellings are our first clue to this change: the scribes become confused in their use of the letters *z* and *s,* apparently because they now sounded (in most positions) the same. Earlier *waz* "what" and *was* "(he) was" are now no longer clearly distinguished in spelling; so also *ez* "it" and *es* "of it" (genitive). As these examples show, fortis *ss, s* changed in most positions to the sound of fortis *zz, z,* though the spelling with the letters *ss, s* was continued and even expanded; cf. modern *was, es, Wasser, gewisser, gewiß.* Initially before consonants, however, fortis *s* changed in the other direction, namely to /š/. Before *m, n, l, w* the spelling was gradually changed to match this change in sound: earlier *smal, snel, slafen, swarz,* but modern *schmal, schnell, schlafen, schwarz.* Before *p* and *t,* however, the old spelling has remained unchanged: *spinnen, stellen,* etc.

The period from 1350 to about 1600 is a transitional one, commonly called (for the south) Early New High German. Its beginning is marked only negatively: the Middle High German courtly culture and its narrowly based semi-standard language have largely disappeared. Its end is more positively marked: by about 1600 two supra-dialectal forms of language have begun to develop in the Netherlandic-German area. One, in the extreme northwest, based largely on the speech of Amsterdam, will become standard Netherlandic (modern Dutch-Flemish); the other, arising largely in east middle Germany, will become standard German. The period as a whole is also marked by the rise and fall of what almost became a standard language: the Low German, especially of Lübeck, employed as the commercial language of the Hanseatic League, which for a time was widely used not only in northern Germany but also at Hanseatic trading centers in Scandinavia, the Baltic countries, and even Russia. Before this could become a true standard language, the age of discovery began, trade shifted from the Baltic to the Atlantic, and the Hanseatic League —with its language—went into decline. The influence of this language lives on, however, in the many Low German words that entered the Scandinavian languages during this period.

The development of East Middle German into a standard language stands in marked contrast to the rise of standard English and standard French. These latter two grew and spread and became standard because they were the languages of great political, cultural, and commercial centers: London and Paris. No such powerful sociological forces supported East Middle German. Why, then, did it eventually spread and become the standard language of so large an area? There were surely many reasons—linguistic, political, and even personal. Linguistically this was newly Germanized territory, and the dialect differences here were far less prominent than in the long settled west. In addition, though the speech of this area was clearly High German, it also represented to a considerable extent a compromise between the extremes of north (Low German) and south (Upper German). Politically, East Middle German gained prestige because it was the language of some influential chanceries (*Kanzleien,* offices issuing governmental documents), notably those of Prague and Saxony. With all these advantages, however, this type of written German would hardly have become standard without some special impetus, some type of writing that came to be widely read throughout all but the Netherlandic area.

This special impetus was provided by the fact that Martin Luther used East Middle German for his translation of the Bible (New Testament 1522, entire Bible 1534). As Luther himself tells us: *Ich red nach der sächsischen cantzeley*

"I speak (i.e., write) according to the Saxon chancery." Luther was an extraordinarily skillful writer and translator: his style had wide popular appeal because it was unusually simple and direct. And popular appeal was important because the recent invention of printing with movable type (by Johann Gutenberg in Mainz, ca. 1450) had now for the first time made it possible to reach a mass readership. Yet we must not exaggerate the speed with which this East Middle German written language became standard. It had many competitors: in the various *Druckersprachen* of the sixteenth century (each printer tended to follow the usage of his local area), and especially in the so-called *Gemeines* (=*allgemeines*) *Deutsch* of Catholic Bavaria and Austria that was used by the imperial chancery of the Habsburgs.

We must mention some of the features of modern standard German which reveal its largely East Middle German origin. Four vocalic features are especially characteristic:

1. Most striking is the diphthongization of long /ī ū ǖ/ to modern /ai au oi/ and their merger with the /ai au oi/ that already existed. Cf. MHG *mīn, hūs, hiuser* vs. *ein, troum, tröume*, but modern *mein, Haus, Häuser* with the same vowels as *ein, Traum, Träume*. This so-called "New High German diphthongization" seems to have started as early as the twelfth century in the extreme southeast, and then to have spread north and northwest during the following centuries. Though it eventually covered a large area, including East Middle German, it is by no means universal; it still has not spread into the dialects of the southwest, or into Low German.

2. The places vacated by the diphthongization of /ī ū ǖ/ have been filled, as it were, by a second striking vowel change: the monophthongization of /iə uə üə/ to modern /ī ū ǖ/. Cf. MHG *tief, guot, güete* but modern *tief* (/'tīf/), *gut, Güte*. (The spelling *ie* has been retained as a useful way of symbolizing long /ī/.) In the dialects, this so-called "New High German monophthongization" is limited to Middle German; Upper German dialects still have the old /iə uə üə/.

3. MHG short vowels have remained short where they occurred in a so-called "closed syllable" before a long fortis consonant: MHG *sip-pe, mit-te, brüc-ke, of-fen, waz-zer, gewis-ser, waschen* (/'waš-šən/), *machen* (/'max-xən/), modern *Sippe, Mitte, Brücke, offen, Wasser, gewisser, waschen, machen*. But they have become long where they occurred in a so-called "open syllable" before a short lenis consonant: MHG *ni-der, le-sen, sa-gen, o-fen, stu-be* with short vowels, but modern *nieder, lesen, sagen, Ofen, Stube* with long vowels. The lengthening of short vowels in open syllables originated in the north around the twelfth century and has spread into all but the most southern dialects. The old long fortis consonants have now been shortened in the standard language; hence the difference between single and double consonant letters can now be used to indicate the length of the preceding vowel; cf. *schaffe* (short vowel) vs. *Schafe* (long vowel), *Ratte* (short vowel) vs. *rate* (long vowel), etc.

4. By and large, MHG final -*e* has been retained in the standard language;

cf. *ich trinke, zu Hause, zwei Tage*, etc. In the dialects, *-e* has been kept only in a rather narrow band running roughly east and west across middle Germany. The dialects to the south, in particular, have lost final *-e* and have forms equivalent to *ich trink, zu Haus, zwei Tag*.

Modern standard German reveals its East Middle German origin also in the use of shifted initial *pf-* (*Pfund*, etc.), where West Middle German keeps unshifted *p-* (*Pund*, etc.). But it also reveals a strong southern influence in the use of shifted *-pf-* (*Apfel*, etc.) where the East Middle German dialects keep unshifted *-pp-* (*Appel*, etc.).

Three consonant changes deserve brief mention. (1) MHG *w* was clearly a semivowel, like English *w*; but in the standard language it has become the consonant /v/, though the old spelling is still kept: *Wasser* /'vasər/, *Löwe* /'lövə/, etc. (2) Perhaps in reaction to this change, MHG lenis *f*, *v* has become fortis; but the old lenis spelling *v* (never consistently used) has often been kept: MHG *vater* beside *fater*, *vier* beside *fier*, *vuoz* beside *fuoz*, *veder* beside *feder*, modern *Vater, vier, Fuß, Feder*. (3) MHG medial *h* has been lost, cf. MHG *sehen, stahel* (with short vowel plus /h/), but modern *sehen, Stahl* (with long vowel and no /h/). This loss of medial *h* began during MHG times and is now nearly universal in the modern dialects. It permits the letter *h* to be used as a method of indicating that the preceding vowel is long.

In addition to the above changes in sounds, there were also changes in the grammatical forms of words. Many weak verbs of MHG had different vowels in the present and past, for example, present *hæren* "to hear" with /ö/, but past *hōrte* "heard" with /ō/. This phenomenon is customarily called *Rückumlaut*, that is, "back umlaut," as if an umlaut in the past had somehow been eliminated. (The term is misleading, since in actual fact the *i* of an earlier **hōrita* was dropped before it could cause umlaut.) In modern standard German the vowel of the present has analogically been extended to the past of nearly all such verbs, giving present *hören*, past *hörte*, etc. The only modern verbs that still show "Rückumlaut" are *brennen brannte, kennen kannte, nennen nannte, rennen rannte, senden sandte, wenden wandte*.

Another analogical change affected the many strong verbs of MHG that showed different stem vowels in the singular and plural of the past. Compare the following MHG and modern forms:

	MIDDLE HIGH GERMAN				NEW HIGH GERMAN		
Present	*Past Sing.*	*Past Plural*	*Participle*		*Present*	*Past*	*Participle*
1. helfen	half	hulfen	geholfen		helfen	half(en)	geholfen
2. trinken	trank	trunken	getrunken		trinken	trank(en)	getrunken
3. rīten	reit	riten	geriten		reiten	ritt(en)	geritten
4. geben	gap	gāben	gegeben		geben	gab(en)	gegeben
5. biegen	bouc	bugen	gebogen		biegen	bog(en)	gebogen

Sometimes the vowel of the past singular was analogically extended into the past plural, as in 1 and 2; sometimes the vowel of the past plural was analogically extended into the past singular, as in 3 and 4; and sometimes the vowel of the participle was analogically extended into the whole past, as in 5. The only modern survival of the old stem vowel alternations between past singular and past plural is the archaic past singular *ward*, past plural *wurden*—though analogical past singular *wurde* is of course the usual form today. The fact that modern standard German has any past tense at all again betrays its East Middle German origin. Throughout the entire south, the modern dialects have given up the past tense altogether. There is no equivalent of standard German *ich kam, ich sah*, etc.; one can only say the dialect equivalent of *ich bin gekommen, ich habe gesehen*.

Still another analogical change has affected the present tense of many strong verbs. Compare the following, in which modern analogical forms are italicized:

	1sg.	2sg.	3sg.	1pl.	2pl.	3pl.
MHG	trage	tregest	treget	tragen	traget	tragent
MODERN	trage	trägst	trägt	tragen	tragt	*tragen*
MHG	hilfe	hilfest	hilfet	helfen	helfet	helfent
MODERN	*helfe*	hilfst	hilft	helfen	helft	*helfen*
MHG	ziuhe	ziuhest	ziuhet	ziehen	ziehet	ziehent
MODERN	*ziehe*	*ziehst*	*zieht*	ziehen	zieht	*ziehen*

All verbs have changed the 3pl. ending *-ent* of MHG to modern *-en*, probably in analogy with the past tense where 1pl. and 3pl. both had *-en*. Many verbs (like *helfen*) have changed the 1sg. stem vowel, probably in analogy with verbs like *tragen*. And some verbs (like *ziehen*) have changed the stem vowel of the entire singular, in analogy with the many verbs that had the same stem vowel in present singular and plural.

Further analogical changes, too numerous to detail here, have also affected the inflection of nouns. In particular, the use of umlaut as a mark of the plural has spread to large numbers of nouns which did not originally show umlaut. This process began in MHG times and has continued right on down into the present.

Somewhat arbitrarily, we may choose 1600 as the beginning of the New High German period; and we can divide the years that follow roughly into three periods: (1) 1600 to 1750; (2) 1750 to 1900; and (3) 1900 to the present.

1. The years 1600–1750 saw the gradual acceptance of a single standard written language, based largely on Luther's East Middle German though with numerous minor additions from other areas. The period is rounded off rather neatly by the publication in 1748 of Johann Christoph Gottsched's *Grundlegung einer Deutschen Sprachkunst*. The fame of this work, and the importance attached

to it, show clearly that the concept of a single standard written language had by 1750 been almost universally accepted.

2. The years 1750–1900 saw the adoption and consolidation of this single standard language, notably in the works of the great writers that soon followed. The consolidation culminated in two conferences (1877 and 1901) which fixed the spelling system that we now use, and in an additional conference on pronunciation which led in 1898 to the publication of the *Siebs*. This latter for the first time provided a standard *spoken* form of the written language.

3. The period since 1900 is too close for us to see it in reasonable perspective; yet three matters deserve brief mention. First, the end of World War II saw a drastic reduction in the size of the German-speaking area, since most of the German-speaking populations east of the Oder and Neisse rivers and in the many German speech islands of eastern Europe were resettled in the area to the west. Second, though local dialects are by no means dying out, their use is probably becoming more and more restricted. The arrival of the thousands of eastern refugees is in part responsible for this. Before their arrival, a small-town storekeeper had little occasion to try to speak the standard spoken language; all his customers were local people. But when newly resettled East Prussians, Silesians, Sudeten Germans, and so on, came to make up a considerable proportion of his customers, he had no choice but to try to speak standard German with them—and they with him. Third, Germany is now split into a western, capitalistic German Federal Republic (*Bundesrepublik Deutschland*) and an eastern, communistic German Democratic Republic (*Deutsche Demokratische Republik*). Political divisions such as this have always affected language in the past; there is no reason to believe that this will be an exception—if it continues. The first twenty years of this division have produced no differences in sounds or grammar, but there are already obvious differences in vocabulary and, more subtly, in the meanings of old familiar words.

In the preceding paragraphs we have sketched the history of German almost as if it had developed independently, with no influence from other languages. But no language develops in total isolation (unless, of course, its speakers are actually quite isolated from speakers of other languages—a most unusual situation). Every language is influenced to a greater or lesser extent by other languages with which its speakers come in contact, and this influence is most obvious in the words which its speakers borrow from these languages. Where two languages are in close contact, one of them usually has the status of the "upper language" because its speakers are politically dominant, or culturally more advanced, or both; the other language is then the "lower language." In such cases the upper language usually makes only limited borrowings from the lower language. American English, for example, has made only limited borrowings from the many Indian languages of America: chiefly cultural novelties (such as *tomahawk*, *wigwam*) and place names (such as *Massachusetts*, *Mississippi*). A lower language, on the other hand, may make massive borrowings of all sorts from an upper language. Witness the huge numbers of French words borrowed into English following the Norman Conquest in 1066.

During the course of its history German has borrowed many thousands of words from other languages. By and large it has held the status of a lower language as against the languages to the west and south (though the period of Frankish rule in France is a notable exception to this); hence it shows extensive borrowings from the Romance languages, notably French. On the other hand, German has by and large held the status of an upper language as against the languages to the east and north; hence it shows relatively few borrowings from the Slavic and Scandinavian languages—though these languages in turn, as lower languages, show extensive borrowings from German. In addition to such "contact borrowings" (where speakers of the two languages were in direct contact with one another), German—like all other modern languages of Europe —has made extensive "learned borrowings" from classical Latin and Greek.

Though this process of word-borrowing has been a continuous one, we can conveniently distinguish a number of different periods. The earliest of these is prehistoric: words borrowed from Celtic into Germanic, long before there was a distinguishable "German" language. A number of loan words suggest the superior political and legal status of the Celts: the noun *Reich* and the adjective *reich* (cf. English *rich*), derived from an earlier word **rīk-* meaning "ruler" (cf. Gothic *reiks*) which was borrowed from Celtic *rīg* "king"; the word *Eid* (cf. English *oath*), from a Celtic word that appears in Old Irish as *óeth* "oath"; and the word *Amt*, Middle High German *ammet*, older *ambet*, Old High German *ambaht*, from a Celtic word which Julius Caesar wrote as *ambactus*. A number of other words suggest the Celts' superior knowledge of early metallurgy: *Eisen* (cf. English *iron*), *Lot* (cf. English *lead*), and *Blei*—all apparently early borrowings from Celtic. During this same prehistoric period a number of words seem to have been borrowed from Germanic (as the upper language) into Finnish (as the lower language). An example is the Finnish word *kuningas* "king," apparently a borrowing of the Germanic word for "king" which we reconstruct as **kuningaz*.

The earliest period of word-borrowing which we can clearly document has already been mentioned: the many words borrowed into Germanic from Latin immediately before and after the beginning of the Christian era. These were not "learned borrowings" from Latin but rather "contact borrowings": borrowings made by Germanic speakers who came into direct contact with the Romans, especially in the area of the lower Rhine. Because these borrowings were made before the High German consonant shift, their modern German forms show the results of this shift. Hence Latin /p/ in *pālus, campus, caupō* appears as English /p/ in *pole, camp, cheap*, but as German initial /pf/ in *Pfund*, postconsonantal /pf/ in *Kampf*, postvocalic /f/ in *kaufen*. Latin /t/ in *tegula, menta, catillus* appears as English /t/ in *tile, mint, kettle*, but as German initial /ts/ in *Ziegel*, postconsonantal /ts/ in *(Pfeffer)minze*, postvocalic /s/ in *Kessel*. And

Latin /k/ in *coquus, calcem, secula* appears as English /k/ in *cook, chalk, sickle* (the *ch* of *chalk* is the result of a later change within English), and as German initial /k/ in *Koch, Kalk*, as postconsonantal /k/ in *Kalk*, but as postvocalic /x/ in *Koch, Sichel*.

The one historical period in which German functioned as an upper language in relation to French is the period of Frankish rule in northern France, under the Merovingians and Carolingians during the fifth to ninth centuries. Because the German-speaking Franks were the politically dominant people, word borrowings were primarily from Frankish (the upper language) into French (the lower language). Large numbers of loanwords entered French (and other Romance languages) during this period: French *nord, est, sud, ouest* (cf. German *Nordern, Osten, Süden, Westen*, English *north, east, south, west*); French *guerre, guarder, garnir* (German *Wehr, warten, warnen*, English *war, ward, warn*); and personal names such as *Henri, Louis, Gautier* (German *Heinrich, Ludwig, Walter*; English *Henry* and *Louis* are from French, whereas *Walter* is from Germanic). Some of these French loans from Frankish were later borrowed into English (like the names *Henry* and *Louis*). They account for such "doublets" as English *ward* and *guard*: *ward* directly from Germanic, but *guard* via French *guarder* from Frankish (cf. German *warten*); or *yard* and *garden*: *yard* directly from Germanic, but *garden* via north French (cf. standard French *jardin*) from Frankish (cf. German *Garten*).

The first great period of borrowing from Latin specifically into German (rather than into Germanic in general) was connected with the Christianization of the Germans during Old High German times (eighth to eleventh centuries). By this time the High German consonant shift had long since been completed; hence borrowings during this period do not show any shift of /p t k/ to /pf ts/ or /f s x/, as previously. Cf. Latin *praedicare, templum, speculum*, borrowed into OHG as *predigōn, tempal, spiagal*, modern *predigen, Tempel, Spiegel*. On the other hand, borrowings of this period do show certain sound changes which had by this time taken place in popular Latin. Compare the change of Latin *c* before *e* to *ts* in *cella, crucem*, borrowed into OHG as *zella, krūzi*, modern *Zelle, Kreuz*; or the change of Latin medial *-b-* to *-v-* in *tabula*, borrowed into OHG as *tavala*, modern *Tafel*.

During the classical period of Middle High German (twelfth to thirteenth centuries) German borrowed from French many words associated with the courtly culture of knighthood. Some of these borrowings have since died out: cf. Old French *bohourt, joste, gavelot*, MHG *būhurt, tjoste, gabilōt* "attack, joust, small spear." But others still survive: cf. Old French *aventure, flëute, pris*, MHG *āventiure, vloite, prīs*, modern *Abenteuer, Flöte, Preis*. When French verbs in *-ier* (such as *logier* "to give lodging to") were borrowed, the usual MHG verb endings were added to them (for example, infinitive *loschieren*); this is the origin of the modern verbal suffix *-ieren* that appears in such words as *regieren, halbieren, buchstabieren*, etc.

During the fourteenth to sixteenth centuries, when the Italian city states were the leading commercial centers of the western world, many Italian words were borrowed into German. Examples are such commercial terms as *Bank, Konto, Kasse, Kredit, Risiko, Kapital, Bilanz, netto,* and *brutto*. This was also the period of Humanism, when many learned borrowings were made from Latin and Greek: *Philosophie, Logik, Metaphysik, Medizin, Advokat, Hypothek, Prozeß,* and many others. It is worth noting that these words were in general borrowed with their foreign stress patterns: *Kre'dit, Kapi'tal, Philoso'phie, Medi'zin.* During earlier periods the stress was usually shifted to the first syllable, to match the stress pattern of native German words. This was done consistently during Old High German times and earlier (cf. Latin *praedi'care,* but modern German *'predigen*); it was frequently done still in Middle High German times (cf. Old French *aven'ture,* but modern German *'Abenteuer*), though not always (cf. the foreign stress pattern of verbs in *-ieren* such as *re'gieren*).

The closer we come to modern times, the larger becomes the number of loan words that have entered German. French influence was particularly strong during the seventeenth and early eighteenth centuries, when France was at its political zenith (Louis XIV, reigned 1643–1715) and "Germany" was a collection of hundreds of large, small, and tiny kingdoms, duchies, and principalities. English influence first became significant during the eighteenth century (examples from that century: *Klub, Toast, Mob, Humor, sentimental*), continued throughout the nineteenth and early twentieth centuries, and has reached flood proportions since World War II. Recent loan words (now mostly from American English rather than British English) include such items as *der Teenager* and even *der Twen* "person in his twenties" (modeled on the English word *twenty*).

We cannot conclude this section on loan words in German without at least brief mention of the German attitude toward such words. It is a plain linguistic fact that most foreign words borrowed during recent centuries stick out like a sore thumb in German. Consider such a "General European" word as *Distribution,* which happens to be a learned borrowing from Latin *distributio,* accusative *distributionem.* English /ˌdistri'bjūšən/ and French /distribüsjõ/ cause no particular difficulty: each language has dozens of words of this general type. German /distribū'tsjōn/, on the other hand, sounds very "foreign" with its full unstressed vowels (rather than the usual unstressed /ə/) and its primary stress on the final syllable. Many German speakers like to use such words, however, especially in learned discourse and writing. When the writer of these lines once gave some lectures on linguistics in Germany, he was faced with the problem of finding a suitable translation for the English technical term "complementary distribution." The word "complementary" simply had to be translated with the foreign word *komplementär,* since there is no good native German equivalent. But what of the word "distribution"? Should he use the native German word *Verteilung* or the foreign word *Distribution*? He asked his German colleagues for their preference, and they were unanimous in preferring the foreign sounding *Distribution*. As a result of this preference, modern German is full of such *Fremdwörter* (literally: "foreign words"): words that sound strange and foreign precisely because they differ from native German words in having full unstressed vowels (rather than the usual unstressed /ə/) and in being stressed on the final syllable (rather than on the first or stem syllable). The very "foreignness" of such words, however, makes many German speakers feel uneasy about using them. This has led, on the one hand, to repeated attempts to "purge" the language of such foreignisms, and, on the other hand, to innumerable dictionaries of *Fremdwörter* which explain their use and pronunciation. One of the dilemmas of modern German is its inability to borrow such "General European" words *without* making them sound strange and foreign.

Every human language is constantly subject to change. The sources of this change are partly internal (regular sound changes, which may lead to changes in grammar), and partly external (borrowings from other languages, which may lead to new patterns of word structure). These changes are usually imperceptible to the speakers themselves: we notice only trivial differences between speakers four generations apart—between ourselves and our great-grandparents, for example. Yet the cumulative effect of these trivial differences is astonishingly great. Ten times four generations is forty generations; and, allowing twenty-five years per generation, forty generations takes us back a thousand years, or nearly to the Old English of King Alfred the Great (d. 899) and to the Old High German of the first Lord's Prayer given on page 46 (from about 830). Learning to read Alfred's Old English, or Old High German, is almost like learning to read a totally foreign language—even though it is our own language a mere forty generations back. And if we could somehow hear either of these languages actually spoken, we would probably not understand a single word.

BIBLIOGRAPHY

Sounds and Spelling

MOULTON, WILLIAM G., *The Sounds of English and German*. Contrastive Structure Series. Chicago: University of Chicago Press, 1962. Pp. xiii, 145. Contains a description of the sound systems of English and German. Gives a contrastive analysis of the two systems, emphasizes the particular difficulties of Americans learning German, and suggests corrective drills. Intended for teachers and those preparing to be teachers.

SIEBS, THEODOR, *Deutsche Hochsprache, Bühnenaussprache*. 17th ed. by Helmut de Boor and Paul Diels. Berlin: Walter de Gruyter, 1958. Pp. 353. The standard authority on correct pronunciation. Contains 91 pages of historical and explanatory material, a 135-page word list (with pronunciations), and a 111-page list of German and foreign names (with pronunciations).

Duden: Aussprachewörterbuch. Mannheim: Dudenverlag, Bibliographisches Institut, 1962. Pp. 827. An 86-page introduction gives general information on German phonetics and spelling. The main body of the book consists of an alphabetical list of words (including many foreign ones), first in regular spelling and then in the phonetic transcription of the International Phonetic Alphabet.

Duden: Rechtschreibung der deutschen Sprache und der Fremdwörter. 15th ed. Mannheim: Dudenverlag, Bibliographisches Institut, 1961. Pp. 794. The standard authority for matters of spelling, punctuation, inflection, etc. Indispensable for any German teacher, student, or writer.

Grammar

KUFNER, HERBERT L., *The Grammatical Structures of English and German: A Contrastive Sketch.* Contrastive Structure Series. Chicago: University of Chicago Press, 1962. Pp. xi, 95. Contrasts the grammatical structures of English and German, with particular emphasis on syntax and on those areas where the structures of the two languages differ the most. Intended for teachers and those preparing to be teachers.

GRIESBACH, HEINZ, AND DORA SCHULZ, *Grammatik der deutschen Sprache.* 4th ed. Munich: Max Hueber, 1966. Pp. xv, 445. An excellent reference book, skillfully arranged and convenient to use, based on the modern *Umgangssprache.*

Duden: Grammatik der deutschen Gegenwartssprache. Revised edition edited by the Duden staff under the direction of Paul Grebe. 2nd ed. Mannheim: Dudenverlag, Bibliographisches Institut, 1959. Pp. 774. A scholarly reference book covering all aspects of grammar and spelling, with a brief section on sounds.

CURME, GEORGE O., *A Grammar of the German Language.* 2nd ed. [1922], 7th printing. New York: Frederick Ungar, 1952. Pp. xii, 623. The most thorough grammar of German ever written in any language. Though the theoretical approach is in many respects outdated, the collection of materials is still immensely valuable.

History and Dialects

LOCKWOOD, W. B., *An Informal History of the German Language*, with chapters on Dutch and Afrikaans, Frisian and Yiddish. Cambridge: W. Heffer & Sons, 1965. Pp. viii, 265. The first half of the book sketches briefly, and very readably, the historical development of German, including both Low and High German. Especially valuable is the second half, which discusses modern dialects (including a special section on Pennsylvania German), the use of dialect especially in Switzerland and Luxemburg, the extent of the German-speaking area through the centuries, and the closely related languages Dutch, Afrikaans, Frisian, and Yiddish.

WATERMAN, JOHN T., *A History of the German Language*, with Special Reference to the Cultural and Social Forces that Shaped the Standard Literary Language. Seattle & London: University of Washington Press, 1966. Pp. xiii, 266. A thorough and readable history of German, arranged according to historical periods: Indo-European, Germanic, Old High German, etc. Extensive and up-to-date bibliography.

BACH, ADOLF, *Geschichte der deutschen Sprache.* 8th ed. Heidelberg: Quelle & Meyer, 1965. Pp. 495. A thorough scholarly treatment of the subject. Widely used at universities in the German speaking countries. Extensive bibliography.

KELLER, R. E., *German Dialects: Phonology and Morphology, with Selected Texts.* Manchester: Manchester University Press, 1961. Pp. xi, 396. Contains an introductory chapter on the study of German dialects, and then eight chapters on eight dialect areas: Zurich, Bern, Alsace, Darmstadt, Upper Austria, Luxembourg, Westphalia, and North Saxon (Lower Elbe region).

German-English, English-German Dictionaries
(A small sampling of those available)

MOULTON, JENNI KARDING, *The German Vest Pocket Dictionary, German-English, English-German.* New York: Random House, 1959. Pp. xi, 388. Small but very useful.

SCHÖFFLER-WEIS, *Taschenwörterbuch der englischen und deutschen Sprache.* Stuttgart: Klett. Vol. I, *Englisch-Deutsch,* 3rd ed., 1954, pp. x, 628. Vol. II, *Deutsch-Englisch,* 3rd ed., 1955, pp. xvi, 1174. Remarkably complete despite its relatively small size.

CASSELL, *The New Cassell's German Dictionary, German-English, English-German.* Completely revised and re-edited by Harold T. Betteridge. New York: Funk & Wagnalls, 1958. Pp. xix, 630, 619. Adequate for all but highly specialized use.

Langenscheidt's New Muret-Sanders Encyclopedic Dictionary of the English and German Languages. Ed. by Otto Springer. Part I, *English-German.* Vol. 1, A-M, pp. xl, 1-883; vol. 2, N-Z, pp. viii, 885-1844. New York: Barnes & Noble, 1962, 1964. The most comprehensive English-German dictionary. Part II, *German-English,* will follow. The firm of Langenscheidt also publishes a number of smaller English-German, German-English dictionaries.

All-German Dictionaries

Der Sprach-Brockhaus: Deutsches Bildwörterbuch für jedermann. 7th ed. Wiesbaden: F. A. Brockhaus, 1956 and later printings. Pp. 800. An extremely useful all-German dictionary, full of helpful drawings and tables.

PAUL, HERMANN, *Deutsches Wörterbuch.* 5th ed. by Werner Betz. Tübingen: Max Niemeyer, 1966. Pp. x, 841. A splendid scholarly work with much historical information.
Trübners Deutsches Wörterbuch. Vols. 1-4 ed. by Alfred Götze, vols. 50-8 ed. by Walther Mitzka. Berlin: Walter de Gruyter, 1939-1957. Pp. 4850. A large scholarly work full of information on the history of forms and meanings.

GRIMM, JACOB AND WILHELM, *Deutsches Wörterbuch.* Vols. lff. Leipzig, 1854-1962. A mammoth dictionary of German on historical principles, comparable to the unabridged *Oxford English Dictionary.*

Specialized Dictionaries

PFEFFER, J. ALAN (ed.), *Dictionary of Everyday Usage, German-English, English-German.* New York: Holt, Rinehart and Winston, 1945. Pp. xxvi, 369, 504. Contains ca. 10,000 entries in each part. Not meant for use in connection with reading, but rather for the intermediate student who wishes to speak and write. Extremely helpful because most entries are illustrated in one or more sentences.

Duden: Stilwörterbuch der deutschen Sprache. 5th ed. Mannheim: Dudenverlag, Bibliographisches Institut, 1963. Pp. 800. The use of words is illustrated in large numbers of examples and phrases. Very helpful to the foreigner who wishes to write German.

Duden: Bildwörterbuch der deutschen Sprache. 2nd ed. Mannheim: Dudenverlag, Bibliographisches Institut, 1958. Pp. 672, 112. Contains drawings and pictures on an almost endless variety of subjects, with the names of the objects depicted given on the facing page. Fascinating for those who love words.

Duden: Vergleichendes Synonymwörterbuch, Sinnverwandte Wörter und Wendungen. Mannheim: Dudenverlag, Bibliographisches Institut, 1964. Pp. 792. Useful for finding synonyms and related expressions.

KLUGE, FRIEDRICH, *Etymologisches Wörterbuch der deutschen Sprache.* 19th ed. by Walther Mitzka. Berlin: Walter de Gruyter, 1963. Pp. xvi, 917. The standard etymological dictionary of German.

Bibliography

Subsequent to the writing of the above chapter on "The German Language" the article given below was published. It includes a more recent and more comprehensive bibliography on the German language:

REICHMANN, EBERHARD (ed.), *The Teaching of German: Problems and Methods.* Philadelphia: National Carl Schurz Association, 1970, pp. 496–97.

k gihorta dat seggen dat sih urhettun ænon muo
tin · hiltibraht enti hadubrant untar heriun tuen ,
sunu fatarungo · iro saro rihtun garutun se iro
gudhamun · gurtun sih iro · suert ana · helidos
ubar ringa do sie to dero hiltu ritun · hiltibraht
gimahalta heribrantes sunu · her uuas heroro
man ferahes frotoro · her fragen gistuont fohem
uuortum · per sin fater pari fireo In folche eddo
pelihhes cnuosles du sis · ibu du mi enan sages · ik
mi deo dreuuet chind In chunincriche · chud ist
mir alirmin deot · hadubraht gimahalta hiltu
brantes sunu dat sagetun mi usere liuti alte anti
frote dea erhina parun · dat hiltibrant haetti
min fater : ih heittu hadubrant · forn her ostar
gih uuetc floh her otachres nid hina miti theotrihhe
enti sinero degano filu · her furlaet In lante luttila
sitten prut In bure barn unpahsan arbeo laosa
her raet ostar hina dat sid detrihhe darba gi
stuontun · fateres mines · dat uuas so friuntlaoso
man · her par otachre ummet tirri dega
no dechisto unta deotrihhe darba gistontun ·
her par eo folches at ente imo puas eo pehta a ti leop ·
chud par her · chonnem mannum ni paniu ih
iu lib habbe ... nu minget ot quad

German Literature to Goethe

GEORGE SCHULZ-BEHREND

The University of Texas at Austin

OLD HIGH GERMAN LITERATURE

Before the Germanic tribes encountered Christianity they probably possessed no written literature. Tacitus and other mediterranean authors report that the Germans sang war songs and had heroic lays, but the reports are vague, and no actual examples of this oral literature have come down to us. Shortly after the birth of Christ the Roman emperors Drusus and Tiberius extended their rule far into German territory; but although Roman technology and Latin left their mark on the German language, no considerable artistic or intellectual awakening took place among the German tribes.

The Goths, who were first to leave their Scandinavian homelands, were also the first to come under the influence of the Hellenistic world and of Christianity. Constantine the Great, emperor of the Eastern Roman empire, made peace with the troublesome raiders and invaders in 332 A.D. and one of the most influential among them, Ulfilas (or Wulfila, meaning "little wolf," ca. 311–83)

George Schulz-Behrend received his early training in the Gymnasium of his home town, Greifswald, Germany, his B. A. and M. A. from the University of Colorado, and his Ph.D. from the State University of Iowa. He has been teaching in the University of Texas at Austin from 1946 to date and has been a guest professor at Marburg and the Free University, Berlin. Publications include his translation of Grimmelshausen's *Simplicius Simplicissimus*, 1965, the first two volumes of his critical edition of the works of Martin Opitz, as well as numerous articles on Opitz, Holz, Kafka, Werfel, and others in scholarly journals.

became ambassador to the imperial court in Byzantium. Possibly already a Christian at the time, Ulfilas benefited enormously from his encounter with Latin and Greek and the ideas which at that time could be expressed only in these languages. For forty years he worked among his people in behalf of Christianity as a missionary bishop and acted as spokesman for the Goths at various councils and synods. As "the apostle of the Goths" he translated the entire Bible into Gothic (except for the Book of Kings which he considered too inflammatory for his warlike countrymen). Unfortunately only portions of this translation have been preserved, the largest fragment being the "Codex argenteus," 117 (of originally more than 330) purple parchment leaves inscribed with silver ink. The Codex contains much of the Gospels and is today kept in the University Library at Uppsala, Sweden. In order to write Gothic, Ulfilas had to adapt to his purpose Germanic runes (letters until then used only for short inscriptions) and to supplement them with characters from the Greek and Roman alphabets. But he also had to bend old words to new uses and to make up new ones for concepts previously unknown in Gothic. Superficially viewed, his task was similar to that of Luther who translated the Bible into modern German eleven centuries later; but intrinsically Ulfilas' task was incomparably more difficult. Luther could look to a number of predecessors from whose experiences he benefited in rendering largely familiar words and concepts for readers who were well established in Christianity, whereas Ulfilas had to acquaint his people with new ideas and to mold new attitudes through a host of novel words and unfamiliar constructions. In doing so he remained faithful to the Greek text and rendered it with poetic imagination and boldness of expression. His is one of the world's great Bible translations.

After centuries of strife and rivalry among the Germanic nations, there gradually emerged a relatively stable kingdom under Franconian rulers. Clovis (or Chlodwig, 466–511), by conquering Gaul as far south as the Loire and becoming a Christian, had firmly established Franconian rule in the West. He and his successors rounded out their realm by subduing the Swabians, Thuringians, Hessians, Allemanians, Bavarians, Lombards, and lesser nations. Christianity became well established under Wynfrith Boniface, the apostle of the Germans (672–754). Finally Charlemagne conquered and Christianized the Saxons and Frisians in the North.

Charlemagne—crowned emperor of the West Roman empire on Christmas day of the year 800 in Rome—carried Franconian rule to its greatest extent and splendor. Charles, realizing that sheer power bestows neither permanence nor prestige, made the Church a partner to his rule. He furthered its aims by appointing clergymen to important administrative posts and by protecting the Pope. Furthermore he enhanced the importance of the Church by erecting substantial buildings on the model of Italian churches. But most significant, he endeavored to strengthen the intellectual and moral fiber of his subjects through education. For this purpose he called to his court at Aachen (Aix la

Chapelle) prominent scholars and teachers from all over Europe, a number of them from England, where Anglo-Saxon genius had already been permeated with Christianity and where a rich and varied literature existed. From the headship of the cathedral school at York he called Alcuin, who became his advisor and the foremost member of the Palatine Academy, to which belonged many scholars, courtiers, and even the ladies of the royal family. For children of the royal household and those of the courtiers a palace school was founded.

Though Charles himself had never learned to write, he could speak several languages and between campaigns he took lessons in Latin grammar and other subjects from a learned Italian, Peter of Pisa. Charles also induced the historian of the Lombards, Paulus Diaconus, who knew Greek, to spend a few years in Aachen. More than ever before, the monasteries now became centers of learning and education. Alcuin, now abbot of St. Martin's at Tours, trained a number of outstanding teachers, one of whom, Hrabanus Maurus, headed the monastery school at Fulda, which he transformed into one of the best in Germany. Other centers of learning were located at Reichenau, where Hraban's student Walafrid Strabo became the headmaster; at St. Gall, founded by Irish monks in 613, where still another student of Hraban's was now abbot; and at Salzburg and Cologne.

Although Latin was and remained the language of government and church, of law and learning, Charlemagne was sympathetic to the use of the German language and ordered the recording and preservation of extant vernacular poetry. We possess nothing of the collection which may have resulted, but chance saved a fragment of one heroic song that ranks among the best of its kind, the *Hildebrandslied*. It was written down ca. 820 at Fulda on two empty leaves at the front and back of a Latin theological work.

The *Hildebrandslied* (*Song* or *Lay of Hildebrand*) is written in *Stabreim* (alliterative verse), the verse form common to all old Germanic poetry. The line constitutes the metrical unit; divided into two half lines, it contains four stressed syllables and an unfixed number of unstressed ones. Two or three of the accented syllables begin with the same consonant (or have vowel onset), that is, they alliterate. The first stressed syllable of the second half line is always alliterative, for example:

> fur*l*aet in *l*ante   *l*uttila sitten
> *p*rut in *b*ure,   *b*arn unwahsan[1]

The anonymous poet tells us that Hildebrand, a warrior returning with an army after thirty years of exile among the Huns, is challenged to single combat by a man half his age. Hildebrand recognizes the challenger as his son Hadubrant and tries to avoid the confrontation. But when Hadubrant, sensing the old man's reluctance to fight, calls him a coward, the duel becomes a matter of honor and cannot be avoided. The two men get ready for the fight, their shields are splintered—and here the fragment ends. From an Old Norse poem we know that the elder, more experienced fighter kills his son.

The language has the sonorousness of all the older Germanic dialects; run-on lines testify to the craftsmanship of the poet in giving the verses power and sweep. But the concentrated excitement is due to still another device: the poet describes very little; instead he reveals what is going on in the minds of the heroes through terse speeches. Dialogue thus lends this short epic fragment of some sixty lines a remarkable dramatic quality.

Of other pre-Christian writings little has survived and the few documents we have concern the folklorist rather than the literary historian. We refer particularly to two Old High German incantations, called the *Merseburger Zaubersprüche* (*Merseburg Charms*), from the place of their discovery. The first of these intends to help a prisoner of war escape; the second one, longer and more skillfully constructed, is intended to cure a horse's sprained leg. It mentions several Germanic deities, whose specific names are significant, for in contrast to extensive information on Scandinavian Germanic mythology, we have very little evidence of a strictly German mythology.

Many more documents with Christian content have survived from the ninth century. At that time poet priests were busy adapting and translating Christian writings from Latin so that Christian ethics and dogma could be asserted in words that were widely understood. One such work, written ca. 830 by an anonymous cleric, is the Old Saxon *Heliand* (*The Savior*), a Gospel harmony of some 6,000 lines of alliterative verse. The poet, who is said to have written it at the request of Louis I, the Pious, a son of Charlemagne, based his story on Tatian's synopsis of the Gospels, the *Diatessaron* (second century, but translated into German only shortly before the *Heliand*); the *Heliand* poet knew contemporary theology, and by skillful use of epithets, kennings, variations, and enjambment proves that he was well acquainted with Germanic epic poetry, particularly the Anglo-Saxon Biblical epic. Though he tells his story at a leisurely pace, he hardly ever wastes a word. His sense of what is poetically effective proves him a master of the older Germanic wordcraft—perhaps he was its last great practitioner on the continent.

The poet uses familiar language and situations to make an alien story clear to his audience; since towns were still unknown, he speaks of Rom*burg* and Bethlehem*burg*; Christ retreats not into a desert but into the forest; and in the nativity scene the *shep*herds become *horse*herds. Thus the story of Christ is Germanized and assumes Saxon local color. But when it comes to Christian ethics the poet makes no concessions whatever. He does not try to explain the great mystery according to which Christ is unable to defend himself, nor why he does not ask his "retainers" to ward off the attackers in Gethsemane. He makes the most of the sword stroke with which Peter severs the ear of Malchus, but Christ's passion has been foreordained by God the Father and his suffering must be borne so that mankind can be saved.

Some fifty years after the *Heliand*, one of Hraban's pupils, the Alsatian monk Otfried of Weissenburg, composed a similar work, the *Evangelienbuch*, a Gospel harmony of more than 15,000 lines in Rhenish Franconian. Writing for a sophisticated audience of clergymen and educated courtiers, Otfried explains in one of his four introductions that the Frankish tongue, though rude, is indeed as worthy and capable a language as Latin for retelling the life of Christ. In the selection of the episodes Otfried is fairly independent, and at the end of some he gives a symbolic or practical-moral interpretation. While his approach smells of the lamp and his style is anemic, his versification is remarkable. Here largely pure end rhyme and essentially regular alternation of stressed and unstressed syllables are used for the first time in German. These devices—end rhyme and alternation—derive from Latin Ambrosian hymns and remain important metric principles of poetry down to the present time.

The so-called "Otfried line" soon began to be used for poems of widely varying subject matter. Before the year 900 we find it in the *Ludwigslied*, a song of praise for the West Franconian king Louis III and his victory over the Normans at Saucourt in 881; in the *Georgslied*, a saint's life, and in the *Petruslied*, a short prayer for God's grace and the first German hymn. All of these "Lieder" were sung by skilled soloists; the listeners were, however, allowed to join in such refrains as the "Kyrie eleison, Christe eleison!" of the *Petruslied*.

THE POST-CAROLINGIAN ERA. CLUNY

At the beginning of the tenth century the so-called Carolingian Renaissance had run its course, and as the empire passed into the hands of Saxon rulers (919–1024), a new *Lebensgefühl* (attitude toward life) asserted itself. While not hostile to the world, this attitude was not one of optimism. It had expressed itself in the founding (910) of the monastery of Cluny in France. From there a mood of seriousness and strictness emanated: it reached England as early as 920 and was brought to Germany by way of Lorraine through the Swabian monastery of Hirsau. Cultural life was still almost exclusively in the hands of churchmen, and Latin predominated over German as the language of literature. But whereas a century ago Latin had been used primarily for theoretical and scientific writings—Eginhard had composed a Suetonian *Vita Caroli*, and historians and theologians had employed it—now it also became the language of belles lettres. And though some of the subjects treated were classical (or close to the classics), many others were German and upon these the Latin garb hung somewhat awkwardly.

One of several monks named Ekkehard of St. Gall wrote the epic called *Waltharius manu fortis* (*Walter of the Strong Hand*), a poem whose popularity is well proven by twenty-nine extant manuscripts. Ekkehard knows how to tell a story: Three children have been sent as hostages to Etzel, King of the Huns in Pannonia: Walter, son of the king of Aquitania; Hagen from the Frankish court; and Hildgund, daughter of the king of Burgundy. Hagen escapes when Gunter, the new king of the Franks, refuses to continue paying tribute to the Huns. Thereupon, to prevent Walter's escape, Etzel makes him the leader of a group of warriors. At a victory celebration Walter encourages the Huns to carouse till they fall into a stupor. Then he and Hilde, to whom Walter was betrothed in childhood, steal a good horse, load it with treasure, and escape under cover of night. Forty days later they cross the Rhine near Worms. When the ferryman tells King Gunter about the rich strangers, Hagen surmises who they are and is glad that his friend Walter has made good his escape. But greedy Gunter follows the pair and demands the horse, the girl, and the treasure. Walter refuses and has to fight successively eleven of Gunter's men, all of whom he kills. Hagen, who has been reluctant to enter the fray, is drawn in after Walter threatens and humiliates his lord Gunter. But darkness intervenes. Next day Walter must fight Gunter and Hagen at the same time, and the fighting stops only after each man has been severely wounded. Now Hildgund binds up the wounds and brings strengthening food. Amid coarse joking about the mayhem, peace is made and the treasure divided evenly. Walter and Hilde continue on their way, and after the death of his father, Walter rules for thirty happy years.

The poet, in utilizing an older Germanic saga, could not avoid endowing his characters with the old-fashioned warlike virtues of courage and defiance of death, but as a monk he could hardly approve of them. To his hero he assigned a somewhat superficial Christianity and in the joking between Hagen and Walter he views with a bitter smile such heroics as had been accomplished. What Ekkehard disapproves of most severely is greed: avarice is Gunter's chief trait, and even the hero is guilty of it when he steals from his generous host. Ekkehard states emphatically that avarice is the root of all evil. Revealing also is the role he assigns to Hildgund: she is a tomboy and, aside from being helpful to the wounded, her chief characteristic is unquestioning obedience to her fiancé.

With another anonymous Latin poem, the *Ruodlieb*, written in rhyming hexameters ca. 1060 by a monk of Tegernsee in Bavaria, we are already approaching the age of chivalry. Since the poem is fragmentary, it is not easy to recognize its basic intent, but ideals of Christian knighthood clearly pervade it. A young knight, eager for new experiences, has ingratiated himself with a king. When he is called home, the king offered him for a parting gift the choice between a rich reward or wisdom. Ruodlieb chooses wisdom and receives twelve maxims and two loaves of bread; close inspection reveals that the loaves are filled with jewels and gold. On his homeward journey Ruodlieb has to try out the maxims, and at home is able to avoid a mésalliance with a lady his relatives want him to marry. In a last fragment we see him fighting with a dwarf, and a fairy-tale element enters an otherwise realistic story.

The poet's Latin is not so good as Ekkehard's, but he knew more of the world, of men and ladies at court, of village life and games, of music and customs. If, as has been suggested, Walter represents the last of the Germanic heroes, then Ruodlieb is the first hero of the chivalric age. As a Christian knight he seeks adventure and through experience he proves and improves his mettle. To find such stories written in the German language we shall have to wait another century.

Along with the epics of Walter and Ruodlieb we must mention the *Ecbasis captivi* (*The Escape of the Prisoner*), the first example of the "beast epic" on German territory, ca. 1040. It was written by a monk of Lorraine in Latin hexameters and tells of the escape of a calf from prison; but the wolf takes it and holds it captive until a number of other animals release it. Now the calf is glad to return to its original prison. In general the allegory of the story is obvious: the author satirizes himself for trying to escape from monastic discipline only to get caught in far greater trouble; humbly he returns to his monastery.

Around the year 1000 there worked in St. Gall a monk by the name of Notker, first nicknamed "Labeo" (the Thicklipped), later also called "Teutonicus" (the German). As headmaster of the monastery school he had observed that pupils grasped thoughts and concepts more easily in their native tongue than in Latin; so he prepared translations (interspersed with some Latin and brief explanations in German) of such classical texts as the *Disticha Catonis*, Gregory's Commentary on Job, or books by Boethius and Aristotle. He also wrote a *Rhetoric* and created a host of words for theological, philosophical, and scientific uses. The only translator among many monastic authors of his time, he seems to have been unaware of any predecessors in the field. With his death in 1022 St. Gall ceased to be an important center of literary activity.

At a time when classical plays were read, or at best recited but never performed, the canoness Hrotsvita (ca. 935–after 973) in the north German convent of Gandersheim wanted to provide students with reading material more suitable than the six wicked comedies of heathen Terence. Thus she composed half a dozen prose dialogues in Latin dramatizing saints' legends and extolling the chastity and fortitude of Christian maidens. One of the saints' legends she wrote in Latin hexameters deals with a medieval Faust: the ambitious Theophilus sells himself to the devil in exchange for worldly prosperity, and only the intervention of the Virgin Mary saves him from eternal damnation.

About the year 1100 a general fear was rampant that the world was coming to an end. The spirit of Cluny which exalted the spiritual far above the temporal did nothing to dispel this apocalyptic mood, and as witness to it we have a number of German poems that express contempt of the world and preach remembrance of death and of eternal values. An example is Noker of Zwifalten's *Memento mori* (*Remember Death*) which moans:

Trohtîn, chunic hêre,   nobis misere!
tu muozist uns gebin ten sin   tie churzun wîla, so wir hie sîn,
daz wir die sêla bewârin: wanda wir dur nôt hinnan sulen varn.[2]

But thanks to the ironic principle that always contradicts generalizations, there now also began to flourish among the educated the songs of the *clerici vagantes*, poets who traveled from one university to another and left behind rollicking and ribald Latin songs. Quite a few of these are found in a manuscript collection made in the Bavarian monastery of Benediktbeuern and hence named *Carmina Burana*. The phenomenon was European, however. In our century Carl Orff has set a number of these poems to modern melodies.

THE AGE OF COURTLY LITERATURE

ca. 1150–ca. 1250

The Lyric

In the Middle Ages the leading social classes were the clergy and the knights; these two exercised leadership in matters of the spirit and of power. A third class, the burghers and the peasants, was as yet without much influence; they did the world's work and provided the means of subsistence. Until the beginning of the twelfth century literature had almost exclusively been the domain of the clergy, and most literature had been concerned with matters spiritual. But soon after 1100 German knights began to assert themselves in literature; we have already seen that knightly themes were utilized in such epics as the *Ruodlieb*. Cultural leadership, however, passed to France, particularly Provence, Burgundy, and the Low Countries (Brabant), and Provencal troubadours now originated an entirely new kind of poetry—lyric song in praise of a lady. Scholars have tried to trace this encomiastic poetry to secularization of the worship of the Virgin Mary; they have sought and found Moorish traces of Oriental love poetry in it; and they argue that at least for the German equivalent of troubadour songs, native vernacular song furnished the basis. Be that as it may, courtly German poetry, both the lyric and epic variety, is based on a new feeling of life which contrasts sharply with the previous, pessimistic *Lebensgefühl* advocated by the Church. In an enumeration of knightly virtues, one would have to include such concepts as *mâze* (moderation), *triuwe* (faithfulness), *zuht* (discipline), *milte* (generosity), *êre* (honor), *staete* (steadiness), *saelde* (the certainty that one's luck will hold), and—*minne*. This last concept needs explaining even more than the others, none of which can be exactly conveyed by the words here used to translate them. *Minne* means reverence for womanhood and the conviction that woman, representing the gentler part of humanity, needs protection; in turn she inspires a man to noble deeds and brings out his best qualities. Sex is all but excluded from this concept, for, as in the French convention, the lady revered by the poet is unattainable; often she is the wife of the poet's liege lord. Thus *minne* can adore from afar only and without hope of reward. The knight seeks hardly more than a smile from his always anonymous lady, but *hoher muot* (idealism) buoys him up and in celebrating *his* lady he celebrates the beauty, the gentleness, the purity of all ladies. Such high-mindedness is possible only in an unrealistic world, in a world of dreams and symbols. The world of courtly literature, with whose ideals we are vaguely familiar even today, possesses a fairy-tale geography, but by and large it is a joyful rather than a tragic world. Knighthood and with it courtly literature reached its zenith in Germany from about 1180 to 1250, that is, during the reign of the Hohenstaufens; yet it was at the many smaller courts rather than at the imperial one that the great epics were cherished and minnesong was performed. For "publication" in those days meant presentation by the singer of an original melody along with the words before a social gathering. It is only toward the end of the era that the words were written down, and only a few melodies have been preserved.

> Dû bist mîn, ich bin dîn,
> des solt dû gewis sîn.
> Dû bist beslozzen in mînem herzen;
> verlorn ist daz sluzzelîn.
> Dû muost immer drinne sîn.[3]

These lines are found at the end of a Latin letter written by a nun and their preservation was a lucky accident. We may assume that many more such poems existed, for we know that Austrian minnesingers based their more artful love poems on them before the French conventions began to assert themselves. The Lord of Kürenberg (der Kürenberger), writing in the archaic form of the Nibelungenstrophe, often lets the lady express her longing, her joys and disappointments, as for example, in this *Song of the Falcon*:

> Ich zôch mir einen valken   mêre danne ein jâr.
> dô ich in gezamete   als ich in wolte hân
> und ich im sîn gevidere   mit golde wol bewant,
> er huop sich ûf vil hôhe   und floug in anderiu lant.
>
> Sît sach ich den valken   schône fliegen:
> er fuorte an sînem fuoze   sîdîne riemen,
> und was im sîn gevidere   alrôt guldîn.
> Got sende sî zesamene,   die gerne geliep wellen sîn![4]

Reinmar von Hagenau (also called Reinmar the Old, who flourished in Vienna from about 1190 to 1210) may be regarded as a typical, even a classic minnesinger. He frequently uses the tripartite strophe which consists of two melodically and metrically identical sections, called *Stollen* and a somewhat more complicated conclusion, called *Abgesang*.

Reimar sings of the sadness of *minne*, of its melancholy and of his resignation. But he enjoys the tension between longing for fulfillment and the impossibility of it. To be permitted to serve his lady is all the privilege he desires. His poems have an almost Byronic touch in their self-analysis and frustration.

> Und wiste ich niht, daz sî mich mac
> vor al der welte wert gemachen, ob si wil,
> Ich gediende ir niemer mêre tac:
> sô hat si tugende, den ich volge unz an daz zil,
> Niht langer, wan die wîle ich lebe.
> noch bitte ich sî, daz sî mir liebez ende gebe.
> waz hilfet daz? ich weiz wol, daz siez niht entuot.
> nu tuo siz durch den willen mîn
> und lâze mich ir tôre sîn
> und neme mîne rede für guot.[5]

More colorful is Heinrich von Morungen, a Thuringian knight who died about 1222; he knew the French troubadours as well as he knew Ovid. His carefully constructed stanzas underscore his graceful diction; his images are vivid and fresh, so that even the greatest genius of the era, Walther von der Vogelweide, was able to learn from him by emulating him. Like Reinmar he confined himself to convention, but unlike Reinmar he was able to infuse it with personal enthusiasm and imaginative variation. The one poem that represents the highest reaches of Morungen's art—and oversteps convention slightly—is his "Tagelied." The French, from whom this kind of poem is derived, call it *aubade*; the situation is that of lovers' parting in the morning, and the best-known (but belated) example of it in English is Shakespeare's "It was the nightingale and not the lark . . ." in *Romeo and Juliet*.

> Owê, sol aber mir iemer mê
> geliuhten dur die naht
> Noch wîzer danne ein snê
> ir lîp vil wol geslaht?
> Der trouc diu ougen mîn:
> ich wânde, ez solde sîn
> des liehten mânen schîn.
>   do taget es.
>
> Owê, sol aber er iemer mê
> den morgen hie betagen?
> Als uns diu naht engê,
> daz wir niht durfen klagen:

"Owê, nû ist ez tac,"
als er mit klage pflac,
do'r jungest bî mir lac.
   dô taget ez.

   Owê, si kuste âne zal
in deme slâfe mich.
Dô vielen hin ze tal
ir trêne nidersich.
Iedoch getrôste ich sî,
daz sî ir weinen lî
und mich al ummevî.
   dô taget ez.

   Owê, daz er sô dicke sich
bî mir ersêen hât!
Als er endahte mich,
sô wolte er sunder wât
Mich armen schouwen blôz.
ez war ein wunder grôz,
daz in des nie verdrôz.
   dô taget ez.[6]

On the purely formal side, the stanzas contain much art: consider the gently varied rhyme scheme; note how the refrain falls into place without obtruding; observe how alternately (in the ancient manner of the *Wechsel*) the man and the lady speak. In many ways the poem is unconventional: no watchman calls the hour or warns the lovers of the approaching dawn; no birds sing, nor are vows of eternal faithfulness exchanged, But what chiaroscuro imagery, what joy of union and what intensity of passion! One marvels at the sophistication and maturity of the audiences that could appreciate such poetry.

The greatest lyric poet of the era was Walther von der Vogelweide, a noble poor knight, born about 1170. He spent his early years in Vienna where Reinmar taught him the conventions of composing words and melody. With the death of his patron in 1198 there began for Walther a life of wandering that did not stop until Emperor Frederick II bestowed a fief on him. He died about 1230 in Würzburg.

Politically his were difficult times. Philipp of Swabia, the strongest contender for the throne of the empire, was murdered by a relative in 1208. Now his opponent, dour Otto IV gained the ascendancy until generous young Frederick II came forward. The turmoils of history, far from discouraging Walther's poetic endeavors, inspired him to write lyrics that make him Germany's first politically articulate poet. Before him, traveling entertainers (invariably of the lower class) had sung out the news, and occasionally they had added praise or censure. Now Walther adapted this tradition and elevated it to a courtly level. Avoiding all abstract diction, Walther creates a characteristic situation from which comment emanates naturally. Although most of Walther's *Sprüche* (pronouncements) contain only one strophe, their structure is varied and often intricate, and they deal with a wide range of subjects: he praises generosity in one prince and deplores indiscriminate hospitality in another; he advises Philipp to put on the imperial crown and to put arrogant princes in their place; he chides the young people for their rude manners and gives advice on the rearing of children ("Spare the rod, but don't spoil the child."); he complains of his own poverty and hopes for rewards; he rejoices in his fief and praises his old teacher Reinmar; he recommends self-discipline and composes a morning prayer.

A number of the more important *Sprüche* are devoted to the relationship of Church to empire, of emperor to pope. Walther supported the Church as the guardian of spiritual values, but in the struggle for wordly power he sided throughout his life with the empire, a position that could hardly have displeased any of the contenders for the throne.

From some of Walther's *Sprüche* we can learn a good deal about the realities of medieval life, realities that are never glimpsed in the idealized situations of courtly literature. We learn, for example, that Gerhart Atze killed Walther's horse. When the time came to pay for the damage, Atze resorted to a silly subterfuge. Other *Sprüche* tell of the deplorable conditions prevailing in the empire. In the poem

> Ich saz ûf eime steine
> und dahte bein mit beine[7]

Walther assumes the thinker's traditional posture and wonders how a man can harmoniously combine honor, wealth, and the grace of God. These three will never harmonize unless peace and justice prevail.

Incisive and varied as Walther's *Sprüche* are, his pure lyrics are even more attractive. Beginning with conventional minnesong, Walther soon wearied of its narrow compass and, neither parodying nor destroying the existing usage, extended its range. He introduces joy and humor where elegant sobriety had prevailed; speaking of genuine affection, he often granted fulfillment to his lovers; his nature scenes took on added meaning where previously they had been mere set pieces. The following is one of the most ingratiating of his *Lieder*:

> Under der linden
> an der heide,
> dâ unser zweier bette was,
> dâ muget ir vinden
> schône beide
> gebrochen bluomen unde gras.
> vor dem walde in einem tal—

tandaradei!
schône sanc diu nahtegal.

Ich kam gegangen
zuo der ouwe,
dô was mîn friedel komen ê.
dâ wart ich enpfangen,
hêre frouwe,
daz ich bin saelic iemer mê.
kuster mich? wol tûsentstunt!
tandaradei!
seht, wie rôt mir ist der munt.

Dô het er gemachet
alsô rîche
von bluomen eine bettestat.
des wirt noch gelachet
innéclîche,
kumt iemen an daz selbe pfat.
bî den rôsen er wol mac—
tandaradei!
merken, wâ mirz houbet lac.

Daz er bî mir laege,
wessez iemen,
—nu enwelle got—sô schamt ich mich.
wes er mit mir pflaege,
niemer niemen
bevinde daz, wan er unt ich
und ein kleinez vogellîn!
tandaradei!
daz mac wol getriuwe sîn.[8]

The girl (who is not a noble lady) tells us of her joyous experience indirectly and delicately. No courtly convention is flouted and all remains on an aesthetic level; true feeling is the keynote and the setting contributes to the mood.

Another poem has for its subject the praise of German women. Pale praise of one courtly lady could be heard everywhere, but now Walther bids us listen to him, the poet who had observed ladies and women throughout Europe:

. . .
der iu maere bringet, daz bin ich.
allez daz ir habt vernomen,
daz ist gar ein wint; nû frâget mich!

Tiusche man sint wol gezogen.
rehte als engel sint diu wîp getân.
Swer si schiltet, derst betrogen:

> ich enkan sîn anderst niht verstân.
> Tugent und reine minne
> swer die suochen wil,
> der sol komen in unser lant: da ist wünne vil.
> lange müeze ich leben dar inne![9]

Frederick's crusade of 1227 had inspired the poet to support a worthy cause, but about that time, too, he takes a melancholy last look at the world:

> Owê war sint verswunden   alliu mîniu jâr!
> ist mîn leben getroumet,   oder ist ez wâr?[10]

The world has changed for the worse and only heaven remains as a hope and a comfort for those who have been deceived by the world. The mood of this elegy is only in part due to old age; an era and an imperial idea were coming to an end.

As the splendor and strength of the Hohenstaufen empire declined, so did the influence of the relatively small number of knights and nobles who had produced or at least supported literature and the arts. A considerable falling-off in poetic and moral quality can be noticed in the two collections of poems by Neithart von Reuental (1180–1250). In the *Sommerlieder* (*Summer Songs*) Reuental paints relatively innocuous scenes of village exuberance, while in the *Winterlieder* (*Winter Songs*) his attitude toward the villagers has changed to envy and derision. He makes fun of the rustic swains who imitate their betters; but then he also uses the forms and phraseology of courtly *minne* to parody village behavior. That his intentional mixture of style, his wit, and his cynicism were very popular is proved by the fact that Neithart became the hero of many stories and songs: they are the kind not exactly distinguished by delicacy and decorum.

While many minnesingers continued writing, no new developments took place. The time had come for collecting the harvest of a passing age. The most famous of several collections of minnesongs is the so-called "Manessische Handschrift," ("Manesse Manuscript"); it was commissioned by a rich Zürich merchant and gorgeously illustrated; today it is kept at Heidelberg.

The Courtly Epic

As in the lyric, so in the epic the German writers followed the French. This was true even in the transitional era, when the chivalric ethos had not yet been fully realized, in the *Alexanderlied* (between 1130 and 1150) by the priest Lamprecht or in priest Konrad's adaptation (ca. 1170) of the *Chanson de Roland*. In these romances and several others of that time, adventure predominates over all other aspects, although the spiritual intent is not neglected.

The first altogether chivalresque epic in the German language was Heinrich von Veldeke's *Eneit*, an adaptation of the Norman French *Roman d'Eneas*. Here Virgil's famous story of Aeneas' flight from Troy, his adventures, and the ultimate establishment of his rule in Italy is retold in contemporary courtly terms. Specifically this means that the two love stories assume great importance. The precipitous love of Aeneas for Queen Dido ends in disaster, but like a brave knight, our hero wins Lavinia after achieving success by deeds of valor. Sinful love and true *minne* are contrasted—as in many a later knightly romance.

Veldeke, who came from the lower Rhine, wrote the *Eneit* in rhyming couplets of regular, four-stressed lines without stanzaic grouping; his rhymes are pure and there is much enjambment. Veldeke is given credit for introducing these features which helped to bring about a Middle High German poetic language and to establish the emerging epic form.

With Hartmann von Aue we meet the first "classic" author of Middle High German epics. Hartmann (ca. 1160–ca. 1220) was a Swabian, of the *ministerial* class (that is, serving a higher lord, but himself of knightly rank); he was well educated, knew Latin and French, could read and write; all of his works were written between 1180 and 1200. He composed a few lyric poems (as did most epic writers of the time), but he is chiefly known for his four great epics: *Erec, Iwein, Gregorius,* and *Der arme Heinrich.*

The first two are based on two of Chrétien de Troyes' renditions of Arthurian legends. Both deal with the conflict of enjoyment and honor. In *Erec* the hero, having won poor Enite for his bride, forgets his knightly duties over the demands of *minne*. Being chided, he takes his wife along on a quest for adventure, but forbids her to speak to him. However, she cannot help warning him of dangers and he rebukes her while proving his honor as a knight. In the end, having recognized her loyalty and love, he asks her forgiveness and both return to King Arthur's court and ultimately to his father's country. In *Iwein* the knight promises his newly-won wife to return after a year's adventuring. When he overstays his time he loses her favor and goes insane. He is healed by a fairylike noble lady and after freeing a lion from the clutches of a dragon he becomes the champion of ladies in distress. When Iwein returns to his wife the two are reconciled.

Both epics deal with the same vital problem, and the solution is sought both times in the poetic context of King Arthur's court. The enthusiastic endorsement of married love being understood, the poet seems to suggest that a knight's honor (*êre*) must be based on loyalty and faithfulness (*triuwe*), and that happiness can be attained only through moderation (*mâze*) and kindness (*rehte güete*). In *Gregorius* Hartmann tells us a saint's legend in chivalric terms. Gregory, offspring of an incestuous marriage between brother and sister, is set adrift on the sea, rescued by a fisherman, and brought up by an abbot. As a youth he frees his widowed mother from unwanted suitors and unwittingly marries her. When the secret of his birth is revealed the couple separate and Gregory atones for his and his parents' sins by having himself chained to a bleak rock in the ocean. After seventeen years he is declared by God to be the holiest of sinners, is made pope and as such forgives his mother. And so this medieval version of the Oedipus story finds a happy ending.

In retelling a local legend concerning an ancestor of his liege lord, Hartmann has given the world one of the most charming tales of the Middle Ages. The hero of *Der arme Heinrich* is a nobleman of great renown and wealth, a poet even, but he neglects to think of God. Suddenly he is struck with leprosy, and impatiently consults one physician after another in search of a cure. A doctor in Salerno tells him that he can be healed if a virgin will sacrifice her blood for him. In despair he sells all he owns and retires to an outlying farm to await death. The caretaker's twelve-year-old daughter soon develops a special liking for her lord and when later she finds out how Henry can be cured, she determines to sacrifice herself for him. In Salerno the doctor warns her once more, but when he is about to start the operation, Henry refuses to accept the sacrifice and together they return home. Now Christ, seeing the girl's readiness to give her life and noting the nobleman's act of humility (*triuwe* and *bärmde*: loyalty and mercy), restores health to Henry who, in turn, makes the girl his wife. After many God-fearing years they both attain life eternal.

Der arme Heinrich is brief and reads like a short story. But in all of his works Hartmann is the same master of language in all of its aspects. He says what he wants to say with clarity and elegance, whether he utters thoughts or describes situations and actions.

Wolfram von Eschenbach (d. ca. 1220) exceeds his contemporaries in power of expression, depth of feeling, and earnestness of intention. His masterpiece, the most important work of the MHG classical period, is *Parzival*.

In order to illustrate the four-stressed rhyming couplets of the courtly epic in general and Wolfram's style in particular we quote from the Introduction to *Parzival*:

> . . .
> ein maere wil i'u niuwen,
> daz seit von grôzen triuwen,
> wîplîchez wîbes reht,
> und mannes manheit alsô sleht,
> diu sich gein herte nie gebouc.
> sîn herze in dar an niht betrouc,
> er stahel, swa er ze strîte quam,
> sîn hant dâ sigelîchen nam
> vil manegen lobelîchen prîs.
> er küene, traeclîche wîs,
> (den helt ich alsus grüeze)
> er wîbes ougen süeze,

unt dâ bî wîbes herzen suht,
vor missewende ein wâriu fluht.
den ich hie zuo hân erkorn,
er ist maereshalp noch ungeborn,
dem man dirre âventiure giht,
und wunders wil des dran geschiht.[11]

Parzival, whose father died in battle away from home, is brought up by his mother in the loneliness of the woods, where she wants to conceal from her son all knowledge of knighthood in order to protect his life. This attempt fails. With a group of errant knights Parzival goes to King Arthur's court, where he gains some renown but is not accepted yet as a member of the Round Table. He delivers the lady Condwiramur from a siege, marries her, and after various adventures comes to the Grail Castle, where a wounded man, King Amfortas, introduces him to the wondrous grail, symbol of spiritual power. Amfortas will be released of his suffering if Parzival asks concerning the king's ever bleeding wound. But out of false politeness Parzival suppresses the question and on the next morning is rudely dismissed. For years he wanders about, at odds with God, with himself, and with the world. On Good Friday he comes to a pious hermit, Trevrizent, and confesses that he is guilty of *zwîvel*—bitterness, resentment, doubt in the goodness of God. Trevrizent, noting Parcival's contriteness, forgives his sin. Now Parzival restores his blemished reputation as a knight and becomes a member of the Round Table by overcoming Gawan, who is the ideal worldly knight. After a duel with Feirefiz, his heathen half brother, Parzival returns with his wife and two sons to the Grail Castle where he asks the question that releases Amfortas from his suffering and becomes King of the Grail.

Wolfram wrote this work of about 25,000 lines between 1205 and 1215. His French model—another of Chrêtien's romances—offered him little more than a series of adventures, interesting enough, but without deeper meaning. Wolfram enriched this material with an ethical and religious significance that goes beyond anything Hartmann might have dealt with; Wolfram's thought gives the story relevance far beyond its time and class. Parzival is man; we see him in the guise of a knight, to be sure, but he is an exemplary human being nevertheless. Having outgrown childish naiveté, he tries to become a perfect knight; when he follows the rules of polite conduct too literally he falls into error: he should have sensed that the promptings of mercy in his heart were more important than even the rules of chivalry. Now he compounds his error by yielding to *zwîvel*, and rebelling against God. Yet, his yearning for perfection is never stilled and in the end, remorse and renewed effort win him *saelde*. But all his efforts would have come to nought if he had not also regained God's grace. It is almost as if Wolfram had tried to answer Walther's question of how a man should live in harmony when God and the world make incompatible claims on him.

In a sense *Parzival* is the first developmental novel (*Bildung-* or *Enwicklungs-roman*, a story in which the hero's psychological development is traced from its beginnings to maturity), a forerunner of Goethe's *Wilhelm Meister*, Novalis' *Heinrich von Ofterdingen*, Keller's *Der grüne Heinrich*, and Thomas Mann's *Der Zauberberg*.

The shorter epic *Willehalm* (ca. 1215) tells of the noble knight William of Orange's fight against the heathen Mohammedans. The spirit of fairness and tolerance pervading this work is characteristic of Wolfram and remarkably advanced for its age.

The fourth great epic writer of the era was Gottfried von Strasbourg, whose romance *Tristan und Isolde* is one of the world's incomparable love stories. Gottfried followed the French version by Thomas, which in turn goes back to Celtic origins.

Tristan, having been wounded with a poisoned sword while regaining his father's kingdom, comes in disguise to the court of Morold, the man he killed in battle. Here he is healed by Morold's sister and her daughter Isolde. Upon his return Tristan is sent by his uncle Marke, the king of Cornwall, to woo Isolde in his behalf. He wins her for Marke, but on the way a magic potion meant for Isolde and Marke is accidentally drunk by Isolde and Tristan, and thus these two will be forever in love with one another. After the wedding Marke suspects that his bride and his nephew are lovers and banishes them from his court. Together they live in a *minne* grotto which is described in terms of religious significance. The lovers determine to leave the grotto: Isolde returns to Marke; Tristan goes to Normandy, where he wins the love of another Isolde, Queen Isolde of the White Hands. Not being able to forget his first love, he languishes in unhappiness. At this point the poem breaks off; Gottfried probably was unable to finish it. Two later poets who tried to supply an ending did so in a superficial sense only.

While Wolfram's theme had been man's struggle for God, in the attainment of whose kingdom knightly virtues and *minne* are considered important, Gottfried seems to assign highest value to *minne*. He is the poet of love in all its ramifications, its happiness, and despair. God is present in *Tristan* by implication only. The problems Gottfried deals with are by no means simple: though the lovers commit adultery, they have been deprived of free choice through magic; therefore they are innocent. They both suffer torments of conscience for their violation of human and courtly conventions; yet they can not help themselves. They voluntarily leave the *minne* grotto—and are the unhappier for it. Gottfried easily excels his contemporaries in the grasp and analysis of passion, in sophistication, psychological insight, and in awareness of beauty in the face of sin. The fact that the ready-made answers of aristocratic society—answers which other writers were still accepting as valid—seem to have lost validity indicates to us that with Gottfried an era was coming to an end. He had no choice but to accept uncertainty, unresolved conflict, and hopelessness as part of existence. If this conclusion sounds grim, the reader of *Tristan und Isolde* will be surprised to find abundant humor in Gottfried's graceful, musical, and clear style. It may be significant that he was not a knight but a burgher.

Walther had already complained that the young men of his day showed little enthusiasm for knightly values. In *Meier Helmbrecht* by Wernher the Gardener (1250 or slightly later) we are told the story of how a cocky young peasant, eager for the glamor of knighthood, becomes a highway robber. His father, a man of simple habits, happy in his appointed place in the scheme of things, warns the son: "dîn ordenung ist der pfluoc" ("your place is at the plow"), but young Helmbrecht spurns such advice and ends on the gallows. The author has an eye for detail and he observes the niceties of MHG classical poetry, but his mind is worried and he deplores the changes all about him.

The Heroic Epic of the Nibelungs

Even though many plots of German epics were borrowed from French sources, German stories going back to events of the time of the migration of the Germanic nations had never been entirely forgotten. Now an Austrian poet joined a number of these stories, cautiously modernized them in courtly terms, and cast them in an archaic strophe, the Kürenberg stanza. Anonymity being a characteristic of national epics everywhere, it seems to be by design that the Nibelungen poet took such excellent care to conceal himself and he has never been identified.

Obviously the poet does not care to discard older Germanic values, for he makes no effort to Christianize his heroes or to give psychological explanations of their behavior. Overweening fate governs all; *triuwe* (loyalty) is the supreme virtue; revenge must be exacted; forgiveness and love of enemy are unknown. Where Christianity and knightly attitudes appear, they do so marginally and not altogether convincingly.

The plot of the *Nibelungenlied* falls into two divisions. Part one ends with Siegfried's death; at the end of part two Kriemhild, his avenger, dies. From the very first stanza, a serious mood prevails:

> Uns ist in alten mæren   wunders vil geseit
> von heleden lobebæren,   von grôzer arebeit,
> von fröuden, hôchgezîten,   von weinen und von klagen,
> von küener recken strîten   muget ír nu wunder hœren sagen.[12]

Siegfried, prince of the Low Countries comes to the Burgundian court at Worms to demand from King Gunther the hand of his beautiful sister Kriemhild. To obtain her he is asked to help Gunther in winning Brunhilde, a magic queen who will marry only a suitor who defeats her in games of prowess. While Gunther goes through the motions of the contest, it is Siegfried who defeats Brunhild: a magic cap has given him strength and made him invisible. On their return to Worms, Siegfried is given Kriemhild and the couples are united in a double wedding, but during the second night after the wedding Siegfried has to come to Gunther's relief by subduing Brunhilde once more. He takes a ring and a belt from her and naively gives these tokens to Kriemhild. About a year later the wives have a violent quarrel.

If Siegfried had not won Brunhilde for Gunther he would not have been given Kriemhild for a wife. If he had not given the ring and belt to Kriemhild she could not have humiliated Brunhilde when Brunhilde insulted her by calling Siegfried a mere retainer of *her* husband's. A peaceable and honest solution of the quarrel between the wives being out of the question, grim Hagen, resentful of Siegfried and loyal to his queen, offers to kill Siegfried and shortly thereafter does so. When Kriemhild finds Siegfried's corpse at the door of her room she knows at once who murdered her husband.

Years later Kriemhild marries Etzel, King of the Huns, for only thus will she be able to avenge Siegfried's death. Again years have passed when the Burgundians accept an invitation to visit Kriemhild. On the journey Kriemhild's youngest brother is betrothed to the daughter of Rüdiger, the man who had wooed Kriemhild for Etzel, had promised to help her whenever she called on him, had lately invited the Burgundians, and is their guide now. Even as the Burgundians arrive, hostile feelings erupt and actual fighting ensues almost at once. Etzel is ready to call off his men if Gunther will hand over Hagen, but loyalty forbids him to do so. Kriemhild orders the banquet hall set on fire: if she cannot wreak vengeance on Hagen alone, she will destroy him and her three brothers with him. However, the Burgundians survive the fire and next morning Rüdiger, who has sworn allegiance to Kriemhild and who is by kinship and hospitality bound to spare the Burgundians, is forced into a conflict of loyalty. Reluctantly he decides in favor of Etzel and against the Burgundians; after the courtly gesture of giving his own shield to Hagen, Rüdiger is killed in the fight. Dietrich von Bern, a guest at Etzel's court, is then forced to enter the fray. He overcomes both Gunther and Hagen and delivers them to Kriemhild. She promises to spare Hagen's life if he will reveal the whereabouts of a treasure that Siegfried had once won and which Hagen has hidden. Hagen replies that he has sworn an oath not to tell while his lord is alive. Kriemhild then has her brother's head cut off and shows it to Hagen. He still refuses to speak. Thereupon Kriemhild pulls Siegfried's own sword from Hagen's side and slays him with it. When Dietrich's armorer, old Hildebrand, sees this fiendish deed he strikes Kriemhild dead. The survivors break into bitter lamentation.

The two main themes of the *Nibelungenlied* are the inevitability of Fate and loyalty to one's liege lord, both matters with which the ancient Germanic epics were deeply concerned. And though these are not neglected in the courtly epics of the era, the emphasis there is altogether different. Hagen exemplifies the ideal Germanic hero: with unswerving, unquestioning loyalty he follows his weak lord and in the very face of death he remains hard and heroic. Fate changes Kriemhild from a beautiful maiden into a fiend driven by one passion —revenge for her husband's murder. Rüdiger, the most modern of the characters, is the only one who has to choose between conflicting loyalties.

Under these gloomy, pre-Christian aspects the poet has fashioned a compelling story out of diverse plot elements. He does not always motivate perfectly; he does not always avoid banalities and platitudes; and he does not even attempt to create suspense from intensely dramatic situations. But these are minor shortcomings in a monolithic work by a great poet. His contemporaries appreciated the *Nibelungenlied*, for it has come down to us in more than thirty manuscripts (not all of them complete). Since its rediscovery in the eighteenth century, the *Nibelungenlied* has been a source of wonder and inspiration to dramatists, poets, and musicians. That its qualities were misinterpreted and perverted by self-aggrandizing German nationalists in the twentieth century is one of the mockeries of our age.

Since the *Nibelungenlied* was composed about the year 1200, we might well have begun our discussion of MHG literature with it. But the fact is, it lies like a gigantic erratic block athwart a landscape that had been ameliorated and enhanced by many a poet. Courtly lyrics and romances continued to be written and read in Germany (as well as in the rest of Europe) for a long time, long after the class which originated the genres had declined from power. The idealism of the early poems vanished, poetic diction turned to cliché and was finally abandoned for prose. But it was not until 1605 that Cervantes in *Don Quijote* laughed their heroes out of court. Two hundred years later the German Romanticists revived serious interest in them by editing and translating them.

But even to the present day the epic themes and motifs keep exerting a powerful interest: Richard Wagner used their themes in *Tannhäuser*; *Tristan und Isolde*; in the Nibelungen tetralogy *Der Ring des Nibelungen* (*Das Rheingold, Die Walküre, Siegfried*, and *Die Gotterdämmerung*); and in *Parsifal*. Friedrich Hebbel fashioned a dramatic interpretation of the old lay in *Die Nibelungen* (1862), a trilogy in eleven acts. Gerhart Hauptmann dramatized the story of *Poor Henry* in *Der arme Heinrich* (1902); and Thomas Mann utilized Hartmann von Aue's *Gregorius* for his humorous novel *Der Erwählte* (*The Holy Sinner*, 1945). These are but a few of the many modernizations that could be mentioned.

THE LATE MIDDLE AGES
1250–1550

Middle High German literature had flourished for little more than a generation before the courtly society that produced and supported it fell into a severe decline. The rising urban middle class, the burghers, assumed leadership for the next two or three centuries. Towns and cities became the centers of life and magnificent Gothic churches, great city halls, and splendid town houses were built. The Gothic churches in Cologne, Strasbourg, Ulm, Marburg, and Freiburg were begun in the thirteenth century; many more followed in the fourteenth. City halls of architectural significance were built in Breslau, Nürnberg, Lübeck, Münster, Braunschweig, and Stralsund. Rothenburg, Freiburg, Lübeck, and many other towns erected gates that were both practical and beautiful. Examples of patrician houses of this period can be seen in Greifswald, Hildesheim, Frankfurt/Main, Nürnberg, and in many other places.

Yet, despite these indications of prosperity, many authors write in a pessimistic mood and enviously look back on past splendor; they appear unable to give adequate expression to the needs of the era or come to grips with its problems. The old genres lingered, but form and content were at odds and this imbalance makes the works less relevant and less enjoyable. In the fourteenth and fifteenth century a trend toward the realistic, the utilitarian, and didactic became noticeable, while in the sixteenth the Reformation absorbed much of the available intellectual and aesthetic energy. At no time did the clergy regain the power it had held in the earlier Middle Ages; but new religious orders (of mendicant friars) were founded to minister to the urban dwellers and great preachers like Bertold von Regensburg (d. 1272) commanded a large following. In scholasticism, the official philosophy of the Church, the German Albertus Magnus (1193–1280) labored alongside Thomas of Aquino and Duns Scotus to justify faith through philosophy. But mysticism, an undogmatic approach to God, also found many adherents. Meister Eckhart (1260–1327); Heinrich Seuse (d. 1366), author of the first autobiography in German; Johannes Tauler (d. 1361); and Thomas a Kempis, who wrote *De imitatione Christi* (*The Imitation of Christ*, before 1420); as well as a number of devout women like Hildegard von Bingen (d. 1179) and Mechthild von Magdeburg (d. ca. 1282) should be mentioned here. By their awareness of a more personal relationship to God, an approach that softens the claims of exclusive mediation on the part of the Church, these mystics satisfied a deep need of the time.

Nicolaus von Cues (or latinized, Cusanus, 1401–1464) began as a student in the school of the Brethren of the Common Life in Deventer in the Low Countries and developed into one of the continent's leading theologian-philosophers, mathematicians, scientists, and churchmen. On the basis of mysticism he wanted to improve and modernize the spiritual life of his time. In many ways he anticipated not only humanistic intentions but also the ecclesiastic reforms of the coming age.

The drama of the Church originated at the altar as part of the liturgy; it was in Latin and international in scope. Two monks at St. Gall, Notker Balbulus (the Stammerer, 840–912) and Tutilo (d. 915), developed tropes and sequences, Latin words in prose or verse that were sung during the worship service. Tutilo is probably the author-composer of the trope that enhanced the Easter service and lead to the earliest rudimentary drama of the Church: priests representing angels would sing the Latin equivalent of "Whom seek ye in the sepulcher, Christians?" The three women, also represented by priests, answered: "Jesus of Nazareth, you dwellers of heaven." The angels then replied: "He is not here. He has risen as he predicted. Go and announce that he has risen from the grave."

This simple group dialogue was later extended to more elaborate interchanges, for example, between single voices and the choir, and in time simple action and costuming appeared. Other church holidays were similarly embellished: a crib at the altar was the place to which the shepherds came at Christmas, or the wise men at Epiphany. About the year 1100 the first of a long series of non-Biblical interpolations was added: a merchant sells cosmetics to the three women, one of whom, Mary of Magdala, had been pictured as a wayward hussy in a previous scene; and when the disciples Peter and John, instead of walking, race each other to the grave, that scene introduced situational comedy. Thus an ever increasing number of non-Biblical elements, use of the vernacular, and the sheer extent of the theatrical action forced these representations out of the church and onto the market place.

In the Easter play of Muri, ca. 1250, we have the first of many later plays on religious topics presented in German. Muri already had eighteen speaking parts. Soon some of the more ambitious passion plays required hundreds of participants and took two or even three days to perform. The actors came from the craft guilds whose members often organized annual presentations of these plays. The "stage" was distributed over several locations, and the actors walked from one to the other, for example, from heaven by way of the temple to Gethsemane, to the house of Caiaphas and Pilate, and to Golgotha. Crassly realistic histrionics entered: hell was a definitely circumscribed place from which grotesquely dressed devils sallied forth to threaten the spectators until Christ released the lost souls. Certain speeches and gestures anticipate the Shrovetide plays of the sixteenth century. Plays based on the lives of saints are called miracle plays. A late form of passion play is still performed every ten years in Oberammergau, Bavaria.

A systematic attempt to continue courtly poetry was undertaken by the schools of the mastersingers, where the art of song making was taught as if it could be mastered by apprenticeship and examinations. Needless to say, not much came of these efforts except that they inspired Richard Wagner to write *Die Meistersinger von Nürnberg* (1867). The hero of this opera is the shoemaker-poet Hans Sachs, whose historical prototype lived from 1494 to 1576 and produced more than 7,000 works—master songs, rhymed stories, a few hundred tragedies and comedies, and several dozen *Fastnachtsspiele* (Shrovetide plays). Hans Folz and Hans Rosenplüt had preceded Sachs in writing such skits and Jacob Ayrer was to continue the tradition. But Sachs was the most ingenious fabricator of these short plays that were performed by amateur actors in taverns or in private houses. The skits are written in rhymed couplets, eight or nine syllables per line (*Knittelvers*), and their subject matter ranges from satire against peasants and priests, and ridicule of stupid husbands and wives, to the portrayal of adulterers, thieves, and other unsavory persons. A neatly formulated moral like the one quoted here from *Der Bauer im Fegefeuer* (*The Peasant in Purgatory*, 1552) usually concludes the work:

> Es gibt kein größre Sünd auf Erden
> Als Eifersucht. Drum Nachbarn mein,
> Laßt euch vor ihr gewarnet sein,
> Weil man sie straft so ungeheuer
> Mit Ruten unten im Fegefeuer.[13]

Sachs is good at dramatic structure and characterization, while his humor is anything but delicate. It was not until Goethe, recognizing the homespun genius of Hans Sachs and incorporating *Knittelvers* into his *Faust*, that the Nuremberg cobbler-poet was rehabilitated. While Sachs supported the Reformation, he does not deal with it in any of his Shrovetide plays. In Switzerland, on the other hand, Nicolaus Manuel freely used the *Fastnachtsspiel* for anti-Catholic propaganda.

Meistergesang was confined to a small circle of urban enthusiasts, but folksong flourished throughout the country. Romanticists later mistakenly assumed that the "folk" itself had produced the songs. The fact is rather that they were created by individual singers whose identity became lost. Folksongs deal with the universal themes of life's joys and sorrows, childhood, love, parting, and loss; but they also tell of hunters, soldiers, shipmen, miners, and many others. They do so in simple poetic terms that everybody can understand and enjoy. Often the Church utilized a popular melody and put its words to it; when political events or battles were treated the song is known as a historical ballad. Occasionally old epic themes like that of the *Hildebrandslied* or parts of the *Nibelungenlied* were made into ballads.

Our example, entitled "Erntelied" (Harvest Song) has religious overtones:

> Es ist ein Schnitter, heißt der Tod,
> hat Gewalt vom großen Gott,
> heut wetzt er das Messer,
> es schneid't schon viel besser,
> bald wird er drein schneiden,
> wir müssen's nur leiden.
> Hüt dich, schöns Blümelein!
>
> Was heut noch grün und frisch da steht,
> wird morgen weggemäht:
> die edel Narzissel,
> die englische Schlüssel,
> die schön Hyazinth,

die türkische Bind.
Hüt dich, schöns Blümelein!

Viel hunderttausend ungezählt
da unter die Sichel hinfällt:
rot Rosen, weiß Lilgen,
beid wird er austilgen.
ihr Kaiserkronen,
man wird euch nicht schonen.
Hüt dich, schöns Blümelein!

Trutz, Tod! komm her, ich fürcht dich nit,
trutz! komm und tu ein Schnitt.
Wenn er mich verletzet,
so werd ich versetzet,
ich will es erwarten, in himmlischen Garten.
Freu dich, schöns Blümelein![14]

It should be remembered that the lyrics of a song are unsatisfactory when they are separated from the melody. This is particularly true of folk songs.

Similar to the songs, folk tales were also current. Many of these originated in France, but the stories clustering around Doctor Faust, Till Eulenspiegel, and the good burghers of Schilda are of German origin. According to the *Historia von D. Fausten, dem Weitbeschreyten Zauberer und Schwartzkünstler* (*History of Dr. Faustus, the Notorious Magician and Necromancer*), the hero, eager for fame and power, makes a pact with the devil, but he finds out that he has struck a bad bargain, for after twenty years he must go straight to hell. Till Eulenspiegel is a merry rascal who wanders about the country and points out the shams and weaknesses of human society. He is the typical man of the people, witty, intelligent, and resourceful, but unlucky in the end. Richard Strauss translated his life into one of his best-loved tone poems. The citizens of Schilda, finally, (*Das Lalebuch*, 1499) defy the laws of nature and psychology because they think they are smarter than anyone else. In comic-strip fashion they commit old errors and invent new ones, thereby delighting children young and old.

Collections of *Schwänke*—witty anecdotes, jolly stories, and erotic tales— enjoyed a long and extensive vogue. The sources are often medieval, but following the model of the Italian humanist Poggio, an author like Heinrich Bebel (1472–1518) gave a polished form to his Latin *Facetiae* (1509/14). The monk Johannes Pauli (ca. 1455–1530) in his *Schimpf und Ernst* (*Fun and Seriousness*, 1522) stressed the didactic virtues and the moralizing purpose of his stories, though the collection contains its share of ribaldry and unabashed coarseness.

Satirical didacticism was a genre popular throughout this period. In his *Renner*, (*The Runner*, ca. 1300), a poem of 24,600 lines, Hugo von Trimberg inveighs against sin in all its aspects. He uses parable, examples, moralizing sayings, and popular stories to make and reiterate his point; though he strongly condemns courtly life, his appraisal of Walther von der Vogelweide is often quoted:

> Her Walther von der Vogelweide,
> swer des vergaeze, der taet mir leide.[15]

The view of life presented in Wittenweiler's *Ring* (ca. 1400, just under 10,000 lines) is similarly satirical, but here the plot figures more prominently. After the peasant lad Bertschi Triefnas has won and wed Mätzli Rührdenzumpf, a war between their respective villages ensues. Heroes of the great epics, giants, and even Neithard von Reuental participate in chaotic battles until destruction is complete. Bertschi, a lone survivor conscious of man's stupidity and wrongheadedness, retires into the wilds of the Black Forest.

Sebastian Brant in his *Narrenschiff* (*Ship of Fools*, 1494) lets the characters board a ship bound for Narragonia. But this frame is only a device for satire directed at most professions and occupations. Brant combines material culled from the classics of Greece and Rome with homely stories and proverbs; woodcuts by Dürer contributed to the success of the book which was enjoyed by naive readers and learned humanists, poets and preachers alike. Translations into Latin, French, and English followed in rapid succession and the *Narrenschiff* was reprinted well into the seventeenth century.

The beast epic, which began in the Middle High German period, continued to enjoy considerable popularity. Toward the very end of the fifteenth century there appeared in low-German dialect a book that criticized with special vigor the ills of church and society through the figure of Reynard, the clever, amoral fox, who for all his villainy is eventually made chancellor of the realm. *Reinke de Vos* (*Reynard the Fox*) by an anonymous adaptor appeared ca. 1498, and Goethe, who also tried his hand at this ancient theme, later called the book "an unholy Bible of the world."

HUMANISM AND THE REFORMATION
1400–1624

Within the larger framework of the Renaissance, humanism represents the endeavor to realize the dignity and worth of man as an individual under the ideals of ancient Greek and Roman philosophy and literature. Humanists were concerned more with discovering, editing, and emulating ancient authors than with the religious and scientific quarrels of the day, though there was of course much interaction. Inseparably connected with the Renaissance itself, humanism had developed in the Italian city states, and students and scholars had quickly carried it north of the Alps, where it gradually became dominant in the faculties of the universities. By its very nature humanism represents a rebuff to almost everything medieval. With the coming of humanism Man was to be the measure of all things; he would be master in the realm of the intellect and the spirit. Life would no longer be a mere prelude to the hereafter. It is easy to understand that the Reformation benefited to a considerable extent from humanistic attitudes; nevertheless, German humanists by and large were not adherents of Luther and Zwingli.

The earliest contact with humanism in the German empire took place in Bohemia, where Charles IV had founded the university of Prague in 1348. Here Italian humanists like Petrarch and Cola di Rienzo were well known and it was here that the earliest document of German humanism originated, *Der Ackermann aus Böhmen* (*The Plowman from Bohemia*) by the town scribe Johann of Saaz, ca. 1400. In moving prose the author accuses Death of having wantonly robbed him of his wife. Eventually God himself renders the decision: Death, having but done his duty, is in the right; but the plaintiff should be honored for pleading his cause so well. Though *Der Ackermann* contains many medieval features, it asserts man's new dignity and independence. The work was widely read, first in manuscript, and later, after the invention of printing, in numerous illustrated editions.

Unfortunately, *Der Ackermann* had been the harbinger of a spring that was late and not very promising. Translators like Niclas von Wyle, Albrecht von Eyb, and Heinrich Steinhöwel had by about 1475 rendered Poggio's fabliaux, Aesop's *Fables*, some of Plautus' plays, and a number of Italian *novelle*, but they had proved incapable of remaking the German language to their purpose: their style is Latinate; lexicon and rhythm remain inadequate. Unfortunately German humanists did not pursue the use of their native tongue with as much vigor as humanists in, for example, Italy and England, and the Renaissance tended to become chiefly the concern of scholars.

For the purpose of teaching their students Latin conversation, humanists everywhere wrote dialogues like the *Colloquia* of Erasmus. Such dialogues could be adapted to special occasions, as when, for example, the commencement speaker at Heidelberg in 1480 incorporated in his address on the advantages of humanism a dramatic reading in which the hero, a bright young humanist, gets the better of an opportunistic ignoramus. From this, the *Stylpho* of Jacob Wimpfeling, to the slightly more dramatic inventions of Celtis, Locher, Grünpeck, and others it is but a short step. However, with Johannes Reuchlin's *Henno* (1480)—an adaptation of the French farce *Maître Pierre Pathelin*—we get the first lively and rather modern play. It is the story of the servant who not only cheats his master but even the smart lawyer who had helped him; but in contrast to *Pathelin* with its medieval staging, we find here the technical innovation that various acts represent different locales. *Henno* was presented many times and had a decisive influence on school plays, both in Latin and German, until well into the seventeenth century.

Reuchlin's chief interest, however, was Hebrew studies. From Jewish scholars he had learned the language of the Old Testament and had written a Hebrew grammar. When a certain zealot, the convert Johannes Pfefferkorn, advocated that all Hebrew books should be confiscated, Reuchlin denounced such narrow-mindedness and was promptly attacked by Pfefferkorn and his scholastic friends. In reply Reuchlin published letters written by friends in support of his arguments, the *Litterae clarorum virorum* (*Letters of Famous Men*, 1514). A year later there appeared an anonymous volume entitled *Litterae obscurorum virorum* (*Letters of Obscure Men*). These, while apparently endorsing Pfefferkorn's position, were a subtle but sharp attack on scholasticism and its methods, on stupid monks and defenders of the status quo, and writers of execrable Latin. The *Litterae obscurorum virorum* written by Crotus Rubeanus and Ulrich von Hutten, contain some of the cleverest satire ever invented: the question of how many angels can dance on the point of a needle was never asked by serious schoolmen; it comes straight out of this satire! It does not seem to matter much that years later Reuchlin was condemned by the pope himself.

The leading figure in humanism, at least north of the Alps, was Desiderius Erasmus of Rotterdam (1466–1536). By editing the Greek portions of the Bible, by translating them anew into Latin and providing them with philological and historical commentary, he applied the new scholarship to sacred texts and freed them from error. In his Latin writings—the *Adages*, *Colloquies*, and *In Praise of Folly*—he criticised self-righteousness and stupidity, and demanded freedom, reason, tolerance, and insight instead. His attitude was always such that he would try to reconcile opposites rather than provoke open conflict.

Such a conciliatory attitude was alien to Martin Luther (1483–1546), the German reformer. Luther came from very simple people: his father, a miner who had prospered in a modest way, wanted his son to study law and so he sent him to the University of Erfurt. But self-doubt and the fear that in spite of ceaseless efforts his life was worthless in the sight of God made young Martin join the order of the Augustinian Eremites. Although he worked hard at his theological studies, was ordained, and enjoyed the confidence and respect of his superiors, he still felt deserted of God. His worries and conflicts persisted until he became convinced that only through the gift of God's grace is salvation possible and that no man can earn his way into heaven by good works. As a young professor at the newly founded University of Wittenberg, Luther's forceful teaching attracted many students and gained him the support of the Elector of Saxony.

In 1519 Luther proposed to discuss in an academic setting the nature and validity of papal indulgences. However, the ninety-five theses that were to be the basis of the discussion caused such widespread and violent reaction that attempts were made to silence him. Luther did not answer a summons from Rome, and when he was excommunicated in 1520 he publicly burned the papal decree. During this year he also published his three "primary treatises":

Von der Freiheit eines Christenmenschen (*On the Liberty of a Christian Man*), *Von der babylonischen Gefangenschaft der Kirche* (*On the Babylonian Captivity of the Church*), and *An den christlichen Adel deutscher Nation von des christlichen Standes Besserung* (*To the Christian Nobility of the German Nation on the Improvement of the Christian Estate*). The break with the Church being complete, Luther's fate now rested with the worldly authorities, that is, in the hands of twenty-one-year-old Emperor Charles V and the imperial diets. Even though the enormous consequences for the unity of the German empire were pointed out to him, Luther insisted at the Diet of Worms (1521) that neither Pope nor Church were infallible, that every Christian stood in direct relationship to God, and that the Church was not needed for the attainment of salvation. Soon Emperor and Diet were at odds about Luther's heresies and their political consequences, and while the wrangling went on, Luther, already under the ban of the Empire, disappeared. His sovereign, Frederick the Wise, had spirited him away to the Wartburg, one of his castles, and there Luther started translating the Bible, a task which was to occupy him almost to the end of his days: the *New Testament* appeared in 1522, the entire Bible in 1534, a revision in 1541. Rioting and violence on the part of radicals prompted Luther to return to Wittenberg so that he could direct the changes into the channels of deliberate reform rather than allowing the revolutionaries to take over his movement. In the ensuing Peasant Revolt he was on the side of the feudal lords who crushed the uprisings and imposed ever harsher conditions on the peasants.

Luther, who wanted every German to be able to read the Holy Bible in his native German, was of course aware that several German Bibles already existed, but those versions were based on the Vulgate, the authorized Catholic Latin text of the Scriptures. Luther went back to the older, more authoritative Hebrew and Greek texts which scholars like Reuchlin and Erasmus had edited. In that respect Luther acted like a humanist, but in translating he strove for a quality that was a far cry from humanistic elegance. "For one should not ask the letters in the Latin language how to speak German; rather one must ask the housewife, the children in the street, the common man in the market square, and look at their mouth how they speak and translate accordingly. That way they understand what's meant and take notice of what one says to them in German." The language Luther used was that of Upper Saxony, specifically the East Middle German dialect of the Saxon Elector's Secretariat. His feeling for native rhythm, his use of concrete rather than abstract diction, his felicitous and often poetic phrasing made Luther's Bible translation at once the standard among German Protestants. Moreover, the language of Luther's Bible translation helped to unify and envigorate the German language even in the Catholic sections up to and beyond the days of Klopstock and Goethe.

In comparison to the Bible translation, Luther's voluminous other writings, his theological tracts, propaganda pamphlets, speeches and table conversations, letters, etc., though they have their importance in the history of ideas, are aesthetically less significant. We should, however, mention a number of his hymns, for example, the battle song of the Reformation, a paraphrase of Psalm 46, "Ein feste Burg ist unser Gott" ("A mighty fortress is our lord"), and the Christmas hymn "Vom Himmel hoch da komm ich her," ("From heaven high I have arrived"), a folk song to which Luther set new words.

In 1525 Luther had married Catharina von Bora, a former nun, with whom he lived in happy marriage in a big house full of children, relatives, and visitors. While various diets wrestled with the problem of reconciling the claims of Catholics, Lutherans, and Zwinglians, Luther withdrew from the realm of politics and devoted his energies to building up the organization of his church, devising new forms of worship, providing a hymnal, establishing schools, and acting as advisor to numerous princes.

On school stages and elsewhere we find many plays in Latin or German which deal with the Reformation. We had already seen that in Switzerland Niclas Manuel (1484–1530) used the *Fastnachtsspiel* to ridicule monks and to point an accusing finger at the pope. Luther's reliance on grace alone was exemplified by Burkart Waldis in his play about the prodigal son, *Vam verlorn Szohn* (1527); Naogeorgus in *Pammachius* (1538) struck at the pope and in *Mercator* (1640), gave a Lutheran version of *Everyman*. The Protestants had many such plays, while on the Catholic.side they were less frequent until the schools of the Jesuits made them a regular part of their educational program.

Prose was now more extensively used than ever before, especially for satire, pamphlets in the religious struggle, and for the emerging novel of the bourgeois class. Jörg Wickram (ca. 1520–62) was one of the originators of the German novel. In *Der Knaben Spiegel* (*The Boys' Mirror*, 1554) he juxtaposes the development of an ambitious son of a poor peasant to that of the spoiled scion of a nobleman. Literary historians have called *Der Knaben Spiegel* the first example of the developmental novel, a genre that was to become the favorite of German novelists up to Kafka. While Wickram's *Goldfaden* (*Golden Thread*) has a rather conventional plot—poor boy marries daughter of a rich count—his *Von guten und bösen Nachbarn* (*Of Neighbors Good and Evil*, 1556) deals with the fate of three generations of a merchandising family. In all of these novels plot predominates over psychology, but Wickram does draw pictures of idealized bourgeois life.

A writer of considerable talent was Johann Fischart (1546–90). His short epic *Das glückhaft Schiff von Zürich* (*The Lucky Ship of Zürich*, 1576) praises the civic solidarity of Strasbourg and Zürich in times of need as well as of joy. His anti-Catholic pamphlets and a rhymed version of Till Eulenspiegel are rather old-fashioned and conventional, but in his *Geschichtklitterung* (*Story-conglomeration*, 1575), which started as an adaptation of Rabelais' *Gargantua et Pantagruel*, he created one of the world's most monstrous, yet humorous books. Where Rabelais had satirized hidebound scholasticism, spiritual and intellectual intransigency, Fischart expands the original and castigates all immorality, grossness, and crude manners. Exaggeration, breathless rhythm, neologism, puns and verbal pyrotechnics, whole catalogs of synonyms, Joycean extravaganza, asides provoked by association of sound, quotations of popular songs in their entirety, proverbs, catch phrases, wise cracks, and nonsense refrains— all this and much more is poured out upon the reader and threatens to overwhelm him, as it seems to have hypnotized the author. Contemporaries must have been keenly aware, however, of what Fischart's moral-satiric glossomania was aiming at, for by 1594 a fourth edition had become necessary.

Fischart, who has been called the harbinger of the baroque era, is really one of the last writers of the medieval bourgeois age. In him humanism and satire were blended just as they had been in Brant, though the proportion was different. With Fischart the pre-eminence which the southwest part of Germany had long held in literature came to an end. Innovation and new impulses for the next century or so were to come from the east central section, a part of Germany that was becoming culturally more important.

THE AGE OF THE BAROQUE:
COUNTERREFORMATION, ABSOLUTISM
1600–1720

The sixteenth century in Germany had been a period of deep unrest: the Reformation of Luther, Zwingli, and Calvin had affected the princes and the commoners, rich and poor alike. Social unrest had been manifest in a rebellion of the knights against the spiritual princes in 1522, and in the bloody Peasant Revolt of 1524–25. When Luther refused to lend his support to the peasants, the "left wing" of the Reformation was taken over by men like Thomas Münzer who felt that religious reform must also involve social betterment. In Münster the so-called Anabaptists established on principles of early Christianity a commune which lasted over a year. In the southeast of the empire the Turks were moving into Hungary and threatening Vienna, while Charles V was busy defeating the Protestant princes of the Schmalkaldic League. Fortunately the Peace of Augsburg (1555) ended overt warfare between Catholic and Protestant princes, but tension continued and was increased by the Church and with the active support of a number of Catholic princes. The most obvious result of the Counterreformation was the most extensive armed conflict up to that time, the Thirty Years War (1618–48). Almost from the beginning the war aims shifted and instead of settling the religious questions, foreign powers with dynastic ambitions of their own invaded Germany. Large armies of hired soldiers (*Landsknechte*) had to be maintained, or they would live off the land and loot and destroy. Peasant, burgher, and nobleman suffered enormous losses, and as the middle class was wiped out, absolutism gained. For over a century after the war ended, conditions created by that war would determine economic and mental attitudes. Such modest achievements as literature and the arts could register under so much discouragement are a monument to human resilience. Small wonder that the literature of the Baroque period is a literature of extremes in spirituality and worldliness, resignation and abandon.

In other countries life had not been exactly tranquil, but science, literature, and the arts managed to flourish amid the turmoils a little more luxuriantly than in Germany. England had experienced a magnificent literary outburst in the reign of Queen Elizabeth I: after Spenser, Sidney, Shakespeare, Bacon and others, a transition to the Baroque era was made by Donne and Milton. In France, where the Pléiade had flourished under Ronsard in the second half of the sixteenth century, a similar development toward the orderly neoclassicism of Corneille, Racine, and Moliére took place. Spain was enjoying her *siglo de oro*, her golden age, with Lope de Vega, Calderon, Cervantes, Alemán, Quevedo, Góngora, and Guevara. The Netherlands, emerging from the tyranny of Spain, could boast of great painters and dramatists, among whom Rembrandt and Joost van den Vondel were outstanding; her lyric poets included Hooft, Bredero, Huygens, Cats, and others; her scholars were Hugo Grotius and Daniel Heinsius. After Tasso's death in 1595 Italy did not have a writer of European stature, but Italian universities were still great centers of learning where men like Copernicus the Polish astronomer studied, and where Galileo taught that the Ptolemaic system was outmoded and that a heliocentric conception of the universe would have to be accepted by theologians. Italian architects like Bernini and Borromini, having modified the Renaissance style into more sweeping, undulating designs, were emulated by builders of churches, palaces, and theaters from Vienna to Mexico City.

German intellectuals deplored the backwardness of their country, and were thinking of remedies. The great Middle High German period of poetry was forgotten, and changes in the language would have made it impossible to start where Walther had left off. Attempts to take over Romance forms like the sonnet, the ode, the Alexandrine, or *vers commun* had failed so far, and German poets wanting to speak with beauty and dignity preferred to use Latin with its vast and ready-made store of forms and phrases. For a while it seemed that the problems of metrics and diction might be solved by Schede and Weckherlin, court poets at Heidelberg and Stuttgart respectively, but then an approach was taken that was new for Germany: in 1617 a concerned group of noblemen founded the *Fruchtbringende Gesellschaft* (*Fruitbearing Society*). The purpose of this society, which was modelled after the Florentine *Accademia della Crusca*, was to "purify" the language and to produce translations which creative minds could follow. Despite the fact that much energy was spent on social rigmarole, the "Fruitbearing Society" managed to call attention to literary problems and within its limited resources tried to solve them.

At exactly the same time, 1617, a brilliant young man, Martin Opitz (1597–1639), published a Latin speech he had delivered at his school in Beuthen on Oder. In the two dozen pages of *Aristarchus* Opitz argues that in the past great poetry had been written in German (and he quotes a passage in Middle High German), that the language is capable of great poetry now—and he quotes himself! When Opitz found out that in the Netherlands problems similar to the ones in Germany had already been solved, he began translating from the Dutch, especially from Daniel Heinsius, and in a remarkably short time he had mastered the art of writing poetry in which the stress required by poetic meter and natural word stress coincided. As for words, he used—no easy task!—the vernacular equivalents of the vocabulary with which the neo-Latin poets had achieved elegance and eloquence; that is, he avoided dialect and the careless diction of his predecessors.

His first book of lyrics, *Teutsche Poemata* (*German Poems*), was a collection of translations from the French, Dutch, Italian, and Latin; but it also contained original pieces. The manuscript had been assembled during Opitz' year and a half of studying in Heidelberg, where he had been the leader of a group of lively young poets; but the outbreak of the war scattered them and delayed publication until 1624.

In order to explain the principles of the new German poetry, Opitz quickly threw together his *Buch von der deutschen Poeterey* (*Book of German Poesy*, 1624), in which he leaned heavily on authorities like Ronsard and Scaliger to define the kind of poetry that was regarded as good beyond considerations of time and national boundaries. Again he demonstrated by examples how such poetry could be written in German. This slender treatise became an immediate success and from then on Opitz was the acknowledged authority on German poetics, a position he retained until the days of Klopstock and the Storm and Stress.

In 1625 Opitz produced a translation of Seneca's *Trojan Women*; one year later followed the German version of *Argenis*, a widely read neo-Latin *roman à clef* by the refugee Scotsman John Barclay; and in 1627 Opitz adapted the text of Rinuccini's opera *Daphne* for a new musical setting by Heinrich Schütz. His translation of Sophocles' *Antigone* (1636) proved that even Greek tragedy was no longer beyond the reach of the German language.

If the translations were meant to be models for emulation, Opitz' *Trostge-dicht in Widerwärtigkeit des Krieges* (*Poem of Consolation in the Adversity of War*, written 1620-21, but left unpublished until 1633) is his most important original work. Under the pervading sentiment of Christian stoicism Opitz here expresses strong personal sympathies for the victims of war and its cruelties, sympathies which he either suppressed or sublimated in his other works.

By way of illustration let us look at one of his lyric poems:

Liedt im thon: *Ma belle je vous prie*

Ach Liebste, laß uns eilen,
  Wir haben Zeit.
Es schadet das Verweilen
  Uns beiderseit.
Der schönen Schönheit Gaben
  Fliehn Fuß für Fuß,
Daß alles, was wir haben,
  Verschwinden muß.

Der Wangen Zier verbleichet,
  Das Haar wird greis,
Der Äuglein Feuer weichet,
  Die Flamm' wird Eis.
Das Mündlein von Korallen
  Wird ungestalt.
Die Händ' als Schnee verfallen,
  Und du wirst alt.

Drum laß uns jetzt genießen
  Der Jugend Frucht,
Eh dann wir folgen müssen
  Der Jahre Flucht.
Wo du dich selber liebest,
  So liebe mich,
Gib mir, daß, wann du gibest,
  Verlier auch ich.[16]

The *carpe diem* theme of this poem is expressed in words whose meter alternates regularly between stress and nonstress; yet the rhythm is skipping rather than striding, and the diction is not yet so burdened with metaphors as it will be later. The emotional impact is overbalanced by reason, and a witty last line closes the poet's appeal to a beloved who remains slightly indefinite. The total effect of the poem is one of rather conventional elegance. More than that was not possible at the time and under the circumstances, but through such poems Germany once more was linked to the traditions of European art.

One of Opitz' great admirers was the Saxon poet Paul Fleming (1609–40). As a student in Leipzig he began writing neo-Latin poetry in the tradition of humanism and Petrarcism. (The latter, extending and varying motifs familiar from minnesong, consists of poetic exercises in praise of a beautiful, unyielding lady whom the poet professes to love.) Before finishing his studies, Fleming accepted a minor position in an expedition that was to explore the overland route to Persia for purposes of stimulating the silk trade. During a delay in Reval (Estonia) Fleming fell in love and became engaged, and now the conventional poetic motifs of Petrarcism proved inadequate. The poems he wrote on his trip sound a new and personal note: He speaks of constancy in the face of misfortune, of faithfulness and the hopes he has for the future. The intensity of his feeling brings Fleming close to Christian Günther or even young Goethe. Unfortunately Fleming died before he had a chance to establish himself. The epitaph he wrote a few days before his death is one of his most characteristic poems:

Ich war an Kunst und Gut und Stande groß und reich.
Des Glückes lieber Sohn. Von Eltern guter Ehren.
Frei. Meine. Konnte mich aus meinen Mitteln nähren.
Mein Schall floh überweit. Kein Landsmann sang mir gleich.

Von Reisen hoch gepreist, für keine Mühe bleich,
Jung, wachsam, unbesorgt. Man wird mich nennen hören,
Bis daß die letzte Glut dies alles wird zerstören.
Dies, deutsche Klarien, dies Ganze dank ich euch.

Verzeiht mir, bin ich's wert, Gott, Vater, Liebste, Freunde!
Ich sag euch gute Nacht und trete willig ab.
Sonst alles ist getan bis an das schwarze Grab.

Was frei dem Tode steht, das tu er seinem Feinde.
Was bin ich viel besorgt, den Atem aufzugeben?
An mir ist minder nichts, das lebet, als mein Leben.[17]

Poets who followed Opitz' theories and practices used to be called members of the First Silesian School and those who carried them to extremes were designated as poets of tumescence (*Schwulst*) or members of the Second Silesian School. Since the twenties, however, the term "baroque" has gained wide acceptance. Though in German criticism it does not carry the pejorative connotation which still clings to it in English, the controversy about the extent and applicability of the term continues. But one author who is without question characterized as baroque is Andreas Gryphius (1616–64). He is both a lyric and a dramatic writer. Born in Silesia, he studied (and taught) in Leyden, traveled in France and Italy. In Holland he came to know the plays of Vondel, but he was also influenced by Jesuit dramatists and the English comedians.

The heroes of Gryphius' tragedies are martyrs of stoic constancy. The Christian queen in *Catharina von Georgien* (*Catharine of Gruziya*, 1651), held captive by the heathen King of Persia who wants her for his wife if only she will give up her faith, triumphs over the tyrant in death. In *Carolus Stuardus* (1650) Gryphius expresses his horror of regicide while Charles I is apotheosized as a martyr of the divine rights theory. *Cardenio and Celinde* (1657) is a tragi-comedy with middle-class characters in which two lovers, having been made to see the errors of their way, are led to a satisfactory marriage.

Of Gryphius' three comedies, one, *Herr Peter Squentz* (*Master Peter Quince*, 1657), was inspired by the tradesmen's scenes in *A Midsummer Night's Dream*. *Horribilicribrifax* (1663) incorporates the braggard soldier in an atmosphere of mixed-up languages and love affairs, while in *Die geliebte Dornrose* (*The Beloved Briar Rose*, 1660) Gryphius depicts Silesian peasants with benevolent humor, but not without satire on the vanity of their behavior.

Gryphius' poetry, mostly odes and sonnets, paints a somber picture of his time; through unusual metaphors and far-fetched similes he tries to capture—and overcome—the suffering, the gruesomeness of the era which only the promptings of faith enable him to bear. Vanity, futility, and death—these are the themes to which he is committed, to which he gives ever varying expression as in "Menschliches Elende":

> Was sind wir Menschen doch? Ein Wohnhaus grimmer Schmerzen,
> Ein Ball des falschen Glücks, ein Irrlicht dieser Zeit
> Ein Schauplatz herber Angst, besetzt mit scharfem Leid,
> Ein bald verschmelzter Schnee und abgebrannte Kerzen.
>
> Dies Leben fleucht davon wie ein Geschwätz und Scherzen.
> Die vor uns abgelegt des schwachen Leibes Kleid
> Und in das Totenbuch der grossen Sterblichkeit
> Längst eingeschrieben sind, sind uns aus Sinn und Herzen.
>
> Gleich wie ein eitel Traum leicht aus der Acht hinfällt
> Und wie ein Strom verscheusst, den keine Macht aufhält,
> So muß auch unser Nam', Lob, Ehr und Ruhm verschwinden.
>
> Was itzund Atem holt, muss mit der Luft entfliehn,
> Was nach uns kommen wird, wird uns ins Grab nachziehn.
> Was sag ich? Wir vergehn wie Rauch von starken Winden.[18]

In Strasbourg and many other towns the schools presented plays in Latin or German and, as we have seen, Gryphius gave the German stage a powerful impetus. From about 1585 on, traveling English actors also presented plays at courts and in towns. These so-called "English comedians," doubling as musicians and dancers, brought with them their repertory of flamboyant plays and used an exaggerated style of acting which was designed (in the beginning at least) to overcome the language barrier.

Now the Jesuits began to use the theater in the service of the Counterreformation by presenting Latin plays that showed the strength of the Church and sought to gain converts. A typical example of these plays is Jacob Bidermann's *Cenodoxus, the Doctor of Paris* (1602). The hero, a kind of Faust figure, is an apparently pious and successful physician obsessed with intellectual pride, for which he must go to hell. Elaborate productions of opera also were popular, especially at the larger courts. Comparison with other countries suggests that Germany's lack of a national capital was a serious cultural handicap, particularly to the theater.

Among the many religious writers of the era Jacob Böhme (1575–1624) is outstanding. A simple shoemaker, he penned his speculations about God in a personally determined prose and called them *Aurora oder die Morgenröte im Aufgang* (*Aurora or Dawn Arising*, 1612), a book that made him the leader of a local circle of mystics. When the Lutheran clergy became aroused over his unorthodox statements, Böhme was enjoined from further publication. Nevertheless, his treatises circulated in manuscript and exerted a wide influence. Böhme is no visionary; through contemplation alone he looked into God's heart and tried to express what he had seen there. To him it was perfectly clear that from this *Urgrund* or *Ungrund* came all polarities, all harmonies and discords. Like Meister Eckhart and other mystics, Böhme in his struggle to express the inexpressible enriched the German language at considerable remove from language academies and academic reformers.

A mystic who acknowledged indebtedness to Böhme is Johannes Scheffler (1624–77); when he became a Catholic in 1653 he took the name of Johannes Angelus, and as a poet he is known as "Angelus Silesius," the Silesian messenger. The logician among the mystics, he used the epigram—mostly the Alexandrine couplet—to express his witty, often paradoxical thoughts on God. He called the first edition of his collected epigrams *Geistreiche Sinn- und Schlußreime* (*Witty Rhymed Epigrams and Conclusions*, 1657); the second edition, renamed *Der cherubinische Wandersmann,* (*The Cherubic Wanderer*, 1674), is greatly increased in scope. Here we find such oxymoric lines as:

Zufall und Wesen
Mensch, werde wesentlich; denn wenn die Welt vergeht,
So fällt der Zufall weg; das Wesen, das besteht.

Wer ganz vergöttert ist
Wer ist, als wär er nicht und wär er nie geworden,
Der ist, o Seligkeit, zu lauter Gott geworden.

Man weiß nicht, was man ist
Ich weiß nicht, was ich bin; ich bin nicht, was ich weiß;
Ein Ding und nicht ein Ding, ein Tüpfchen und ein Kreis.[19]

A much more deeply lyrical mood prevails in the poems of the Catholic mystic Friedrich von Spee (1591–1635). As father confessor he walked to the pyre with scores of women condemned as witches. At personal risk he demanded justice and a fair trial for those accused of witchcraft, and he endangered himself caring for the wounded on battlefields and the victims of the plague. While recovering from an attempt on his life he wrote *Trutznachtigall* (*Better than the Nightingale*, published posthumously in 1649). Spee is justly famous for his tender nature lyrics; yet to him nature meant something different from what it meant to the Romantics who rediscovered him. In nature Spee loves and praises God and in tender words he expresses his religious involvement. Though a close contemporary of Opitz, Spee's metrics and diction owe little to the reformer.

There is nothing mystical or ecstatic in the religious poems of Paul Gerhardt (1607–76), Germany's greatest hymn writer. Many of his approximately 130 hymns are still sung, and many have found their way (in translation) into English hymnals. In most of his hymns Gerhardt gives voice to the individual Christian, in contrast to Luther who had emphasized the congregation. Gerhardt is intensely aware of human suffering, but faith in the Lord and a cheerful expectation of grace and salvation determine the mood of his poems; when he writes of nature, it is with a certain poetic sobriety.

Twenty years after the close of the war there appeared a novel with autobiographical overtones which at once became a favorite of the reading public and has remained so almost without interruption ever since—*Der abenteuerliche Simplicissimus* (*The Adventurous Simplicissimus*, 1668)[20] by Hans Christof von Grimmelshausen (ca. 1620–76). At first glance the hero, Simplicius Simplicissimus or Simplex for short, is a rogue, a cousin of the Spanish picaro Lazarillo de Tormes; but closer examination reveals that Simplex is troubled by metaphysical problems that never occurred to Lazarillo.

As a ten-year-old Simplex is robbed of home and parents by the war. Wandering through the woods he comes upon a hermit who gives him shelter and instructs him in the precepts of Christianity. When the hermit dies the boy is brought to the commander of Hanau fortress and is made into a court jester. Soon he realizes that it is impossible to live by Christian principles and that the world wants to be deceived. Having been kidnapped, he becomes a soldier and prospers until he is captured. Forced into a marriage he escapes to Paris and a life of lucrative erotic excesses. Smallpox disfigures him and he returns to soldiering and even highway robbery when he runs into his evil spirit, an unsavory character named Olivier. Fortunately Olivier is killed and Simplex makes up for his misdeeds by taking care of his sick friend Heartbrother. A second marriage brings no happiness to Simplex, but he meets his foster father again and finds out that the hermit was his real father. A journey to the center of the earth acquaints him with a strange utopia of sylphs and sprights, and a stay in Russia teaches him more of earth's sordid realities. On his return home he becomes a recluse like his father, but he stays in touch with the world and the author warns us that his hero may not remain a hermit forever.

Shortly after the novel had been published, Grimmelshausen furnished a sequel, the *Continuatio* (1669). In it Simplex undertakes an adventurous pilgrimage. On his way to Campostela he is shipwrecked and washed up on an uninhabited island. Here he leads a simple life and refuses a chance to return to Europe, for only in the wilderness can he live a life pleasing in the sight of God. Grimmelshausen was the only author who made the war the scene of his novel. *Simplicissimus* is in part autobiographical, but it is much more than that. Whatever corner of the world Grimmelshausen looks at, he sees it and lets *us* see it with extraordinary vividness. Moreover, his descriptions are complicated by the fact that he probes behind the scene as well and lets us discover how deceptive appearances are. He would like this world to be a better place and by irony and satire he tries to nudge his fellow creatures in the direction of improvement. But he knows that generally not much can be done and that what is can be borne more easily with a sense of humor. Using the events of this time, Grimmelshausen really deals with the timeless problems of mankind, and the figure of Simplex speaks for all of us. The author's subsequent "Simplician writings" are less important, but one of them, *Die Landstörzerin Courage* (*The Adventuress Courage,* 1670), must be mentioned, for its heroine inspired Bertolt Brecht's *Mother Courage.* Courage is the female counterpart of Simplex, but unlike Simplex, she has few redeeming features.

If Grimmelshausen was a "folk author" who showed his readers the lower strata of society, a large number of authors deals only with the noble, the mighty, the learned, and the exotic: Duke Anton Ulrich of Brunswick created interminable historical novels; Daniel Casper von Lohenstein dealt with Germanic tribal history and Roman intrigue in more than 3000 pages (*Arminius,* 1689); and Heinrich Anselm von Zigler takes us to bloody adventures in Burma with *Die Asiatische Banise* (*Princess Banise of Asia,* 1689). Only Philipp von Zesen (1619–89) managed to tell a relatively simple love story: Markhold, the hero of *Die Adriatische Rosemund* (*Rosemund from the Adriatic,* 1645), is a middle-class German who falls in love with a Catholic girl from Venice. Markhold's religious convictions prevent a marriage and Rosemund dies of grief. The novel contains elements of psychology; it is sentimental and reflects social attitudes that were close to readers of that time; it is the first original modern novel in Germany.

The era had its share of satirists and moralist: Hans Michael Moscherosch (1601–69) rendered Quevedo's *Sueños* as *Die Gesichte Philanders von Sittewald* (*The Visions of Philander von Sittewald,* 1642). The voluble and popular Viennese preacher Abraham a Santa Clara (1644–1709) entertained even as he railed against sin. Friedrich von Logau (1604–55) wrote more than 3500 finely chiseled epigrams, most of which are critical of his time. Finally Christian Reuter (1665–ca. 1712) ridicules the absurdities of many-volumed, learned adventure novels by making a bumpkin the hero of his satirical novel *Schelmuffsky* (1696).

The tendency toward extremes of pathos in diction, structure, and themes continued as the seventeenth century neared its end. The six exotic tragedies of Daniel Casper von Lohenstein (1635–83) follow in the path blazed by Gryphius, but Lohenstein's theme remains the same throughout: tragedy engendered by absolute power and absolute pleasure. His affinity to Seneca has been observed more than once. His poetry, like that of his Breslau compatriot Christian Hofmann von Hofmannswaldau (1617–78), is no longer Gryphius' salvation in despair. The late Silesians, like virtuosi of language, handle the old themes with wit and objectivity; the erotic bulks large. But Boileau's influence was making itself felt and critics were beginning to demand the "natural" and the "unforced." The first two volumes of a seven-volume anthology, beginning in 1695 and edited by Benjamin Neukirch (1665–1729), contain typical examples of *fin de siècle* Silesian mannerism; the later volumes already bring poems characteristic of early rationalism.

Christian Günther (1695–1723) is sometimes called the "last of the Silesians." He wrote pastoral and amorous poems, hymns, and drinking songs, and in all of them he sounded a note of personal involvement which struck his contemporaries as embarrassing. His tragic life and early death were not understood, his great achievements not fully appreciated until the days of the Storm and Stress movement.

THE AGE OF ENLIGHTENMENT
1720–1750

While German literature could not yet assert a position of independence at the turn of the seventeenth to the eighteenth century, Germany possessed in Johann Sebastian Bach (1685–1750) a genius who brought baroque music to its highest perfection. In philosophy Gottfried Wilhelm Leibnitz (1646–1716) was able to bridge the chasm between the creator and the created, the hereafter and the here and now, reconciling thereby the extremes which had plagued man during the baroque era. Leibnitz was a universal scholar who wrote mostly in Latin or French, and some of his most important thoughts were not published till long after his death. In the *Essai de Théodicée* (1710) he argued that evil is a logical necessity and that our world, while not perfect, is the best of all possible worlds. Four years later in his *Monadologie* he tried to reconcile the concepts of mechanical science as developed by Galileo, Kepler, and Newton with religion by postulating a system of carriers of energy, called "monads" each of which is a reflection of the universe, each existing independently in a harmony pre-established by God, who himself is the highest monad. Leibnitz' metaphysics, which contains a good deal of baroque irrationality, was interpreted, popularized, and—as invariably happens—modified in the process by Christian Wolff (1679–1754), professor of philosophy at Halle. What resulted was one variety of the philosophy of rationalism.

Rationalism is not a specifically German philosophy. The English empiricists Francis Bacon, John Locke, and David Hume, the Frenchmen Descartes, Pierre Bayle, and Voltaire, and many others contributed to this world view which significantly influenced the creation of literary works during this era, not only in Germany but even more so in France and England. Rationalism is primarily a bourgeois philosophy of confidence, joy, and optimism: the God-given, universally valid power of human reason can explain and improve everything. Having done away with such constraints as dogma and prerogatives of the nobility, it becomes man's destiny now to eliminate ancient errors and superstitions, and to spread enlightenment, tolerance, and virtue. From these springs happiness, and the greatest happiness lies in man's universal "humanity," that is, humanness, a quality which is impeded rather than aided by nationalism. This era was proudly proclaimed to be the Age of Man. Without Enlightenment and concomitant rationalism neither the French Revolution nor the constitution of the United States would have been possible.

Under a rationalistic world view God plays a relatively minor role. Having built the clock of the universe, the clockmaker retires, for direct intervention in the affairs of the world through revelation or miracles is neither necessary nor possible. The belief in "natural religion" and a benevolent but distant personal God—deism—was widespread among intellectuals of the time. Many of them joined the Freemasons, an organization which had come to Protestant Germany in 1737 from England by way of Hamburg. The churches, as might be expected, were opposed to "free thinkers" of any kind, be they deists or Freemasons, but church authority had been severely weakened by infighting among the theologians on matters of dogma and doctrine, so that even the common folk were disaffected by the frosty atmosphere prevailing in the major churches. Among those for whom religion was a necessity of the heart rather than cause for argument Pietism found many adherents.

Pietism developed as early as 1670 when Jacob Spener (1635–1705) established small groups of the devout, so-called *collegia pietatis*, in Frankfurt on Main. Spener combined elements of medieval and baroque mysticism with practical benevolence and an undogmatic, rather emotional approach to religion. August Hermann Francke (1663–1727), professor of theology at Halle, elaborated on Spener's ideas and exemplified them by founding the Halle Orphanage which gave a Christian education to orphaned children that had been left to fend for themselves until then. For literature, Pietism is significant because, favoring self-observation and introspection—listening to the voice of God within—, it produced keen psychological and religious insights that cried out to be communicated in letters, diaries, poems, and aphorisms. The words appropriate for expressing these nicely differentiated observations are still enriching the German vocabulary. Pietism exerted a literary influence to the days of young Goethe and beyond.

During the baroque era the beauties of nature had been regarded as symbols of paradise or an earthly prelude to it; now philosophy taught the poet to look upon nature as the manifestation of God's wisdom and to admire and revere it accordingly. Barthold Heinrich Brockes (1680–1747), a well-to-do Hamburg merchant, does just that in the nine volumes of his *Irdisches Vergnügen in Gott* (*Earthly Joy in God*, 1721–48). With joyful and loving dedication he describes an object, a flower, a tree, or a view only to conclude his poem with teleological observations. Albrecht Haller (1708–77), a physician and scientist from Bern in Switzerland, looks at nature with similar eyes. The beauty of the mountains in *Die Alpen* (*The Alps*, 1729) proves God's kindness and wisdom;

in anticipation of Rousseau he contrasts the natural life of the mountaineers to the complicated existence of city dwellers. Largely because of his contemporary success we mention here the Swiss artist Salomon Gessner (1730–88). In gentle prose he painted his *Idyllen* (*Idylls*, 1756) as rococo pictures with shepherds and shepherdesses seeking happiness through virtue and contentment. His sentimentality foreshadows Klopstock.

In 1554 the humanist Henricus Stephanus published in Paris a number of Greek poems in praise of friendship, wine, love, and song and attributed the collection to Anacreon. These pseudo-Anacreontics had already enjoyed a vogue in France and England when they were translated into German by three friends, Johann Wilhelm Gleim (1719–1803), Johann Peter Uz (1720–96), and Nicolaus Götz (1721–81). This translation signaled others to write poems in the same mood and the genre became extremely popular, particularly since the philosophy in vogue encouraged the pursuit of happiness. (It may be recalled that our national anthem is sung to the melody of a poem entitled "Anacreon in Heaven.") Many a sedate parson or official composed Anacreontics by refurbishing the requisite motifs and arranging them elegantly, wittily, and gracefully. These poets no longer lived by the favor of a prince; therefore if the term *rococo* is pervaded by a courtly aura it would be incorrect to apply it to the German Anacreontists who were burghers almost to a man.

Umkränzt mit Rosen eure Scheitel
(Noch stehen euch die Rosen gut)
Und nennet kein Vergnügen eitel,
Dem Wein und Liebe Vorschub tut.

Was kann das Toten-Reich gestatten?
Nein! lebend muß man fröhlich sein.
Dort herzen wir nur kalte Schatten:
Dort trinkt man Wasser, und nicht Wein.[21]

Friedrich von Hagedorn (1708–59), author of the above little poem, lived in Hamburg and was a friend of Brockes. His Anacreontics preceded those of the three translators, but even Lessing, Klopstock, and young Goethe still cultivated this crowded field.

Another facet of an increasing English influence on German life and letters is represented by the *moralische Wochenschriften* (moral weeklies, but *moral* is to be taken in the widest possible sense), periodicals which took for their models Addison and Steele's *Tatler* (1709–11), *Spectator* (1711–12) and *Guardian* (1713). The first German journal of this kind was the *Vernünftler* (*Reasoner*), Hamburg, 1713. In Zürich, Switzerland, Bodmer and Breitinger published *Die Discourse der Mahlern* (*Discourses of the Painters*, 1721–23), and in Leipzig Gottsched issued *Die vernünftigen Tadlerinnen* (*Ladies Who Reasonably Reproach*, 1725–27) and *Der Biedermann* (*The Honest Man*, 1727–29). Later titles are *Neue*

Beiträge zum Vergnügen des Verstandes und Witzes (*New Contributions to the Enjoyment of Reason and Intelligence*), published in Bremen 1744–57, but its contributors were members of an anti-Gottsched group that lived in Leipzig; this is the journal in which Klopstock published the first three cantos of the *Messias*. Dozens of other titles could be named.

Although these weeklies never quite reached the quality of their models—Germany had as yet no national capital, no political parties, no freedom of the press, and no coffee house—their effect was nevertheless broad and salutary. Being read by parsons and teachers, officials, merchants, physicians, landowners, shopkeepers—and their wives—, they helped to spread the ideas of the Enlightenment by means of essays, satires, poems, letters, etc. in which common sense, morality, and "good taste" were the important ingredients. Their aim was to teach while entertaining, and a circulation of 5000 for the heyday of the Hamburg *Patriot* (begun 1724) tends to confirm the soundness of the enterprise.

In an age stressing reason, the two didactic genres of fable and satire enjoyed great popularity. For the fable, La Fontaine (d. 1695) remained the unexcelled model. In 1738 Friedrich von Hagedorn whom we have already met as an Anacreontist, published a verse tale that is typical of the rhymed fable: "Johann der muntere Seifensieder." Johann, a jolly craftsman, a soap maker, is constantly singing—during work and after. This annoys his rich, crabbed neighbor who by a lavish gift persuades Johann to give up singing and working. But guarding his treasure makes Johann unhappy and he returns it, glad to be his own jolly self again. The moral, partly expressed by Johann, partly stated by the poet in his own person, is not hammered home. The poem, to which time has given the patina of old-fashionedness, is pleasant and instructive; most Germans know it even today. Christian Fürchtegott Gellert's fables, versified like Hagedorn's, bear down a little harder on the Christian moral. Gellert (1715–69), who also wrote hymns, a novel in the style of Richardson's *Pamela*, and a number of moralizing comedies, was a very popular professor of moral philosophy at Leipzig; young Goethe was his student there. Frederick the Great of Prussia, who admired only French literature, called Gellert "le plus raisonnable de tous les savants allemands." Satire, which in England was brilliantly handled by Pope in verse and Swift in prose, would have found plenty of subject matter in Germany, but ever-present censorship restricted authors like Gottlieb Wilhelm Rabener (1714–71) to general and harmless topics: the Germans' eagerness for titles, foolish fashions, etc.

Even though Frederick II did not think very highly of German authors, the king who called himself the first servant of his state was a sort of national German hero, at least among the Protestants. The Seven Years' War inspired Ludwig Gleim (1719–1803) to write *Preußische Kriegslieder von einem Grenadier* (*Prussian War Songs by a Grenadier,* 1758), poems highly praised by Lessing, Goethe, and Herder. Gleim also wrote Anacreontics and fables, and he corresponded with most German authors of the time. Always eager to help young talents, he put his genius for friendship in the service of the younger generation of poets, to whom he was known as "Father Gleim."

Johann Christoph Gottsched (1700–66), professor of poetics and philosophy at Leipzig, the intellectual capital of Germany at the time, was the man who dominated German literary life from about 1725 till close to the middle of the century. We have already met him as the editor of two "moral weeklies." However, his most influential work deals with the theory of literature and the reform of the stage. His *Versuch einer critischen Dichtkunst vor die Deutschen* (*Attempt at a Critical Theory of Poetry for Germans,* first edition 1730, fourth augmented 1751) was philosophically based on Christian Wolff's interpretation of Leibnitz, while esthetically it relied on Boileau and his neoclassical theories. According to Gottsched the lofty purpose of literature is to aid in spreading knowledge of the good and the true by giving concrete examples of it. On the one hand, the poet must avoid everything mean and commonplace; on the other, he must stay within the bounds of the natural, the reasonable, and the probable. The contents of a literary work might be stated in prose, except that meter, rhyme, and poetic diction make the work more attractive. In drama the unities of time, place, and action, as understood by the French, and the rules of decorum must be observed.

Gottsched was keenly aware of the backwardness of German letters and he believed that imitation of the Greek, Latin, and French masterpieces was the way to remedy the situation. Conscious of the fact that he was not a genius, Gottsched encouraged other writers and came forward with a program of improving the German theater: he wanted to bring together the dramatist and the actor for the benefit of the spectator. As yet there was no resident theatre in Germany. Plays were presented by groups of wandering players, descendants of the "English comedians" who were by now altogether German. The repertoire consisted of prose adaptations of English, French, Italian, or Spanish plays. But these adaptations were totally irregular, full of digressions and bluster, and the clown—"Hans Wurst" or "Pickelhering"—always stole the show since he was played by the manager himself. These "*Haupt- und Staatsaktionen*" (plays of bombast) were held in contempt by the educated; yet, except for the plays rector Christian Weise in Zittau wrote for performance at his school, no serious drama existed in Germany. Gottsched realized that he would have to rid the theater of its excesses in order to give it status. In Frau Neuber he found a manager willing to try out the necessary reforms. The venture proved a success, and now the search for suitable plays began. Gottsched himself had written *Der sterbende Cato* (*Cato Dying,* 1732) in which he had liberally borrowed from Addison and Deschamps; now he translated from the French, in Alexandrines, of course, and got his wife and students to do likewise. Thus the six volumes of *Die Deutsche Schaubühne nach den Regeln der alten Griechen und Römer eingerichtet* (*The German Stage Arranged According to the Rules of the*

Ancient Greeks and Romans, 1740–45) were assembled. Louise Adelgunde Gottsched, herself the author of several comedies, also translated Moliére's comedies, and together with authors like Gellert she inaugurated what the literary histories call "Saxon comedy"—rather sentimental plays with didactic intentions.

Gottsched's attack on the opera was less successful: opera had been firmly established at several courts and in cities like Hamburg and Leipzig, and though it was a highly baroque, that is, unnatural, unreasonable, and improbable form of entertainment, princes and patrons liked it so well that mere arguments failed to stop it. On the whole, Gottsched's reforms of the theatre were beneficial, and when Lessing in 1759 categorically denied that Gottsched had improved the German theatre he was clearly being unjust.

But criticism of Gottsched had come long before Lessing's sledgehammer blows fell. In 1740 two Swiss critics, Johann Jakob Bodmer (1698–1783) and Johann Jakob Breitinger (1701–76) of Zürich published a *Kritische Dichtkunst* (*Critical Theory of Poetry*), a descriptive rather than a normative work, in which they stressed the importance of the creative imagination and of original, forceful diction for literature. Bodmer had translated Milton's *Paradise Lost* into German prose; he wrote several Biblical epics and translated Homer in unrhymed hexameters. Although there were large areas of agreement among Gottsched and the Swiss, an acrimonious fight broke out which was carried on in the journals and which ended with the defeat of Gottsched. Klopstock, the most original genius of the younger generation, was decidedly on the side of the Swiss.

FOOTNOTES

[1] Ließ im Lande die Kleine sitzen, die Braut im Hause, das unerwachsene Kind.

Left in the land the little one sitting, the bridge in the bower a bairn not grown.

[2] Herr, hoher König, habe Mitleid mit uns! Mögest Du uns die Einsicht geben, die kurze Zeit, da wir hier sind, daß wir unsere Seele retten, denn dahinfahren müssen wir unbedingt.

Lord, sublime king, take pity on us! Give us the good sense to save our soul during the short time that we are here, for of necessity we must depart.

[3] Du bist mein, ich bin dein, dessen sollst du gewiß sein. Du bist in meinem Herzen eingeschlossen. Das Schlüsselein ist verloren. Du mußt immer darin sein.

You are mine; I am yours. Of this you can be sure. You are locked inside my heart. The key is lost. You must always be inside.

[4] Ich zog mir einen Falken, länger als ein Jahr. Als ich ihn gezähmt hatte wie ich ihn haben wollte, und ich ihm sein Gefieder mit Gold wohl verziert hatte, erhob er sich und flog in andere Länder.

Seither sah ich den Falken wie er schön flog. An seinem Fuße führte er seidene Riemen und sein Gefieder war rotgold. Möge Gott die zusammenbringen, die einander lieb haben!

I raised a falcon longer than a year. When I had trained him as I wanted him and had decorated his feathers lavishly with gold he rose and flew into other lands.
Later I saw the falcon skillfully flying. Tied to his leg were silk ribbons and his plumage was reddish gold. May God bring those together who love each other.

5 Und wüßte ich nicht, daß sie mich über alle Welt wert zu machen vermag, wenn sie's nur will, ich dient' ihr länger keinen Tag. Nun hat sie aber Tugenden, denen ich nur so lange diene wie ich lebe. Gleichwohl bitte ich sie, mir Erfüllung zu schenken. Was hilft's? Ich weiß wohl, daß sie's nicht tun wird. Doch tue sie's denn, nur weil ich sie darum bitte und erlaube sie mir, ihr Narr zu sein und möge sie meine Rede nicht für ungut nehmen.

And if I did not know that she can make me (feel) worthy beyond this world—if she cares to do so—I would not serve her one day longer. But she has virtues which I shall serve only as long as I live. Still, I am asking her to grant me fulfillment. But what good does the request do me? I know for sure she will not. But let her do it because I beg her to, and let me be her fool, and may she not be offended at my words.

6 [Ritter:] Ach, wird mir je ihr schöner Leib, weißer als Schnee, wieder durch die Nacht leuchten? Der betrog mir die Augen; ich wähnte, es sei des Mondes Schein. Da wurd's Tag.
[Dame:] Ach, wird er hier je wieder den Tag anbrechen sehn, daß wir nicht zu klagen brauchen, während die Nacht vergeht, "Weh, jetzt ist's Tag," wie er klagte, als er mir zur Seite lag? Da wurd's Tag.
[Ritter:] Ja, sie küßte mich vielmals in dem Schlafe. Ihre Tränen rannen herab. Doch ich tröstete sie, so daß sie mit Weinen aufhörte und mich umfing. Da wurd's Tag.
[Dame:] Ach, daß er sich so oft an meinem Anblick erfreut hat. Mich Arme wollte er ohne Kleidung sehen, als er mir die Decke abzog. Es verwunderte mich, daß er nie des Anblicks satt wurde. Da wurd's Tag.

[Knight] Alas, will her beautiful body, whiter than snow, ever again appear to me in the night? It deceived my eyes: I thought it was the moonlight. Then the day broke.
[Lady] Alas, will he ever again see the dawn here so that we need not complain while the night is passing "Alas, now it is day," as he was lamenting recently while he lay by my side? Then the day broke.
[Knight] Alas, she kissed me many times in that sleep. Her tears ran down, but I comforted her and she stopped crying and embraced me. Then the day broke.
[Lady] Alas, that he enjoyed looking at me so often. When he uncovered me he wanted to see poor me without clothing. It is a great marvel to me that he did not tire of the view. Then the day broke.

7 Ich saß auf einem Steine
und schlug ein Bein über das andere

I was sitting on a rock
With my legs crossed

8 Unter der Linde bei der Heide, wo unser beider Bett war, da könnt ihr schönstens Blumen wie auch Gras geknickt finden. Vor dem Walde in einem Tal, tandaradei, sang die Nachtigall so schön. Ich kam zu der Au gegangen; mein Geliebter war schon da. Dort wurde ich 'hehre Dame' empfangen, so daß ich immer wieder beglückt bin. Küßt' er mich? Wohl tausendmal—tandaradei—; seht, wie rot mir der Mund ist.

Dann machte er eine herrliche Bettstatt aus Blumen. Darüber wird noch inniglich gelacht, wenn jemand den Pfad benutzt. An den Rosen sieht er wohl, tandaradei, wo mir das Haupt lag.

Dass er bei mir gelegen, wenn's jemand erführe—und Gott verhüt's—, so schämt' ich mich. Möge niemand je erfahren, was er mit ihm und mir und einem kleinen Vögelein, tandaradei, welches das Geheimnis wohl bewahren kann.

Under the linden by the heath where the two of us had our bed, there you may find both flowers and grass neatly matted down. By the woods in a valley, tandaradei, the nightingale sang prettily.

I came walking to the meadow. My sweetheart had gone there earlier. I was received as 'Noble Lady'; I've been happy ever since. Did he kiss me? A thousand times: tandaradei! See, how red my mouth is.

Then he made a rich bed of flowers. If someone comes along that path he will still quietly laugh to himself. By the roses he can see, tandaradei, where my head lay.

If—God forbid!—anyone should find out that he had lain by me, I'd be ashamed. May no one ever learn what he did with me except he and I and a little bird, tandaradei, and it can keep a secret.

9 Wer euch diese Neuigkeit bringt, das bin ich. Alles, was ihr bisher vernommen habt, das ist etwas, was gar nicht zählt. Nun fragt mich!

Deutsche Männer sind wohl gebildet. Recht wie Engel sind die Frauen. Wer sie beschimpft, der betrügt sich. Anders kann ich mir seine Haltung nicht erklären. Tugend und reine Minne, wer die finden will, der komme in unser Land. Da ist der Wonne viel. Lange möge ich darin leben.

I am the one to bring you this news. Whatever you have heard before, it is like nothing; now ask me!

German men are well educated. The women are like angels. Whoever faults them is deceived. That is the only way I can explain his attitude. Virtue and pure *minne*, whoever wants to find them, let him come to our country: there is much joy there. May I live in it a long time.

10 Wehe! Wohin sind all' meine Jahre entschwunden?! War mein Leben geträumt oder ist es wirklich?

Alas, what has become of all my years?! Was my life a dream or is it real?

11 Eine Geschichte will ich euch neu erzählen, die von grossen Treuen (von Liebe und Treue) handelt, von echter Weiblichkeit des Weibes und gerader Männlichkeit, die sich nie dem Druck beugte. Sein Herz betrog ihn nie in dieser Hinsicht: er war wie Stahl, wo es zum Kampfe kam. Seine Hand gewann als Sieger manchen ruhmvollen Preis. Obgleich kühn, wurde er erst langsam weise. So begrüße ich meinen Helden, der den Augen der Frauen gut tat, ihnen im Herzen aber weh tat, und der immer die Schande mied. Den ich hierzu erkoren habe, von dem diese Geschichte handelt und dem darin Wundersames zustößt, der ist noch nicht einmal geboren.

I will tell you once again a story that deals with great loyalties, with the true womanliness of woman and man's proper manliness, such as never shrank from hardship. His heart never deceived him in this respect: he was like steel when it came to a fight. His hand won many a worthy prize. He was bold, but slow to become wise. I greet my hero thus. He was sweet to the eyes of women but a sickness to their hearts; he would always flee from disgrace. As far as my adventure story is concerned and the miraculous events of it, its hero is not even born yet.

12 Uns wird in alten Geschichten viel Ungewöhnliches erzählt: von lobenswerten Helden,

von großer Mühsal, von Freuden und Festlichkeiten, von Weinen und von Klagen,
vom Kampfe kühner Recken mögt ihr nun Wundersames hören.

Many old stories tell of unusual events. Of praiseworthy heroes, of great troubles, of
joys and feasts, of crying and of plaints, of struggle by brave warriors you will now be
wondrously informed.

13 There is no greater sin on earth
Than jealously. Therefore, neighbors,
Let me warn you of it,
For it is punished monstrously
With whips below in purgatory.

14 There is a reaper called Death; he has his power from the great lord. Today he is sharpen-
ing his knife; it is already much sharper. Soon he will be cutting. Our fate is to submit.
Beware, pretty flower!

Whatever is green and fresh today, tomorrow it will be cut down: the noble narcissus,
the angelic key [key to heaven = the cowslip], beautiful hyacinth, the Turk's-cap lily.
Beware, pretty flower!
Many hundreds of thousands fall under his scythe. He will eliminate both the red rose
and the white lily. Your Crowns Imperial will not be spared. Look out, pretty flower!
Defiance to you, Death, defiance! I do not fear you; come and cut. If he hurts me I
expect to be transplanted into heaven's garden. Be joyful, sweet flower!

15 Walther von der Vogelweide, wer ihn vergässe, der täte mir weh.

Whoever forgot Walther von der Vogelweide would inflict sorrow on me.

16 Song to the Melody of *Ma belle je vous prie*.
Beloved, let us hurry; now is our time. To tarry will harm either of us. The pretty
gifts of beauty fly step by step, and everything we own must disappear.
Red cheeks will soon be blanched and hair turn white; the fire in eyes burn dimmer and
flame be ice. Your lips of coral color will lose their shape, and snowy hands be ugly
and you'll grow old.
Therefore let us enjoy now the fruits of our youth before we needs must follow the
flight of the years. If you but love yourself, please love me too; and give me—if you
grant it—what I'll lose too.

17 I was great and rich in art, goods, and position, was Fortune's darling son. Of honorable
parents. Free. Independent. Could support myself. My fame spread exceedingly far.
No German sang like me.
For my travels (I was) highly praised, not loth to exert myself. Young, alert, carefree.
My name will be heard until the final holocaust destroys this world. For this, German
muses, I am indebted to you.
If you deem me worth it, forgive me, God, father, beloved, friends. To you I say "Good
night" and exit willingly. All else is done—except for the black grave.
Whatever Death may do, let him do it to his enemy. Why should I be troubled about
breathing my last? Nothing less of me will live than my life [= fame].

Human Misery

18 What are we human beings? The residence of grim pain, a plaything of false Fortune, a
will-of-the-wisp of our time, a theater of bitter fear, beset by excruciating suffering, a
snow that will melt soon, and burnt-out candles.
This life flies away like gossip and banter. Those who put aside before us the garment of
their frail body and those inscribed long ago in the record book of great mortality, they
are erased from hearts and minds.

As an idle dream easily escapes attention, and as a stream rushes by when nothing impedes it, so too our name, reputation, honor, and glory must disappear.

Whatever draws breath now must like breath escape. What comes after us will follow us into the grave. What shall I say? We disappear like smoke blown by a strong gale.

19   Accident and Essence

Man, become essential, for if the world decay
Your accident drops out; but essence, it will stay.

      He Who Is Altogether Deified

Whoever is as if he were not and never has been created, he has become—o bliss—pure God.

      One Does not Know What One Is

I know not what I am. And what I know I'm not.
A thing and not a thing, a circle and a dot.

20 The complete title of the first edition is: *Der Abentheurliche Simplicissimus Teutsch/ Das ist: Die Beschreibung deß Lebens eines seltzamen Vaganten/ genant Melchior Sternfels von Fuchshaim/ wo und welcher gestalt Er nemlich in diese Welt kommen/ was er darinn gesehen/ gelernet/ erfahren und außgestanden/ auch warumb er solche wieder freywillig quittirt. Überauß lustig/ und männiglich nutzlich zu lesen. An Tag geben Von German Schleifheim von Sulsfort. Monpelgart/ Gedruckt bey Johann Fillion/ Im Jahr MDCLXIX.* The place given is not the actual city of publication.

21 Encircle your heads with roses while roses still become you and do not call vain any joys encouraged by wine and love.

What can the realm of the dead offer us? No, to be joyful one has be alive. There we shall only embrace cold shadows. There they drink water, not wine.

BIBLIOGRAPHY

Abbreviations of Editions and Series

ATB   *Altdeutsche Textbibliothek*, founded by Hermann Paul, Halle, 1881, now Tübingen.

DLD   *Deutsche Literaturdenkmale des 18. Jahrhunderts*, founded by B. Seuffert, 151 vols., Heilbronn, Tübingen, Berlin, 1881–1924.

DLE   *Deutsche Literatur, Sammlung literarischer Kunst- und Kulturdenkmäler in Entwicklungsreihen*, H. Kindermann, Leipzig, 1928ff. Over 100 vols. in various series; scholarly instructions; many volumes have been reprinted in recent years.

DNd 18   *Deutsche Literaturdenkmale des 18. Jahrhunderts*, Heilbronn, Henninger, 1881ff. Later Berlin and Leipzig.

DNL   *Deutsche National-Literatur*, initiated by J. Kürschner, 164 in 222 vols., Berlin, 1882–99. Most German authors of any importance are represented in this scholarly collection. A number of volumes have been reprinted.

DTM — *Deutsche Texte des Mittelalters*, formerly issued by the (Royal) Prussian Academy, now the Deutsche Akademie der Wissenschaft, Berlin.

Nd — *Neudrucke deutscher Literaturwerke des 16. und 17. Jahrhunderts*, founded by W. Braune, Halle, 1876.

Nd, N.S. — *Neudrucke*, Neue Serie, Tübingen; Supersedes Nd.

Reclam — *Reclams Universalbibliothek*, since 1867 in Leipzig; one of the first paperback series. At present two firms are producing these well-known booklets: VEB Reclam, Leipzig, and Philip Reclam Jun., Stuttgart. Virtually the whole range of German literature is represented, but introductions are brief, the print is small, and few aids are provided for the reader.

Slg. M — *Sammlung Metzler: Realienbücher für Germanisten*, Stuttgart, 1961ff. Concise reports on the research concerning topics and authors.

SLV — *Bibliothek des Literarischen Vereins in Stuttgart*, Tübingen, Leipzig, Stuttgart (in that order) since 1843, 295 vols. to date. Texts from the Middle Ages to the nineteenth century in scholarly editions. Some of the introductions and even some of the editions have become obsolete, but many have been reprinted lately.

UNCS — *University of North Carolina Studies in the Germanic Languages and Literatures*, Chapel Hill, 1949ff. Monographs, translations, and bibliographies in the field indicated.

General Reference Works and Bibliographies

ARNOLD, R., *Allgemeine Bücherkunde zur neueren deutschen Literaturgeschichte*, Berlin, 4th ed., 1966. While this work contains nothing on medieval literature, it lists book titles on German literature in all its ramifications, on biography, bibliography, and fields (like music or philosophy) impinging on German literature.

HANSEL, J., *Bücherkunde für Germanisten*, Studienausgabe, Berlin, 5th ed., 1969. New editions keep this handy reference tool up to date.

———, *Personalbibliographie zur deutschen Literaturgeschichte*, Studienausgabe, Berlin, 1967. Bibliography of bibliographies grouped according to authors of primary literature.

KORNER, J., *Bibliographisches Handbuch des deutschen Schrifttums*, Bern, 3rd ed., 1949. The most important single-volume bibliographical tool.

KOSCH, W. A., *Deutsches Literatur-Lexikon*, 4 vols., 2nd ed., 1948–58, 3rd ed., 1963ff. Concise information on critical concepts, metrics, authors, scholars, titles, etc.; bibliographical information.

MERKER, P., and W. STAMMLER, *Reallexikon der deutschen Literaturgeschichte*, 4 vols., 1925–26, 2nd ed., 1955ff. Brief discussion of genres, literary and critical concepts by experts in the field; bibliographies.

STAMMLER, W., and K. LANGOSCH, *Die deutsche Literatur des Mittelalters. Verfasser-*

Lexikon, Berlin, 1933–55. Concise information on all medieval authors and anonymous works; editions and secondary literature are enumerated; also consult the supplement.

Histories of German Literature

BOESCH, B., et al., *Deutsche Literaturgeschichte in Grundzügen*, Bern, 3rd ed., 1967. Each period is treated by a specialist. The Swiss view is stressed.

DE BOOR, H., and R. NEWALD, *Geschichte der deutschen Literatur von den Anfängen bis zur Gegenwart*, München, 1949ff. I: *Die deutsche Literatur von Karl dem Grossen bis zum Beginn der höfischen Dichtung* (770–1170); II: *Die höfische Literatur* (1170–1250); III, part 1: *Die deutsche Literatur im späten Mittelalter* (1250–1400); all by De Boor; V: *Die deutsche Literatur vom Späthumanismus bis zur Empfindsamkeit* (1570–1750), by Newald. Very detailed treatment of each period; bibliographies for further study; the emphasis is not always even.

EHRISMANN, G., *Geschichte der deutschen Literatur bis zum Ausgang des Mittelalters*, 4 vols., München 1918–35; reprint, 1959. The great standard history of the period, indispensable for study and further research; bibliographies.

FRENZEL, H. A. and E., *Daten deutscher Dichtung*, I: *Von den Anfängen bis zur Romantik*, paperback dtv 28, München, 1970. A concise survey with useful summaries of the intellectual situation of each period. Inexpensive.

FRICKE, G., and V. KLOTZ, *Geschichte der deutschen Dichtung*, Lübeck, 1949, many editions. A one-volume history of German literature eminently suitable for the student reading German.

KOHLSCHMIDT, W., *Geschichte der deutschen Literatur von den Anfängen bis zur Gegenwart*, II: *Vom Barock bis zur Klassik*, Stuttgart, 1965. Treats forms, genres, styles, as well as the ideas and motifs embodied in the literature of the period.

NEUMANN, F., *Geschichte der altdeutschen Literatur (800–1600)*, Berlin, 1966. The basic works of the period are treated in detail; enough minor works are discussed to characterize the times. Particularly valuable for the later Middle Ages.

ROBERTSON, J. G., *A History of German Literature*, revised by E. Purdie, Edinburgh, 1959; originally 1902. Objective presentation from an essentially nineteenth-century point of view, updated in successive revisions.

ROSE, E., *A History of German Literature*, New York, 1960. The author stresses aesthetic criteria and presents German literature against a background of cultural history.

Many more histories of German literature could be named; see J. HANSEL, *Bücher-kunde*, sections entitled "Literaturgeschichte in ihrer Gesamtheit," " . . . nach Epochen," and " . . . nach Gattungen."

Anthologies

ANGER, A., *Dichtung des Rokoko*, Tübingen, 1968.

BRAUNE, W., *Althochdeutsches Lesebuch*, 14th ed., E. A. Ebbinghaus, Tübingen, 1962. This reader contains many of the Old High German documents plus valuable philological and bibliographical references.

CYSARZ, HERBERT, *Barocklyrik;* Vol. I: *Vor- und Frühbarock;* Vol. II: *Hoch- und Spätbarock;* Vol. III: *Scwund- und Kirchenbarock,* DLE, Leipzig, 1937, reprint, Hildesheim, 1964. The most extensive anthology of Baroque poetry presently available.

Epochen der Lyrik; Vol. I: 1100–1500; Vol. II: 1500–1600; Vol. III: 1600–1700; Vol. IV: 1700–1770; dtv. 1969/70. Inexpensive paperback volumes.

KILLY, WALTHER, et al., *Die deutsche Literatur: Texte und Zeugnisse,* München, 1963ff. I: *Mittelalter,* 2 parts, H. de Boor, 1965; II: *15. und 16. Jahrhundert;* III: *Das Zeitalter des Barock,* A. Schöne, 2nd ed., 1968; IV: *18. Jahrhundert.* Selections arranged under characteristic headings; the "Werkregister" at the end gives exact information about the original imprints. The reader is aided by translations of some of the older documents and annotations on difficult words and passages.

SCHOOLFIELD, G., *The German Lyric of the Baroque in English Translation,* UNCS 29, 1961. Representative poems in good translations; biographical sketches and explanatory notes.

Old High German Literature

WULFILA. Text in photoreproduction: *Codex argentus,* Uppsala, 1927; text and commentary: W. Streitberg, *Die gotische Bibel,* 2 vols., Heidelberg, 3rd ed., 1960.

Hildebrandslied. Text in photoreproduction with commentary: G. Baesecke, Halle, 1945; Braune.

Merseburg Charms. Text: Braune; De Boor. Lit.: G. Eis, *Altdeutsche Zaubersprüche,* Berlin, 1964.

Heliand. Text: O. Behagel, rev. W. Mitzka, ATB 4, 7th ed., 1958; Eng. trans.: M. Scott, UNCS 52, Chapel Hill, 1966; Ger. trans.: F. Genzmer, Reclam, Stuttgart.

OTFRIED VON WEISSENBURG. Text: L. Wolff, *Evangelienbuch,* ATB 49, 5th ed., 1965; Ger. trans.: J. Kelle, Prag, 1870, Osnabrück, 1965.

Ludwigslied, Georgslied, Petruslied. Text: Braune.

Post-Carolingian Era. Cluny

Waltharius manu fortis and *Ruodlieb.* Text and trans.: K. Langosch, *Waltharius, Ruodlieb, Märchenepen,* Darmstadt, 1965; Eng. trans. of *Ruodlieb:* E. Zeydel, UNCS 23, 1959. Lit.: W. F. Braun, *Studien zum Ruodlieb,* Berlin, 1962; G. B. Ford, Leiden, 1965.

Ecbasis cuiusdam captivi. Introduction, text, and Eng. trans.: E. Zeydel, UNCS 46, 1964.

HROTSVITA VON GANDERSHEIM. Text: K. Strecker, Leipzig, 1909; B. Nagel, *Sämtliche Dichtungen,* München, 1966; Eng. trans.: C. St. John, London, 2nd ed., 1966; Ger. trans.: O. Baumhauer et al., München, 1966. Lit.: B. Nagel, *Hrotsvita von Gandersheim,* Slg. M 44, 1965.

Memento mori. Text: Braune; with commentary R. Schutzeichel, *Das alemannische Memento mori,* Tübingen, 1962.

Carmina Burana. Text and commentary: A. Hilka and O. Schumann, 3 vols. (incomplete), Heidelberg, 1930–41; Eng. trans.: J. A. Symonds, London, 1931; Ger. trans.: K. Langosch, *Vagantendichtung*, Fischer Bücherei, Berlin, 1963.

The Age of Courtly Literature

THE LYRIC

Representative selections from this era can be found in Killy et al., *Die deutsche Literatur: Texte und Zeugnisse*, I. The "Werkregister" contains additional references. See also the following standard collections: K. Lachmann and C. von Kraus, *Des Minnesangs Frühling*, 32nd ed., Stuttgart, 1959; C. von Kraus and H. Kuhn, *Deutsche Liederdichter des 13. Jahrhunderts*, 2 vols., Tübingen, 1952–58.

WALTHER VON DER VOGELWEIDE. Text: H. Paul, A. Leitzmann, and H. Kuhn, *Die Gedichte*, ATB 1, 1959; Peter Wapnewsky, *Gedichte* (75 poems, original text and trans.), Fischer Bücherei 732, 4th ed., 1966; Eng. trans.: E. Zeydel and B. Morgan, Ithaca, 1952; Ger. trans.: H. Böhm, Berlin, 1964, and many others. Lit.: K. Halbach, *Walther von der Vogelweide*, Slg. M 40, 1965.

THE COURTLY EPIC

PFAFFE LAMPRECHT, *Alexanderlied.* Text: F. Maurer, DLE series "Geistliche Dichtung des Mittelalters" 5, Leipzig, 1940, 2nd ed., Darmstadt; Ger. trans.: R. Ottmann, Halle, 1897. Lit.: W. Fischer, *Die Alexanderliedkonzeption des Pfaffen Lambrecht*, München, 1964.

PFAFFE KONRAD, *Rolandslied.* Text: C. Wesle, Bonn, 1928, 2nd ed., Halle, 1952; Maurer.

HEINRICH VON VELDEKE, *Eneida.* Text: T. Frings and G. Schieb, DTM 58, 1964; Ger. prose trans. with commentary: M-L. Dittrich, Darmstadt, 19—. Lit.: G. Schieb, *Henric van Veldeken. Heinrich von Veldeke*, Slg. M 42, 1965.

HARTMANN VON AUE. Text: A. Leitzmann and L. Wolff, *Erec*, ATB 39, 3rd ed., 1963; G. Benecke, K. Lachmann, and L. Wolff, *Iwein*, Berlin, 5th ed., 1966; Ger. prose trans. of *Erec* and *Iwein* with commentary: E. Schwarz, Darmstadt, 1967; text: H. Paul and L. Wolff, *Gregorius*, ATB 2, 10th ed., 1963; text and Ger. trans.: B. Kippenberg, Ebenhausen, 1959; Eng. trans.: E. Zeydel and B. Morgan, UNCS 14, 1955; text: E. Gierach, *Der arme Heinrich*, Germani. Bibliothek, III, 3, Heidelberg, 2nd ed., 1925; H. Paul and L. Wolff, ATB 3, 1966; text with Ger. trans. and commentary: E. Schwarz, Darmstadt, 1967; text and trans.: De Boor, Fischer Bücherei, Berlin, 1963. Lit.: P. Wapnewski, *Hartmann von Aue*, Slg. M 17, 2nd ed., 1964.

WOLFRAM VON ESCHENBACH. Text: A. Leitzmann, *Parzival*, ATB 12–14, 1960–63; Eng. trans.: E. Zeydel and B. Morgan, UNCS 5, 1960; modern Ger. trans.: W. Stapel, München, 1968; Reclam 7451; prose trans. with commentary: G. Weber, Darmstadt, 2nd ed., 1967; text: A. Leitzmann, *Willehalm*, ATB 15–16, 5th ed., 1963. Lit.: J. Bumke, *Wolfram von Eschenbach*, Slg. M 36, 2nd ed., 1966.

GOTTFRIED VON STRASBOURG, *Tristan und Isolde.* Text: F. Ranke, Berlin, 1930, 2nd ed., 1958; Ger. prose trans. with commentary: G. Weber et al., Darmstadt, 1967. Lit.: G. Weber and W. Hoffmann, *Gottfried von Strasbourg*, Slg. M 15, 2nd ed., 1965.

WERNHER DER GARTENAERE, *Meier Helmbrecht*. Text: F. Panzer, ATB 11, 6th ed. by K. Ruh as *Die Märe vom Helmbrecht*, 1960.

THE HEROIC EPIC OF THE NIBELUNGS

Nibelungenlied. Text, Manuscript A: K. Lachmann and U. Pretzel, Berlin, 1960; text, Manuscript B: K. Bartsch and H. De Boor, Deutsche Klassiker des Mittelalters 3, Wiesbaden, 15th ed., 1959; text, Manuscript C: F. Zarncke, Leipzig, 6th ed., 1887; Ger. trans.: F. Genzmer, Reclam, Stuttgart, 1955; Eng. trans.: F. Ryder, Wayne State University Press, Detroit, 1962; A. Hatto, Penguin Books, Baltimore, 1965. Lit.: G. Weber and W. Hoffmann, *Heldendichtung II. Nibelungenlied*, Slg. M 7, 1961.

The Late Middle Ages

DRAMA OF THE CHURCH. History: Karl Young, *The Drama of the Medieval Church*, 2 vols., Oxford, 2nd ed., 1951. Texts: R. Froning, *Das Drama des* Mittelalters, DNL 14, n.d.; E. Hartl, DNL series "Drama des Mittelalters," I, "Osterfeiern," II, "Osterspiele," IV, "Passionsspiele," 1937–42, reprints Darmstadt.

SHROVETIDE PLAYS, MASTERSONG. HANS SACHS. Texts: A. von Keller and E. Goetze, *Sämtliche Werke*, 26 vols., SLV, 1870–1908, reprint Hildesheim; E. Goetze, *Sämtliche Fastnachtspiele*, 7 vols, Nd, 1880–87; E. Goetze and K. Drescher, *Sämtliche Fabeln und Schwänke*, 6 vols., Nd, 1893–1913, 2nd ed., L. Markschies, 1953; selections in DNL 20–21; modern spelling editions in Reclam UB. NIKLAUS MANUEL. Text: J. Baechtold, *Sämtliche Dichtungen*, Bibliothek alterer Schriftsteller der deutschen Schweiz 2, Frauenfeld, 1878. Lit.: E. Catholy, *Fastnachspiel*, Slg. M 56, 1966; B. Nagel, *Meistersang*, Slg. M 12, 1962.

FOLKSONG. Texts: R. von Liliencron, *Deutsches Leben im Volfslied um 1530*, DNL, 1884; L. Erk and R. Böhme, *Deutscher Liederhort*, 3 vols., 1893–94. Lit.: W. Suppan, *Volkslied*, Slg. M 52, 1966.

FOLK TALES. Bibliography: P. Heitz and F. Ritter, *Versuch einer Zusammenstellung der Deutschen Volksbücher* . . ., Strassburg, 1924. Texts: H. Kindermann, DLE series "Volks- und Schwankbücher," 1, 2, and 7; reprint of vol. 2 available; R. Petsch, Faustbuch *Das Volksbuch vom Doctor Faust*, Nd 7-8, 2nd ed., 1911; H. Knust, *Till Eulenspiegel*, Nd 55–56, 1884.

SCHWÄNKE. J. PAULI, *Schimpf und Ernst*. H. Oesterley, SLV 85, 1866; K. von Bahder, *Das Lalebuch (1597) mit den* . . . *Erweiterungen der Schiltbürger*, Nd 236–39, 1914; see also DNL 24.

SATIRE AND DIDACTICISM. HUGO VON TRIMBERG, *Der Renner*. Text: G. Ehrismann, SLV 247–49 and 252–56, 1908–11. H. WITTENWEILER, *Ring*. Text: E. Wiessner, DLE series "Realistik des Spatmittelalters" 3, 1931, commentary 1936, reprint Darmstadt, 1963; Eng. trans.: G. F. Jones, UNCS 18, 1956. S. BRANT, *Narrenschiff*. Text: F. Zarncke, Leipzig, 1854, reprinted; also see DNL 16, 1889.

BEAST EPIC. *Reinke de Vos*. Text: A. Leitzmann and K. Voretzsch, ATB 8, 1925.

Humanism and the Reformation

HUMANISM. R. Newald, *Probleme und Gestalten des deutschen Humanismus: Studien,* H.-G. Roloff, Berlin, 1963.

JOHANN VON TEPL (or SAAZ), *Der Ackermann aus Böhmen.* Text with full bibliography: W. Krogmann, Deutsche Klassiker des Mittelalters, N.S. 1, Wiesbaden, 2nd ed., 1964; K. Spalding, Blackwell's German Texts, Oxford, 1950 (introduction, notes, vocabulary in English); Eng. trans.: E. Kirrmann, *Death and the Plowman,* Chapel Hill, 1958; Ger. trans.: Reclam 7666 and many others.

JACOB WIMPHELING, *Stylpho.* Text: H. Holstein, Lateinische Literaturdenkmäler des 15. und 16. Jahrhunderts 6, Berlin, 1892.

JOHANNES REUCHLIN, *Kömodien.* Text: H. Holstein, Halle, 1888; *Henno* (with Sachs's trans. of 1531), Konstanz, 1922. Lit.: L. Geiger, *Johannes Reuchlin,* Leipzig, 1871.

Epistolae obscurorum virorum. Text: A. Bömer, 2 vols., Heidelberg, 1924; Ger. trans.: P. Amelung and W. Binder, *Briefe der Dunkelmänner,* München, 1964; Eng. trans. (with Latin text): F. Stokes, London, 2nd ed., 1964.

ERASMUS. Texts: J. Le Clerc, *Opera omnia,* Leiden, 1703–06, reprint, 1961–62; A. and H. Holborn, *Ausgewahlte Werke,* München, 1933, reprint, 1964; Eng. trans.: N. Bailey, *Colloquia,* 3 vols., London, 1900; C. R. Thompson, Chicago, 1965ff. Lit.: J. Huizinga, *Erasmus,* available in Dutch, English, 1952, and German, 4th ed., 1951; W. Kaegi, *Erasmus and the Age of Reformation,* New York, 1957.

MARTIN LUTHER. Texts: J. Knaake, G. Kawerau, et al., *Werke,* 62 vols., Weimar, 1883ff.; L. E. Schmitt, *Von der Freiheit eines Christenmenschen,* Nd 18, 3rd ed., 1954; E. Wolfel, *De captivitate Babylonica ecclesiae,* München, 1961; W. Braune, *An den christlichen Adel deutscher Nation,* Nd 4, 1884; *An den christlichen Adel . . . , Von der Freiheit . . . , Ein Sendbrief vom Dolmetschen,* Reclam, Stuttgart, 1958; Eng. trans.: *Three Treatises,* Muhlenberg Press, Philadelphia, 1960; J. Dillenberger, *Selections from his Writings,* Garden City, 1961; text: G. Hahn, *Sämtliche deutsche geistliche Lieder,* Nd, N.S. 20, 1967. Lit.: Carl Franke, *Grundzüge der Schriftsprache Luthers,* 3 vols., Halle 1913–22, reprint, 1967. Biography: G. Ritter, *Luther,* München, 5th ed., 1949, Eng. trans., New York, 1963; H. Lilje, *Martin Luther,* Nürnberg, 3rd ed., 1952; also in the series Rowohlts Monographien 98, Eng. trans., Philadelphia, 1952.

BURKARD WALDIS, *Der verlorene Sohn.* Text: G. Milchsack, Nd 30, 1881; A. E. Berger, DLE series "Reformation" 5, Leipzig, 1935.

TH. NAOGEORGUS (KIRCHMAIER). Texts: J. Bolte and E. Schmidt, *Pammachius.* Lateinische Literaturdenkmaler des 15. und 16. Jahrhunderts 3, Berlin, 1891; J. Bolte, *Mercator,* in *Drei Schauspiele vom sterbenden Menschen,* SLV 269–70, 1927.

JÖRG (GEORG) WICKRAM. Texts: H.-G. Roloff, *Sämtliche Werke,* Berlin, 1967ff.; J. Bolte and W. Scheel, *Werke,* SLV 241; *Von guten und bösen Nachbarn,* SLV 223; DLE series "Volks- und Schwankbücher" 7, 1933. Lit.: G. Fauth, *Jorg Wickrams Romane,* Strassburg, 1916.

JOHANN FISCHART. Texts: G. Baesecke, *Das gluckhafft Schiff von Zürich*, Nd 182, 1901; A. Alsleben, *Geschichtklitterung*, Nd 65–71, 1891; Ute Nyssen, Düsseldorf, 1963; selections in DNL 18. Lit.: H. Sommerhalder, *Johann Fischarts Werk*, Berlin, 1960.

The Age of the Baroque : Counterreformation, Absolutism

CRITICISM. R. Alewyn, ed., *Deutsche Barockforschung*, Köln, 1965. A collection of the most valuable essays published in the twenties and thirties on the subject of German Baroque literature; bibliographies.

MARTIN OPITZ. Texts: G. Witkowski, *Aristarchus und Buch von der deutschen Poeterey*, Leipzig, 1888; R. Alewyn, *Buch von der deutschen Poeterey*, Nd, N.S. 8, 1963; G. Witkowski, *Teutsche Poemata (1624)*, Nd 189–92, 1902; G. Schulz-Behrend, *Trostgedicht in Widerwärtigkeit des Krieges*, SLV 295, 1968; *Argenis*, SLV 297, 1970. Lit.: M. Szyrocki, *Martin Opitz*, Berlin, 1957.

PAUL FLEMING. Text: J. Lappenberg, *Deutsche Gedichte*, SLV 82–3, 1865, reprint, Darmstadt, 1965; selections in DNL 28.

ANDREAS GRYPHIUS. Texts: M. Szyrocki and H. Powell, *Gesamtausgabe der deutschsprachigen Werke*, Nd, N.S. 5–15ff., 1963ff.; H. Palm, *Trauerspiele, Lustspiele, Lyrische Gedichte*, SLV 162, 168, and 171, 1878, 1882, 1884; W. Flemming, *Catharina von Georgien*, Nd 261–2, 4th ed., 1968; H. Powell, *Carolus Stuardus*, Leicester, 1955 (Eng. intro. and notes); Powell, *Cardenio und Celinde*, 1961 (Eng. intro. and notes); Reclam 8532; Powell, *Absurda comica oder Herr Peter Squenz*, 1957 (Eng. intro. and notes); Reclam 917; W. Braune, *Horribilicribrifax*, Nd 3, 1883; Reclam; W. Flemming, DLE series "Barockdrama" 4; W. Flemming, *Verlibtes Gespenst* and *Die gelibte Dornrose*, DLE series "Barockdrama" 4; Komedia 4. Lit.: M. Szyrocki, *Andreas Gryphius: Leben und Werk*, Tübingen, 1964; W. Flemming, *Andreas Gryphius*, Stuttgart, 1965.

ENGLISH COMEDIANS. W. Creizenach, *Die Schauspiele der englischen Kömodianten*, DNL 23, 1889.

JACOB BIDERMANN. Text: *Cenodoxus* in Meichl's trans., DLE series "Barockdrama" 2; Reclam 8958–9.

JACOB BÖHME. W.-E. Peuckert, *Sämtliche Schriften* (facsimile of Ueberfeld's ed. of 1730–31), 11 vols., Stuttgart, 1955–61. Lit.: H. Grunsky, *Jacob Böhme*, Stuttgart, 1956; J. J. Stoudt, *Sunrise to Eternity*, Philadelphia, 1957.

JOHANNES SCHEFFLER (ANGELUS SILESIUS). Text: H. L. Held, *Sämtliche poetische Werke*, 3 vols., München, 3rd ed., 1949–52; G. Ellinger, *Der cherubinische Wandersmann*, Nd 135–38, 1901. Lit.: E. Sporri, *Der 'Cherubinische Wandersmann' als Kuntswerk*, Zurich, 1947; G. Ellinger, *Angelus Silesius: Ein Lebensbild*, Breslau, 1927; J. Sammons, *Angelus Silesius*, New York, 1967.

FRIEDRICH VON SPEE. Text: G. Arlt, *Trutznachtigall*, Nd 292–301, 1936; E. Rosenfeld, *Sämtliche Schriften*, München, 1968ff. Lit.: *Friedrich von Spee von Langenfeld*, Berlin, 1958; E. Rosenfeld, *Neue Studien zur Lyrik von Friedrich von Spee*, Milano, 1963.

PAUL GERHARDT. Text: E. von Cranach-Sichart, *Dichtungen und Schriften*, München, 1957. Lit.: B. Hewitt, *Paul Gerhardt as a Hymn Writer*, New Haven, 1918.

HANS CHRISTOF VON GRIMMELSHAUSEN. Text: *Simplicius Simplicissimus*, editions in SLV, DNL, Nd, Reclam, etc.; best is R. Tarot, *Der Abentheuerliche Simplicissimus Teutsch und Continuatio*, Tubingen, 1967; Eng. trans. G. Schulz-Behrend, Indianapolis, 1965; text: W. Bender, *Lebensbeschreibung der Ertzbetrügerin und Landstortzerin Courasche*, Tübingen, 1967; Eng. trans: H. Speier, Princeton, 1964; R. Hiller and J. C. Osborne, Lincoln, 1965. Lit.: G. Herbst, *Die Entstehung des Grimmels-Hausenbildes in der wissenschaftlichen Literatur*, Bonn, 1957; W. Welzig, *Beispielhafte Figuren . . . bei Grimmelshausen*, Graz, 1963.

ANTON ULRICH VON BRAUNSCHWEIG. Lit.: B. L. Spahr, *Anton Ulrich and 'Aramena,'* Berkeley, 1966.

DANIEL CASPER VON LOHENSTEIN. Texts: K. G. Just, *Trauerspiele* (*Türkische, Römische, Afrikanische*), 3 vols., SLV 292-4, 1953-57; F. Bobertag, *Cleopatra*, DNL 36/I; Reclam; W. Flemming, *Sophonisbe*, DLE series "Barockdrama" 1, 1931, reprint, Darmstadt. Lit.: E. Verhofstadt, *Daniel Casper von Lohenstein*, Brugge, 1964: L. Laporte, *Lohensteins Arminius'*, Berlin, 1927.

HEINRICH ANSELM VON ZIGLER. Text: F. Bobertag, *Asiatische Banise*, DNL 37. Lit.: W. Pfeiffer-Belli, *Die asiatische Banise*, Berlin, 1940.

PHILIPP VON ZESEN. Text: M. Jellinek, *Adriatische Rosemund 1645*, Nd 160-63, 1899. Lit.: P. Baumgarten, *Die Gestaltung des Seelischen in Zesens Romanen*, Zurich, 1942.

HANS MICHAEL MOSCHEROSCH. Text: *Die Gesichte Philanders von Sittewald* (selections), DNL 32.

ABRAHAM A SANTA CLARA (JOHANN ULRICH MEGERLE). Text: K. Bertsche, *Werke*, 3 vols., Wien, 1943-45; F. Bobertag, *Judas der Erzschelm* (selections), DNL 40, 1884.

CHRISTIAN REUTER. Text: G. Witkowski, *Werke*, 2 vols., Leipzig, 1916; A. Schullerus, *Schelmuffsky*, Nd 57-8, 1885. Lit.: W. Hecht, *Christian Reuter*, Slg. M 46, 1966.

CHRISTIAN HOFMANN VON HOFMANNSWALDAU. Lit.: E. Rotermund, *Christian Hoffmann von Hofmannswaldau*, Slg. M 29, 1963. See also next item.

BENJAMIN NEUKIRCH. Text: A. G. de Capua and E. A. Philippson, *Benjamin Neukirchs Anthologie: Herrn von Hoffmannswaldau und andrer Deutschen auserlesener und bissher ungedruckter Gedichte erster* (and *anderer*) *Theil*, Nd, N.S. 1 and 16, 1961, 1965.

JOHANN CHRISTIAN GÜNTHER. Text: W. Krämer, *Sämtliche Werke*, 6 vols. (incomplete), SLV 1930-37, reprint, Darmstadt, 1964. Lit.: H. Dahlke, *Johann Christian Günther*, Berlin, 1960.

The Age of Enlightenment

GOTTFRIED WILHELM LEIBNITZ. Texts: E. Cassirer and A. Buchenau, *Hauptschriften*, 4 vols., Hamburg 3rd ed., 1904-25; *Monadologie*, Reclam 7852; Eng. trans.: Mary Morris, *Philosophical Writings*, Everyman 905, 1961.

FREEMASONRY. M. Steffens, *Freimaurer in Deutschland*, Flensburg. 1964.

PIETISM. A. Ritschl, *Geschichte des Pietismus*, 3 vols., Bonn, 1880-86, reprint, 1966.

BARTHOLD HEINRICH BROCKES. Text: *Auszug der vornehmsten Gedichte aus dem Irdischen Vergnügen in Gott*, DNd 18, 1965; selections, Reclam 2015.

ALBRECHT VON HALLER. Text: H. Maync, *Gedichte*, Leipzig, 1923; *Die Alpen und andere Gedichte*, Reclam 8963–4; also see DNL 41, part 2. Lit.: C. Siegrist, *Albrecht von Haller*, Slg. M 57, 1967.

SALOMON GESSNER. Text: J. L. Klee, *Schriften*, 2 vols., Zürich, 1841; H. Hesse, *Werke* (selections), Leipzig, 1922.

ANACREONTISTS. Text: F. Muncker, *Anakreontiker und preussisch-patriotische Lyriker*, DNL 45, 1884. JOHANN WILHELM GLEIM. Text: W. Körte, *Sämtliche Werke*, Halberstadt, 1811–13; A. Sauer, *Preussische Kriegslieder von einem Grenadier*, DLD 4, 1892. NICOLAUS GÖTZ. Text: C. Schüddekopf, *Gedichte*, DLD 42, 1893. JOHANN PETER UZ. Text: A. Sauer, *Samtliche poetische Werke*, DLD 33–38, 1890.

FRIEDRICH VON HAGEDORN. Text: *Sämtliche poetische Werke*, 3 vols., Hamburg, 1757, reprint in 1 vol., Bern, 1967.

CHRISTIAN FÜRCHTEGOTT GELLERT. Texts: *Sämtliche Schriften*, 10 vols., Leipzig, 1769–74, reprint, Bern, 1967; *Fabeln*, Insel-Bucherei 679; *Die schwedische Gräfin von Gellert*, Reclam 8536. Examples of Gellert's sentimental comedies: *Die Betschwester*, Komedia; *Die zärtlichen Schwestern*, Reclam 8973–4.

GOTTLIEB WILHELM RABENER. Text: F. Muncker, *Bremer Beiträger* (selections), DNL 43–44, 1889. Lit.: H. Wyder, *Gottlieb Wilhelm Rabener*, Zürich, 1953.

JOHANN CHRISTOPH GOTTSCHED. Texts: J. Birke, *Ausgewählte Werke*, Ausgaben deutscher Literatur des XV. bis XVIII Jahrhunderts, Berlin, 1968ff.; *Versuch einer critischen Dichtkunst vor die Deutschen*, Leipzig, 1751, reprint, Darmstadt, 1962; *Der sterbende Cato*, Reclam 2097/97a. See also J. Crüger, *Gottsched und die Schweizer*, DNL 42, 1884.

JOHANN JAKOB BODMER and JOHANN JAKOB BREITINGER. Texts: Th. Vetter, *Discourse der Mahlern. 1721–1722*, Frauenfeld, 1891; *Kritische Dichtkunst*, 1740, facsimile reprint, DNd 18, 1966.

Lessing's *Laokoon:* a manuscript page and the title page of the first edition.

Laokoon:

oder

über die Grenzen

der

Mahlerey und Poesie.

Ὕλη καὶ τρόποις μιμήσεως διαφέρουσι.

Plut. vet Ἀθ. κατα Π. ἑ κατα Σ. ἐδ.

Mit

beyläufigen Erläuterungen

verschiedener Punkte

der alten Kunstgeschichte;

von

Gotthold Ephraim Lessing.

Erster Theil.

Berlin,

bey Christian Friedrich Voß.

1 7 6 6.

The Age of Goethe

WOLFGANG LEPPMANN

University of Oregon

The Age of Goethe differs from the classical periods of other national literatures in that it was not accompanied by any corresponding political, military,
or economic achievements. Periclean Greece, Augustan Rome, Elizabethan
England, and the France of the Sun King mark high points in the *total* development of these countries and are therefore named after rulers, not poets
or artists; although more generic in nature, the terms *renaissance* and *siglo de
oro* likewise indicate a flowering not only of the intellectual but of the entire
national life of Italy and Spain. The fact that the high point of German literature has been named not after a ruler but a writer tells us something about
the respective order of magnitude. Indeed, it would have been inconceivable
to call this period after any one of the countless German princes or statesmen who were contemporaries of Goethe; the only possible candidates might
have been Frederick the Great of Prussia, who was already on the throne
when the poet was born, or Bismarck who came to power long after he had
died. Goethe, in other words, looms larger not only in German letters but in
German life than Sophocles, Vergil, Shakespeare, or Racine did in that of their
countries, and it is no coincidence that an entire phase of German history, the

Wolfgang Leppmann received his B. A. and M. A. from McGill University,
and his Ph.D. from Princeton University. He taught at Princeton University, Brown University, the University of Toronto, and Vassar College,
and is now at the University of Oregon. He has twice been a Guggenheim
Fellow, and wrote *The German Image of Goethe* (Oxford, 1961, German
version, 1962), *Pompeji, eine Stadt in Literatur und Leben* (Munich, 1966,
English version, 1968), and *Winckelmann* (New York, 1970, German version, 1971), as well as articles in scholarly and other journals.

Weimar Republic of 1919–33, should have been named after the city in which he had resided a century before. Goethe is gigantic not only because he *was* very great, but because his country was then so very insignificant.

What made it so insignificant is the fact that in Goethe's day, "Germany" was little more than a geographical term applied to the conglomeration of kingdoms, duchies, bishoprics, free cities, and other petty states which made up the Holy Roman Empire. Its rulers, the Habsburg emperors, resided on the periphery of the German language area, in Vienna. Although the political capital and a center of musical life, that metropolis carried no more weight in other respects than several smaller cities within and without the Empire: Hamburg, an important trade center in which Lessing and Klopstock resided for some time; Leipzig, the fountainhead of worldly fashion and the home of Gottsched, Germany's arbiter of literary fashion; the Königsberg of Hamann, Herder, and Kant; Zürich, where Bodmer and Breitinger stressed the exemplariness of English literature in contrast to Gottsched's praise of the French; and the Berlin of Frederick the Great, a stronghold of Rationalism as well as a focus of political power. Within Goethe's lifetime and due in large measure to his residence there, the little town of Weimar, capital of a duchy with a total population of perhaps 100,000, was to surpass all these cities and become the cultural center of the entire country, which formed no nation at all in the modern sense, but so loose a confederation of disparate states that it disintegrated altogether under the impact of the Napoleonic Wars and was formally laid to rest in 1806. The political division of Germany into so many small administrative units brought about a corresponding fragmentation of the country's economic life (different laws and currencies, customs at every border) and of its military potential, so that with the exception of the Kingdom of Prussia, the individual states could hope to survive only by adjusting themselves to the whims of their more powerful neighbors on whom they were dependent for dynastic reasons (England and Hanover, for example, were ruled by the same family), or through fear of being invaded (the Palatinate by France), or annexed (Silesia by Prussia). The analogy sometimes drawn between Athens and Florence on the one hand and Weimar on the other, is therefore mistaken: neither the Athens of Pericles nor Medicean Florence were the most powerful states of their time, but they did represent viable political and economic commonwealths supported by a population with a strong feeling of cohesiveness and civic pride, whereas the Duchy of Sachsen-Weimar lacked all national identity and existed only by sufferance of Prussia, Saxony, and the Empire.

The Age of Goethe, then, is a cultural phenomenon which took place in what was for all practical purposes a political vacuum. In literary life, this void was filled by France. As late as 1781, French was spoken at all German courts except that of Weimar, and Frederick the Great habitually preferred that language to his own, which he spoke badly and thought fit only for servants, soldiers, and others of little social importance. French literature, and especially the classical French theatre, was the model which Germans were supposed to follow but could scarcely hope to equal. Parisian manners and fashions were imitated by all who possessed, or hoped to achieve, any degree of distinction. If this ascendancy of French culture was not restricted to Germany, it was more pronounced there; sophisticated Englishmen, Spaniards, and Italians also took their cue from Paris, but the literature of these countries was less affected by this subservience than was that of Germany, which possessed neither a political nor an intellectual capital from which this influence might have been countered. Hence the time and effort, so incomprehensible in retrospect, which men like Herder, Goethe, and above all Lessing expended in specifically disproving the doctrine of the innate superiority of the language and literature of France.

A further distinguishing feature of the Age of Goethe is that its constituent trends and phases cannot be clearly separated in chronological order. They did not so much follow one another as exist side-by-side, so that the method, arbitrary at best, of dating the onset of a particular movement from this or that event—English Romanticism from the publication of *Lyrical Ballads* in 1798, French Realism from the fiasco of Hugo's *Burgraves* in 1843—cannot be applied at all to the German literature of that period. For example, if the course of English literary history were to be represented graphically in diagram or profile, it would show a fairly clear alternation of high points and low, of peaks designated by works (for example, *Beowulf*, *The Faerie Queene*, *The Waste Land*), movements (such as Renaissance, Restoration, Romanticism), or poets (Shakespeare, Milton, Pope, etc.), set off from one another by valleys of lesser productivity. The same applies to other Western literatures, to that of France from the *chansons de geste* to Gide and St. John Perse, that of Spain from the *Cantar del mío Cid* to the Generation of 98 and beyond, that of Italy from Dante, Petrarch, and Boccaccio to Montale, Quasimodo, and Lampedusa. The literary history of Germany, on the other hand, shows no such structured profile. Despite a few minor rises here and there, it shows only two plateaus, the MHG poetry of the late Middle Ages and the early twentieth century with Rilke, Mann, Kafka, and their contemporaries—and one gigantic mountain: the Age of Goethe. In this respect as in some others (centuries of domination by foreign models, nonsynchronization of literary and political greatness) it rather resembles Russian literature, which, to foreigners at least, is so largely concentrated in the nineteenth century, that of Pushkin, Tolstoi, and Dostoevski.

This peculiarity springs not only from Goethe's overwhelming stature but from the fact that no fewer than four distinct movements flourished in his lifetime: Enlightenment, Storm and Stress, Classicism, Romanticism. If we remember that one of these, *Sturm und Drang*, was an almost exclusively German phenomenon and that two others, *Klassik* and *Romantik*, bear no more than a superficial resemblance to the analogous phases of French and English letters, it is clear that they cannot be measured by the same tokens, and that some definitions are in order. These will be given in due course, and it is well to keep in mind for now that instead of following one another, these phases took place contemporaneously in the period here under discussion, that of 1750–1830. The five years from 1795 to 1800 alone saw the publication of the following major works which run the whole gamut of literary expression from Rationalism to Romanticism, from translation through adaptation to original creation, from prose to poetry, from the lyric through the dramatic to the epic: Goethe's *Römische Elegien*, *Wilhelm Meisters Lehrjahre*, and *Hermann und Dorothea*; Schiller's *Wallenstein* and *Maria Stuart*; Herder's *Briefe zur Beförderung der Humanität*; Tieck's translation of *Don Quijote*, and the beginnings of the Schlegel-Tieck translation of Shakespeare's plays; Jean Paul's *Das Leben des Quintus Fixlein* and Wackenroder's *Herzensergiessungen eines kunstliebenden Klosterbruders*; Goethe's and Schiller's main ballads; the Schlegel Brothers' *Athenaeum*; Novalis' *Hymnen an die Nacht* and Hölderlin's *Hyperion*; Friedrich Schlegel's *Lucinde* and Tieck's *Der gestiefelte Kater*.

Complicating matters for the student, but adding to the impressive sum total of this achievement is one final trait of the Age of Goethe which should be stressed here by way of introduction: the simultaneousness of several major literary trends with a high level of musical and speculative activity as well. Whereas the great days of Italian music (Scarlatti and Pergolesi in the early eighteenth, Rossini and Verdi in the mid-ninteenth century) and the great days of French painting toward the end of the last century were not complemented by similar achievements in the literary life of these countries, we find in Germany a synchronization of musical and philosophical with literary excellence. The life span of the poet after whom the whole period is named encompassed the birth and death of Fichte and Hegel, Mozart and Beethoven, Weber and Schubert. During his youth and manhood, Goethe was for many decades a contemporary of Kant and Haydn; when he died, Schopenhauer and Wagner were grown men.

JOHANN JOACHIM WINCKELMANN

Needless to say, Goethe did not create single-handedly the literature of his age. He was preceded by a number of near-contemporaries each of whom pencilled a characteristic note, as it were, into the symphony that he was to conduct. The first of these men—in the order in which they will be discussed here—was Johann Joachim Winckelmann, who gave to German classical literature, and indeed to a whole phase of Western art, its Greek orientation. Born as a cobbler's son in 1717, he managed, after difficult years as a schoolteacher, to become librarian and private secretary to a Saxon nobleman who resided near Dresden, where Winckelmann developed an avid interest in art which was nourished by many visits to the local museum, the *Antikensaal* which housed Raphael's

"Sistine Madonna" and a number of Roman reproductions of Greek sculptures. He soon saw himself faced with a major decision: a Protestant by birth, he found that only the Roman Church seemed able to provide him with the opportunity to carry out what he henceforth considered to be his life's work: proclaiming the exemplariness of classical Greek art to a public awed by the Baroque and enchanted by the Rococo. In order to do this, he would have to take up residence in Rome, where so many Greek and Hellenistic works had been preserved. Penniless as he was, he would be in a position to do so only if he attached himself in some fashion to the Roman Catholic Church and thus gained access to the many museums and collections which were then administered by the Vatican. In 1754, Winckelmann accordingly became a convert, and shortly thereafter received a stipend from the Saxon court which enabled him to set out for Italy. As a learned man with a sound knowledge of history and a command of half a dozen languages, he was now able to test at first hand the theories he had developed in the long, dull years spent as a schoolteacher and librarian. He was helped in this by his connection with an influential cardinal who eventually took him into his home. For over a decade, the shoemaker's son lived at the side of a Prince of the Church, whom he advised on art purchases and the preservation of ancient monuments.

Winckelmann repeatedly visited Herculaneum, the Graeco-Roman town which had been destroyed along with Pompeii by the eruption of Mount Vesuvius in 79 A.D. and was then being excavated. The observations that he made on the spot bore out many of his conjectures about the characteristics of ancient art, and his criticism and suggestions in regard to the excavations themselves were so fruitful that he became, for all practical purposes, the founder of archaeology as we know it and as it is now practised all over the world. What had formerly been a hurried search for hidden treasure now became a careful identification, cataloguing, and preservation of every object dug up by the workmen. As a result of these and other labors, his fame spread far and wide. It must have been with a deep satisfaction that he learned that no less a personage then the mighty King of Prussia had begun to take an interest in his erstwhile subject: Frederick charged the writer Friedrich Nicolai with bringing Winckelmann back to Berlin as Director of the Royal Collection of Antiquities, and the negotiations were well underway when the Francophile ruler, aghast at the archaeologist's demand of a salary of two thousand thalers, terminated them with the characteristic remark that "one thousand are quite sufficient for a German." Successful as he was, especially for his century which by and large knew no such thing as a self-made man, there was one prize that still eluded Winckelmann: a journey to Greece, the home of that art and literature which he so admired. It might have been granted to him had he not first taken a trip to Germany, on the return from which he was murdered, in 1768 in Trieste, by a robber to whom he had foolishly shown the medals and decorations which the emperor had bestowed on him in Vienna.

The Classical Revival that swept Europe in the second half of the eighteenth century, and extended to America with Jefferson's Monticello and the work of such sculptors as Hiram Powers and Horatio Greenough, was not the result of any one man's labors. In France, the archaeologist De Caylus, the writer Diderot, the painter Clérisseau, and others had begun to sing the praises of classical art; in England, the Society of Dilettanti and similar groups of classicist orientation had launched a fashion which became dominant with the publication of the first volume of Stuart's and Revett's *Antiquities of Athens* in 1762; even in far-away Russia, palaces were being built in Graeco-Roman style. But it was Winckelmann who formulated the theoretical basis of this movement and raised it to doctrinal status in his main works, *Gedanken über die Nachahmung der griechischen Werke in der Malerei und Bildhauerkunst* (*Thoughts on the Imitation of Greek Works in Painting and Sculpture*, 1755) and *Geschichte der Kunst des Altertums* (*History of Ancient Art*, 1764). He believed that the art of classical Greece, that of the era of Phidias and Praxiteles in the fifth and fourth centuries B.C., represented an absolute standard of perfection characterized by a "Noble Simplicity and Quiet Grandeur"—"Edle Einfalt und Stille Grösse" —that had not been achieved before or since, neither by the Egyptians nor the Romans, neither by the Italians of the Renaissance nor the later artists of France, Italy, and Germany. Modern painters and sculptors, he thought, can attain this perfection only by studying these masterpieces and putting themselves into the state of mind out of which the Greeks had spontaneously created them. Far from being merely interesting or pleasing, such art also has a moral impact on the beholder, in cleansing him of the impurities of ephemeral fashion and raising him to a higher level: "I forget all else," Winckelmann wrote about the Apollo Belvedere, "at the sight of this miraculous work of art, and assume a more exalted standing myself in order to be worthy of it." Great art molds those who behold it: an idea which was to recur in German literature as late as Rilke, whose poem *Archäischer Torso Apollos* ends with the thought that "you must change your life"—"Du musst dein Leben ändern."

Winckelmann, however, was not content merely to postulate such theories without attempting to buttress them with detailed observations, measurements, and comparisons. When he looked at a statue he did not "gush," but deduced from it the underlying concept of harmony which had actuated its creation. He thus arrived at a precise evaluation of the historical development of Greek art, which he divided into four main phases, and of the ethnic, social, and other factors that had determined its rise and eventual decline. If his approach was primarily aesthetic and speculative (it had to be because Greece, then under Turkish rule, was difficult to visit, and the genuinely Greek works which Winckelmann had been able to examine were few in number), he also possessed a sharp eye for the functional and technical aspects of ancient tools and implements, such as the lowly *stylus* which had served the ancients for writing on wax tablets. Although he was neither the first nor the last man to do so, he formulated more tellingly than others a number of theses which, one-sided though they may be, have long become part and parcel of Western aesthetics: that Greek art is superior to that of Rome (which was by no means self-evident to his contemporaries); that beauty, while partly a subjective value, is also a rational factor which can be proved to exist in a great work; and that some statues, such as those in the Vatican, represent an absolute measure of perfection.

Although Boswell had been among his English and Diderot among his French admirers, it was in Germany that Winckelmann's observations had their greatest effect. Lessing respected him even while disputing his analysis of the "Laocoön" group, Herder and Goethe devoted essays to him, and even such twentieth-century authors as Hauptmann and Bergengruen wrote novels about him. Winckelmann not only wrote in German, at a time when that language was not commonly used for scientific works, but imparted to the classical phase of German literature an image of Greece as a non-Christian paradise, a country in which there had once prevailed a state of preordained beauty and harmony, a lost Eden which men must yearn for and strive to recreate, in modern times and on German soil, through that imitation of the Greeks in which he had seen the key to artistic perfection. Goethe's *Iphigenie* and the second part of his *Faust* are as inconceivable without Winckelmann's Greek ideal as are Hölderlin's odes or Schiller's essays, or for that matter, as is much of later German literature up to the days of George, Hofmannsthal, and Benn. It little matters in this connection that the "real" ancient Greece, as far as we now know from archaeological, literary, and other evidence, is not likely to have been as peaceful and harmonious as Winckelmann had imagined. His notion of an "Apollinian" Greece has since been balanced by Nietzsche, Burckhardt, Freud, and others, by the modern view of a tense, somewhat neurotic, "Dionysian" Greece; but while it lasted, Winckelmann's influence on German thought and letters was incalculable.

GOTTHOLD EPHRAIM LESSING

If Winckelmann spent his last years in mundane splendor, Gotthold Ephraim Lessing was condemned to a life of obscurity. The son of a Protestant minister, he belongs to that large group of German writers (Klopstock, Wieland, Schiller, Hölderlin, Nietzsche, Hesse) who were educated, as wards of Church or State, in schools designed for the training of indigent but promising children of the clergy and the professional classes. Born in Saxony in 1729, Lessing attended the *Fürstenschule* at Meissen, and because it was expected of him eventually took up the study of theology in Leipzig. Although a provincial town in size and mentality, Leipzig was Germany's wickedest city, the place where one sowed one's wild oats and acquired such worldly graces as dancing, fencing, and gambling. Young Lessing quickly developed an interest in the theatre, and according to a famous anecdote was peremptorily ordered home when his mother discovered that he had shared the Christmas cake she had sent him with a group of freethinkers and stage people. The reaction strikes us as odd, but it must be remembered that actors were then looked down upon as social outcasts and that not only Gottsched but Lessing, Goethe, and Schiller harbored strangely ambivalent notions about the theatre as such, considering it on the one hand as a hotbed of vice and intrigue and on the other as an institution of great potential significance, a training ground not only of literary taste but of moral and civic rectitude (in the first part of *Wilhelm Meister*, Goethe was to do justice to both these dimensions). It was one thing for Winckelmann, in Rome, to go about in clerical garb and to call himself *abbé*, but it was quite another for Lessing or Goethe to be seen in the company of actors in Leipzig.

After his theological studies and an equally desultory interlude as a medical student in Wittenberg, Lessing went to Berlin and in 1751 took up his real calling, that of a free-lance writer and critic. He was, in fact, the first major German author to make a living, precarious but sufficient, as an independent man of letters instead of deriving his support from private means, from the patronage of temporal or spiritual rulers, or from the proceeds of a profession such as teaching. Lessing wrote for newspapers, did some translations, and became a friend of the publisher Friedrich Nicolai and the philosopher Moses Mendelssohn, the first of many Jews to play a role in German literature (although an autocrat, Frederick the Great was also a freethinker, and an advocate of religious tolerance who did much for the emancipation of the Jews). It was thus fitting that two of Lessing's early plays should have been entitled *Der Freigeist* and *Die Juden*, respectively, and that their heroes despite some individualizing traits should still have represented types rather than flesh-and-blood characters. It was not until he wrote *Miss Sara Sampson* (1755) that he advanced beyond the satirizing of human weaknesses on the one hand and the depiction of Virtue Unsullied on the other. This play was not only his first success on the stage, but remains one of the earliest examples of what came to be called *bürgerliches Trauerspiel* or "domestic tragedy"; as such, it represents a departure from previous dramatic practice which was the more radical as Gottsched had just reiterated his conviction that only the great figures of history were worthy of being made heroes of a play. Sara Sampson, however, is not an historical personage but an ordinary English girl who is seduced by her lover and eventually poisoned by his discarded mistress, whereupon the scoundrel stabs himself over Sara's dead body. Melodramatic though it sounds, it is a cogently argued work which was to be followed by a whole subgenre of German dramas written by various hands and based on an attractive but weak man's infatuation with an evil woman, and his subsequent betrayal of an innocent girl. Although no *Stürmer und Dränger*, Lessing foreshadows the language of that movement when he has the cast-off mistress rave: "With eager hands will I tear limb from limb, vein from vein, sinew from sinew, and not stop cutting and severing the smallest remnant even when there is nothing left but a lifeless carcass. . . . At least I shall know then how sweet revenge can be!" In other respects, again, the play is curiously old-fashioned; the mistress' nine-year-old daughter, for example, is too precocious to be believable—a reminder that in the history of literature as in that of painting, the realistic representation of a child is a relatively late development.

The outbreak of the Seven Years' War in 1756 found Lessing in Amsterdam. He returned to Prussia and eventually became secretary to the Prussian governor of Breslau, who put him to work on such prosaic tasks as the procurement of remounts, uniforms, and the like. Many nice touches in his next play, *Minna von Barnhelm* (1767), were drawn from his observations not only of the military sphere in general but of that particularly critical time in a soldier's life, his return to civilian status. Although he was indebted for some details to foreign models, these borrowings do not detract from the author's distinction of having created, with this work, the first German comedy that has truly weathered the ages and still forms part of the standard repertory. Its theme, the reconciliation of the warring factions as symbolized by the eventual marriage of a Saxon lady and an officer who had fought in the Prussian army, must have come straight from the heart of Lessing, a Saxon who had taken up residence in Prussia. It is, of course, an ageless theme, and the nationalities are not so narrowly drawn that one cannot with a little good will sympathize both with Major Tellheim, the wounded and discharged officer whose reputation is endangered by an alleged financial irregularity committed during the war, and with Minna, who loves her former enemy, and, like any smart woman, not only gets her man, but in so doing cures him of his overly punctilious notions of honor. The comical characters, Just, Franziska, Werner, and the foppish Riccaut de la Marlinière who speaks a sort of "fractured German," are effective on the stage but actually less original than Minna, the motive force in this comedy of courtship, or Tellheim, who as a sympathetically described soldier supplants the military braggarts and strutting warriors that had hitherto occupied the European stage.

In his other great plays, *Emilia Galotti* (1772) and *Nathan der Weise* (1779), Lessing's strengths and also his weaknesses show up even more clearly. The first work is in essence the story of the Roman Virginia, but transposed into an Italian court whose prince threatens to violate one of his subjects, the heroine, who thereupon asks her puritan father to kill her, in order to preserve her from shame and perhaps also from the turmoil of her own senses, which have been awakened by the prince's ardor: "My blood, father, is as youthfully warm as any other girl's," she cries out, "my senses, too, are senses. I can vouch for nothing." The play is so tautly constructed that Friedrich Schlegel once called it "a very model of mathematical dramaturgy"—"ein Rechenexempel drama- tischer Algebra"; indeed, no knot is left untied and no word or gesture unnecessary. Perhaps it is due to this perfection that *Emilia Galotti* leaves one cold; it may be that we are too aware, when reading it or seeing it performed, that the author *intended* to provide the German stage with a faultlessly designed work, and that this work in turn represents an important step on the road toward a drama of social significance.

Lessing's last play, *Nathan der Weise*, is set in the Holy Land at the time of the Crusades and represents in part an elaboration of the parable of the three rings told in Boccaccio's *Decameron*. It demonstrates a truth that was very dear to the Enlightenment, namely, that a man's worth lies not in the letter of the religion he professes, but in the degree to which he lives its spirit: here, the Jew Nathan and the Mohammedan Saladin are more "Christian" than the Templar who ostensibly professes that faith. *Nathan der Weise* is possibly the most impressive paean to religious tolerance in all of world literature; by raising the Jew, who in Boccaccio's story is merely clever, to a figure whose innate nobility conquers evil, Lessing created a timeless symbol of humanity at its best, much as Goethe was to do with *Iphigenie* and Schiller with *Maria Stuart*. Indeed, the cleansing of an imperfect mortal and his or her growth into an exemplary figure is one of the hallmarks of German *Klassik*, and a token of its idealistic orientation. Outwardly, this development is reflected in the use of a blank verse patterned after that of Shakespeare; this iambic pentameter now replaces the French alexandrine and becomes the standard verse of the German classical drama.

When he died in 1781, after a late marriage tragically terminated when his wife died in childbirth, Lessing could look back on great achievements as a playwright. If he nonetheless failed to reach the stature of a Shakespeare or a Schiller, the cause may be found not only in his times, in the lack of a great stage peopled by competent performers and supported by an educated public, but in himself. He was a cerebral person, easily angered (and magnificent in his anger) but not otherwise given to deep passions. He thought out his dramas more than he "lived" them, and his characters resemble nothing so much as fencers who probe for weaknesses, make brilliant sorties, and parry these with grace and verve. What they engage in, all too often, is a game of dialectical one-upmanship, and although their verbal pyrotechnics are fired off in the service of worthy causes, they seldom awaken in the audience the deeper feelings of pity and fear. On the other hand, it was precisely this dialectical skill that made Lessing such a formidable critic.

First and foremost, he was a great critic because he addressed himself to issues of prime importance. His main theoretical work, *Laokoön oder über die Grenzen der Malerei und Poesie* (*Laocoön, or the Boundaries of Painting and Poetry*, 1766), postulates a vital difference between the plastic arts and literature. Whereas the former aim at the representation of bodies and are able to suggest action only indirectly, the latter, whose function it is to represent action, should suggest bodies only in so far as it describes them in action. As related by Vergil,

Laocoön cries out when attacked by the serpent, while he is not shown as doing so in the famous sculpture—not, as Winckelmann had assumed, because the ancients considered the expression of human suffering as indecent, but because they considered pain as inexpressible in the plastic arts: in other words, not for ethical but for artistic reasons. Again, when Homer wants to describe Agamemnon's clothing to us, he does not list the garments but has the king put them on one after the other, with the result that "we see the garments as the poet describes the act of getting dressed; someone else [that is, a lesser poet, or a painter] would have detailed the garments down to the last tassel without giving us anything of the action." With that, Lessing put an end to the allegorical and descriptive poetry which had so long been considered a major literary form. Although his definitions strike the modern reader as too narrow in their dismissal of landscape painting and much else that did not fit into these somewhat arbitrarily drawn categories, they did clear the air at the time in assigning to each art from its own characteristic theme. "All the critical guidelines by which we hitherto judged," Goethe later wrote, "were cast aside like a worn coat."

Equally fundamental was the distinction which Lessing made between the French drama and that of Shakespeare in *Hamburgische Dramaturgie* (*Dramatic Notes from Hamburg*, 1767–69). He had been called to that city in order to aid, as a critic, stage author, and translator, in the establishment of a national stage. Lessing accordingly went to a great many performances, and in reporting on them came to feel that the critic's function encompassed not only judging the work itself but also the manner in which it was put on, since the actor's art is so ephemeral that its effect usually ceased, in the days before movies and tape recordings, with the moment the curtain was rung down. He eventually dropped all mention of the performers, after singling out this one for praise and that one for censure had led to difficulties within the troupe; but it is indicative of the man's sense of fairness that he should at least have attempted to preserve for posterity the efforts of these long-forgotten men and women. What remains are many fine essays on the repertory of the Hamburg theater, in which Lessing discusses, among many other problems, such questions as the feasibility of ghosts on the stage (permissible, and in fact very effective in *Hamlet* where the ghost appears at midnight and addresses himself only to one person, but ridiculous in Voltaire's *Semiramis* where Nimus' spirit enters in broad daylight before the assembled Estates-General of France), the plausibility of a given plot (what matters is not whether it has taken place but whether it could have taken place under the given set of circumstances), and the nature of catharsis (tragedy should awaken fear and pity, but not the kind of abhorrence created by the representation of a totally and unbelievably wretched character). The conclusions at which he arrived may thus be termed common-sense precepts for that German national theater at whose birth he had hoped to be present (like other such attempts to build a national theater, the Hamburg project soon died of malnutrition). Lessing had already formulated similar rules in his *Briefe, die neueste Literatur betreffend* (*Critical Letters on the most Recent Literature*, 1759 ff.), an evaluation of contemporary writing in the guise of letters addressed to a Prussian officer who lay wounded in hospital and wanted to keep abreast of new literary developments. The most famous *Brief* is the seventeenth which ends with Lessing's fragment of a *Faust* and contains the delightful sally against Gottsched: "'Nobody,' [it has been said], 'can deny that the German stage owes much of its recent improvement to Professor Gottsched.'—Well, I am this nobody: I deny it outright! It would have been much better if Mr. Gottsched had never meddled with the theater. Where his alleged improvements do not concern irrelevant details, they actually represent changes for the worse . . . . Knowing a little French, he started to translate and encouraged all those who could versify a little and understand '*Oui, Monsieur*,' to do likewise." Instead of translating from the French, Lessing thought, Gottsched should have studied Shakespeare, whose works are more in harmony with the German spirit, and incidentally with the ancients, than Corneille ever was.

Aside from his great dramatic and critical opus, Lessing wrote a number of fables, religious treatises, and *Rettungen* or vindications of dead authors who had been mistranslated. Here again, he appears as a writer of common sense and good taste, a scrupulously honest judge of his own work and that of others. As a human being, as a man of unimpeachable character tempered by wit, he was perhaps the most appealing among Goethe's predecessors. "I am neither an actor nor a poet," he said of himself, "[although] I have sometimes had the honor of being taken for the latter . . . I do not feel in me the living spring that gushes forth out of its native strength and breaks out in copious, fresh, and clear streams. I must force everything out of myself by pressure and pipes . . . and am therefore always ashamed or annoyed when I hear or read anything in disparagement of criticism. It is said to suppress genius, and I flattered myself that I had gained from it something very close to genius. I am a lame man who cannot possibly be edified by abuse of his crutch."

JOHANN GOTTFRIED HERDER

It was as a young student at the University of Königsberg that Johann Gottfried Herder (1744–1803) first came under the influence of the two men who shaped his development: Immanuel Kant and Johann Georg Hamann. The former examined the limits of human cognition and showed that reason alone cannot satisfactorily define such ideas as God, Freedom, or Immortality. These concepts, he thought, derive their meaning not from cogitation but from being based on Man's innate scale of moral values, which in turn asserts itself in a "categorical imperative" that makes us act in conformity with what we recognize to be our duty; not only the ideal but the proper action is thus one which could be held up as a universal precept for all men. By disputing the primacy of reason, and in effect postulating as the prime mover of life a power that transcends both reason and emotion, Kant exerted a profound influence not only on Herder but on Schiller and Kleist. Hamann more particularly stressed the importance of such irrational elements as intuition, emotion, and revelation both as counterpoise to the exercise of reason and as true wellsprings of poetry. His works are largely forgotten now, and were in any event so aphoristic in concept, fragmentary in form, and obscure in style that he was called *Der Magus des Nordens* or the "Northern Oracle" (like Kant and Herder, he spent many years in Königsberg). Hamann drew his young disciple's attention to Shakespeare, to the collection of Celtic poetry called *Ossian*, and altogether to *Urpoesie*, which was later enlarged to *Volkspoesie*, or a type of writing that came to be contrasted with *Kunstpoesie* as the original with the derived, the spontaneous with the constructed, poetry of the "heart" with that of the "mind." Shakespeare, to be sure, had not been quite as original as Hamann and Herder believed, and *Ossian* quickly turned out to be no more than a clever imitation; but the distinction between these fundamental types of literature has been very fruitful, and has not altogether lost its validity even in modern times.

In his later years, which he spent as a teacher, court preacher, and finally, through Goethe's intervention, as *Generalsuperintendent* of the Protestant clergy of Sachsen-Weimar, Herder refined these and other theses about the origin, nature, and function of literature. In *Fragmente über die neuere deutsche Literatur* (*Fragments on Recent German Literature*, 1767), he claimed the existence of a close relationship between a people's ethnic endowment and its literature, and denounced, as an act of violence against the very nature of writing, the composition of a work in a foreign language (a frequent phenomenon in that cosmopolitan era). In *Kritische Wälder* (*Critical Forests*, 1769)—after the *silvae* of Latin poets—he demanded, in literature, much the same return to nature that his contemporaries Rousseau and Pestalozzi were advocating in other fields. In the treatise *Über den Ursprung der Sprache* (*On the Origin of Language*, 1770), he expressed his belief in the human origin of language, and its importance not just for an elite but for all people. The collection *Volkslieder* represents, especially in its enlarged posthumous edition as *Stimmen der Völker in Liedern* (*Voices of Nations in Songs*, 1807), the first scientifically conceived anthology of lyrical poems collected and translated from several languages. The fragmentary *Ideen zur Philosophie der Geschichte der Menschheit* (*Ideas on a Philosophy of Human History*, 1784–91) is an attempt to arrive at a typology of national characteristics. Herder's last major work, *Briefe zur Beförderung der Humanität* (*Letters on the Advancement of Humanism*, (1793–97), is marked by a certain animosity against Goethe and Schiller, who had by then exhibited not only critical gifts of a high order but something that Herder himself lacked for all his brilliance:

creative powers. He died as an embittered man who realized that he would be remembered as an initiator, a predecessor of greater men rather than a poet in his own right. The impact of his thought made itself felt later than that of Winckelmann and Lessing; he was a forerunner of *Sturm und Drang* and *Romantik* as well as *Klassik*, and, unlike the other two, lived long enough to enter into personal contact with Goethe and Schiller, to whom he imparted a sense both of the uniqueness of their own national and popular heritage (especially the *Volkslied*, a term which he coined) and of its connection with a world literature that transcends all boundaries of time and place.

FRIEDRICH GOTTLIEB KLOPSTOCK

Although the early eighteenth century was for Germany a period of intellectual ferment rather than creative vitality, mention must here be made of two men who were not so much critics as writers. Friedrich Gottlieb Klopstock (1724–1803), the foremost lyric poet of his time, lives on in history as the author of a number of odes (among them *Die Frühlingsfeier* which was to play such a catalytic role in Goethe's *Werther*) and the religious epic *Der Messias* (1748 ff.). Reminiscent in many details of *Paradise Lost*, it deals with the passion and redemption of Christ:

> Sing, unsterbliche Seele, der sündigen Menschen Erlösung,
> Die der Messias auf Erden in seiner Menschheit vollendet . . .[1]

One of the sublimest of all themes is here treated in German, a language which was until then considered arid and clumsy, but now so to speak throws off its fetters and expands almost visibly under the poet's hands. As a result of the success of this work, both the hexameter and the hymnic free verse in which it was written became so popular in Germany that some of the greatest poets—Goethe, Hölderlin, Hauptmann—later made use of these originally foreign forms. *Der Messias* is borne by a cheerful, masculine faith which not only contrasts strongly with the general texture of the period's spiritual life, the Pietists' all-pervading consciousness of sin as wel las the scepticism of the Rationalists, but also reflects Klopstock's awareness of himself as a poet-prophet whose function lies not in entertaining but in praising, exhorting, and censuring his fellow man. These very qualities which were new at the time and made the work so famous in its day, have brought about the decline into which it has since fallen in popular and critical opinion. For the modern reader is no longer able to sustain, through twenty long cantos, so tense a religious emotion couched in so rhapsodic a language; as Schiller, himself often an exalted poet, observed long ago, Klopstock divests everything of its body that he treats, in order to turn it into pure spirit. It is only in the later portions of *Der Messias* that the poet descends from ecstatic vision to concrete imagery, in the description of the fallen angel Abbadona. Like Dante and Milton, he discovered that the evil principle possesses a greater plastic density than the good. Be that as it may, parts of *Der Messias* and certain poems are still read (*Der Zürcher See, Die frühen Gräber*), and some facets of Klopstock have had a lasting influence on later writers. His view of the poet not as a spare-time rimester but as a spiritual force in the nation's life was shared by many from Goethe to George. His disciples, the members of the *Göttinger Hain* who published their *Musenalmanach*, were merely the first of several such groupings in German literary history. His interest in Germanic and specifically Nordic themes led to a flourishing of *Barden-* or *Skaldendichtung*, or Norse poetry, and although most of it is as antiquated now as Klopstock's Biblical dramas were even in his lifetime, it did constitute in subject matter a much-needed alternative to the perennial glorification of Greek and Roman heroes, and in form a relief from imitations of French neoclassicism. Finally, Klopstock's sovereign handling of the language, both in making it a worthy vehicle for the expression of religious and metaphysical concepts and in the actual coining of new words, was a prerogative which, once he had claimed and exercised it, was to be granted automatically to later German poets.

CHRISTOPH MARTIN WIELAND

If Klopstock was what Germans call a *Dichter*, Christoph Martin Wieland (1733–1813) was primarily a *Schriftsteller*. After studying at the University of Tübingen he went to Zürich, where he came in contact with the Swiss patrician J. J. Bodmer, a patron of the new antirationalistic literature and himself the translator of *Paradise Lost* into German. Bodmer had already befriended Klopstock, only to be shocked on finding that the German Milton was not otherworldly in personality at all, but a cheerful young man not averse to such earthly pleasures as hiking, skating, and drinking. Although he had been reared in a Pietist home, Wieland also eventually disappointed his straitlaced mentor and host: he had no sooner returned to his native Biberach in Swabia than he renounced religious poetry and became a *philosophe*, a tolerant bon vivant whose favorite literary habitat was not the Old Testament but a pagan Greece seen through Rococo eyes. If some of Wieland's contemporaries were distressed at this change, Lessing welcomed it with the comment: "He has returned to the common fold"—"er wandelt wieder unter den Menschenkindern."

Typical of Wieland's attitude to life is *Musarion* (*Musarion, or the Philosophy of the Graces*, 1768), an elegant little verse epic in which a seductive Greek beauty uses her wits and her charms in order to reconvert to the enjoyment of life a former lover who, surfeited with sensual indulgence, had renounced all pleasures and devoted himself to solitary speculation. Even though his basic theme, that of a man's education through a process of aesthetic refinement and the development of his common sense, remained a fairly constant one, Wieland's works are not all cut of the same cloth. If *Der Sieg der Natur über die Schwärmerei, oder die Abenteuer des Don Silvio von Rosalva* (*The Victory of Sense over Exaltation, or the Adventures of D. S. v. R.*, 1764) shows his indebtedness to Cervantes, *Oberon* (which, in turn, inspired Karl Maria von Weber to his opera) is borrowed in large measure from Shakespeare, most of whose dramas Wieland later translated into German. *Agathon* (1766) is one of the earliest biographical novels or *Erziehungsromane* in German literature, a not unworthy precursor of Goethe's *Wilhelm* Meister, while *Die Abderiten*, again set in ancient Greece, is a thinly veiled parody of the good people of Biberach, whom Wieland had come to know only too well during his tenure as town clerk. Wieland's Greece, to be sure, is not the austere home of Winckelmann's Noble Simplicity and Quiet Grandeur but a carefully trimmed *ancien régime* park in which men and women, and indeed the gods themselves, lead lives of civilized leisure. With all that, his didactic streak, that common denominator of much of the century's writing, is never far below the hedonistic surface; it was, in fact, quite as genuine as his tolerance and understanding even of those, who, like Goethe and Kleist, were greater men than he was. The kindness that Wieland showed them is more than an expression of the cult of friendship, which flourished in that period when letters of ardent admiration were often exchanged among men who scarcely knew one another. It was also a token of that lifelong concern with the quality of the country's intellectual life which made him edit the review *Der teutsche Merkur* and set down in a political novel, *Der goldene Spiegel* (*The Golden Mirror*, 1772), his belief in an enlightened monarchy as the form of government under which the arts are most likely to flourish. It was as a result of this novel that one of the most enlightened of all German rulers, the Dowager Duchess Anna Amalia, called him to Weimar as tutor of her sons.

Like the other works mentioned in this brief account of German literature in the days of Goethe's youth, Wieland's political treatise was not the only one of its kind: Klopstock wrote *Die deutsche Gelehrtenrepublik*, and the Swiss A. v. Haller a whole sequence of state novels in which he compared the Roman Republic with Oriental despotism and the English constitutional system. The search for an ideal form of government was a European fashion in the period immediately preceding the French Revolution. Again, if Klopstock praised the beauties of Nature in his odes, Haller did much the same in his own, somewhat ponderous fashion in *Die Alpen* (*The Alps*), C. E. v. Kleist in *Der Frühling* (*Spring*), and B. H. v. Brockes in *Irdisches Vergnügen in Gott* (*Earthly Delight in God*); disparate poets though they were, their concerns were much the same. If Lessing wrote didactic fables, he followed the example of F. v. Hagedorn and

C. F. Gellert; if Wieland is at times pastoral, he follows in the wake of S. Gessner and approaches the type of Anacreontic poetry practised not only by men like J. P. Uz, J. N. Götz, and J. G. Jacobi, but by young Klopstock and young Goethe (it was the time of Dresden china and Marie Antoinette's Trianon, when nymphs and shepherds cavorted in Arcadian groves, symbols of a charming if artificial and stylized Return to Nature). In short, men like Winckelmann, Lessing, Herder, Klopstock, and Wieland were not solitary eminences in a vacuum but representatives of the major tendencies of their era: of Pietism and rationalism, of dying *Anakreontik* and of a *bürgerliche* or middle-class literature that was struggling to be born, of the demise of the French classical theatre and the discovery of that of Shakespeare, of the first stirrings both of a German national literature and of the concept of a universal or world literature.

JOHANN WOLFGANG GOETHE

1749–1788

These developments found their culmination, their union, and their lasting literary expression in the works of Johann Wolfgang von Goethe, whose life is here discussed in some detail—not out of pedantry and still less from a belief (once fashionable) that his works can best be explained on that basis, but because this life was highly representative both of the man himself and of the age that bears his name.

Goethe was born in Frankfurt am Main in 1749. His father, a somewhat dogmatic man who was as dour as the poet's mother was cheerful, gave him the best education that tutors could provide: a solid background in the Bible and in contemporary theology, instruction in the rather speculative science of the time, both an applied and a theoretical grounding in arts and languages, and such social and athletic skills, from horsemanship to dancing, as were favored by the upper bourgeoisie of Germany. Goethe was an indefatigable worker all his life, intent on keeping abreast of new developments and on practising and applying the talents that Nature had given him; contrary to many other poets, however, he never had to learn in later life entire disciplines in which he had lacked instruction in his youth. This sound basis was further strengthened at the University of Leipzig, where he took lectures in various subjects for almost three years. There he fell in love, wrote his first poems, and returned to Frankfurt in 1768 in poor health but essentially a mature if somewhat restless young man. The following year he spent at home, recuperating from a series of minor illnesses underscored by a religious crisis. His father wanted him to study law, as he had done himself, and Goethe accordingly went to Strasbourg in 1770 in order to finish his formal education with the acquisition of a degree. In the main, however, his studies were again eclectic rather than professional, and if he discovered in Strasbourg what he did not like jurisprudence, and writing in the manner of Gottsched and Gellert, (both of whom he had met in Leipzig), he also found much that was germane to his spirit. He met Herder, who, opening his eyes to Shakespeare, *Ossian*, and the *Volkslied*, encouraged him to write in his own manner instead of following the Anacreontic and other fashions of the day. He saw Strasbourg cathedral and other examples of a Gothic architecture that was then thought barbaric, but which he learned to respect as a genuine expression of the medieval spirit. Above all, he fell in love with a rural clergyman's daughter in nearby Sesenheim, and wrote some poems that were so unmistakably personal that a whole new period of German literature can be said to date from them. *Mailied* and *Willkommen und Abschied* are spontaneous lyrical expressions of what this young man felt at this particular time (and, because they are so perfect, what every young-man-in-love feels). They contain no references to literary, mythological, or historical models, no conceits or learned similes, no hackneyed expressions or stylized turns of phrase. Without any desire to be original, he wrote as if no one had ever written before, with that utter simplicity possessed only by the very great, as in *Mailied* (1771):

> Wie herrlich leuchtet
> Mir die Natur!
> Wie glänzt die Sonne!
> Wie lacht die Flur!
>
> Es dringen Blüten
> Aus jedem Zweig
> Und tausend Stimmen
> Aus dem Gesträuch
>
> Und Freud und Wonne
> Aus jeder Brust.
> O Erd', o Sonne,
> O Glück, o Lust.
>
> O Lieb', o Liebe,
> so golden schön
> Wie Morgenwolken
> Auf jenen Höhn,
>
> Du segnest herrlich
> das frische Feld—
> Im Blütendampfe
> Die volle Welt!
>
> O Mädchen, Mädchen,
> Wie lieb' ich dich!

Wie blinkt dein Auge,
Wie liebst du mich!

So liebt die Lerche
Gesang und Luft,
Und Morgenblumen
Den Himmelsduft,

Wie ich dich liebe
Mit warmen Blut,
Die du mir Jugend
Und Freud' und Mut

Zu neuen Liedern
Und Tänzen gibst.
Sei ewig glücklich,
Wie du mich liebst.[2]

In the course of the next four years, from his return from Strasbourg in 1771 to his departure for Weimar in 1775, Goethe became a poet in the fullest sense. As always, the outward aspects of his life were commonplace enough: he traveled around a little in southwest Germany and Switzerland, spent a few months in Wetzlar and in various places along the Rhine, dabbling in law, visiting friends, meeting luminaries such as Klopstock and the theologian J. K. Lavater. He fell in love with a young woman who was engaged to a friend of his, and, somewhat later, with the beautiful wife of a much older man; for a while he was engaged to the daughter of a prominent Frankfurt banker, the most society-minded of his many loves. None of this would be important had it not given impetus to a truly outstanding literary production. In the grip of these and other emotions, Goethe wrote some magnificent poems, love lyrics as well as hymns in which the titanic urges of youth are immortalized in mythological and nature settings as in *Ganymed*, *An Schwager Kronos*, and *Prometheus*. After some earlier dramatic experiments he now created, in *Götz von Berlichingen*, a historical play in the *Sturm und Drang* manner, and followed it up with *Clavigo*, a weaker but theatrically more effective work, and *Stella*. In twelve weeks, he composed his first novel, *Die Leiden des jungen Werther* (*The Sorrows of Young Werther*, 1774), which made him famous overnight. He tossed off, so to speak, a number of smaller dramas which were later set to music like *Erwin und Elimire*, and began work on more ambitious themes like *Mahomet* and *Der ewige Jude*. One of these early heroes, Faust, was to accompany him all his life. He wrote reviews and essays, translated from foreign languages, and corresponded with numerous men and women. It was an outburst of vitality such as the world has not often seen and such as Goethe, for all his lifelong activity, was not to experience again. When an acquaintance wrote of him in 1774 that "there is reason to fear that his own fire will consume him," he merely stated what was in many minds.

Not the least remarkable of Goethe's gifts was his ability for growth, for developing his talents and interests in more directions and for a longer span of time than other men. Having arrived in Weimar in 1775, as guest of the same Duke Carl August to whom Wieland had been a tutor, Goethe was so quickly absorbed by his new sphere of life that he could report to a friend as early as the following January: "I am involved in all sorts of court and political affairs, and doubt that I shall ever be able to leave again"—[*Ich bin*] *in alle Hof–und politische Händel verwickelt und werde fast nicht wieder weg können.*" He became a senior civil servant and eventually a cabinet minister, taking charge, at various times, of such disparate administrative tasks as mining, road construction, the conscription of soldiers, finances, and the supervision of the Duchy's theatres and its institutions of higher learning. During the early Weimar years, these duties were rendered more onerous by two anomalies in his situation: his standing as a commoner, and Carl August's extreme youth. The former, a severe handicap at a time when all social and most political authority lay in arisocratic hands, was remedied when the Emperor bestowed on him, at Carl August's request, a patent of nobility which enabled Goethe (who, while no snob, was enough of a realist to appreciate and accept the gesture) to call himself "Herr von Goethe." No such solution could be found for the other problem; only time itself could make of the ebullient eighteen-year-old duke a mature and responsible ruler. Goethe, who kept him company in drinking, hunting, and what used to be referred to as "wenching," endeavored to restrain the good-natured but touchy young prince by his own example of cheerful self-control; in the end, of course, there developed between the two a deep friendship which at times entailed the use of the familiar *du.*

The value of Goethe's work as an executive minister of state lay less in the position itself (he acquitted himself well in it, but the Duchy of Sachsen-Weimar was only a tiny cog in the Empire's creaking machinery) than in the discipline which it forced on his volatile nature. It taught him to work hard even on matters in which he had lost interest. It imbued him with a meticulousness and a drive for perfection that, although they occasionally degenerated into fussiness, eventually stood him in good stead when he had to finish, with Part II of *Faust* and *Wilhelm Meisters Wanderjahre* (*W. M.'s Travels*), works that he had begun much earlier and which had to be continued at an age when the creative fires burned low. Last but not least it enabled him, the scion of a middle-class family, to move whenever necessary among the great of his time, not excluding such personages as Napoleon and Metternich. The protracted interlude as a practical man of affairs constituted a much-needed balance to the sensitivity which was Goethe's hallmark as a poet and to which he had just given expression in *Werther*. It is surely no coincidence that the flights of fancy of the dramatic heroes of that time should be counterpoised by the common-sense of such antiheroes as Oranien in *Egmont*, Antonio in *Torquato Tasso*, Pylades in *Iphigenie in Tauris*, and Mephistopheles in *Faust*.

It was only by a strong effort of will that Goethe was able to maintain his equilibrium against the demands made on him, at one and the same time, by affairs of state and by his poetic calling. He was helped in this by his awakening interest in natural science—at this stage mainly mineralogy and anatomy, the latter a field in which he first gained distinction with the discovery, in 1784, of the intermaxillary bone in the human embryo—and above all by his relationship with Charlotte von Stein, intellectually the most stimulating of the many women in his life. A court official's wife, she was the mother of several children and Goethe's senior by some years. She was not beautiful, but seems to have possessed a remarkable gift for divining and soothing the turmoil that threatened to upset the poet's mental and emotional balance. Reflections of her being have undoubtedly gone into the figure of Iphigena, and some fine poems like *Warum gabst du uns die tiefen Blicke* and *An Lida* were likewise written under the spell of this attraction, which lasted a decade. All in all, the literary output of the years 1775–86 differs both in kind and in quantity from that of the pre-Weimar phase. His nature poetry continued to flow both in the manner of the traditional ballad (*Der Erlkönig, Der Fischer*) and in highly personal settings (*Seefahrt, Harzreise im Winter*), but the titanism of the *Sturm und Drang* and of his own youth gradually gave way to a maturer and more philosophical spirit; if Prometheus is an example of the former kind, *Grenzen der Menschheit* (*Limits of Man*) and *Edel sei der Mensch* (*Noble be man, charitable and good*) may be said to epitomize the latter. An ethical component, an awareness of man's duty as well as his fate, pervades many poems of this period in which the novel *Wilhelm Meisters theatralische Sendung* (the later *W. M.'s Apprenticeship*), much of *Egmont*, and the prose version of *Iphigenie* were completed. *Faust*, a part of which he seems to have taken with him to Weimar, grew by a number of scenes, but work on *Tasso* stopped at the end of the second act. Goethe needed a rest and a change before completing it, and he found both on his visit to Italy in 1786–88.

What he looked for and discovered for himself in Italy was not the home of the Roman Church or the birthplace of the Renaissance, but the locale of so much of classical antiquity. His preference for classical art and architecture made his itinerary a highly selective one, causing him to neglect Renaissance Florence in favor of neoclassical Vicenza and to disregard, in Assisi, all traces of Saint Francis in order to devote himself to the study of the town's only surviving Roman structure. Equally arbitrary, at least in comparison with the modern tourist's predilections, were the interests that he cultivated elsewhere on this journey. Yet if he seemed more concerned, in Venice, with a sheep's skull that he chanced to find on the beach than with the great Titians, and if one of the major discoveries of his Sicilian sojourn was the conviction, arrived at in the Botanical Gardens of Palermo, of the principle of "the original identity of all segments of a given plant," he was again merely being true to himself and to his ever-growing fascination with anatomy and botany. In his own way, then, he gained much from this, the only major journey of his life: a first-hand knowledge of classical art, even if it was conveyed to him through Winckelmann's one-sidedly idealistic vision; a personal exposure to the Mediterranean way of life, which he henceforth contrasted with that of his native land, often to the detriment of the latter; the recognition of his own limitations in painting and sketching, a hobby of many years' standing in which he had gained much skill but failed to achieve true mastery; and an insight into ethnic and social problems which did not exist within the narrow confines of the Duchy of Sachsen-Weimar. He got to know the world as well as himself on this journey, from which he returned a changed man. Once and for all, his artistic habitat now came to be that of a *Klassik* patterned after, but not necessarily imitative of, that of ancient Greece. His working life would henceforth be devoted almost exclusively to literature and science (at Goethe's request, Carl August relieved him of most of his administrative duties upon his return to Weimar). Under the impact of recent experiences, his relationship with the other sex became for a while so unplatonic that upon returning home he took a pretty young woman, Christiane Vulpius, into his house and lived with her for many years as husband and wife (he did not marry her until 1806, when their son was seventeen).

The terms *Sturm und Drang* and *Klassik* have repeatedly been used in these pages, and it is well that they should now be defined because the Italian journey forms a rough dividing line between them in Goethe's own life and production. As a forerunner of Romanticism and also as a reaction to Rationalism fed by such sources as Rousseau's Return to Nature, Young's *Conjectures on Original Composition*, and Herder's praise of *Urpoesie*, the *Sturm und Drang* emphasized above all else the primacy of *Gefühl*, of feeling and emotion, in life and in literature. Not only do great, exemplary emotions tend to be harbored by great, exemplary men and women; they also tend to be actuated and expressed in extraordinary circumstances like family strife, political upheaval, and other situations in which the individual is brought face to face with a hostile environment. The typical *Sturm und Drang* hero is motivated by love of freedom, by a view of nature as an all-embracing power of which he himself forms a part, by a predilection for simple and uneducated folk, and by other emotions of the kind, which in the aggregate make his very life seem a protest against the existing order of things. Whether he grows to full stature as a *Kerl* or—ultimate accolade in the language of the time—as an *Originalgenie* in the manner of Schiller's Karl Moor, or whether he quietly succumbs to the established order in the manner of Werther, his is essentially a tragic fate. Intense, white-hot emotion, to be sure, is not the stuff whereof long and involved novels are written, and with the exception of Goethe's *Werther*, the *Sturm und Drang* has not left any. An overflow of feeling can, however, find expression in lyric poetry and in the drama. It is, indeed, in the latter genre that we find the lasting achievements not only of Goethe (the early scenes of *Faust*, *Götz von Berlichingen*) and Schiller

(*Die Räuber, Kabale und Liebe*) in their *Sturm und Drang* period, but of those of their contemporaries who never outgrew this brief phase in German literature (about 1770–80): of H. L. Wagner, J. A. Leisewitz, H. W. v. Gerstenberg, F. Müller, J. M. R. Lenz, and of F. M. Klinger from the title of one of whose dramas the whole movement had taken its name. The admiration of the *Stürmer und Dränger* for a type of literature that flowed intuitively from men's hearts rather than being manufactured in their minds, made them translate Homer, Shakespeare, and others whom they considered to have been *Original-genies*. It made them substitute a genuine lyricism for the playfully flirtatious love poetry of the Rococo, dismiss both Pietism and Rationalism in favor of a highly personal and visceral religiosity, and dismantle the carefully wrought syntax of literary German in order to clear the ground for an expressionist type of speech, so larded with expletives and exclamation marks that it sometimes achieves a mesmerizing effect as in Goethe's *An Schwager Kronos*:

> Spude dich, Kronos!
> Fort den rasselnden Trott!
> Bergab gleitet der Weg;
> Ekles Schwindeln zögert
> Mir vor die Stirne dein Haudern.
> Frisch den holpernden
> Stock Wurzeln Steine den Trott
> Rasch in's Leben hinein!...[3]

Since their passionate protest could not find much practical, let alone political, expression in the staid Germany of the 1770's, the *Stürmer und Dränger* sometimes turned back upon themselves and became self-destructive not only in their works but in their lives. Such at least was the case with the lyric poet G. A. Bürger, who became infatuated with his sister-in-law and spent his best years in a veritable morass of domestic misery, and with Lenz, another gifted poet and the author of two dramas of ferocious social criticism, who went insane and died drunk in a Moscow street. Although the members of the *Göttinger Hain* were among its protagonists and Herder's writings were looked upon by some as a manifesto, the movement as such was less a school or a program than an attitude: a stance of revolt against the social, political, religious, and above all the literary establishment of the time. Its long-term effects were chiefly potential: if the *Sturm und Drang* created little of permanent value, it nonetheless turned over and fertilized the soil from which *Klassik* and *Romantik* were to spring.

If we turn from a typical *Sturm und Drang* product like *Götz von Berlichingen* to *Iphigenie auf Tauris*, we enter such a different world that it is difficult to believe that one and the same man wrote both works within a mere fifteen years. Here, we find five actors instead of dozens; ancient Greeks, and mythological barbarians, instead of medieval Germans of established historical significance; an almost total lack of action on the stage instead of frantic goings-on distributed over fifty-odd changes of scene; the stately pentameter and other meters derived from classical models, instead of an artless prose which is on occasion purposely crude; and a heroine who instead of thrashing about in the manner of the old robber knight, rises before our eyes from a captive woman to a human being of such nobility that she civilizes, by her very example, a whole tribe of savages. Götz von Berlichingen's ethical impact on his time had been nil: at the end of the drama, we see history moving on while the hero is left to wither on the vine; in *Iphigenie*, on the other hand, the heroine's ethical impact on her surroundings is the very marrow of the play, and it is indicative of the difference between *Sturm und Drang* and *Klassik* that the former work ends in rejection ("Woe to the posterity that misjudges you!"—"*Wehe der Nachkommenschaft, die dich verkennt!*") and the latter, in conciliation ("Farewell! And give me your right hand as a token of old friendship"—*Leb wohl! und reiche mir zum Pfand der alten Freundschaft deine Rechte*). In changing the play's "message" from a triumph of Greek cunning sanctioned by the intervention of the gods, as it was in Euripides' version, to the triumph of a person who in overcoming herself not only releases her brother from madness but overcomes her own fate, Goethe gave expression to one of the finest ideals of the *Klassik*: the *schöne Seele*, or the person who is so pure in spirit that he or she becomes inviolate. Despite its Christian connotations, it is not a Christian ideal because it considers man a self-contained individual, perfectible without divine grace; despite the Greek setting which it is given in this and other plays, it is not a Greek ideal because it is in essence inward and unworldly. It is, rather, a fusion of Greek *kalok' agathia* and Christian ethos, and its representatives share with other figures of classical German literature, and indeed with the great classical figures of other literatures, a characteristic way of expressing themselves. Whether Iphigenia says:

> Wohl dem, der seiner Väter gern gedenkt,
> Der froh von ihren Taten, ihrer Grösse
> Den Hörer unterhält, und still sich freuend
> Ans Ende dieser schönen Reihe sich
> Geschlossen sieht![4]

or Tasso:

> O glaube mir, ein selbstisches Gemüt
> Kann nicht der Qual des engen Neids entfliehen.
> Ein solcher Mann verzeiht dem andern wohl
> Vermögen, Stand und Ehre; denn er denkt:
> Das hast du selbst, das hast du, wenn du willst,
> Wenn du beharrst, wenn dich das Glück begünstigt.[5]

or whether Maria Stuart says:

> Denkt an den Wechsel alles Menschlichen!
> Es leben Götter, die den Hochmut rächen!
> Verehret, fürchtet sie, die schrecklichen,
> Die mich zu Euren Füssen niederstürzen—
> Um dieser fremden Zeugen willen, ehrt
> In mir Euch selbst . . .[6]

or Wilhelm Tell:

> Wer frisch umher spät mit gesunden Sinnen,
> Auf Gott vertraut und die gelenke Kraft,
> Der ringt sich leicht aus jeder Fahr und Not:
> Den schreckt der Berg nicht, der darauf geboren.[7]

they all address themselves not only to the situation at hand, to the problem that faces them at the moment when the statement is made, but to the human condition as such. By foregoing, as the Greek dramatists had done before them, any thought of startling or shocking the audience by the introduction of a new plot (Goethe's and Schiller's public was as instantly familiar with the stories of Iphigenia and Wilhelm Tell as that of Aeschylus and Sophocles had been with the fate of Agamemnon and Oedipus), the German poets were free to concentrate on the inner development of heroes who, suspended as it were within a traditionally established frame of dramatic reference, now acquire under their hands an extraordinary symbolic density. What had previously been a character whose actions are feasible only within the context of a specific historical period—as Götz von Berlichingen's were in sixteenth-century Germany—now becomes an archetype stripped of all regional and temporal restrictions. The parallel transformation of a specific dramatic plot into a universal existential problem is both facilitated and enhanced by the mythological setting of *Iphigenie*, and by the exalted verse in which these truths are expressed in this and other plays of the *Klassik*.

If Goethe had limited himself to adapting and updating certain motifs from the Greek drama, he would have been a mere neoclassicist. *Klassik*, however, is something different: extending far beyond the use of neoclassical forms, it encompasses an entire philosophy of life which Goethe shared with Schiller and Wilhelm von Humboldt, and at one remove with Lessing, Wieland, and many others. It includes, for example, the belief that the path of human progress, in literature and art and science as well as in politics, is marked not by violent upheavals but by a conciliation of extremes, of polarities which, so to speak, bracket a given idea or phenomenon and, moderated through experience, common sense, and practical application, determine its characteristics. Hence, in large measure, Goethe's rejection of an uncompromising tragedy in literature, of the French Revolution in politics, and of absolute postulates in the sciences. It entails a form of *Humanität* based less on doing good works or on advocating grandiose schemes for the betterment of mankind, than on the precept that every man must manage his own life before advising his neighbor on how to live his. With Goethe, not only charity, but freedom and tolerance began at home. Hence his scant sympathy for chauvinists, religious fanatics, radical social reformers, and others who believed that the world would have to be turned inside out before it could be improved. A knowledge of oneself founded on the awareness of one's own worth and shortcomings, he thought, was an essential prerequisite to success and happiness. This self-knowledge was to be gained not through introspection but through activity, through measuring oneself against the world not as it was or should be but as it is, for the Here and Now is the arena in which we must prevail. Hence, in large part, his distrust of the Romantics who neglected the present in favor of the Middle Ages, and his impatience with men like Kleist and Beethoven who not only appeared to be waiting for an utopian stage and concert hall, but who for all their genius were unable to cope with so many problems of practical, everyday life.

JOHANN WOLFGANG GOETHE
1788–1832

The biographical details of the second half of Goethe's life may be summarized by stating that he resided continuously in Weimar from 1788 until his death in 1832, with frequent excursions to the Bohemian spas and a brief trip to France, to Switzerland, and to Northern Italy. While he continued to take an interest in the affairs of the Duchy, his active participation in them was limited to the supervision of its theatres and the University of Jena. He was by now the most respected writer of his time, a celebrity comfortably ensconced in a large house where he lived surrounded by his family, friends, books, and collections. He was visited by travelers from all corners of the globe, whom he received graciously if somewhat pontifically while drawing forth from them, in the course of a sometimes quite brief conversation, such a wealth of details about their own spheres of life that he remained to the end one of the best informed of men. His very fame brought it about that he was consulted by many German writers; he knew them, sometimes intimately and over a span of years, and he read and often criticized the works which they sent him. He talked with Hegel and Schelling, heard Beethoven and Mendelssohn play, was received by Napoleon and Metternich, corresponded with Byron and Manzoni; but although much of his time was spent with artists, statesmen, scientists, and writers, his social milieu was as often aristocratic as intellectual. In view of the lowly rank to which German authors had been consigned in his youth, it is significant to note that Goethe kept company, in Marienbad in the spring of 1810 and at other times, not only with his friends, the musician Zelter and the philologist Wolf, but also with the Empress of Austria, the Duchess of Courland, the ex-King of Holland, and the Princes August and Heinrich of Prussia. But above all, he worked: not feverishly, but with an inobtrusive heroism that enabled him to carry his work forward a little each day in the face of his own unstable nature, of the diminutions of old age, and of such shocks as the death of his wife and his only son.

If this was the tenor of his later life, what were its achievements? With the publication, in the immediate post-Italian period, of *Egmont, Iphigenie*, and *Tasso*, Goethe entered upon his own *Klassik*, a dimension to which he returned again and again throughout the remainder of his life, in the epic with *Hermann und Dorothea* (1797) and *Achilleis* (1799), in poetry from *Römische Elegien* (*Roman Elegies*, 1795), to *West-östlicher Divan* (*West-Eastern Divan*, or *Cycle of Poems*, 1819) and beyond, in criticism with *Winckelmann und sein Jahrhundert* (*W. and his Century*, 1805) and countless other essays. But if this was henceforth the true North of his compass, he explored other directions as well. Some were familiar to him from the days of his youth, such as the ballads (in friendly competition with Schiller, he wrote some of his best ones in 1797) and the kind of simple lyric statement at which he excelled and which continued to flow from his pen until the very last. Many of these are occasional poems—*Gelegenheitsgedichte*—in a particular sense: they commemorate not great historical events, royal weddings, victorious battles, etc., such as were celebrated by the Poets Laureate of England, but significant moments in the poet's own inner life. An example of this genre is *Gefunden*, written not as one might surmise by a man of twenty-four, but by one of sixty-four:

> Ich ging im Walde
> So für mich hin,
> Und nichts zu suchen,
> Das war mein Sinn.
>
> Im Schatten sah ich
> Ein Blümchen stehn,
> Wie Sterne leuchtend,
> Wie Äuglein schön.
>
> Ich wollt es brechen,
> Da sagt' es fein:
> Soll ich zum Welken
> Gebrochen sein?
>
> Ich grub's mit allen
> Den Würzlein aus,
> Zum Garten trug ich's
> Am hübschen Haus.

Und pflanzt' es wieder
Am stillen Ort;
Nun zweigt es immer
Und blüht so fort.[8]

It is to poems of this nature that Goethe owes much of his distinction as a lyricist. They are so perfect in form and limpid in language that they have made him, among all the world's poets, the one whose works have been most often set to music (*Gefunden* alone has attracted seventy different composers, from H. Ambrosius through Richard Strauss to C. Fr. Zelter); the frequent fusion of theme and symbol have encouraged those of his readers who feel so inclined, to consider them on an autobiographical as well as an aesthetic level (there is reason to believe, for example, that the flower represents Christiane, whom Goethe had met and taken into his house exactly twenty-five years before he sent her this poem); at the same time, his frequent modulation of old themes makes him one of the most constant of poets (*Gefunden* is a variation on a better-known poem, a *Heidenröslein* in reverse). Yet his astounding lyrical gift developed even while it seemed to stand still. Among other things, it served him for the expression of scientific thought in *Metamorphose der Tiere* (1820) and elsewhere; it took on the most varied colorations in entire lyric cycles written in the manner of Propertius and other Latin poets in *Römische Elegien*, in that of Petrarch and other Italians in *Sonette*, in that of the Persian Hafiz in *West-östlicher Divan*: works in which he not only adapted foreign forms but recreated them as autonomous lyrical utterances. As late as 1823, when he had fallen in love a last time, a man of seventy-four with a girl young enough to be his granddaughter, this gift enabled him to express the torments that raged in his soul, in such an exemplary fashion that in banishing the specters of defeat and resignation he gave to German literature one of its greatest poems, the *Marienbader Elegie*. As his Tasso had done so many years before, Goethe, too, found consolation in the healing powers of poetry:

Und wenn der Mensch in seiner Qual verstummt,
Gab mir ein Gott zu sagen, was ich leide.[9]

It was with his great novels, *Die Wahlverwandtschaften* (*Elective Affinities*, 1809) and *Wilhelm Meisters Lehrjahre* (*W. M.'s Apprenticeship*, 1796) with its sequel *Wilhelm Meisters Wanderjahre* (*W. M.'s Travels*, 1828), that Goethe most often found favor in the eyes of the Romantics. His own attitude toward that movement, while very complex in its shadings, may be called one of reserve toward its first and dislike of its second wave. Specifically, he objected to the later Romantics' leanings toward Roman Catholicism, to their glorification of the medieval German world, and to their patriotism which became stridently anti-French during the years of Germany's struggle against Napoleon. These tendencies, he felt, were retrograde and escapist (indeed, it was easier to hate

Napoleon than to emulate his many administrative successes from highway building to codifying the law) and vitiated the accomplishments of Goethe's own generation, especially its attitude of tolerance and cosmopolitanism. The Romantics, on their part, began by admiring, and in some cases ended by detesting Goethe as an unreconstructed heathen in practice and outlook, a reactionary in politics, and a classicist fossil in aesthetics. Yet it is easy to see why the novels should have appealed to them. Both *Die Wahlverwandtschaften*, one of the subtlest books ever written about the institution of marriage, and the two parts of *Wilhelm Meister*, the story of a young man's self-discovery and discovery of the world (exemplified, in the beginning, by the stage), contained much that was Romantic in spirit, and more that was Romantic in form. Marriage, and the search for identity, were among the Romantics' favorite topics; the leisurely, rambling progress of the novels themselves, their frequent interruption and retardation by lyric and epic insertions, the profound influence on human fate and behavior here granted to dreams, premonitions, and other irrational and supernatural forces, the view of nature not as decorative background but as an all-pervading influence on human affairs, and the gentle irony with which the author looks upon the men and women of his creation— all this appealed to the Romantics and foreshadowed in many instances their own works.

By the time these novels saw the light of day, the public had long ceased to consider Goethe a popular author, such as he had been in the days of *Werther* and *Götz von Berlichingen*. He had long ceased so to consider himself, and in his autobiography *Dichtung und Wahrheit* (*Poetry and Truth*, 1811 ff.) had even set about giving a stylized version of his own youth. This habit of considering himself *sub specie aeternitatis* had been strengthened by a growing disillusionment with the times, with the rise of Romanticism in literature and the arts, with the political situation in Germany (ruled by Napoleon, whom Goethe admired, and rising up against him only in order to relapse, or so it seemed, into its prerevolutionary coma), and last but not least, with the critical reception accorded to his scientific work. "I am more and more driven into the arms of science," he had confessed to a friend as early as 1790, and his interest in optics, plant science, and comparative anatomy eventually resulted in the publication of *Beiträge zur Optik* (*Contributions to Optical Science*, 1791 ff.), *Zur Farbenlehre* (*On the Theory of Colors*, 1810), and a number of lesser treatises. This is not the place to analyze these contributions, or to assess in detail their scientific value which is considerable in some areas (recent developments in color photography, for example, have borne out the validity of his observations on the physiology of the visual sense) and negligible in others (his acrimonious attempt to discredit Newton was based on a number of misconceptions). The range of this work, in any event, was sufficient to take in half a dozen disciplines; its methodology was marked by a distrust of laboratory experiments, including microscopic work and all manner of mathematical calculation, with a compensatory reliance on what might be termed "comprehensive observation" (the results of which, to be sure, must stand up to precise measurement); its results were particularly rewarding in the developmental and morphological areas. What interested him was not the individual detail, but the underlying law of which it is an expression. It was his interest in such problems as the relationship which a particular aspect or stage of a phenomenon bears to the whole phenomenon, and the degree to which that aspect or stage is shaped by its function as component part of a larger unit, that led him to such postulates as that of an *Urpflanze* or primeval plant, or of the human skull as a modified vertebra. In relation to the sum total of his achievement it may be said that Goethe, while no Leonardo or Einstein, was far more than an amateur scientist, and that he would occupy a small but honored place in the history of science even if he had never written anything else.

The question presents itself: what, precisely, is the "sum total of his achievement"? It is impossible, and probably undesirable as well, to attempt to "prove" that he was one of the greatest of all poets; but since it is equally undesirable to categorize him, History of Literature-Fashion, by means of a more or less felicitous selection of titles, dates, and adjectives, we might now take a look at *Faust* and define, in this greatest and most famous work in all of German literature, at least some of the qualities that have caused its author to be regarded, by practically universal consent, the most outstanding German writer. While looking at this drama, we must of course remember that its creator was also a competent government minister, an original scientist, a gifted painter, in the opinion of most of his contemporaries an extraordinarily magnetic personality, a fine and handsome physical specimen of a man, and a person who successfully mastered his life in a period of intense historical conflict.

FAUST

Faust is a many-faceted work which can be examined from a number of rewarding viewpoints. One of the more obvious approaches to it is the autobiographical one, in which parallels are drawn between certain scenes and figures in the play and specific incidents and persons known to have played a role in the poet's life. It is, for example, very likely that Goethe's friend J. H. Merck lent some traits to Mephistopheles, that Goethe's experiences as a stage author and theatre director are mirrored ironically in "Vorspiel auf dem Theater," and that the students in "Auerbachs Keller" were sketched after types that he had encountered in just that locale. In the final instance, however, such parallels are imprecise if merely conjectured, and irrelevant even if they could be proved to form a bridge between life and work: Goethe, after all, was not the only writer to have satirized the theatre-going public or to have been repelled by the inanities of drunken students. More productive is the search for "period" elements. Clearly, Gretchen's execution meant more to Goethe than a social problem, processions more than a dramatist's retarding device, and sudden conflagrations more than a means of bringing a scene to a close; but although their main dimension is a symbolic one, these elements are also reflections of a period in which the unwed mother's fate was invariably a tragic one, the staging of fanciful allegories a popular form of entertainment, and fire a major hazard to life and property. The highest level on which autobiographical and period connections can be established is the typological one in which Goethe is partially identified with Faust, and the latter with "modern man" as such. For it has early been recognized that Faust is not only an individual, but a personality type seen in historical as well as psychological perspective: the driving, ever-discontented, inventive, and on occasion ruthless type of man, now sometimes called "Faustian," who has created the world in which we live. Without putting too fine a point on it, it may be said that Goethe endowed both Faust and Mephisto with many of his own talents, and that the hero and antihero not only embody but were meant to embody, in their character as well as their fate, a portion of all mankind. Socrates was not the first, and Galileo not the last man whose "Faustian" drive to extend the limits of knowledge brought him into conflict with his social environment. One reason for the ambiguous relationship between the author and his hero lies in the fact that in writing *Faust*, Goethe in a sense merely modified by one more version a literary theme that had existed before and continued to exist after him. His is the best-known installment of a story to which many others contributed chapters of their own, from the days of Christopher Marlowe to those of Thomas Mann and beyond. It is a testimony to the unimpaired vitality of this theme that Faust is cast, in a contemporary Russian version, as a Soviet cosmonaut.

Aside from these and other biographical and characterological aspects, *Faust* may of course also be considered as belonging, with St. Augustine's *City of God*, Dante's *Divine Comedy*, and Shakespeare's dramas, to that select group of literary works which represent a summing-up of an entire historical period (a group more recently represented by Balzac's novels, Proust's *Remembrance of Things Past*, and Mann's *The Magic Mountain*). Indeed, if all other written records were to be lost in some cataclysmic upheaval, we would still be able to reconstruct from Goethe's *Faust*, in broad outline and in some cases with considerable exactitude, many of mankind's hopes, fears, and accomplishments from the Reformation to the beginnings of the Industrial Age: the late Middle Ages in which so many of its scenes are set and from which the historical figure of Dr. Faustus sprang, the Renaissance that imparted so many traits to the hero's personality from his pursuit of knowledge to his admiration for classical antiquity, the Baroque to which the play is indebted for much of the setting in Part II, the Enlightenment so expertly persiflaged in Mephisto and especially in Wagner, the French Revolution and the Romantic Era which have left their traces in "Walpurgisnacht" ("Walpurgis Night") and the first two acts of Part II, and much else besides from Luther's language through Shakespeare's plays and Mozart's operas to Fichte's philosophy. *Faust*, to be sure, is more than a polyhistoric compendium of knowledge; but it is also that.

If these are some well-tried approaches to the play's content (there are many others, including its interpretation as a religious parable, an existentialist manifesto, a proto-Freudian case study, and an indictment of capitalist society), its form can likewise be analyzed from many points of view. As a drama, *Faust* has been the object of some of the most extravagant praise and most scathing criticism heaped upon any example of the genre. Part I is a loosely joined sequence of scenes ranging in length from a very few lines to several hundred, in verisimilitude from the naturalistic "Vor dem Tor" ("Before the City Gate") to the surrealist "Hexenküche" ("Witches' Kitchen"), in language from the lyric flow of Gretchen's songs to the staccato prose of "Trüber Tag: Feld" ("Desolate Day: Field"), in stageworthiness from "Garten" ("Garden"), which can be played by almost anyone on almost any stage, to "Walpurgisnacht" which cannot be adequately performed at all. *Faust I* contains a scene as timeless as "Dom," and one so restricted in appeal that it cannot be understood without reference to some perfectly obscure contemporaries of Goethe ("Walpurgisnachtstraum" ("Walpurgis Night's Dream"). Nevertheless, Part I is a unit held together by the action, by the continuity in character development, and by a number of recurrent motifs (for example, that of *Vernunft* or reason, which man cannot disregard except at his own risk) and images, like that of flight. *Faust II*, on the other hand, is a regular five-act drama in itself, dealing with the hero's progress in *die grosse Welt* of the Emperor's court, in contrast to *die kleine Welt*, the small university town which had encompassed the action of Part I. The high point of Part II, and, in some eyes, of the entire tragedy, is the third act in which Faust meets Helen. This union differs from the Gretchen episode in that it forms an integral portion of the *Faust* legend. In Goethe's version, it has been considered a synthesis of many opposites, among the more obvious of which are those of the male and the female principle, intellectual power and physical beauty, North and South or Germany and Greece, the Middle Ages and classical antiquity or *Romantik* and *Klassik*, Christianity and Paganism. A trilogy in form, this act is probably the most convincing recreation of a Greek drama in German literature, with few *dramatis personae* and a chorus which comments the action, written in a variety of Greek measures (from eight-foot trochees for animated speech to anapests for marching rhyme) skillfully adapted to German, containing numerous Greek devices from stichomythy to lines addressed, in the manner of Aristophanes, to the audience, and presenting, in the heroine, a woman who might have stepped forth from the pages of a Sophocles—not a Frenchwoman in Greek costume but a stately queen resigned to her fate and yet ever sensitive to that which behooves her regal position.

Goethe's *Faust* is an extraordinary work not only on account of its theme —Man's life between Heaven and Hell, painted on a canvas as gigantic as that filled by Dante and Milton—but also because it contains a great many individual jewels that shine even if taken out of their setting. As an expression of a young girl's yearning for her lover, Gretchen's

> Meine Ruh ist hin,
> Mein Herz ist schwer;
> Ich finde sie nimmer
> Und nimmermehr[10]

has perhaps no rival in any language, in the depth of its feeling and the simplicity of its language. The thumbnail sketch of the smug burgher:

> Nichts Besser's weiss ich mir an Sonn—und Feiertagen
> Als ein Gespräch von Krieg und Kriegsgeschrei,
> Wenn hinten, weit, in der Türkei,
> Die Völker aufeinander schlagen . . .[11]

immortalizes a type that must have existed ever since man first became a social animal. The description of fallen Troy:

> Durch das umwölkte, staubende Tosen
> Drängender Krieger hört' ich die Götter
> Fürchterlich rufen, hört' ich der Zwietracht
> Eherne Stimme schallen durchs Feld,
> Mauerwärts[12]

with the last line reverberating in the distance, is a haunting evocation of all conquered cities and of the nightmares suffered by their inhabitants. Baucis' characterization of her ancient husband's life:

> Langer Schlaf verleiht dem Greise
> Kurzen Wachens rasches Tun[13]

exemplifies, in its monumental briefness, the very essence of old age: frantic, last-minute activity interrupted by periods of exhaustion. It is the frequency of passages like these, and as different in nature as these, no less than the transformation of the theme itself from the traditional story of sin and damnation to one of striving and salvation, that make the poem so unique.

We have said that Goethe's life was characteristic not only of the man but of his whole age, and so indeed it is from its bourgeois orientation to its lack of nationalistic engagement. Perhaps its most typical feature, as far as the *Klassik* as a whole is concerned, is the air of almost studied understatement which surrounded it. Goethe was far from otherworldly, to be sure; to give but one example of his fitness for life, we may recall that he derived an uncommon satisfaction out of extracting from his publisher the lordly sum of sixty thousand thalers for a single edition of his collected works. Yet there is nothing remotely "glamorous" about his life. Unlike so many other poets, Goethe did not fight duels, drink to excess, seduce beautiful ladies, travel to exotic lands, experiment with drugs, take part in a revolution, affect flamboyant clothes, fight in a war, attempt suicide, or engage in other acts likely, let alone calculated, to attract attention to himself. Among all of Byron's contemporaries and admirers, he was surely the least Byronic of men. This lack of the colorful attributes of the "creative personality"—more than that: the subordination of personality to work—is a trait which he shared with Kant, Beethoven, Schiller, Hegel, Kleist, and many other contemporaries, not to mention later compatriots of his whose tendencies toward self-effacement may well have been strengthened by his august example, which was eventually held up to them in home and school. Indeed, it is only a slight exaggeration to state that our world has to a large extent been shaped by Germans who "just sat and thought." The names of such admirers of Goethe as Marx, Nietzsche, Freud, and Einstein come to mind, men whose unadventurous lives were not redeemed, by and large, by any pleasure or even activity save that of work. Among other things, it is the sedentariness of so many contemporaries of Goethe that strikes even the casual observer. To sharpen the contrast, we need only remember that the journeys of Mme. de Staël, Chateaubriand, and Lamartine extended from Russia to America and from Scandinavia to Africa, while those of Eichendorff, E. T. A. Hoffmann, and Hölderlin amounted to a few hesitant steps taken into France and Poland, or that Byron, Keats, and Shelley lie buried far from their homeland while Novalis, Wackenroder, and Brentano never left theirs. Goethe never visited Paris, London, or even Vienna; Schiller, Beethoven, and Hegel did not leave the German language area at all, and Kant never stirred from his home town. Incalculable as the achievements of these men were, they were clearly the fruits of a withdrawn and sedentary life and not the result of familiarity with the world at large.

FRIEDRICH SCHILLER

Friedrich Schiller's life (1759–1805) was an unrelenting struggle—against so weak a constitution that his health was continually imperiled and broke down just as he approached his creative peak, against a poverty so dire that he could never afford a trip to the mountains or the sea (which he nonetheless described so well in *Wilhelm Tell* and *Der Taucher*), against a spotty education that he later had to flesh out by autodidactic work especially in history, classical studies, and philosophy, and in a way even against Goethe in whose shadow he had to live for many years before asserting himself as a major poet in his own right. It is a measure of the man's worth that his work bears little trace of this struggle, and that even his earliest play, *Die Räuber* (*The Robbers*) far transcends the circumstances under which it was written: secretly, during his final year in the military academy which the Duke of Württemberg, in whose service Schiller's father was employed, had forced him to attend. So rigid were the prohibitions under which he labored that Schiller had to absent himself from duty in order to be able to attend the play's triumphant première in Mannheim in early 1781. But although he belongs, with Keller, Mann, Hesse, and Rilke, to that large and characteristic group of German writers whose school years were a period of intense suffering, he never made this, or any other experience taken from his own life, the subject of a major work.

The main theme of *Die Räuber*, hostility between two brothers, had already occurred in Schiller's immediate source, a novel by his fellow-Swabian C. D. Schubart, and was so dear to the *Sturm und Drang* that it was also treated in Leisewitz' *Julius von Tarent* and Klinger's *Die Zwillinge*, and taken up again by Schiller himself in *Die Braut von Messina* (*The Bride of Messina*, 1803). Strong medicine as *Die Räuber* is—Karl Moor, a young man of noble mind whom his evil brother Franz had artfully displaced in their father's affection, assumes the leadership of a robber band and takes revenge not only on his own kin but on a social order which seems to countenance such a monstrous perversion of family life—it rises above the black-and-white technique and the hyperbolical language when Karl voluntarily hands himself over to justice, and thus becomes a true Schillerian hero who in making a free ethical choice strips off the fetters that tie him to an imperfect world.

Although his next drama, *Die Verschwörung des Fiesko zu Genua* (*The Conspiracy of Fiesco in Genoa*, 1782), was less successful on the stage, it was with this play about a Genoese statesman corrupted by power that Schiller established himself in a genre of which he was to become a master second only to Shakespeare himself: the historical drama. He had developed, early in life, a marked historical awareness (which among other things enabled him to judge the greatest event of his own time, the French Revolution, more rationally than Goethe did); he later wrote two major historical works of his own, and in time became a professor of history at the University of Jena. With the exception of *Die Räuber*, *Kabale und Liebe* (*Love and Intrigue*, 1783) in which the criticism of social conditions overshadows all else, and *Die Braut von Messina* which he freely invented, Schiller took as a background for his dramas some large historical setting on which he could depict that conflict between freedom and necessity which formed the core of much of his thought. Inevitably, the question arises: to what extent do the works of this dramatist who was also a part-time historian correspond to historical fact? It can be answered by stating that Schiller's procedure never varied: whether he treated an episode from Italian history as in *Fiesko*, or one from that of Spain in *Don Carlos* (1787) or that of Germany in *Wallenstein* (1799), or that of England in *Maria Stuart* (1800) or that of France in *Die Jungfrau von Orleans* (*The Maid of Orleans*, 1801) or that of Switzerland in *Wilhelm Tell* (1803) or that of Russia in *Demetrius* (1805), he began as an historian by studying the sources, and ended as a dramatist who took only such liberties with the truth as seemed warranted by the exigencies of the stage. This is of course a playwright's privilege, and the moderate and highly effective use that Schiller made of it is perhaps best illustrated by the meeting of the two queens in *Maria Stuart*; although history records no such event, Schiller's invention of it remains one of the most convincing of all such confrontations in dramatic literature. Only twice did he appreciably fall short of fusing into a harmonious unit the disparate elements of history, philosophy, and the theatre: in *Die Jungfrau von Orleans* whose history he retold without much reference to its core, the trial, and in the *Wallenstein* trilogy (not so much the introductory *Lager* as *Die Piccolomini* and *Wallensteins Tod*) which is focused upon a character of such doubtful dramatic yield and whose plot is, as Schiller himself said, so "utterly inflexible"—"*im höchsten Grade ungeschmeidig*"— that the play may well have faltered on the stage if the author had not suspended historical reality long enough to let the audience warm to the fictitious love story of Max and Thekla.

His third, and the last of his *Sturm und Drang* plays is *Kabale und Liebe*, a powerful accusation against the absolutist system of government as practised not under the more or less benign eye of the Sun King, but at an obscure German court. The ruthless, self-made minister of state who thwarts his son's impending marriage to a commoner, Luise Miller (hence the title of Verdi's opera); the toadying secretary and foppish courtier, aptly called Wurm and Kalb (epithets too close for comfort, as it turned out, because Schiller later thought of changing the latter's name in order not to offend his friend and admirer, Charlotte von Kalb); the prince's discarded mistress who in disgust retreats to her native England; the old groom who gnashes his teeth as he describes the departure of the subjects whom the prince had sold to the British as cannon fodder; the irascibly honest Miller and his brainless wife, and above all the star-crossed lovers themselves, Ferdinand and Luise—they are not only powerfully drawn figures in their own right but men and women caught, like so many flies, in the transparent web of this *Kabale* which triumphs over *Liebe* in setting son against father, wife against husband, servant against master. Much later, Schiller was to say that a poet ought to discomfit his readers and shake them out of their moral torpor—"die Leute inkommodieren, ihnen die Behaglichkeit verderben, sie in Unruhe und Erstaunen versetzen." With *Die Räuber* and *Kabale und Liebe*, the cathartic shock was so great that the Director of the Mannheim *Nationaltheater*, Schiller's protector Freiherr v. Dalberg, insisted on a number of changes before he would consent to having the plays staged; thus the action of *Die Räuber*, which the poet had intended to be contemporary, had to be placed back into the less explosive late Middle Ages, with which the public had recently become familiar through Goethe's *Götz von Berlichingen*. *Kabale und Liebe* "hit home" even closer than the earlier work, in which the fratricidal conflict and the generation conflict overly and to some extent mute the programmatic exposure of the dying *ancien régime*'s rottenness. Schiller was no political revolutionary, and in any case soon turned away from a drama of social protest; but it is no coincidence that these plays should have been written a few short years before the outbreak of the French Revolution—whose leaders, in turn, made the poet an honorary *citoyen* of the Republic.

Although Schiller typically worked in a very concentrated if not feverish fashion, the composition of *Don Carlos* took four years. It is, of course, a transitional work, in form because it was begun in the same prose in which the *Sturm und Drang* dramas had been written, and then recast in blank verse, and in theme because Schiller fell under the spell of Marquis Posa, much as Goethe had become infatuated with the figure of Gretchen and retarded his account of the traditional *Faust* legend until after he had done full justice to her. The older motifs of Don Carlos' love for his stepmother, and the conflict of generations and philosophies between Philipp and Don Carlos, were so relegated to the background that the work can be said to change direction in midplay. It is a transitional work even in the poet's life because it was begun under the influence of Dalberg and finished far from the Mannheim stage, in Dresden, where Schiller had found a new friend in C. G. Körner, who encouraged him in every possible way by offering him not only a home and a circle of friends, but a measure of financial security. A reflection of the lifelong attachment of the two men may be found in the friendship of Carlos and the noble Posa, as well as in Schiller's ode *An die Freude*, later immortalized in Beethoven's Ninth Symphony.

During the years which elapsed between the completion of *Don Carlos* and that of *Wallenstein*, Schiller grew from a promising young playwright and lyric poet into the second greatest figure in German letters. Safeguarded in his material existence through Körner's generosity and later through an unexpected gift from the Danish royal family, he now found recognition as a writer, and even a measure of happiness in his marriage to Charlotte von Lengefeld. Wieland invited him to contribute to the *Teutsche Merkur* which first published the poems *Die Götter Griechenlands* and *Die Künstler*; Goethe and Wilhelm v. Humboldt became Schiller's friends, and his successful interlude as a university professor, cut short by sickness as it was, showed him how popular he had become, especially with the young. He taught, he studied and wrote history, he edited a journal to which Goethe and others contributed, and in so doing he gained, chiefly through the prism of Kant's philosophy, a clearer insight into the nature of history and of aesthetics.

Having come to believe, with Kant, that history is not a haphazard conglomeration of dates and names but a record of mankind's groping toward the development of a rational social order, Schiller was shocked into the realization, forcibly brought home by the earthshaking events that were taking place across the Rhine, that man's presumed ascent to perfection could more justly be seen in terms of a return to barbarism. The high-water mark of civilization, he came to think, was as likely to have been passed long ago, in ancient Greece, as it was to be reached in the future. Although gained in this dialectical rather than idiosyncratic fashion, Schiller's commitment to the postulate of a preter-naturally harmonious classical Greece was almost as strong as Goethe's. It found expression in an adaptation of classical form in the late dramas (especially *Die Braut von Messina* with its choruses) and the choice of Greek settings for such poems as *Das Ideal und das Leben, Die Kraniche des Ibykus,* and many other examples of *Gedankenlyrik* or reflective poetry, which differs from Goethe's late lyrical production in its tendency to be morally uplifting and in a hymnic flow of language which contrasts with Goethe's plasticity of expression. Kant's influence may also be seen in the philosophical essays, the most important of which, *Über Anmut und Würde* (*On Gracefulness and Dignity,* 1793), *Über die aesthetische Erziehung des Menschen* (*On the Aesthetic Education of Man,* also 1793), and *Über das Erhabene* (*On the Sublime,* 1801), stress the ethical component of art and its function in raising man to a higher level, and in the treatise *Über naive und sentimentalische Dichtung* (*On Naive and Sentimental Poetry,* 1795–96), in which Schiller designed what amounts to a typology of writers: those in harmony with the world who work inductively by advancing from the obser-vation and experience of life to the identification of universal ideas, and those others who write as the result of cogitation, and, in constant awareness of the tension between themselves and the world at large, proceed deductively from the abstract to the concrete. Goethe, Schiller believed, was a "naive," and he himself a "sentimental" poet. Superimposed upon the concepts of *Volkspoesie* and *Kunstpoesie,* and modifying not only the idea of *Dichter* and *Schriftsteller* but the more generic literary terms "ancient" and "modern," these Schillerian categories were to stimulate all later German literary criticism.

It was in the few years that remained to him that Schiller wrote the magni-ficent sequence of classical dramas—the *Wallenstein* trilogy, *Maria Stuart, Die Jungfrau von Orleans, Die Braut von Messina, Wilhelm Tell,* and the *Demetrius* fragment—on which his reputation rests in the main. Vastly different as they are in plot, they share certain qualities which may be defined in the course of a very brief examination of *Wilhelm Tell,* the last completed play; for if one reads or sees these works in the chronological order of their genesis, one finds that they represent an ascending order of quality and a continuous striving on the poet's part to advance beyond himself instead of considering any stage of his development, or any individual work, a *ne plus ultra.* The scene of Tell's shot has come to suffer from its very fame; we can no more face it "naively" than we can listen to certain lines from Shakespeare which have gone stale from constant repetition. Yet shopworn though it may be, the scene is so well con-structed, with the father's inner struggle symbolized by his repeated raising and lowering of the crossbow and the public's attention being distracted, at the moment of highest tension, by Gessler's quarrel with Rudenz, that the actual shot is almost an anticlimax. Any reflections we may entertain about its moral and technical implausibility ("What kind of a father is this, anyway? And how unlikely a shot!") are swept away by the power of this action. If this is an example of his stagecraft, we may see an instance of his sovereign handling of the plot in the unprecedented introduction, in the last act, of an entirely new major figure, that of Johannes Parricida whose wanton murder of his uncle, the emperor, is made to contrast with the murder that Tell committed in self-defense and thus provides a unique built-in catharsis. Admirable is also his use of many small touches, from dress and manner to landscape and history, which identify the setting as well as the hero as Swiss, in so unmistakable a fashion that *Wilhelm Tell* has become the country's national drama, recited and performed at patriotic festivals precisely because it depicts the Swiss "as they think they ought to be" (Gottfried Keller). Indeed, the local color is markedly more realistic than in the early plays although Schiller, never having set foot in the country, had had to rely for it entirely on books and on his conversations with Goethe. Again, all criticism falls silent in the face of this achievement, and we hardly notice that the lake "invites us to bathe"—"zum Baden ladet der See"—even though the season is identified, a few lines farther on, as late October. Like its virtues, *Wilhelm Tell* has certain weaknesses which it shares with Schiller's other classical plays. Thus the love story of Rudenz and Bertha does not come up to the level of the rest of the drama, and is so poorly joined on to the main action that some sutures have remained visible; like the corresponding episode in *Wallenstein*, it was finished last, possibly on account of its unhistorical nature. Also, the pronounced moral orientation of Schiller's works occasionally detracts from their enjoyment, at least in the eyes and ears of a modern audience to which Schiller's praise of freedom—not the freedom of instant gratification demanded by the *Sturm und Drang*, nor that of personality development exemplified by Goethe, nor yet the dialectical *Gedankenfreiheit* for which Posa pleads in a famous passage in *Don Carlos*, but that inner freedom in which duty coincides with inclination so that its performance "comes naturally"—has a hopelessly idealistic ring. Schiller's heroes end by doing their moral duty without regard to such personal and external considerations as fear or ambition, or even the risk that their actions may be misunderstood (as Tell's were to be misunderstood by Bismarck, who considered the assassination of Gessler a cowardly deed). This is a notion which does not always sit easily with us, the contemporaries of Sartre and Ionesco. Yet it was precisely this aspect of Schiller, externalized in such passages as the final line in *Tell* in which Rudenz frees his serfs and in the *Reiterlied* at the end of *Wallensteins Lager*, that brought about his popularity as *Freiheitsdichter* or herald of German political liberty during much of the nineteenth century, a popularity which was so universal that it caused Eichendorff, no mean patriot himself but also a conservative Roman Catholic, to complain that the Germans of his day were no longer raised on the Bible, but on Schiller—"Ach! Dieses Volk ist nicht mehr Bibelfest, es ist Schillerfest!"

This sense of alienation with which many modern readers regard Schiller is sharpened by the high-flown language in which his idealism is clothed; but although it is easy to see in him a preacher whose works, well-knit as they unquestionably are in point of dramatic structure, appeal mainly to the immature, he is in a way the most topical of the classical authors of Germany because his dramas demonstrate, much as do those of Brecht and Dürrenmatt, the incompatibility of the moral and the practical resolution of the existential problem. When he published his English translation of *Maria Stuart*, Stephen Spender rightly observed that the play conveys to us even now "a vision of the role of necessity in history, and a horror of the corruption of power—and these are relevant to a contemporary audience."

Until well into the present century, the question as to whether Goethe or Schiller had been the greater poet was often discussed by German literary historians. Only relatively recently have they been content to accept Goethe's own statement that instead of making pointless comparisons between him and Schiller, the Germans ought to rejoice in having had two poets of such stature. Be that as it may, his friendship with Goethe was the last great experience in Schiller's brief life. On the surface, there was much that militated against any close relationship between them: a decade's difference in age, greatly contrasting personalities and backgrounds (which had made the one an influential writer-turned-statesman while the other, for all his literary fame, had only just found his professional and social footing), and the fact that the younger man had continued the *Sturm und Drang* at a time when the older had already turned his back on it. In the meantime, however, Schiller himself had matured in the course of his historical and philosophical studies and his discovery of classical antiquity, while Goethe, having grown apart from his old Weimar friends in the wake of his return from Italy and as a result of his *mésalliance* with Christiane, was becoming ever more lonely and embittered. The stage was thus set for a series of meetings which took place more or less by chance but soon took on an exploratory character. By 1795, the two had become friendly competitors, and there is no doubt that many of Goethe's works, a number of major lyric poems as well as *Wilhelm Meisters Lehrjahre* and *Faust*, would either not have been finished at all without Schiller's encouragement and advice, or at the very least not have been written in the way in which they have come down to us. Schiller, on his part, gained through Goethe that self-knowledge which can only be acquired in the give-and-take of almost daily contact with a friend of equal but different stature, and received a powerful stimulus toward the completion of his own dramatic projects. In all likelihood, *Wallenstein* (first performed in Weimar under Goethe's direction) and *Tell* (enriched, as we saw, by many folkloristic and regional touches supplied by Goethe) would also have turned out quite differently without this collaboration, which in one instance was so intimate that a work was published under the joint signature of both: *Xenien*, a collection of aphoristic comments on the numerous tendencies of the time of which both poets disapproved. Thus there developed between these two disparate men a deep friendship which is recorded also in their correspondence, published by Goethe after Schiller's death. The close relationship between its two main protagonists is among the more striking of the characteristics that set the *Klassik* apart from the superficially similar epochs of Aeschylus and Sophocles, Vergil and Horace, Cervantes and Calderón, Corneille and Racine.

HEINRICH VON KLEIST

Whereas Goethe and Schiller became famous early in life and were admired and imitated almost from the beginning, Heinrich von Kleist (1777–1811) exerted no influence whatever on his contemporaries or on his immediate posterity. Although his genius had early been recognized by Wieland, as Hölderlin's was by Schiller, the world at large ignored him; like Hölderlin, he was appreciated only by an elite—Tieck, Hebbel, Nietzsche—and not widely read until the present century. Many factors combined to deprive both poets of the encouragement and recognition which should have been theirs from the beginning. In Kleist's case, these were the traditions and attitudes of his family, in whose eyes he remained a misfit, unwilling alike to pursue the military career for which he had been trained and to serve the state in a respected civilian capacity, his poverty (orphaned early in life, he soon exhausted his modest inheritance and would have starved if his half-sister had not repeatedly come to his rescue), his "difficult" personality (stuttering and fits of absent-mindedness were among the many peculiarities which his friends had to condone), and the whole tone of his life (and even his death, a double suicide with a woman incurably ill of cancer). The temper of the times, when Prussia existed in the shadow and by the tolerance of Napoleon, was as much against him as the literary constellation: at the time of Kleist's greatest need, his former mentor Wieland was in his dotage, Schiller had just died, and Goethe signally failed to understand him. Goethe has been blamed for this, and rightly so; but in 1808, when he could most have helped Kleist by staging the comedy *Der Zerbrochene Krug* (*The Broken Pitcher*) in Weimar according to the author's instructions rather than allowing it to turn into a fiasco, he was almost sixty and Kleist just over thirty, a chronological distance aggravated by personality differences as well as sharply contrasting literary aims and practices. This concatenation of unfortunate circumstances brought it about that Kleist never saw a work of his performed on the stage, that his greatest drama was preserved only because Tieck chanced to come upon a manuscript copy long after the author's death, and that his longest and possibly best prose work, a two-volume novel, has been lost altogether.

A glance at the works that did come down to us—eight dramas, a like number of *Novellen*, two or three brilliant short essays and some other criticism, as well as a few undistinguished poems—reveals the deeper reasons for Kleist's failure in his own time and for the recognition he has found in ours. Whether freely invented as in *Die Familie Schroffenstein*, mythological as in *Penthesilea*, or historical as in *Prinz Friedrich von Homburg*, the background against which his dramatic figures are shown can be likened to a thin crust of ice, which may break under them at any time and leave them to drown in the dark depths. The protagonists of the great *Novellen*, whether these end tragically like *Das Erdbeben in Chili* (*The Earthquake in Chile*) and *Die Verlobung von St. Domingo* (*The Betrothal in San Domingo*) or in a measure of reconciliation like *Die Marquise von O . . .* and *Michael Kohlhaas*, are similarly brought into conflict with a world whose institutions are repeatedly characterized as "brittle"—"die gebrechliche Einrichtung der Welt." Kleist's reading of Kant (whose *Critique of Pure Reason* he mistakenly considered as proving that *all* truth remains forever inaccessible to us, and that the very striving for truth and thus knowledge is at bottom futile) and the experiences of his own life convinced him that we are thrown defenseless into an indifferent if not actively hostile environment. Far from providing a stable framework within which we may live, those institutions by means of which Man has attempted to bring order into this chaos—law, marriage, social groupings like state, army, family—are so brittle, so likely to be proven hollow, that they grant us not the reality of order but only an illusionary sense of security. Kafka admired Kleist and learned much from him; but if the former's characters are as a rule the victims of a chain of events incomprehensible to them in causation and sequence, Kleist's characters resemble more closely the traditional ones of dramatic and epic literature. They carry within them the seeds of their own destruction, often in the form of that small excess of virtue which turns a positive trait into a negative one: Homburg's bravery turns into impetuousness, Kohlhaas' sense of justice into righteousness. Superimposed upon this time-honored *hubris* is another and more typically Kleistian element: an uncommonly intense affective life. Ruled by their emotions, or rather by a succession of emotional states, his characters are both victims and heroes; they prevail, or go down as the case may be, not suffering but fighting with all their might, and in so doing lay bare the very fiber of their being. Many of them are, indeed, taken apart and put together again before our very eyes, like Homburg who discovers, in one of the most harrowing scenes on the stage, that he is not only a battle-tried hero but on another level also an abject coward, who after being led past the grave that has just been dug for him renounces all claims to glory and honor and even to the woman he loves. He is, historically and "technically," a victorious Prussian general, and it is easy to see why this play should have found no favor in the official circles of Kleist's time. The most extreme case of Kleistian *Gefühlsverwirrung* or turmoil of affects is Penthesilea, the Amazon queen who loves Achilles and nonetheless (or should we say "therefore," with Kleist and perhaps Freud?) not only kills him but, in another frightful and unforgettable scene, sinks her teeth into his breast. Small wonder that the author of *Iphigenie* should have recoiled in horror from this play, which bears not the remotest trace of a Goethean belief in man's innate goodness, let alone his ability to pattern his actions after a noble example.

The impact of Kleist's work is enhanced by two factors. One is his non-involvement: he relates but does not comment. Kohlhaas, who assuages his outraged sense of justice by taking the law into his own hands, dies while the Marquise lives on to marry the father of the child she unknowingly conceived. They are, objectively speaking, as noble in character as any figures drawn by Goethe and Schiller, but this is irrelevant in Kleist's view and we are not encouraged to sympathize with them. What is brought home to us is the fact that the strength and rightness of their *Gefühl* is vindicated and that they, and the world at large, find out what kind of people they are. The other factor which rivets our attention on everything that Kleist wrote is his extraordinarily compact style. We are not so much led as pushed into the action, as in the opening paragraphs of *Michael Kohlhaas*:

> Toward the middle of the sixteenth century, there lived on the banks of the Havel a horse dealer by the name of Michael Kohlhaas, the son of a schoolmaster, one of the most upright and at the same time one of the most terrible men of his day. Until his thirtieth year this extraordinary man would have been thought the very model of a good citizen. In the village that still bears his name, he owned a farm on which he quietly earned a living by his trade; the children with whom his wife presented him were brought up in the fear of God to be industrious and honest; there was not one of his neighbors who had not benefited from his benevolence or his fairmindedness—the world, in short would have had every reason to bless his memory, if he had not carried one virtue to excess. But his sense of justice turned him into a brigand and a murderer.[14]

and *Die Marquise von O . . . .*:

> In M . . . , a large town in northern Italy, the widowed Marquise of O . . . , a lady of unblemished reputation and the mother of several well-bred children, published the following notice in the newspapers: that, without her knowing how, she was in the family way; that she would like the father of the child she was going to bear to report himself; and that her mind was made up, out of consideration for her people, to marry him.[15]

We are instantly faced with a protagonist, setting, and period, warned to expect action of a violent and unheard-of sort, and familiarized with the brittleness of the institutions of a world which must indeed be out of joint if it can turn an "upright" man into a "terrible" one or place a lady of "unblemished" reputation in that particular predicament. This intensity is maintained throughout, and all obstacles that would normally tend to retard the telling of the story, including the standard syntactical order of the German sentence, are ruthlessly swept away. Under Kleist's hands, the stately flow of verse and even of prose becomes a raging torrent. When a Greek soldier describes an attack launched by Penthesilea's Amazons, he does not proceed in logical sequence, as is the case in many similar reports in Schiller's *Jungfrau*, but by affective emphasis:

> Ein neuer Anfall, heiss wie Wetterstrahl,
> Schmolz, dieser wuterfüllten Mavorstöchter,
> Rings der Ätolier wackre Reihen hin,
> Auf uns, wie Wassersturz, hernieder sie,
> Die unbesiegten Myrmidonier, giessend.[16]

We have come a long way from Winckelmann to Kleist, from Noble Simplicity and Quiet Grandeur to Penthesilea mutilating her lover's bloodied corpse. This artistic, moral, and emotional distance was traversed within the lifetime of Goethe whose figure continues to tower—even as we look back on it from the twentieth century—over the whole sweep of classical German literature.

FOOTNOTES

1
> Sing, immortal soul, the redemption of sinful man
> which the Messiah fulfilled walking with men as man . . .

> How splendidly nature
> beams and dazzles!
> The sun so bright,
> the fields so light!

> The blossoms are bursting
> from every branch
> and choruses of voices
> from bushes and brush,

> and joy and exultation
> from every breast.
> O rapture of all creation,
> delight to be so blessed!

> O love, O love,
> as golden bright

as morning clouds
above that height.

Your radiant blessing
on fertile fields—
on the flowering world
and all it yields!

O darling, darling,
I love but you!
How bright your eyes—
you love me too!

And so the lark
loves song and air,
and morning flowers
the dewy mist they share.

How I love you
with heart and soul!
You bring me youth
and joy, a goal—

inspire me to song
and dance again.
May you be happy,
as you love me.

—K. S. Weimar, trans.

3   Hurry up, Kronos,
Off we go at a trot!
Down hill fast as we can.
Poking along
Makes me sick and dizzy.
Lurching, speeding along,
Sticks, stones bumps our trot,
Dashing onward to life.

4   Happy the man who mindful of his forbears
Delights to tell and celebrate their deeds,
Their fame, and sees with modest satisfaction
Himself a part of this illustrious
Procession . . .

(Act I, Scene iii)

5   Believe me now a self-indulgent heart
Cannot escape the pain of envy's chains:
A man of such a heart may overlook
Another's station, fortune, fame; he thinks,
However, all of this you can possess,
If you but will, persist, be fortune's child.

(IV, ii)

6   But think of how transient all things human are!
The gods endure who arrogance avenge!

Respect, have fear of them, the awesome ones,
Who cast me prostrate here before your feet.
By reason of these unfamiliar witnesses
In me yourselves do honor . . .

(III, iv)

7 Whoever boldly looks about alert
And trusts in God and his own nimble strength,
He extricates himself from every danger:
He fears no mountain who was born in mountains.

(III, i)

8 I once went walking,
just on my own.
I was not looking;
I went to roam.

In forest shade I saw
a little flower,
a radiant star,
a pretty dower.

I went to pluck it
when soft it spoke:
Am I to wither,
to die, thus broke?

With all its roots
I pulled it out
and took it home
to see it sprout.

I planted it again
in sheltered bed;
the shoots keep growing,
the buds are red.

9 And when in sorrow others find no words,
A god gave me to say how much I suffer.

10 My peace is gone,
my heart is sore;
I'll find it never
and nevermore.

11 I know of nothing better Sundays or a holiday
than talk of war and rumors of war,
when off in Turkey far away
they're fighting furiously once more.

12 Through the loud clangor, clouds of the dust of
fiercely attacking heroes' voices I heard,
deities' fearful cry, discord I heard
clanging in brazen tone over the field
on to the walls . . . .

13   Sleep gives this old man the strength for
ready deed in briefest day.

14 From *The Marquise of O———, and Other Stories*, trans. Martin Greenberg, (New York: Criterion Books, 1960), p. 87

15 *Ibid.*, p. 41

16 A new attack, hot and fast as lightning, by these fierce daughters of Mars melted the lines of the brave Etolians all about, and caused these [hitherto] unconquered Myrmidons to come pouring down upon us like a cloudburst.

BIBLIOGRAPHY

ABBÉ, DEREK MAURICE VAN, *Christoph Martin Wieland, A Literary Biography*. London: George G. Harrap & Company, Ltd., 1961. A concise and well-written introduction to the study of a poet on whom not much is available in English.

ATKINS, STUART, *Goethe's Faust, A Literary Analysis*. Cambridge, Mass.: Harvard University Press, 1958. A very detailed interpretation, more to be recommended to the experienced reader than to the neophyte.

BUCHWALD, REINHARD, *Schiller, Leben und Werk* (4th ed.). Wiesbaden: Insel-Verlag, 1959. A general introduction which offers little that is new, but sweeps the cobwebs from much of the old.

CLARK, ROBERT T., JR., *Herder—His Life and Thought*. Berkeley and Los Angeles: University of California Press, 1955. Very detailed, a solid piece of scholarship which must be read as a companion to the works rather than as an introduction to them.

FAIRLEY, BARKER, *A Study of Goethe*. Oxford: Clarendon Press, 1947. A biography "from within," especially of the young poet. Original and most readable.

FREIVOGEL, MAX, *Klopstock*. Bern: A. Francke, 1954. The subtitle, *Der heilige Dichter*, indicates the author's preoccupation with one major aspect of Klopstock's work.

GARLAND, H. B., *Lessing, The Founder of Modern German Literature*. London: Macmillan & Co., Ltd., 1962. A sensible book sensibly subdivided into The Life; The Critic; The Dramatist; Lessing and Religion.

GERHARD, MELITTA, *Schiller*. Bern: A. Francke, 1950. The aesthetician and ideologue Schiller is here treated with rather more sympathy than the poet and human being.

GILLIES, A., *Goethe's Faust*. Oxford: B. Blackwell, 1957. A no-nonsense approach to a complex work; ideal for the beginning reader.

———, *Herder*. Oxford. B. Blackwell, 1945. Shorter and less comprehensive, but livelier than Clark's work.

GRAY, RONALD D., *Goethe, A Critical Introduction*. Cambridge University Press, 1967. With its companion volume of selected and annotated poems, this is perhaps the most readable of all recent introductions to Goethe.

HATFIELD, HENRY C., *Goethe—A Critical Introduction*. Cambridge, Mass.: Harvard University Press, 1964. Brief and to the point, gives all the essentials but inevitably leaves out much that could have been added.

————, *Winckelmann and His German Critics, 1755–81*. New York: King's Crown Press, 1943. A detailed and thoroughly documented discussion of Winckelmann's impact on German thought in the period specified.

HAYM, RUDOLF, *Herder*. 2 vols. Berlin: Aufbau-Verlag, 1954. A reprint of the original edition of 1880. Dependable, positivistic, a little dull.

JUSTI, CARL, *Winckelmann und seine Zeitgenossen*. 3 vols. Leipzig: F. C. W. Vogel, 1866–72. One of the great biographies of nineteenth-century German scholarship. Antiquated in details but unsurpassed in its presentation of an entire age.

KAISER, GERHARD, *Klopstock*. Gütersloh: G. Mohn, 1963. More finely articulated than Freivogel's book, and offering panoramic rather than sectional views of the poet.

KLEIST, HEINRICH VON, *The Marquise of O ————, and Other Stories*, trans. Martin Greenberg. New York: Criterion Books, 1960. An achievement of its kind: a readable translation of the work of an almost untranslatable author.

KOCH, FRIEDRICH, *Heinrich von Kleist*. Stuttgart: J. B. Metzlersche Verlagsbuchhandlung., 1958. As complex and fascinating, with its dichotomy of *Bewusstsein* and *Wirklichkeit*, as Kleist's own works.

MANN, OTTO, *Lessing*. Hamburg: M. v. Schröder Verlag, 1949. One of the better recent biographies, accenting *Sein und Leistung* rather than the traditional Life-and-Works.

ROBERTSON, J. G., *Lessing's Dramatic Theory*. London: Cambridge University Press, 1939. An interpretation that needs to be brought up-to-date in the light of recent developments in the theatre and in Lessing studies.

SENGLE, FRIEDRICH, *Wieland*. Stuttgart: J. B. Metzlersche Verlagsbuchhdlg., 1949. More detailed than von Abbé's book, but not as urbane.

SILZ, WALTER, *Heinrich von Kleist, Studies in His Works and Literary Character*. Philadelphia: University of Pennsylvania Press, 1961. An eclectic work that "does not attempt to be a general book, 'covering' Kleist for the uninitiated reader." Useful for *Amphytrion, Prinz von Homburg, Michael Kohlhaas*.

STAIGER, EMIL, *Goethe*. 3 vols. Zürich: Atlantis-Verlag, 1952–59. One of the best new biographies, it re-establishes many perspectives and proportions that have been distorted by writers (psychoanalysts, New Critics, Marxists, etc.) who had axes to grind.

————, *Schiller*. Zürich: Atlantis, 1967. Less a biography than an attempt to define the characterological and typological basis of Schiller's work, with an interesting final chapter on the poet's significance for our time.

STEINMETZ, H. (ed.), *Lessing, ein unpoetischer Dichter*. Frankfurt a/M: Athenäum, 1969. An anthology of Lessing criticism from 1754 to 1960, with an ideological spectrum that ranges from Franz Mehring on the far left to Mathilde Ludendorff on the far right. Interesting as an example of a popular trend in present-day German scholarship: the documentation of changes in a classical author's influence and reputation (a companion piece: Sembdner [ed.], *Heinrich von Kleists Nachruhm*).

STORZ, GERHARD, *Der Dichter Friedrich Schiller*. Stuttgart: E. Klett, 1959. Like all of Storz' works, this analysis of the poet Schiller reflects a mixture of scholarly knowledge and personal engagement that has become rare in the age of pseudo-"scientific" literary scholarship.

VIETOR, KARL, *Goethe*. Bern: A. Francke, 1949. Briefer, but as good in its way as Staiger. Both these biographies are obligatory reading for the serious student of Goethe.

WIESE, BENNO VON, *Friedrich Schiller*. Stuttgart: J. B. Metzlersche Verlagsbuch-hdlg., 1959. A traditional, solidly worked biography, with many sidelights on the political and cultural background of eighteenth-century Germany.

WITTE, WILLIAM, *Schiller*. Oxford: B. Blackwell, 1949. Contains many sensitive observations on The Letter-Writer, The Poet, and The Playwright, but tends to dismiss the biographical basis.

WOLFF, HANS M., *Heinrich von Kleist*. Bern: A. Francke, 1954. A morsel for the connoisseur.

Between the 18th and 19th Centuries: Hölderlin

MICHAEL HAMBURGER

The uniqueness of Friedrich Hölderlin (1770–1843) is more obvious than his affinities with other German writers of his time. His mature work—that written between 1796 and 1804—belongs neither to Weimar Classicism nor to any of the phases and varieties of German Romanticism. After his apprentice work, under the tutelage first of Klopstock, then of Schiller, Hölderlin went his own way, a way essentially more solitary than that of any other poet of his age, with the possible exception of William Blake. Yet one historical approach to Hölderlin is through certain basic antinomies common to all the major German writers of his time. Ancient and modern, naive and sentimental (in Schiller's peculiar sense of *sentimentalisch*), Nature and Art—these are the most crucial of the antinomies with which Hölderlin was as deeply and dialectically involved as his immediate predecessors and his contemporaries, not excluding the philosophers. To the last, that is until the breakdown of his intellectual faculties in his midthirties, Hölderlin grappled with those antinomies, both in his theoretical writings and in his practice as a poet. The intensity of that struggle has a great deal to do with the prodigious speed and extent of Hölderlin's development within the short period granted to him for mature

Michael Hamburger was educated at Westminster School and Christ Church, Oxford. He taught at the universities of London and Reading and has been a visiting professor at Mount Holyoke College and State University of New York at Buffalo. He has been a Fellow of the Bollingen Foundation and has received four prizes for his work as a translator. His publications include six collections of poems, four critical books and many translations, mainly of German poetry.

work. Those who saw Hölderlin only as an inspired visionary—as the *sacer vates* only, rather than the *poeta doctus*—failed to notice his extraordinary capacity for criticism of himself and his own work. As his essays and letters show, Hölderlin repeatedly questioned, modified, or even rejected the premises of his art. That is the main reason why his *Empedocles*—a tragedy originally conceived in neoclassical or classical terms—remained unfinished, as did the Pindaric hymn *Wie wenn am Feiertage* . . . . In his recent *Hölderlin-Studien* Peter Szondi has traced the connection between the noncompletion of those works and Hölderlin's new insights into the nature of ancient and modern poetry. The same insights that caused Hölderlin to abandon certain of his works drove him on to new modes and possibilities of poetic utterance so daring as to anticipate the stylistic innovations of the late nineteenth and early twentieth centuries.

This aspect of Hölderlin's achievement needs to be stressed because of the persistence of a view of him that attributes more importance to his madness than to his artistry and his intellectual power. Nothing could be more wrong, for instance, than W. H. Auden's recent pronouncement: "Translation also favours poets like Hölderlin and Smart, who were dotty, for their dislocation of normal processes of thinking are the result of their dottiness not their language, and sound equally surprising in any language." Mr. Auden goes on to contrast these "dotty" poets with others "whose principal concern is with the sound of words and their metrical and rhythmical relations." Hölderlin's principal concern as a poet was with precisely those things; even his characteristic dislocation of conventional syntax in his late poems was based on discoveries about the structure of ancient poetry. Nor was Hölderlin ever "dotty"; when his very considerable intellectual powers declined, so did his technical inventiveness and his stylistic innovations.

What Hölderlin struggled for, in fact, was not uniqueness or originality— though his work is highly original and unique—but a "rightness," a balance between ideas of perfection derived from Winckelmann's neoclassicism and what he called "life"—vitality, dynamism, and immediacy. Something of that balance was attained even in his early classical odes, as compared with the rhymed "hymns" that preceded them, with their idealistic impetus always in danger of losing itself in abstraction; but the balance was relatively easy to attain within the narrow scope of brief odes that are little more than epigrams. From these brief odes of 1797 onwards—through the longer odes to the elegies, hexameters, and free verse hymns—all Hölderlin's subsequent development was in the direction of concreteness, of "life," yet without any loss of idealism or of vision. His early epigram about the "descriptive poets" who "report all the facts" remained valid for him even when his poetry had arrived at a sensuous vividness of imagery unparalleled in the poetry of his time. A number of these late poems and fragments point to W. C. Williams' prescription of "no ideas but in things." Yet Hölderlin never aspired to realism for realism's sake.

The more esoteric and intensely personal his vision, the more difficult it became to strike the right balance between the general and the particular, pathos or "drunkenness," as he called it, and the sobriety and measure that were equally dear to him.

The capacity for self-criticism on which I have remarked is apparent even in the poems themselves, from the brief odes to the free verse hymns. In *Menschenbeifall* (*Human Applause*) he comments on the change between his prolix Schillerian verse and the spareness of his new medium:

> Ist nicht heilig mein Herz, schöneren Lebens voll,
> Seit ich liebe? Warum achtetet ihr mich mehr,
>   Da ich stolzer und wilder,
>   Wortereicher und leerer war?[1]

In another ode, also of 1796, *An die Jungen Dichter*, (*To the Young Poets*) he formulates that balance between the great antinomies of the age in which he was to exhaust himself by perpetually adjusting and redressing his art in the light of new experience and of new and more ambitious endeavors:

> Lieben Brüder! es reift unsere Kunst vielleicht,
> Da, dem Jünglinge gleich, lange sie schon gegärt,
>   Bald zur Stille der Schönheit;
>   Seid nur fromm, wie der Grieche war.
>
> Liebt die Götter und denkt freundlich der Sterblichen!
> Hasst den Rausch wie den Frost! lehrt und beschreibet nicht!
>   Wenn der Meister euch ängstigt,
>   Fragt die grosse Natur um Rat![2]

Into the eight sober lines of this seemingly didactic or admonitory poem Hölderlin has packed any number of seeming contradictions that give life to the poem because they are part of Hölderlin's quarrel not with others, but with himself. To begin with, the apparently didactic nature of the poem is contradicted by the injunction not to teach. The Winckelmannian "Stille der Schönheit" (not rendered literally in the English version in the footnote, which transposes Hölderlin's Asclepiadean ode into more amenable Alcaics) is corrected, if not contradicted, by the final reference to the authority of Nature, with the implication that imitation of the Greeks is not enough. Yet neither is Nature to be imitated, in the naturalistic sense of description. Drunkenness and frost, excessive enthusiasm and academic perfection, are placed at either end of a single prohibition, so that the half-line in itself creates a balance between them. Piety toward the Greeks is distinguished from a piety like that of the Greeks, with implications pointing both to Hölderlin's fervent pantheism at this period, a pantheism most explicit in his novel *Hyperion*, and to a whole line of argument extending from Lessing through Herder, Goethe, and Schiller to the early works of Friedrich Schlegel. The dialectical structure of Hölderlin's works, including *Hyperion*, is more apparent in some of the longer odes, with their clear progression from thesis to antithesis and synthesis; but these few random observations may help to indicate some of the tensions contained within so small and relatively unambitious a poem.

Between 1795 and 1798, Hölderlin lived as a tutor in the Gontard household. His love for Susette Gontard, his employer's wife and the "Diotima" of Hölderlin's poems and of his novel *Hyperion* (completed in 1799), is inseparable from his development as a poet in those crucial and highly productive years. As he told his friends in rhapsodic letters, it was Susette who enabled him to reconcile the idealistic impetus of his youth with the sobriety and sensuousness of his maturity. Susette was a real woman, but she was also the re-embodiment of all that Hölderlin admired in the culture of ancient Greece. Yet just as in real life this illicit love was thwarted by the conventions of a barbaric society— Hölderlin was forced to leave the Gontard household and renounce Susette— so the hero of Hölderlin's novel is betrayed and disillusioned in his endeavors to create a free and harmonious society. The Diotima of the novel dies. Like Hölderlin's other hero, Empedocles, Hyperion is left alone with nature. Only pantheistic communion with nature saves him from total alienation and despair.

In the brief odes of 1796, Hölderlin establishes one kind of balance, and defines it in terms still more general than particular. The distinction of these poems is that their diction and cadences enact and exemplify what is said in them, so that mere epigram is transcended; what these poems lack, on the other hand, is the tragic intensity of the longer odes, in which the clash of opposites becomes ever more extreme and more dynamic, the imagery more concrete, the syntax more true to the tensions which it serves to convey. This development from poem to poem cannot be traced here; it would require analyses not only of the odes, and of their successive versions, such as the many later odes that are like variations on themes first stated in the short odes of 1797, but also of the elegies and free verse hymns. Hölderlin's prodigious development must be followed in the poems themselves, in the three successive versions of the *Empedocles* tragedy, and in his essays and letters. Up to 1804, as his letters and theoretical writings confirm, Hölderlin never ceased to reconsider the questions and antinomies most vital to him and to his poetry, and there is an intimate connection between the changes in his theological and philosophical position and the changes in his poetic practice. Nor did he cease to comment on his own poetic practice even in poems as impersonal and oracular as the late hymns, for example when he interrupts the celebration of Christ in *Der Einzige* (*The Only One*, 1802) to confess:

> Diesesmal
> Ist mir vom eigenen Herzen
> Zu sehr gegangen der Gesang,

Gut will ich aber machen
Den Fehl, mit nächstem,
Wenn ich noch andere singe.
Nie treff' ich, wie ich wünsche,
Das Mass. Ein Gott weiss aber,
Wenn kommet, was ich wünsche, das Beste.[3]

True, this poem—quoted here in the first version—remained a fragment, and its fragmentary state, like that of the earlier hymn *Wie wenn am Feiertage . . .* testifies to one of several crises and conflicts so extreme as to leave the poet temporarily unbalanced. The "right measure," as he says, evades him here though he was indeed to restore it, to establish it anew, in related poems like *Patmos.*

Hölderlin's development as a whole can be grasped only through the antinomies with which he struggled until they consumed him, turning into impersonal myths like those of his very last odes, *Ganymede* and *Chiron,* or of the free verse fragments which he published together with them as *Nacht-gesänge.* Already in an earlier ode the antinomy between Nature and Art had been mythologized in terms of the antagonism between Saturn and Jupiter, in such a way as to link up with an even earlier ode *Der Zeitgeist.* The divided allegiance, in the late poems, between Christ and the Greek gods progresses from, but does not nullify, the terms of that earlier conflict. Where a conflict cannot be resolved within a single poem, the resolution is often suspended until new, purely poetic resources have made it possible for Hölderlin to recapitulate and transform it. In such cases he was compelled to evolve new poetic forms, if not a new kind of poetry. Thus in the ode form alone he was able to encompass epigram, pure lyric, tragic conflict and catharsis, and even epic, as in *Stimme des Volks* (*Voice of the People*). That he was critically aware of these possibilities is proved by his theoretical reflections on the interaction of lyrical, tragic, and epic elements within all poetry, whatever its dominant mode or kind.

The opening section of Hölderlin's elegy *Brod und Wein* (*Bread and Wine*) was highly admired in his lifetime; Clemens Brentano praised it, treated it as a separate poem, and in that way gave credit to Hölderlin for excelling even in a mode which he never cultivated for its own sake:

Ringsum ruhet die Stadt; still wird die erleuchtete Gasse,
    Und, mit Fackeln geschmückt, rauschen die Wagen hinweg.
Satt gehn heim von Freuden des Tags zu ruhen die Menschen,
    Und Gewinn und Verlust wäget ein sinniges Haupt
Wohlzufrieden zu Haus; leer steht von Trauben und Blumen,
    Und von Werken der Hand ruht der geschäftige Markt.
Aber das Saitenspiel tönt fern aus Gärten; vielleicht, dass
    Dort ein Liebendes spielt oder ein einsamer Mann

Ferner Freunde gedenkt und der Jugendzeit; und die Brunnen
    Immerquillend und frisch rauschen an duftendem Beet.
Still in dämmriger Luft ertönen geläutete Glocken,
    Und der Stunden gedenk rufet ein Wächter die Zahl.
Jetzt auch kommet ein Wehn und regt die Gipfel des Hains auf,
    Sieh! und das Schattenbild unserer Erde, der Mond,
Kommet geheim nun auch; die Schwärmerische, die Nacht kommt,
    Voll mit Sternen und wohl wenig bekümmert um uns,
Glänzt die Erstaunende dort, die Fremdlingin unter den Menschen
    Über Gebirgeshöhn traurig und prächtig herauf.[4]

In that opening section Hölderlin comes close to descriptive verse evocative
enough to satisfy a Romantic sensibility. Yet the realism of the townscape
here has a special function within the context and structure of the whole
elegy, and already in the closing lines of this section a delicate transition prepares
us for the cosmological and chiliastic significance of Night. The realism,
therefore, serves only to establish one pole of a tension that runs through the
whole elegy, a tension between the particular and the general. The diction
of the elegy, now elevated and sublime, now starkly colloquial (as in the lines
questioning the usefulness of poets in Hölderlin's own time) enacts the same
tension. As in all Hölderlin's mature work, it is the antinomies that impose
the peculiar rightness and balance to be achieved. The poem celebrates Hölderlin's symbiosis of Greek and Christian forces, symbolized by bread and wine
and realized in the last of the gods, the Syrian Christ. The opening section does
not contradict Hölderlin's reservations about descriptive poetry, but it does
show a progression to a stage where description, too, had its place among the
resources available to him as a poet.

At a still later stage, shortly before his final mental collapse (1806), he was
able to dispense not only with regular form and meter, but also with similes
and other rhetorical devices of traditional poetry. The tensions now could be
entrusted to images and to the relationships between them, created by a syntax
no longer governed by the laws of discursive logic. The best-known, though
by no means the only instance of this later practice, is *Hälfte des Lebens* (*The
Middle of Life*, 1803):

Mit gelben Birnen hänget
Und voll mit wilden Rosen
Das Land in den See,
Ihr holden Schwäne,
Und trunken von Küssen
Tunkt ihr das Haupt
Ins heilignüchterne Wasser.

Weh mir, wo nehm' ich, wenn
Es Winter ist, die Blumen, und wo

Den Sonnenschein
Und Schatten der Erde?
Die Mauern stehn
Sprachlos und kalt, im Winde
Klirren die Fahnen.⁵

Of such fragments—and *Hälfte des Lebens* was a fragment of a longer poem
until Hölderlin had the genius and daring to publish it as a poem complete in
itself—Christopher Middleton has written: "Hölderlin's later imagery is the
crystal lava of his unique and perilous inspiration . . . What makes Hölderlin's later work sing is the marvellous balance of energy between disintegration
and articulation, plus the mortal conflict of spirit that is going on between these
poles." Even here, then, there was conflict and balance—on the very verge of
incurable madness.

FOOTNOTES

[1] Has love not hallowed, filled with new life my heart,
    With lovelier life? Then why did you prize me more
        When I was proud and wild and frantic,
            Lavish of words, yet in substance empty?

[2] Quite soon, dear brothers, perhaps our art,
    So long in youth-like ferment, will now mature
        To beauty's plenitude, to stillness;
            Only be pious, like Grecian poets!

Of mortal men think kindly, but love the gods!
    Loathe drunkenness like frost! Don't describe or teach!
        And if you fear your master's bluntness,
            Go to great Nature, let her advise you!

[3]   For this time too much
From my own heart the song
Has come; if other songs follow
I'll make amends for the fault.
Much though I wish to, never
I strike the right measure. But
A god knows when it comes, what I wish for, the best.

[4] Round us, the town is at rest; the street, in pale lamplight, grows quiet
    And, their torches ablaze, coaches rush through and away.
People go home to rest, replete with the day and its pleasures,
    There to weigh up in their heads, pensive, the gain and the loss,
Finding the balance good; stripped bare now of grapes and of flowers,
    As of their hand-made goods, quiet the market stalls lie.
But faint music of strings comes drifting from gardens; it could be
    Someone in love who plays there, could be a man all alone

Thinking of distant friends, the days of his youth; and the fountains,
  Ever welling and new, plash amid fragrance from beds.
Church-bells ring; every stroke hangs still in the quivering half-light
  And the watchman calls out, mindful, no less, of the hour.
Now a breeze rises too and ruffles the crests of the coppice,
  Look, and in secret our globe's shadowy image, the moon,
Slowly is rising too; and Night, the fantastical, comes now
  Full of stars and, I think, little concerned about us,
Night, the astonishing, there, the stranger to all that is human,
  Over the mountain-tops mournful and gleaming draws on.

5 With yellow pears the land
  And full of wild roses
  Hangs down into the lake,
  You lovely swans,
  And drunk with kisses
  You dip your heads
  Into the hallowed, the sober water.

But oh, where shall I find
When winter comes, the flowers, and where
The sunshine
And shade of the earth?
The walls loom
Speechless and cold, in the wind
Weathercocks clatter.

BIBLIOGRAPHY

MICHAEL HAMBURGER, "Hölderlin" in *Reason and Energy* (London 1957) 11–70.

MICHAEL HAMBURGER, *Hölderlin: Poems and Fragments* (London 1966).

ULRICH HÄUSSERMANN, *Friedrich Hölderlin* in Selbstzeugnissen und Bilddokumenten (Hamburg 1961).

MARTIN HEIDEGGER, *Erläuterungen zu Hölderlins Dichtung* (Frankfurt a. M. 1944).

RONALD PEACOCK, *Hölderlin* (London 1938)

ALESSANDRO PELLEGRINI, *Friedrich Hölderlin. Sein Bild in der Forschung* (Berlin 1965) original Italian, 1956.

LAWRENCE RYAN, *Friedrich Hölderlin* (Stuttgart 1962).

PETER, SZONDI, *Hölderlin-Studien. Mit einem Traktat über philologische Erkenntnis* (Frankfurt a. M. 1967).

E. T. A. Hoffmann: a self-portrait.

a. die Nase.
b. die Stirn
c. die Augen
d. Dallashsche Beafsteek
   u. Portwein
e. der Ironische Zug oder
   die Mährchen Muskel
f. das lange Kinn. misfrathe-
   ne Schauspiele (Blandina etc)
g. Neuaptirte Haare oder
   Geistererscheinungen
h. Ein Halstuch
i. Ein Kragen
k. Ein Rokaermel mit
   willkührlichen Falten
l. Der Backenbart oder
   übernächtige Gedanken
   eines Mondsüchtigen
m. die Mephistophelesmusk
   oder Rachgier u. Mordlust
   _ Elixiere des Teufels.
n. fehlt.
o. Das Ohr oder Kreislers
   Lehrbrief der weder ge-
   hört noch verstanden word.
p Und so weiter

The Romantics

Brown University

THE BROTHERS SCHLEGEL

"The French Revolution, Fichte's *Wissenschaftslehre*, and Goethe's *Meister* are the greatest trends of the age." When Friedrich Schlegel made this famous observation in 1798[1] it was not especially perspicacious to identify the eruption of a social, economic, and political revolution as the beginning of a new era, but to call attention to two books of which the clamorous public took little notice and to suggest that these books were to play a still greater role was a bold and original diagnosis (of which the same public took even less notice, of course), Schlegel was expressing his personal enthusiasm for Fichte whose lectures on philosophy he had heard in Jena. But he was also aware of the tremendous significance this philosophy was to have on the young writers, especially Novalis, selections of whose work were also printed in the *Athenaeum*. Fichte's moral philosophy, which argued that the material world was the creation of the ego (*das Ich*) which had to posit its field of action (*das Nicht-Ich*), was to be interpreted aesthetically as the logical and systematic justification of the sovereignty and autonomy of the (romantic) creative imagination.[2] Goethe's novel, *Wilhelm Meisters Lehrjahre* (*Wilhelm Meister's Apprenticeship*,

Karl S. Weimar received his B. A., M. A., and Ph. D. from the University of Pennsylvania. He has taught at the Universities of Delaware, Illinois, Pennsylvania, California at Berkeley, and Rhode Island; he is now at Brown University where he is Chairman of the Department of German. He is author of articles on Stehr, Hauptmann, Thomas Mann, Celan, the modern drama, several textbooks, and translations of German poetry.

1795) signified to Schlegel the first modern romantic work and in the same section of the *Athenaeum* he published an essay on *Meister* which offered his ecstatic tribute. The Goethe novel seems to have realized his own theories of *romantische Poesie*, *Romanpoesie* (poetry of the romance, that is, the novel), and the *Roman* for they are really synonymous concepts for Schlegel. He identified in the novel, or perhaps he in part discovered and in part invented, the essential elements of the romantic work. Briefly they are: the harmony of dissonances, an organic force that informs the whole, romantic songs that reveal poetry to be the natural language and music of *schöne Seelen*, irony, apparent capriciousness, the poetry of poetry, totality, and a sense of infinity.[3] Some of these are rather nebulous, but others are the very same elements which Schlegel had specified, in the celebrated Fragment 116, as the quintessential characteristics of romantic poetry. "Romantic poetry is a progressive universal poetry"; that is to say, in *Meister* it embraces all of life (totality), not just theatre and poetry but the human drama, all the arts, and the art of living. It is progressive in that it constantly changes and develops ("ist noch im Werden"); it is open, and infinite, and free. Thus it recognizes as its first law the poet's caprice (*Willkür*). In *Meister*, however, this caprice is structurally ordered. It is also, though the word itself does not appear in the Fragment, ironic for it mixes and interfuses alternatingly poetry and prose, inspiration and criticism, and the subjective and the objective modes. In *Meister* irony is in the smile of the author's detached stance which actually serves to emphasize his serious intent; it illuminates the contrast between the ideal and reality and the juxtaposition of the prosaic and the poetic. And then romantic poetry reunites all the genres, a feat possible of course only in the novel (or the music drama, a la Wagner, as it turned out). It is interesting to note that in the *Meister* essay the relationship of romanticism to classicism is obliquely implied, for the natural language of the *schöne Seelen* (the ideal, model classical human beings, such as Goethe's Iphigenia) is manifest as music, that is to say, as romantic song. Schlegel's own romantic theories were not initially anti-classical, for they represented an extension and revaluation of his early Hellenism (after all, the magazine was called *Athenaeum*). Two final observations may be in order pertinent to Schlegel's theories and his discoveries: analagous to the progression from spontaneous inspiration to critical consciousness which characterizes the actual creation of a work of literature is not only the reader's experience of involved interest as a result of the work's appeal to his feelings and of detached critical examination as the result of its summons to reflection, but also the critic's progression from empathy to insights, as Schlegel demonstrates by his own example. One should also savor the irony in the fact that the essay does not literally celebrate Goethe's *Meister* as a "romantic" novel (only three times does the adjective appear, twice in respect to Mignon, and once in respect to Nathalie and Therese!) which only proves that this criticism is really itself poetry, for as Schlegel informs us the poetry of poetry (that is Goethe on Hamlet in *Meister*, or Schlegel on Goethe) "knows more than it says and intends more than it knows." And furthermore how delightfully ironic that while he was praising *Meister* in print he was privately attacking it and aspiring to displace it with his own novel *Lucinde*!

Friedrich Schlegel (1772–1829) was a unique phenomenon in some ways and a prototypical romantic in others. His early studies of Greek poetry, very much in the tradition of Winckelmann, emphasized the organic evolution and decline of classical poetry, but Schlegel soon distinguished something anti-thetical to this controlled and harmonious art, namely the open, progressive, universal quality of modern (that is, romantic) poetry. His recognition of the primitive, orgiastic aspect of Greek art and civilization pointed beyond Winckel-mann's formulation of "quiet grandeur and noble simplicity" to Nietzsche's dionysian dissonance. His very catholic interests and critical apprehension (to cite a further example, *Über die Sprache und Weisheit der Indier*, *On the Language and Wisdom of India*, 1808) make him one of the first and most important critics of world literature and one of the earliest practitioners of comparative literature. His disregard for bourgeois convention and his rhapsodic hymn to romantic love and union found expression in *Lucinde* (1799); he married the model for the heroine, Dorothea Mendelssohn Veit, daughter of the Jewish philosopher Moses Mendelssohn, who had separated from her banker husband, in 1804 and together they were converted to Roman Catholicism four years later.

The earliest germination of romanticism in Germany is characterised by the kind of empathetic criticism, aphoristic reflections, and fragmentary insights which appeared in the pages of *Athenaeum* (1798–99). It evolved out of an attempt to find some kind of synthesis of the ideas and ideals of Storm and Stress and of Classicism. Its full flowering is in the novels, *Märchen*, novelle, and poetry of Novalis, Brentano, E. T. A. Hoffmann, Tieck, and Eichendorff. Another aspect is expressed in the patriotic pamphlets, songs, and dramas provoked by the struggle against the foreign invader: Fichte's *Reden an die deutsche Nation* (*Addresses to the German Nation*, 1807–8), E. M. Arndt's *Katechismus für den deutschen Kriegs- und Wehrmann* (*Catachism for the German Soldier*, 1813), F. L. Jahn's *Deutsches Volkstum* (*German National Identity*, 1810), K. T. Körner's poems *Leyer und Schwerdt* (*Lyre and Sword*, 1814), Kleist's furious play *Die Hermannsschlacht* (*Arminius' Victory*, 1818), and his idealistic drama *Prinz Friedrich von Homburg* (1810). The Napoleonic challenge also fertilized the interest in national lore: Arnim and Brentano's collection of folk songs *Des Knaben Wunderhorn* (1805f.), Görres' selections of chapbooks *Die Teutschen Volksbücher* (1807), Jakob and Wilhelm Grimm's *Fairy Tales*, *Kinder- und Hausmärchen* (1812f.). In their rediscovery of the Middle Ages, Catholicism, German legends and folksongs, and the German mystics the romantics established continuity again with their own native tradition.

Schlegel's characterization of romantic poetry has itself many of the values and many of the perils of poetry; it is intuitive and immediate, it is suggestive, evocative, and metaphorical. Postromantic critics and scholars have looked more extensively and objectively to answer the question: What is romanticism? Arthur O. Lovejoy has argued that "romanticism" has so many and such incongruous and opposed meanings that it, by itself, means nothing; he endeavored to show that "the 'romanticism' of one country may have little in common with that of another, that there is, in fact, a plurality of Romanticisms, of possibly quite distinct thought-complexes."[4] René Wellek, on the other hand, argues more persuasively for "a unity of theories, philosophies, and style, and that these, in turn, form a coherent group of ideas each of which implicates the other."[5] He succinctly reviews the history of the term, from the popular usage, to mean romance-like, extravagant, absurd, etc., to its use in criticism and literary history in France, England, and then Germany. It is clear that romanticism is more pervasive and more completely victorious in Germany than elsewhere, for in England it was subject to the indigenous reasonableness of the English spirit and mind and in France to the indigenous rationalism of the French. Pointing specifically to Germany Wellek identifies three central criteria as typical of the unity of European romanticism: a view of poetry as knowledge of the deepest reality, of nature as a living whole, and of poetry as primarily myth and symbolism.[6] The extension of the term from the merely historical to the typological was the contribution of the Schlegel brothers, and especially of August Wilhelm who developed and disseminated the typological distinction in his famous *Lectures on Dramatic Art and Literature* in Berlin (1801–1804) and in Vienna (1808–1809). The Schlegels revised Schiller's antithetical pair "naive and sentimental" to classical and romantic, but emphasized the distinction between the literature of pagan antiquity and that of the Christian modern; in this broader sense romantic literature embraced Dante, Shakespeare, Calderon, Cervantes, and Goethe. Friedrich Schlegel's ideal was the synthesis of the two antithetical aesthetics, the antique and the modern, the classical and the romantic; he tried to mediate between two antagonistic powers within the creative impulse, enthusiasm and skeptical irony; and he knew that conscious irony was the modern bridge across the antinomies of art and the polarity of art and life. Novalis was the first of the contemporaries to consider himself a romantic. For Goethe, as for a number of English poets, romanticism was only a phase through which he had passed, as is testified by his wry remark: "Klassisch ist das Gesunde, romantisch das Kranke."[7] By 1833 Heine considered it proper for the last romantic to comment retrospectively in his *Romantische Schule* on the Schlegels, Goethe, Tieck, Görres, Novalis, Hoffmann, Brentano, Arnim, Z. Werner, Fouqué, Eichendorff, and Uhland. He caustically characterizes the romantic school as "nothing other than the revival of the poetry of the Middle Ages" and bitterly observes that the little romanticists triumphed with the fall of the great Napoleon, thus signalling the victory of "die volkstümlich germanisch christlich romantische Schule" and the "neu-deutsch-religiös-patriotische Kunst." He strikes a more positive note, however, when he contrasts the romantic concern for the infinite with the classical concern for the finite, a formula which Fritz Strich later developed to a compelling thesis in his monumental study *Deutsche Klassik und Romantik oder Vollendung und Unendlichkeit* (*German Classicism and Romanticism or Consummation and Infinity*, 1922). Recent critics have seen in romanticism not only a regeneration of art but a manifestation of a pervasive cultural crisis,[8] "a decisive watershed in the history of mankind."[9]

One other aspect of romanticism merits mention here, the splendid achievement in translating works from world literature: A. W. Schlegel's translations of Calderon, his selections from Italian, Spanish, and Portuguese poetry, Tieck's translation of *Don Quixote*, and Rückert's renderings from the Sanskrit, Hebrew, and Persian. Let one sample illustrate how skillfully the sense and the sound of a well-known passage from *Hamlet* have been recaptured:

> Sein oder Nichtsein, das ist hier die Frage:
> Ob's edler im Gemüt, die Pfeil' und Schleudern
> Des wütenden Geschicks erdulden, oder,
> Sich waffnend gegen eine See von Plagen,
> Durch Widerstand sie enden? Sterben—schlafen—
> Nichts weiter!—und zu wissen, dass ein Schlaf
> Das Herzweh und die tausend Stösse endet,
> Die unsers Fleisches Erbteil—'s ist ein Ziel,
> Aufs innigste zu wünschen. Sterben—schlafen—
> Schlafen! Vielleicht auch träumen!—Ja, da liegt's:
> Was in dem Schlaf für Träume kommen mögen,
> Wenn wir den Drang des Ird'schen abgeschüttelt,
> Das zwingt uns still zu stehn . . . (III, 1)[10]

Goethe's *Meister* was a *Künstlerroman*, a novel with the focus on the artist hero. That this type of figure had a peculiar fascination for the romantics is yet another resonance of the *Geniekult* of Hamann, Herder, and the Stormers and Stressers. Again and again they were attracted to the talented outsider, the painter, musician, poet, or master craftsman, to his peculiar stresses and distresses, his inspiration as blessing and curse, divine and demonic, his contempt for life and his yearning for it, his fulfillment or his despair and destruction. Some of the more significant works of this type are Wackenroder's *Herzensergiessungen eines Kunstliebenden Klosterbruders* (*The Heart's Effusions of an Artloving Monk*, 1796), Tieck's *Franz Sternbalds Wanderungen* (*The Travels of Franz Sternbald*, 1798), F. Schlegel's *Lucinde* (1799), Brentano's *Godwi* (1801), Novalis' *Heinrich von Ofterdingen* (1802), the anonymous *Nachtwachen des Bonaventura* (1804), Eichendorff's *Ahnung und Gegenwart* (*Presentiment and Pre-*

sent, 1815), and E. T. A. Hoffmann's *Kater Murr* (*Tomcat Murr*, 1820). This romantic legacy is still manifest in the works of such disparate writers as Keller, T. Mann, H. Stehr, and H. Hesse.

NOVALIS

The romantic par excellence is Friedrich von Hardenberg (1772–1801), or Novalis as he chose to call himself after the intriguing name he found in the family annals. A number of extraordinary experiences and factors combined to shape the man and the poet. He was born in Saxony, not far from Martin Luther's birthplace (Eisleben) in the Eastern foothills of the Harz mountains, the second of eleven children of whom only two outlived their parents. He grew up in a pietistic family atmosphere, an apparently normal child, until a severe illness seems to have transformed him. The young man was greatly stimulated in the household of a talented and aristocratic uncle; as a student in Jena he came under the influence of Schiller, whose person inspired his poetic aspirations but whose advice dissuaded him; in Leipzig he became attached to Friedrich Schlegel; at the age of twenty-two he was an efficient and dutiful official. At this time he met and immediately fell in love with Sophie von Kühn, who was not yet thirteen. They were engaged but their happiness was brief for in less than two and a half years Sophie died. Novalis' letters and notebooks record the profound and shattering effect her death had upon him. At her grave he experienced "radiant moments of enthusiasm" that united them again; his magic ego leaped over space and time to be with her. He felt compelled to will his own death. His experience of love, death, and religion as one inseparable reality is the prototype of the *Liebestod*, which is consummately realized in Wagner's music-drama *Tristan und Isolde* (text, 1857; completed opera, 1859). Novalis transformed this experience into the strangely beautiful poetry of the *Hymnen an die Nacht* (*Hymns to the Night*, 1800) and *Geistliche Lieder* (*Religious Songs*, 1802); it became the inspiration and formative force of his novel *Heinrich von Ofterdingen* and the fairytale *Die Lehrlinge zu Sais* (*The Apprentices in Sais*), both published in 1802, incomplete. But Novalis did not will his own death. The realization of the meaning of Christ's sacrificial death and the study of the natural sciences drew him back to life. He pursued courses in geology, mineralogy, physics, and chemistry at a mining college. He fell in love again, and was engaged to the daughter of a mine director; in 1799 he was appointed to an administrative post in the salt mines of the Elector of Saxony and died two years later of consumption and the consequences of a shock following his fourteen-year-old brother's tragic death by drowning, himself not yet twenty-nine. He considered poetry an avocation and sought to bring into harmonious synthesis vocation and avocation, science and art.

His fragments and notebooks contain a bounty of fascinating enigmatic reflections and insights about philosophy and religion, psychology and mysticism, the sciences and the arts. Many remain cryptic mystifications; some reveal the very essence of romantic experience: "My book shall become a scientific bible, a real and ideal model and embryo of all books; For Sophie I have religion—not love. Absolute love, independent of the heart, grounded in belief is religion; true mathematics is the proper element of the magician. In music it must take the form of revelation, of creative idealism. Pure mathematics is religion; The ideal of perfect health is merely scientifically interesting. Sickness belongs to individualisation; Every sickness is a musical problem, the cure a musical resolution; The world must be romanticized. Only thus can one rediscover its original meaning. Romanticization is nothing other than qualitative potentialization . . . By giving the vulgar a lofty sense and the commonplace a mysterious aspect, the familiar the dignity of the unknown and the finite an infinite extension I romanticize them. This operation is reversed for the sublime, the unknown, the mystical, the infinite—these are turned into logarithms by means of the correlation—they find expression in familiar terms; We dream of journies through the universe, but isn't the universe within us? The innermost realms of our spirit we do not know.—The mysterious road leads into our own interior world. Within us or nowhere else is eternity with its worlds, the past and the future. The world without is a world of shadows, it throws its shadows into the world of light within." These observations, even more clearly than his poetry and prose works, are reflections of the influence of the thought of the three "romantic philosophers," Fichte, Schelling, and Schleiermacher.[11] Novalis' magic ego is a poetic expression of Fichte's idealism (the ego projecting the nonego); his belief that all roads lead back into the observer's own spirit parallels Schelling's nature philosophy of identity (nature is the visible spirit, spirit is invisible nature), and his equating of love and religion a counterpart to Schleiermacher's theology (religion is not a matter of ethics nor of metaphysics, but a personal and immediate feeling and sense for the infinite, an almost erotic union with God).

The *Hymns to the Night* are a remarkable and controlled expression of the rapture of a mystical experience; the poetry is such that it sweeps away our disbelief, at least for the time of exposure to it, and attests the authenticity of a magic experience and a profound yearning. The hymns celebrate night, love, death, Christ, and the eternal life in love-death; they fuse and confuse the sensual and the spiritual, the past and the future, prose and verse. In the first hymn the poet turns away from the manifold wonders of light and life to "the holy, ineffable, mysterious night" which sends to him his beloved, the lovely sun of the night: "now I awake—for I am thine and mine—thou hast proclaimed night to be my life—and made me human. Consume my body with the fires of the spirit so that I might ethereally commingle more intensely with thee and that the bridal night might then last forever."[12] The second expresses the wish that sleep may not too infrequently bless the votaries of night, the silent messenger of infinite mysteries. The third is the nucleus of the set for it reveals it was the night which released the poet from grieving loneliness beside his beloved's grave to reunite him in the belief in "the heaven of night and its light, the beloved." In the fourth hymn the poet willingly agrees to serve and revere life, but before the end of time when all shall crumble, he will remain faithful to night, love, Christ, and death. The next and longest hymn recounts man's history from the time when once mankind and the gods shared life's festival but feared death, the remote power of incomprehensible night, to the twilight of the gods when nature was lifeless and man no longer at home on earth, without belief and without imagination, and to the time when the advent of the Virgin's Son and the victory of His love in death restored man to eternal life. The sixth and final hymn is a choral song of longing for eternal life and love in death, the song of man lonely, empty, and despairing in the present who seeks his home in the future to join his bride Jesus in the blessed past.

The epitome of romanticism, the romantic work par excellence, is Novalis' novel *Heinrich von Ofterdingen*. The magnitude of its conception, which is so manifestly beyond execution, the apotheosis of poetry and the poet, and the celebration of the magic triad love, death, and religion are all quintessentially romantic; and equally characteristic is the failure to create complete characters and the inability (perhaps more so than the unwillingness) to exercise full control over form and structure. All this is evident in the signs of a gradual diminution of inspiration and artistry and in the increasing tendency to dissolve characters and language into allegory and abstractions that mark the course of the first part and prefigure the second part of which we have only a single episode, some notations, and a sketchy reconstruction. It is an arresting irony that the completed first part is entitled Expectation and the fragmentary unfinished second part Fulfillment, a testimony to the contention that the romantic prefers travelling hopefully to arriving, and that the romantic work is concerned with *werden* and not *sein*.

The setting is the Middle Ages, the theme the making of a poet. The mysterious blue flower envelops characters and events; it informs the life of the hero and the very substance of the work. Its full meaning can only be apprehended, for it has successfully resisted the most intense analysis. Initially we learn that the tale of a stranger has aroused young Heinrich's fervent desire to behold the flower. Then it appears to Heinrich in a dream and he learns that his father had also seen it in a dream. He associates it with the feeling that he is destined to become a poet. At the end of the first part, after a series of formative encounters and experiences which are symbolized in the petals of the blue flower and which culminate in the identification of his beloved Mathilde's face with the fair face reflected in the cup of the flower, he comes to sense that perhaps it symbolizes the life of the poet and is itself the perfect universal work of art, the ideal of the romantic artist. This part, the Expectation, is concluded with a fairy tale related to Heinrich by Mathilde's father, the poet Klingsohr, and it thus becomes the realization of the emblematic flower. Klingsohr interprets Heinrich's journey and reveals to him that his constant companion has been the spirit of poetry for "in the presence of the poet poetry manifests itself everywhere. The land of poetry, the romantic Orient, has greeted you with its sweet melancholy; war has addressed you in its wild splendor; nature and history have revealed themselves to you in the form of the miner and the hermit." Heinrich can now complete the interpretation for he knows that love and religion in the person of his beloved Mathilde have been the culminating experience. But the fulfillment of Heinrich the poet can only follow, according to Novalis, the encounter with death, and his pilgrimage into the realm of the dead, into Sophie's land, and his reunion with the deceased Mathilde were to be the substance of the second part. He is finally to attain the blue flower and experience magic transformations. Novalis knew that his novel was a repudiation of Goethe's *Meister*, for inasmuch as his hero followed the journey inward to the creative self, to the poetic imagination which transforms the world, in a word, to the life of the poet, he was revoking Meister's decision at the end of the novel to renounce art and to serve society, a critical point which Schlegel had chosen to overlook.

This is a strangely uneven, fascinating novel. Klingsohr's fairy tale which is intended to be the model of the romantic work of art is disconcertingly insubstantial and embarrassingly contrived. It fails to effect what every successful fairy tale must do, to fuse and interfuse both worlds, the fantastic and the real, without forcing the one or the other to sacrifice its own peculiar reality. And yet its very position and function in the novel is so characteristically romantic. The *Märchen* is the natural expression of the romantic mythopoeic power, a power generated by a profound need to create new symbols and signs to give form to a feeling of unity and identification with the non-human world and the at the same time by a conscious effort to overcome personal loneliness. Paradoxically Novalis wrote for the abstract, unreal, cosmic setting of the second part one of the most carefully calculated and technically brilliant of all his poems, the "Chorus of the Dead":

Lobt doch unsre stillen Feste . . . (But sing now the praise of these our silent festivals) which magically gives the dead a majestic affirmative voice enjoining the pale captive living to sing the praise of eternal life in death. And so this poem, and not the *Märchen*, becomes the demonstration of Klingsohr's wise words to Heinrich: Begeisterung ohne Verstand ist unnütz und gefährlich, und der Dichter wird wenig Wunder tun können, wenn er selbst über Wunder erstaunt (Fantasy without reason is useless and dangerous and the poet will be able to work few wonders if he himself is struck with awe). It is no wonder that a recent investigator was prompted to observe of this work: "It does not conform to any previously existing standards of literary composition, either as a novel or as a Märchen, and yet it is filled with the quintessential spirit of romantic idealism and optimism. Absurd, and yet moving, it is perhaps the most beautiful, and (among so many strange books) the strangest, of all the poetic works of German romanticism."[13]

CLEMENS BRENTANO

It was altogether appropiate that after the prologue in Jena, where Fichte and Schelling had aroused the young romantics, and the setting of the stage in Berlin, where Friedrich Schlegel had published the *Athenaeum* and his brother had lectured on romantic literature and art, that the scene should shift to Heidelberg, with its castle ruins and idyllic countryside of river, forest, and mountain. Here in 1805 Arnim and Brentano published their collection of German folksongs *Des Knaben Wunderhorn*; here Görres published his collection of chapbooks, and here too in 1808 the circle founded its own journal, *Zeitung für Einsiedler* (Journal for Hermits). Arnim and Brentano may be faulted for their unscholarly editing (they corrected and improved texts, often willfully) but the collection enjoyed great popularity and exerted an enduring effect on German lyric poetry. It stimulated a keen interest in the national past and provided a standard for the simple direct expression of typical experiences in stereotyped images. There is something unconsciously paradoxical in this pursuit of the "sentimental" mind seeking to revive by recreation the "naive" spirit, a situation which especially with Tieck and then Heine was to lead to a conscious irony in treatment and tone. Arnim was an interesting but minor figure, remembered solely for his incomplete novel on the Reformation (*Die Kronenwächter, The Guardians of the Crown*, 1817) and for his marriage in 1811 to Brentano's sister, Bettina.[14]

Brentano is a writer of extraordinary talent and a lyric poet of the first order (if we are to judge by G. Benn's criterion of six or eight perfect poems). His life was a tragically real version of a second rate romantic novel. He was born on the Rhine in Ehrenbreitstein in 1778; his father was a well-to-do merchant, a native of Tremezzo, his mother was Maximiliane la Roche, who had been one of Goethe's loves in the Werther period; his father a widower and Catholic, his mother not yet eighteen, a Protestant. Happy and spoiled at home but often dispatched to relatives, Brentano lost his mother when he was fifteen. He rebelled against his father's sensible plans, suffered through some desultory studies and finally in the stimulating atmosphere of Karoline Schlegel's salon in Jena when scarcely twenty he realized he was destined to be a poet. He lost his first wife in childbirth, married a sixteen-year-old coquette who effected the wedding with threats of suicide. After his separation from her and another period of restless moving about he fell in love with a clergyman's daughter in Vienna who offered him instead friendship (she bore a remarkable likeness to his favorite sister) and helped him find his way back to the Church. He foreswore profane writing and lent his time and talent to charitable purposes. He recorded and poetized the visions of a stigmatized nun at whose bedside he had spent more than four years. He died a penitent pilgrim in 1842.

This troubled and hectic life finds expression in the instability and eccentricity of moods, in extravagant flights of fantasy, and in sudden reverses of attitudes from sensuality to spirituality, from gaiety to melancholy, from childlike simplicity to sophisticated irony which characterize his work. Of his quantitatively modest production, the early novel run wild *Godwi* and the late religious books, two dramas, a dozen *Märchen*, a few stories, a long incomplete verse epic, and some two hundred lyrics, at least two prose works and a half a dozen lyrics number among the finest achievements of the romantics. *Godwi* is still of considerable interest, especially to the reader of today, for its shifting narrative techniques and perspectives; it included some of his best lyric inventions (among them "Lore Lay" and "Die lustigen Musikanten"). The verse epic, *Romanzen vom Rosenkranz* (*Rosary Romances*, posthumously published) is a testimony to Brentano's fantastic technical mastery as well as to his penchant for overly elaborate symbolism.

Die Geschichte vom braven Kasperl und dem schönen Annerl (*The Story of Honorable Kasper and Beautiful Anna*, 1817) is one of the master *Novellen* of German literature; *Gockel und Hinkel* (written in 1816, published posthumously; an enlarged version was published in 1838) is one of the most successful of all *Märchen*. It is both difficult and dangerous to speak of the *Novelle* in generalities and even more so to attempt to postulate a theory of the *Novelle*.[15] Suffice it to say here that the romantic *Novelle* is often a *Märchen*. To say so may not be particularly pertinent to the understanding and appreciation of any single work, but the designations, though somewhat arbitrary, are useful inasmuch as they help to set apart the intentions and technique of writers and the development of the genre. The special nature of the *Märchen* is the creation of an atmosphere in which the distinction between the two worlds, the world of familiar reality and that of inexplicable mystery, recedes and even vanishes. Commonplace events, situations, and lives are juxtaposed and interpenetrated with the unreal, the irrational, and the supernatural and both worlds are accepted and presented as equally real. The narrator is not struck with wonder at the wonders he relates. Beneficent, sinister, and demonic forces intervene; strangeness and mystery prevail. The everyday world becomes unfamiliar, and man estranged (*unbehaust*, without a home, is the current existential designation). Betrayal, or desertion, or loss of faith in the other world is followed by loneliness and punishment. The *Novelle* is more concentrated, more intense; the field of action of the mysterious forces is more often moved into the interior of the characters. The singular, critical event (or events) is generally explicable in terms of the phenomenal social world or of psychology and functions primarily as a catalyst. The event almost always has a special symbolic significance which reflects or suggests the meaning of the whole work. The frame is a traditional hallmark and serves to accentuate the artifice and to allow the narrator a certain objectivity.

The story of Kasper and Anna is a sad and frightening tale of honor, love, justice, and mercy; of robbery and seduction; of portents and fateful circumstances; of death, suicide, and executions. Kasper's grandmother tells his story, recalling how he had been the most industrious and neatest boy in school, but also especially how concerned he had always been with honor. He had earned the reputation of being the most honorable soldier in his lancer squadron. The old woman relates one event which had deeply impressed her grandson. It was the strange story he liked to tell of a French officer who had been forced to follow a royal order to beat a soldier and who then to protest the cruel order had shot himself with the soldier's rifle. The honorable sacrifice effected a rescinding of the order. Because his father and step-brother had ridiculed both the story and Kasper he had come to her for comfort, but had not heeded her reverent admonition: honor God alone! Kasper's story ends with his suicide, for he had been dishonored by his own family. He had been set upon by thieves on his way home and then pursued them only to discover that it was his own father and brother. Holding to honor and justice rather than to love and mercy he turned them over to the authorities and in disgrace shot himself.

Here are the ideal materials for a *Novelle*, but Brentano weaves yet another story into this web, that of Anna, which he developed from one of the ballads in the *Wunderhorn* ("Joseph, lieber Joseph, was hast du gedacht"). He relates the two tales by the simple device of making the grandmother Anna's godmother and Anna Kasper's beloved. A thematic parallel binds them more skillfully for both Kasper and Anna are victims of an exaggerated, false concept of honor. The consummate artistry of the work, however, is the technique of the telling. The grandmother tells the story to the narrator who, in the frame as the work opens, reports that he was concerned to find a woman of eighty-eight on a doorstep so late at night. She explains her presence with the tale of Kasper and Anna; she has come with his wreath to comfort Anna on the morning of her execution. She involves the narrator by requesting him to present a petition to the duke, not for a pardon but for an honorable burial for the two lovers. The narration then passes from the grandmother to the narrator himself, from a rambling account of events recollected, some remote, some recent, often interrupted by digressions and reflections (all beautifully apposite to the eighty-eight year old woman) to a spare almost breathless report of actions as they actually transpire; in a word, from the past to the immediate present. The narrative time had ranged from the childhood of Kasper and Anna to Kasper's suicide that very morning; the narrated time the few hours from midnight to just before daybreak. The denouement is swift and full of suspense as the narrator becomes an active participant. The time can hardly be more than an hour. The narrator leaves the grandmother at the prison, hurries to the duke's palace, frantically gains his hearing despite the guard, rides desperately back with the pardon, only to see the executioner's sword decapitate Anna. The scene quickly changes to the following evening when he attends the honorable burial of Kasper and Anna and witnesses the grandmother's passing at the end of the ceremony. In the exciting closing moments we learn the identity of the man who had wronged Anna and how in remorse he had taken his own life.

In the concluding paragraph another subtle transfer of technique removes the narrator and lends the story a legendary quality. By means of impersonal constructions (man sagt, man will), the subjunctive mood, the future tense, and the modal of supposition and destiny ("das Monument soll . . . errichtet . . . werden; die Idee soll . . . erfunden sein") the time dimension is again shifted. The seducer's sister will be spared a fate like Anna's; the memorial monument at the grave of Kasper and Anna represents false and true honor and symbolically brings stern justice and gentle mercy into balance and concord. It will stand as a benediction, a visible reminder and fulfillment of the blessing the old woman had so piously wished.

The motif of honor, which is implicit in the title (*brav* means good, obedient, upright, brave), shapes the story in manifold gradations and variations. It becomes a superhuman force which determines, in full or in part, the several fates. Kasper is the most honorable of men, but he maintains such honor in all his relations that he sacrifices to it the lives of others and ultimately his own. His father and step-brother have too little honor and ironically dishonor Kasper. Poor Anna, driven to desperation by an overwhelming sense of loss of honor, had suffocated her illegitimate baby and then out of false honor refused a pardon rather than divulge the father's name. Count Grossinger, the father of Anna's child, ironically shields the duke's assignation with the Count's sister and counters the narrator's entreaty in a matter of life and death with the sharp rejoinder that the order not to disturb the duke is a matter of his own honor as a soldier and hence more important. The terrible tragedy awakens the duke's sense of honor and the story ends with the report that he will make the count's sister his wife. Twice Brentano records the impact of the word honor on the narrators of the story. The old grandmother shudders to hear Kasper say that his honor depends upon the return of the stolen horse, for she knows the harsh judgement that awaits him in heaven. And then the narrator despairs to hear the count speak of honor while he is actually preventing him from seeking mercy for Anna.

Especially effective is the way Brentano takes a few simple objects, like a sword, an apron, and a veil, and makes them function both as things in themselves and as symbols which signify the very sense of the story. The fate of Anna is prefigured in an incident that took place when she was only three. The grandmother relates that the child was attracted once to a cupboard in the house of the village executioner—he was also famous for the healing herbs he had—because of a sound she heard like that of a mouse. When the cupboard was opened the executioner's sword was seen swinging to and fro. The executioner's dark warning of some great misfortune is dismissed as superstition. But the next day the head of a murderer rolls from the executioner's sword towards Anna and the teeth clamp upon her skirt. The grandmother covers the hideous head with her apron and following the counsel of the preacher brings her up in the fear of the Lord to save her from Satan's snares. But in vain. Now the teeth and apron take on sexual connotations, for Anna yields to a seducer and suffocates the child in the same apron. It must, of course, be kept in mind that these improbable events are related by the old grandmother and signify for her the ineluctable fate which determines human lives. But the veil is found by the narrator, a writer, who on his way to the duke to seek a pardon for Anna takes it as a favorable sign. The duke snatches it from his hand and dispatching the count to stay the execution bids him wave the veil as a standard of mercy. The count recognizes the fragrance of roses in the veil and identifies it as his sister's. Both sword and veil are then frozen into stone on the monument to represent justice and mercy. These symbols all recur and so also serve as leitmotifs.

The pervading leitmotif, however, is the song of the Last Judgment, which encompasses all the themes and gives them a lyrical voice. Just as the person of the grandmother brings together all the single strands of the story, so her song relates fate and judgment, love, death, and mercy to a higher and more lasting order than human society, an order which, at least to the grandmother, lends to the cruel and terrifying, one is almost tempted to say absurd, events a meaningful context. She sings it for the first time after Kasper's suicide, on the same steps of the house where seventy years earlier singing the same song she had received a rose from the grenadier who was to become her husband. And at the close of the story it echoes on in the narrator's mind, now a sustained prayer of farewell, after Anna's execution and the grandmother's death. Because of its theme and the suspense and tension that characterize it Brentano's dramatic *Novelle* has often been referred to as a parallel phenomenon to the fate tragedies, that peculiar sub-genre which was so popular at the time; but it has greater depth and more perfect form than Kleist's feverish *Familie Schroffenstein* (1803), for example, or Z. Werner's melodramatic *Der 24. Februar* (1810), or Grillparzer's rather stilted *Die Ahnfrau* (*The Ancestress*, 1817), or Platen's labored parody *Die verhängnisvolle Gabel* (*The Fateful Fork*, 1826).

Gockel und Hinkel is an altogether different work. The tale has the simplicity and the charm that is the very essence of the *Märchen*. Author and reader share confidences and credulousness, for so disarming is the tone of the author's jocose belief that the reader is hardly aware of his own unconscious suspension of disbelief. The benign, gay way that the good and the wise are rewarded, the good but foolish converted, and the wicked punished is the comforting demonstration that God is in His heaven and all is right with the world. The story abounds in whimsy and wit; the prose is unpretentious and lyrical; the many songs are much more than decorative arabesques for they narrate events, project moods, and sing the sense of the story. The most delightful and significant of these is the chorus of mice beseeching God's protection and aid in the perilous adventure of regaining the magic ring for their benefactors and earning the reward of tasty tidbits for themselves:

> Kein Tierlein ist auf Erden
> Dir, lieber Gott, zu klein,
> Du liesst sie alle werden,
> Und alle sind sie dein.
>> Zu dir, zu dir
>> Ruft Mensch und Tier.
>> Der Vogel dir singt,
>> Das Fischlein dir springt,
>> Die Biene dir brummt,
>> Der Käfer dir summt.
>> Auch pfeifet dir das Mäuslein klein:
>> Herr Gott, du sollst gelobet sein!...
> Behüt uns vor der Falle.
> Und vor dem süssen Gift.
> Und vor der Katzen Kralle,
> Die gar unfehlbar trifft!
>> Zu dir, zu dir...[16]

The plot is uncomplicated, the structure simple and straight-forward, and the characters, whether human or animal, protagonist or antagonist, ingenuously stereotyped. Brentano adopts such popular themes as the magic ring and the mouse kingdom and grafts them on to his main motif of the rooster and all he represents. A kind of family heirloom, Alektryo the rooster, and the hen Gallina are all that is left to the old, impoverished, unemployed but honest and industrious Count Gockel von Hanau, his wife Frau Hinkel von Hennegau, and their little daughter, Gackeleia. But because of his various virtues and especially his affection for the faithful rooster, Gockel finally learns that Alektryo has preserved hidden in his throat the magic ring, which then comes into his possession only because Alektryo sacrifices his life to reward his master. In the delightful, facetiously pretentious and rhetorical funeral oration Gockel hails the rooster as a noble, useful, sublime creature, one who watches in the dark of night and proclaims to man the light of day, who warns and wakes man, comforts him and protects him, a prophet, a champion, a model pater familias, justly celebrated and revered in myth and history, art and philosophy. From the ashes (he had specified cremation) Alektryo rises phoenix-like and at the close of the story in the beautifully restored chapel of the castle, in accordance with the wishes of Gockel and Hinkel, he is brought back to life by the transformation of a mechanical figure of a golden cock that resembles the faithful

Alektryo. The most exciting adventure after the rooster's sacrifice is the loss and recapture of the ring. In this latter matter the mouse-prince and mouse-princess, who are still grateful for Gockel's friendly aid once before, assist. Gackeleia, as a result of her experience, for it is she who foolishly traded the ring for a doll but then bravely liberated the mouse-princess from the doll, grows up psychologically and physically and marries the prince in the chapel immediately following the resurrection of the rooster.

This kind of story depends so much on the writer's ability to create an atmosphere in which all things, the natural and supernatural, can be viewed afresh, with child-like simplicity and curiosity. This can be effected by involving the reader (who is really considered to be a listener, for the narrator-listener relationship is much more intimate and conducive to the sharing of experience) and by disarming him through gentle humor. The *Märchen* opens this way: "In Deutschland in einem wilden Wald lebte ein altes Männchen, und das hiess Gockel. Gockel hatte ein Weib, und das hiess Hinkel. Gockel und Hinkel hatten ein Töchterchen, und das hiess Gackeleia. Ihre Wohnung war in einem alten Schloss, woran nichts auszusetzen war, denn es war nichts darin, aber viel einzusetzen, nämlich Tür und Tor und Fenster."[17] The short, simple sentences, repetition patterns, alliteration, diminutives, comic inventions (here, the names[18]), and word play are characteristic of the style in general. The closing is an ideal illustration of the *Märchen* technique, the way in which the narrator unobtrusively appears to vouch for the authenticity of the tale: "Oh," said Gackeleia (now the bride, responding to the groom's reminder it is her turn to make a wish), "everything is so splendid and everybody so happy, what else could anyone wish, except that we all were children and the whole story a fairy tale, and that Alektryo were to tell us the story, and that it made us so happy we all clapped our hands for joy." And then Alektryo gobbled up the ring and in the very next moment all were changed into happy handsome children and all the children were sitting around the rooster listening to him tell the story: "and they all clapped their hands so hard that mine still burn, for I was there too, otherwise I would never have heard the story."

Brentano is also one of the half dozen or so great lyric poets in the German language (among them Gryphius, Goethe, Hölderlin, Heine, Mörike, Hofmannsthal, and Rilke). It is curious that he never collected and published his lyrics as poems; almost without exception they appeared in his novel *Godwi*, or in the stories and *Märchen*, or in the plays, or the opera libretto (*Die lustigen Musikanten*). The range of subject is thus somewhat limited and the complete comprehension of a text may frequently depend upon the context, yet the technical virtuosity and the intensity of experience are often combined to produce lyrics of unique beauty. The technical virtuosity, on the one hand, is exercised in the simplicity and restraint of the folksong and, on the other, in the almost pure music of tone-poems. It seems to oscillate between the one extreme of mere verbal legerdemain and the other of sheer magical musicality.

The vibrant intensity of experience finds expression in love poems, cries of psychological and spiritual anxiety (an admirable example is *Frühlingsschrei eines Knechtes aus der Tiefe*), and the songs of religious passion.

The ballad of *Lore Lay* is Brentano's invention and he tells the story with economy of description, direct dialogue, pace, and detachment. There are no subtleties, no irony, and no complicated perspective as in Heine's famous version. It is not the fatal allure of song, but her physical beauty that attracts and destroys. Brentano is concerned with her psychological, existential situation and her desperate desire for mercy and salvation. The rhythm is regular, the rhymes simple, often imperfect (*gross, Schloss; jähe, Höhe*) and with older forms (*gerühret, verführet; gehet, stehet*). Lore Lay is a sorceress, "so schön und feine" that no man can resist her beauty. But her lover has deceived her and abandoned her. She can love no more and so she seeks release from a life that means death for others and begs for God's mercy and pardon. However the bishop before whom she appears is bewitched by her beauty and is unable to condemn her; he has three knights escort her to a convent to prepare herself for the final journey. She requests they allow her one last look at the Rhine and her lover's castle from the lofty rocky cliff above the river. She spies a boatman far below and chooses him to be her lover in death. She plunges down into the river. A Boatman sang the song and from the rock of the three knights there always echoes: Lore Lay, Lore Lay, Lore Lay—"as if there were three of me." The fate of Lore Lay and the knights who were to take her away from life strikes a mysterious echo in the poet's heart. Despite the context (ironically it is sung by the chaste Violette who is in love with Godwi who in turn is having an affair with her mother), one may possibly read into the final line a camouflaged identification on the part of the poet with the tragic situation.[19]

Several of the most characteristic romantic themes coalesce in the splendid poem *Nachklänge Beethovenscher Musik* (*Echoes of Beethoven's Music*, 1814). Brentano celebrates here the artist and his art, patriotism, and liberation. One aspect of what seems to be the romantic obsession with art and the artist is the predilection for the *Künstlerroman*, already mentioned; the most seductive expression of this obsession is a work of philosophy, Schopenhauer's *Die Welt als Wille und Vorstellung* (*The World as Will and Idea*, 1819). This symphony of pessimism presents man as a tragic prisoner of the supra-personal will and the artist as the saint of suffering, for he of all men is most consciously aware of the painful predicament. But he is also the saviour of mankind, for his art offers man one of the few possible escapes from the tyranny of the will. This apotheosis of art culminates in the typically romantic affirmation of music as the supreme art above all the other arts. Analogous to this philosophic argument is the romantic poet's constant preoccupation with sounds (forest murmurs, splashing fountains, singing birds, the posthorn, etc.), the tendency, especially with Brentano, Eichendorff, and Heine, of the poem to become pure song, and the irresistible attraction of romantic poetry for composers (there are almost five thousand published settings to Heine's poetry alone!). Romantic writers felt a deep affinity with musicians and composers; among the most notable tributes are Grillparzer's to Beethoven, Heine's to Paganini, Rossini, and others, and Mörike's to Mozart; of E. T. A. Hoffmann we will speak later. Brentano probably heard Beethoven's "Battle" Symphony (op. 91) in Vienna in the winter of 1813–14. It is not at all surprising that he should have shared Beethoven's enthusiasm for Wellington's victory over the Napoleonic armies in Spain (at Vittoria, June 21, 1813). He did not take up arms against the invader like Körner, Görres, Arnim, and Eichendorff, and his response to the events of the day was as late as it was politically ineffective. The patriotic or political aspect of this particular poem is clearly vicarious and secondary. It was inspired by the composer's glorious work (professional musicians feel differently) and it celebrates the act of creation. It is a work of art about a work of art and not political verse. Only the last two parts commemorate Wellington's military victory, and even the final part hails Beethoven whose harmonies lifted the chariots above the bloody battle fields and assuaged the pain in the music of reconciliation. It is Beethoven's music which immortalizes Wellington's victory and so the poem ends with the hymnic apostrophe: "Wellington, victory! Beethoven, glory!"

The first three parts, and these are the only parts that usually appear in editions and anthologies, hail the inspiration, the mission, and the creative act itself which make the artist. The imagery is bold; the rhythms and rhymes subtly and appositely structured. The first part is a hymn to loneliness and to the eternally divine. Loneliness is a well of the spirit, mother of all sacred springs, a magic mirror of interior suns. Its magic dark waves engulf the singer and the bright astral choirs of his soul begin to resound to the divine beat. His rapture and pain and melancholy take on cosmic dimensions which signify a humble recognition of inner resources, of the omnipotence of his aspiration and the poverty of his earthly existence. This romantic expansion is an upward and outward movement which is a striking contrast to the later inward usurpation of Hopkins' in-scapes and Rilke's *Weltinnenraum*. This mighty inspiration makes the singer mindful of the futility of all things save only the divine. This first part is a masterful demonstration of the consonance of sound and sense. The first rhymes are nouns which relate the images of loneliness (*Geisterbronnen, innrer Sonnen, Wonnen*; the spirit's well, the interior suns, the rapture) and then the rhyme words become verbs signalling the transformation from passive inspiration to dynamic creativity (*mich überronnen, ich begonnen*; overwhelm me, I began [to sing]). This series of alternating rhymes (the first ten lines) terminates with a couplet precisely in tune with a grammatical pause and this couplet is a concentrate of the sense of the whole part: a noun (*Seele*, the singer's soul) is rhymed with a verb (*zähle*, a divinity beats the time). This part ends with a fascinating interlocking of alternating rhymes (*meines Innern*, my inner resources, and *mich erinnern*, remind me [of Thee]; the parallel constructions *Vor der Armut meines Lebens* and *Vor der Allmacht meines Strebens,* [in humble recognition] of the poverty of my life [and] of the omnipotence of my aspiration, rhyme with the final line: "Alles andre ist vergebens" ("all else is futile").

The second part has a central metaphor, that of the statue of Memnon, which when struck by the morning rays of the sun was said to have produced musical sounds. The singer, finding a firm foundation in earthly life and towering like a giant, is this mythical statue, ringing and resounding when seized by the divine inspiration. Its alternating rhymes end again with a couplet. The third part likens the singer-poet to a god, hovering above the winds and tides of time, creating the world which he himself is, lonely and servant to none. The meter of the first part is the dignified trochaic tetrameter, then expanded in part two to pentameter, and in part three to free verse.

A number of Brentano's lyrics seem to be almost pure music, where associations and relationships are suggested by phonic correlatives, or where we might be inclined to say today: the message is the music. A striking illustration is the lyric: "Was reif in diesen Zeilen steht, Was lächelnd winkt und sinnend fleht . . ." ("What is ripe and ready in these lines, What beckons with a smile and beseeches with reflection . . ."; this is, unfortunately, but a poor reproduction) and its hauntingly mysterious closing couplet:

> O Stern und Blume, Geist und Kleid,
> Lieb', Leid und Zeit und Ewigkeit!

Geist, Kleid, Leid, Zeit are all related by the phoneme "ei" to *Ewigkeit*; *Stern* and *Blume* suggest a macrocosm–micrososm parallel, *Geist und Kleid* a contrasting of the abstract and the concrete, and *Liebe*, the only element with no grammatical link, may be the encompassing whole that embraces all the elements.

One last sample to illustrate, among other things, Brentano's effective use of synaesthesia, a favorite romantic technique (Keats was a master practitioner) of confusing and blending sensory impressions:

> Hör', es klagt die Flöte wieder,
> Und die kühlen Brunnen rauschen.
> 3.　Golden wehn die Töne nieder,
> Stille, stille, lass uns lauschen!
>
> 5.　Holdes Bitten, mild Verlangen,
> Wie es süss zum Herzen spricht!
> 7.　Durch die Nacht, die mich umfangen,
> Blickt zu mir der Töne Licht.[20]

The poem is really a duet from the *Singspiel, Die lustigen Musikanten* (1803), a little opera libretto which Brentano developed; it was dashed off in four days from a fantastically grotesque song bearing the same title that had appeared in *Godwi*.[21] The first two lines and lines five and six are sung by the girl Fabiola; the alternating lines by her blind (!) father. The rhymes bring together the two songs. Both father and daughter (and, of course, the poet himself) possess an acute sensibility: the father experiences the sounds as light (golden tones) and the daughter feels the coolness in the splashing sound of the fountains. The duet ends with the bold *der Töne Licht* (the light of the sounds) and this rhymes with *spricht*, which is a manifestation of the daughter's sentient receptivity to the plaintive voice of flute and fountain.

The premiere of an opera to the text by Brentano, score by E. T. A. Hoffmann and conducted by Hoffmann, was held on April 6, 1805, in Warsaw. Neither text nor music deserves the neglect that has been its fate.

E. T. A. HOFFMANN

Hoffmann also wrote an opera to Fouque's fairy tale *Undine* (1811), a typically romantic tale of the water-sprite Undine who gains a soul through the love of a knight, but who must return to the realm of the *Elementargeister* (the spirits of nature) when he proves unfaithful. It enjoyed considerable popular success at the time (1816) but was not revived. Shortly before his death, six years later, Hoffmann turned again to the score with plans to rewrite certain parts.

Much of Hoffmann's life was devoted to music; he was a music teacher, a critic, conductor, and composer. A number of his characters are musicians in whom he often speaks and suffers; in many of his stories, music plays a mysterious, decisive role. Several of his first publications which had appeared in the *Allgemeine musikalische Zeitung* (1809f) he collected along with some other pieces under the title *Fantasiestücke in Callots Manier* (1814–15).[22] The conductor Johannes Kreisler dominates the collection giving it a special tone and dimension. He is Hoffmann's other self, the delicately unbalanced, precariously poised artist, at one moment seized by a fierce creative frenzy, in the next despondently destroying his work, full of melodies and dissonances, possessed by the deity and the demon, eccentric perhaps to the point of madness. Among his rambling effusions are such insights as these: "There are moments, particularly when I have been reading intensely in the works of the great Sebastian Bach, when the numerical relationships of music, especially the mystical rules of counterpoint, make me shudder. Music! with mysterious awe, indeed with terror I speak your name"; "Haydn captures the human element in mortal life romantically; he is more commensurable, more comprehensible for most listeners. Mozart addresses more the superhuman, the wondrous, which resides in the inmost spirit. Beethoven's music releases fear, awe, terror, pain, and arouses that infinite longing which is the essence of romanticism." And this same Kreisler appears again to be the protagonist of the incomplete novel *Lebensansichten des Katers Murr* (*Tomcat Murr's Views of Life*, 1819–21). Offenbach was attracted to these fantastic stories of Hoffmann and for his opera *Tales of Hoffmann* (first produced posthumously by the Opéra-Comique in 1881) adapted four stories, one from the *Fantastic Pieces* (the story of a courtesan who for a flashing diamond steals Hoffmann's reflection), another based on *The Sandman* from *Night Pieces* (about a mechanical doll and magic spectacles), and one from *The Serapion Brethern* (about the daughter of Councillor Krespel—a kindred spirit to Kreisler—who perishes when lured by an evil genius to pour out her heart in song). More recently Hindemith was drawn to the tragic story of the schizophrenic goldsmith in *Das Fräulein von Scuderi* for his opera *Cardillac* (1926).

Ernst Theodor Wilhelm Hoffmann (1776–1822) (he replaced the Wilhelm with Amadeus, an outward sign of his esteem for Mozart), was born in Königsberg, on the Baltic and the borderland between German and Slav, an East Prussian like the three progenitors of romanticism in Germany, Hamann, Herder, and Kant. Hoffmann was one of those rare multiple personalities, not only a composer and conductor but also a caricaturist, theatre-director, and lawyer. He carried out his daytime duties efficiently and even bravely, showing great courage in 1820 when he championed the individual's right before the law in a famous case involving the fanatic Jahn, founder of the *Turnverein* movement. But he was even more brilliant at night, circulating vicious caricatures of his superiors and entertaining his friends with lusty drinking and fantastic storytelling. Hoffmann is the masterful story teller who skillfully spins fairy tales, tales of the occult and of horror, featuring automatons and *Doppelgänger* (mysterious doubles or counterparts), and a bold explorer of the borderlands between the conscious and the unconscious levels of existence, of dreams and supernatural phenomena. Superficially he seems to be the "heir to all preceding romantic gambits of the strange and horrific variety,"[23] but he knows how to transform the impossible into the improbable and to fix an anchor in reality, to plumb the complexes of the psyche and to probe the crisis of identity. He exerted a tremendous influence on writers of the nineteenth century, especially on Nerval, Baudelaire, Poe, and Dostoevsky. If it were possible to single out two stories as the best of his work they would probably be the *Märchen, Der goldene Topf* (*The Golden Pot*, in the *Fantastic Pieces*, 1814) and the *Novelle, Das Fräulein von Scuderi* (*Mlle. de Scudery*, in *The Serapion Brethren*, 1819).

The Golden Pot is the story of the transformation of a rather ordinary student into a poet and of the forces that aid him and oppose him. We are transported magically from the familiar to the fantastic, from the real to the mythical, from Dresden to Atlantis, from the finite to infinity. The hero, Anselmus, is seduced away from the commonplace world of studies, friends, and sweetheart to the mysteriously musical and beautiful world of crystal bells, green serpents, and salamanders, and finally to the eternal bliss of love and poetry. And what is the bridge between these two worlds? What makes it possible to move from the one to the other? The magic moment is a musical moment, the first sound of the serpents' song, accompanied by a rippling and a rustling, a lisping whispering like the tinkle of crystal bells: "Da wurde, er wusste selbst nicht wie, das Gelispel und Geflüster und Geklingel zu leisen halbverwehten Worten: Zwischendurch—zwischenein—zwischen Zweigen, zwischen schwellenden Blüten, schwingen, schlängeln, schlingen wir uns—Schwesterlein—Schwesterlein, schwinge dich im Schimmer—schnell, schnell herauf—herab—Abendsonne schiesst Strahlen, zischelt der Abendwind . . ." Words, yes, but neither the sense nor the image is meaningful here. The alliterative sibilants and the assonance function as music and communicate no more and no less than music. It is because Anselmus can listen and surrender to the sounds that he can understand the song. This in turn awakens in him some longing, some vision of the distant wondrous land to which, having cast away the burden of the commonplace, he can courageously soar, and because he can love the serpent and believe in the wonders of nature and in his own existence amid these wonders the spell is broken and Serpentina becomes his. But there is a moment when he can no longer believe and almost loses all. However the archivist-salamander, Serpentina's father, and the forces of light rout the old apple-vendor-witch who has come to drag him off to a bourgeois marriage, and he is liberated from the crystal prison of doubt. But now the story-teller Hoffmann falters, he cannot find the words to describe the bliss of Anselmus and Serpentina and the beauty of their newly found homeland. At this point the archivist intervenes and prepares a magic potion for Hoffmann which inspires him to finish the story. One final irony—Anselmus ascends to eternal bliss in love and poetry and harmony with all things while his creator sits fast in his attic room in Dresden, his mind preoccupied with the wretched trivialities of everyday life and his vision impaired; this irony is mollified by the comforting words of the archivist that close the fairy tale: "Do not lament so! Weren't you yourself just now in Atlantis and haven't you at least a nice little farm there too to be a poetical possession of your inmost self? And is the happiness of Anselmus really anything other than living in poetry, to which life the sacred harmony of all things is revealed as the deepest secret of nature?"

Thus Hoffmann illustrates beautifully what Shelley so eloquently claimed for poetry: "It makes us the inhabitants of a world to which the familiar world is a chaos. It reproduces the common Universe of which we are portions and percipients, and it purges from our inward sight the film of familiarity which obscures from us the wonder of our being. It compels us to feel that which we perceive, and to imagine that which we know. It creates anew the universe." (*Defence of Poetry*, in *Complete Works* VII, 137.)

Anselmus learns the secret of nature and understands the manifold voices of nature. But how does his creator communicate this? He practices his mythopoeic powers and fashions the myth of origins, harmony, discord, exile, curse, and salvation.[24] Suffice it to mention here that Serpentina's father, the archivist is also a salamander (a creature of light and fire), a remote offspring of Prince Phosphoros, exiled for an indiscretion and punished, for his three daughters must remain serpents until redeemed by young men like Anselmus, capable of belief beyond reason and love without doubt. The reward for such sensibility and capability is the golden pot, nature's dowry, whose polished shining surface reflects the true image of its beholder and which contains a fire-lily, symbolic of the perfect original harmony between man and nature. But there is still another dimension to the Golden Pot for the story of the Golden Pot is itself symbolically a Golden Pot; it is the poetry of poetry, as Schlegel put it; it is itself a revelation of the secret of nature, an artistic manifestation of poetic irony. The concluding episode which brings the archivist-salamander into lively contact with the narrator Hoffmann is an instance of "transcendental buffoonery" which, again according to Schlegel, pulsates in those works informed by the breath of irony.[25] It should, however, also be noted that despite Hoffmann's ridicule of the comfortable materialistic biedermeier life he does allow Veronica, Anselmus' first love before he knows he is unfit for this world, to find happiness in marriage to a man of position and status.

Hoffmann's later stories reduce the centrality of the supernatural and the fantastic and concern themselves more with the human problem. The theme of the engrossing *Novelle*, *Das Fräulein von Scuderi* is the martyrdom of the artist. Cardillac, the master goldsmith, is both a good father and a master craftsman, but he is a victim of a demonic power within him which compels him to murder in order to repossess the beautiful works of his own hand. His agony is to be aware of the curse and to seek deliverance from it. He sends an "offering" to the virtuous Mlle. de Scudery hoping to find a saviour in her. The story is firmly anchored in history, in the dark time of the rule of the Sun King Louis XIV, when Paris was terrorized by cruel street murders and a mysterious fatal poison that left no trace. Superficially it is a gripping, suspenseful story of crime and the detection of crime, of an innocent culprit and an amatuer detective. In this sense the title is appropriate for it is Mlle. de Scudery's legal skill and humanity which establish the innocence of the apparent culprit and help unravel the mystery. But Hindemith is also right in seeing the real protagonist in Cardillac, the tormented, sick artist, destroyed by the demonic aspect of his genius, a murderer and yet beyond good and evil for he is neither apprehended nor subjected to civil justice. Ironically, Mlle. de Scudery is a noble human being, but the inferior artist.[26]

The most ingenious and ironic of Hoffmann's inventions is the incomplete novel which juxtaposes the pretentious views of life of the Tomcat Murr with the inner biography of Kreisler. The life and loves of the *Bildungsphilister* who aspires to culture and the elegant life, but who finds in the adventure of love only boredom and hangover and whose diligent studies produce only insipid rhyming and rank plagiarism are arranged to alternate with the rapture and the torment of the inspired musician who must renounce love and life and bear the curse and the blessing of the artist, a destiny which at times imperils the man with madness. The scattered thoughts and interrupted narrative is skillfully ordered to simulate caprice, in the manner of Schlegel's famous definition. The structure is a study in counterpoint, blending burlesque and romance, bathos and tragedy, punctuated with intriguing ritardandos and accelerandos, suspended notes and delayed chords.

LUDWIG TIECK

In his contentious and ambiguous survey of the Romantic School Heine makes some perceptive observations on Ludwig Tieck (1773–1853). He refers to him as "the best writer of novelle (*Novellist*) in Germany," and "nevertheless still a great poet (*Dichter*)." If one remembers that this judgment was pronounced in 1836 at which time Kleist and Hoffmann are dead, Brentano had renounced secular writing, Stifter, Keller, and Storm have not yet published, and only Eichendorff appears as a contender—and his conservative, Catholic stance could hardly be expected to evoke sympathy in Heine—one is inclined to agree. The qualifying "nevertheless" in the second statement is a warning signal. It is preceded by a remark about the peculiar mesalliance of reason and fantasy in Tieck's work and followed by an ironic observation about a certain deficiency: in all his writings there is manifested no authentic originality (*keine Selbstständigkeit*). "His first period (*Manier*) shows him as nothing at all, his second as a faithful shieldbearer of the Schlegels, and his third as an imitator of Goethe." As so often with Heine, we are treated to a witty exaggeration which nonetheless is much more than a half truth.

The tripartite division of Tieck's work is viable. A number of his early works appeared in the journal of the arch*Aufklärer* C. F. Nicolai. They reflect typical Storm and Stress characteristics with fixation on the cult of the individual and on all kinds of horrific excesses, at the same time they are burdened with the moralizing tendency of the Enlightenment. The epistolary novel *Geschichte des Herrn William Lovell* (1795–96) is still an eighteenth century work in the shadow of Richardson. The Tieck of the second period initiated much of the typical situations and apparatuses of the *Schauerromantik* (the Gothic) and the gambits of the *Kunstmärchen*, this highly conscious and stylized reconstruction of old popular stories. The three volumes of the *Volksmärchen*, a masquerade intended to fool no one, appeared in 1796 and included treatments of the well-known chap-book figure the fair Magelone, and the familiar Bluebeard and Puss in Boots from Perrault's fairy tales. Tieck succeeded in capturing and popularizing two characteristic romantic attitudes epitomized in two magic formulas of his own making: the melancholy loneliness which overcomes the spirit in tune with nature, especially the sense of the mysterious and the sinister in the atmosphere of the dark wild woods evoked in the single word *Waldeinsamkeit* (forest loneliness), and the yearning to escape into the idyllic garden aspect of nature and into the remote glamorous past of legend and fairy tale expressed in the lines:

> Mondbeglänzte Zaubernacht,
> Die den Sinn gefangen hält,
> Wundervolle Märchenwelt,
> Steig auf in der alten Pracht![27]

Waldeinsamkeit is the song of a bird and the leitmotif of the finest story in the collection, *Der blonde Eckbert*; the four splendid lines are from the prelude to the play *Kaiser Oktavianus* (1804), an inflated, diffuse, panoramic glorification of medieval Christianity.

Blond Eckbert is an impressive remorseless tale of innocence and involvement, of an implacable fate, trial, defection, guilt, and retribution meted out by sinister, supernatural, inexplicable forces (here, an old woman in black who also takes the form of at least two men to test and then hound the guilty). It is related with masterful economy, suspenseful pace, and alarming objectivity. The fate of blond Eckbert is unfolded directly, in probably less than a year; his wife Bertha's story is told by her in a flashback from childhood to the present, a story within a story. Eckbert is a quiet, retiring, middle-aged knight, living in what appears to be peaceful married happiness, inclined to melancholy but apparently only because the couple is childless. His desire to withhold no secrets from a dear friend involves him, once his wife has told the strange story of her life, in distrust and fear and drives him, he knows not why, to murder Walther, the friend. Now he seeks to unburden himself in confession to another friend and must flee to avoid violence again, especially since he sees Walther's face in the new friend, Hugo. Completely distracted he wanders into an unfamiliar region and imagines encountering Walther again, this time in a farmer who shows him the way. Distraught, he hears the same bird-song Bertha had described and he meets the same old woman in black who reveals to him that she was Walther and Hugo, and that Bertha was his sister. He becomes completely deranged and as he dies he hears again the bird-song. Bertha's story is that of an unhappy childhood and flight from a cruel father into a remote forest haven with the old woman in black. Here she lives happily tending house for the woman, her dog, and the fantastic bird that sings of the joys of forest-solitude and lays precious stones. But when she becomes a woman (she simply states, "when I was fourteen") a romantic restlessness seizes her and she returns to civilization taking with her the bird and the precious stones. She lives comfortably until the bird, that had not sung since the day Bertha had stolen it away, intones a melancholy song: "Forest-solitude, how remote and far away!"

again and again, until Bertha in anguish and fear strangles the bird. She then marries Eckbert. Her repressed fears burst into feverish sickness when Walther speaks the name of the dog, the name she herself had been unable to recall. The same day that Eckbert murdered Walther, Bertha died. *Der blonde Eckbert* is Tieck's invention and his finest work, a strangely powerful story of human helplessness, in guilt and in innocence, exposed to sinister forces from which there seems to be no escape.

Tieck's *Kindermärchen*, *Der gestiefelte Kater* (*Puss in Boots*, 1797) is generally considered an outstanding satirical comedy and it is true that Tieck succeeds in roundly ridiculing both rationalism and philistinism. It is historically significant that he experimented with new techniques, destroying the illusion by making the audience participants in the play, and thus anticipating to some degree the familiar antiillusionary stage and "epic" theatre of the twentieth century, but the satirical thrusts are too often aimed at unworthy and now forgotten targets, the wit too often labored, and save for the tragi-comic ending—the enforced retirement of the author conceding the triumph of base common sense over poetry and fantasy—it all seems rather trivial and superficial. Tieck's failure is not, however, exceptional; the romantic spirit was not inclined, or perhaps able, to meet the rigorous restrictive demands of the drama. In general the romantic emphasis on the supremacy of feeling (which led to a concentration on content at the expense of form), the intense exercise of the free imaginative powers, and the indulgence of subjectivity are all inimical to the shaping of a drama. German and English romantics appear to have been more aware of this than the French, for one of the interesting differences between French romanticism and German and English romanticism is the prominence given to the drama by the French romantics. This in turn is an aspect of a fundamental difference, for the dominance of feeling over reason is demonstrably less in France than in Germany and England.

Tieck's third period reflects the postromantic climate and his personal situation for, as Heine points out, the one-time mocker of the type *Hofrat* (Privy Councillor, member of the establishment) had himself become a Royal Saxon *Hofrat*. Irony and humor characterize this period. *Des Lebens Überfluss* (*Life's Superfluity*, 1839) is the best example of this stage. It has all the so-called ingredients of the *Novelle*: the unusual situation or event, the twist or turning point (*Wendepunkt* was Tieck's own term), the symbolic object, and the *pointe*. An incident that aroused considerable interest in a Berlin suburb involved a young man and his wife who lived in an upper floor apartment. They had sacrificed family and position to have each other; all their possessions, including a rare edition and the manuscript of the young man's book, were gone. They were penniless but happy in each other's love, dwelling in a paradise that shut out the rest of the world, confident that their ardent love would protect them from the cold winter. But when all else failed the young man decided to stop thinking and writing about the superfluities of civilization and sawed up the railings and chopped up the stairs to feed the stove. They needed no other link with prosaic society than the horizontal view across the roof tops. But the owner appears and demands the return of his stairway and threatens to call the police and the military. At just that critical moment a well-to-do old friend arrives and saves the couple. The young man's book is published and does well; his wife is reconciled with her father, and both return three years later to visit their idyllic first abode and to meditate upon the "necessities and super-fluities of life and the secret of life."

The stairway is the focal symbol of the story, but it is seen only from the young romanticist's perspective, and is made just a little bit too obvious. Accordingly, it is a ladder for upstarts, a fool's bridge for boring visitors, an avenue for dishonest publishers who swindle manuscripts from authors, a means for unscrupulous bookdealers to take advantage of hardpressed bibliophiles, and above all a comfortable way for the bourgeois philistine to descend to the height of his mental capacity, an expendable luxury for the writer who is already at the lofty perch of immediate perception. All of this is not only "the authentic humor of anguish," as the wife neatly puts it, it is, as Tieck knows, foolishness; but ironically Tieck presents it as beautiful foolishness and so he rescues the impractical lovers and even has them triumph over the mundane pragmatism of their society. And again Heine is right when he observes that this humorous irony, or ironic humor, is the only haven and escape from the political censors' restrictions, especially sharp in the Germany of the 1830's. Heine himself, of course, demonstrated this even more tellingly in *Atta Troll* and *Deutschland. Ein Wintermärchen*.

JOSEF FREIHERR VON EICHENDORFF

Eichendorff, writing some ten years before the Tieck *Novelle*, sees it all somewhat differently. The life of his good-for-nothing hero (*Aus dem Leben eines Taugenichts*, 1826) is presented as something beautiful but ultimately foolish. To glorify this life of carefree wandering, of revelling in the sounds and sights of nature, trusting the good Lord, idealizing a fair lady, stumbling into bewildering adventures, and fiddling away merrily, and at the same time to view it satirically for its irresponsibility and even sterility, this is the very essence of romantic irony.[28] In wonderfully lyric prose Eichendorff conducts his guileless child of nature through God's wide world, over mountains and rivers, through forests and fields, into moonlit gardens, by splashing fountains, to Vienna and Rome and back home, where he will marry and settle down. To be sure he will never become the dull earth-bound philistine nor would it be easy for him to become the stolid, circumspect, provident citizen of the Biedermeier type, but it is even more unlikely that he will ever again be the lonesome romantic wanderer. However this is no concern of Eichendorff's nor is the plot so very important. This is a story wholly of mood and atmosphere (*Stimmung*). Everything is animated by the lyrical soul, by the sensitivity and sensibility of the hero-narrator. Again and again he breaks into song and the rhythmic prose dissolves into verse:

> Wem Gott will rechte Gunst erweisen,
> Den schickt er in die weite Welt,
> Dem will er seine Wunder weisen
> In Berg und Wald und Strom und Feld.[29]

Eichendorff's poetry has a special lyrical quality; it is not the sensual, subtle musicality of Brentano, but rather the simple clarity of the folk song. It is a tribute to Eichendorff that his well-loved song "In einem kühlen Grunde/Da geht ein Mühlenrad" ("In a cool valley there turns a mill-wheel") is generally thought to be an anonymous folk song. The key is almost always major; even the sad sweet songs eschew the dark, sombre tones. This predominant buoyancy and serenity is the outward sign of Eichendorff's strong religious faith. He is one of the few Christian poets in the nineteenth century, in the narrowest and at the same time loftiest sense of the word. This also lends to many a poem that particular quality of naiveté and profundity, for there is a sincerity and authenticity of expression and experience in Eichendorff's lyrics which is totally devoid of irony. His themes are not many—nature, God in nature, love, freedom and independence, the poet's calling—nor is his versification varied: primarily the folk song stanza of four lines with alternating rhymes, in iambic trimeter or tetrameter. Visual imagery is restricted, almost stereotyped; description is almost always acoustic. Like most romantics Eichendorff prefers morning and night to gaudy day, for bright clarity inhibits the imagination and nature's voices generally fall silent in the daytime; morning, on the other hand, awakens longing and Wanderlust, while night removes barriers and distance and enhances the feeling of oneness with nature and the sense of infinity. Although he celebrates the pure joy of wandering:

> Fahre zu! ich mag nicht fragen,
> Wo die Fahrt zu Ende geht![30]

his strong moral and ethical sense points beyond romanticism to the Biedermeier:

> Da steht im Wald geschrieben
> Ein stilles, ernstes Wort
> Von rechtem Tun und Lieben,
> Und was des Menschen Hort.[31]

Both quotations are from songs in the novel *Ahnung und Gegenwart* (1815) and they are not contradictory, for Eichendorff combines a fresh eagerness for life's journey with an unwavering sense of its deeper meaning. His heroes have a premonition (*Ahnung*) of this and they turn away from the ephemeral favor, the materialism, and the corruption of the world (conditions of his time, *Gegenwart*) to affirm the "quiet grave message writ in nature, to do right and to love, for this is the true human treasure." The remarkable thing is that so captivating is the lyric spell of the best of his work that the obtrusion of the message seldom disturbs.

Josef Freiherr von Eichendorff (1788–1857) never succumbed to some of the eccentric excesses of other romantics. He was born an aristocrat and so he did not have to look back longingly to older times, to a society of seemingly beautiful stratification, and he was a Catholic and thus was saved from the exaggerated piety of many of the converts. He represented what Hofmannsthal at the end of the century was to call the conservative revolution for he sought to preserve the values of a responsible aristocracy and an idealistic patriotism, and he tried to warn against base materialism, malevolent passions, and barbarous violence.

If his *Taugenichts* is a swan song of romanticism his other fine *Novelle, Das Schloss Dürande* (*Dürande Castle*, 1837) is much more than a mere herald of the Biedermeier. Romantic elements are superficial: the setting of the ruined ancestral castle, the forest and hills of the French countryside, mysterious persons, and an apparent *Doppelgänger*. The focus is not upon the girl who sacrifices her life for love, but upon her brother, a hunter, who is oblivious of nature; consumed by distrust, deranged by a fierce compulsion to avenge an imagined wrong against his sister, he mercilessly pursues the putative seducer. The background is the twilight of a social order, an old order that was not without some beauty and dignity. The brief scene at Versailles is a fine touch. Here Louis XIV appears, a sad, pale man: "a gentle breeze touched the tops of the high trees and scattered the last leaves like a golden rain on the princely figures below." This order is eradicated in a savage onslaught led by a madman that ends in murder and self-destruction. Eichendorff presents the decadence and folly of the landed lords but he selects those who are still capable of courage and self-knowledge, of love and remorse. He is not so much concerned with the cruelty and chaos that attend a revolution as he is with the terrible consequences of the eruption of the bestial element in the individual human being. His theme is the ruination of a man undermined and unhinged by suspicion and distrust, perhaps even jealousy. The frustration and anger that follow the thwarting of his attempts to be heard drive him to pursue vengeance in the name of justice. One thinks here of Kleist's Kohlhaas, but the differences are greater than the similarities. Eichendorff's hunter, Renald, is not at all a man of reason and logic, and because the wrong he seeks to right was a delusion, there is no satisfaction, no ultimate triumph, however ironic, of justice. Renald, appalled to learn of the innocence of his sister and the Count Dürande and the magnitude of his own malefactions, checks the insurgents, sets fire to the castle powder tower and perishes in the conflagration.

LOUIS CHARLES
ADELAIDE CHAMISSO

There remains one more famous figure of the time to mention, a variant of the Faust and Wanderer motifs, again a transition figure from romanticism to Biedermeier: Chamisso's *Peter Schlemihl* (1813). The unhappy, unlucky hero sells his worthless shadow to a mysterious man in gray who possesses magic powers in exchange for a bottomless purse and thus hopes to gain status and security in the elegant society of the rich and the powerful. But though his wealth gains him prestige he is ostracized as an outsider, a man without a shadow. He abuses the power of his money to ruin others until he falls in love. But he cannot win her father's approval, though she loves him unquestioningly. The gray man appears and offers to save all, returning the shadow for another insubstantial thing, Schlemihl's soul. In order to save his beloved from a marriage to a scoundrel, to whom her father has pledged her, he is about to sign away his soul but he is overcome and falls into a faint. Even in retrospect he cannot explain the event, unless it be fate, not an external providential fate, but a necessary act according to his own fate, his character with which he later came to learn to reconcile himself.[32] He frees himself from the devil (the man in gray) by casting away the purse, but his penance is to live without love, outside society. It is his fate, then, to come into possession of seven league boots, which he utilizes to roam through the world as a philosopher-naturalist, recording data on topography, climate, flora, and fauna in service to human society. The curse of shadowlessness has been interpreted in numerous ways; philosophically, sexually, socially. It remains an intriguing mystery. There may very well be some precipitate of Chamisso's own predicament in it, the man without a country.

Louis Charles Adelaide Chamisso was born in France in 1781. His family fled the revolution and finally settled in Berlin in 1796. At twenty Chamisso was commissioned in the Prussian Army, but the family returned to France. In 1806 he was in the service against France. But it was not until after he had moved back and forth between the two countries, travelled around the world (1815–18) on a Russian ship on a scientific expedition and finally obtained a post in the Botanical Gardens in Berlin that he really settled in Germany where he died in 1838.

Romanticism was a more or less general European phenomenon that at least in Germany was manifestly predominant for something like three decades, and it was both a reflection of and a part of that elusive but nonetheless real spirit called the *Zeitgeist*. So diverse and unstable are the components of the *Zeitgeist* that no literary style or mode of thought can flourish long—much less one whose essence was *im Werden*—and the more diverse and the more unstable these elements become the shorter the duration of the style or mode. Economic, political, and social changes were rapid and pervasive in the first two decades of the century. Symptomatic of the consequences is the shift in emphasis from the strongly national feeling that inspired the Germans in the Wars of Liberation, as for instance in Fichte's *Addresses to the German Nation* (1807–8), to a more immediate personal concern with human freedom. This shift is expressed, for example, in Heine's oft-quoted remark that he preferred a sword on his coffin because he was a stalwart soldier in the war for the liberation of mankind (1828) and the less often noted characterization of himself as a modern Don Quixote, a Don Quixote in reverse who intends to demolish the remants of knighthood and who sees in the great political dramas of his day (Metternichean reaction and conservatism) only pathetic puppetshows, which wooden performances, however, he intends to smash like the brave Spaniard (1829). The writers of "Young Germany," Ludolf Wienbarg (who coined the designation), Ludwig Börne, Karl Gutzkow, and Heine, represent this disaffection from romanticism in their dedication of their literary talents to the criticism of current political issues and the cause of liberalism and republicanism. The new, grim realism, pessimism, and surrealist technique of Büchner (who was writing in the thirties) is another sign of things to come. The Biedermeier tendencies in Eichendorff and Chamisso come to the fore in Grillparzer and Stifter who condemn romantic excesses and seek psychological and ethical equilibrium and reconciliation with bourgeois society in gentle moderation (Mörike's "holdes Bescheiden"). The post-Kantian philosophy of Hegel and Schopenhauer also signifies a repudiation of romantic ideas, at least insofar as the restoration of the rational as the real and the deposition of the individual are proposed. But despite the inevitable historical eclipse of romanticism its discovery and exploitation of the subconscious realms, its apotheosis of art and the artist, its refinement of irony, its reanimation of the *Volkslied* and the *Märchen* are a living legacy of which modern German writers are still keenly aware.

Baudelaire's observation (1846) "qui dit romanticisme, dit art moderne" was a prophetic utterance the relevance of which extends beyond the French Symbolists and their affinity with German romanticism to many central aspects of the art of the twentieth century: "Undoubtedly all the anarchic individualism, the ebullient imaginativeness and the emotional vehemence of twentieth-century art are already implicit in Romanticism."[33] Even those writers who are rebelling against it bear its stigma, as is implied in Hugo Friedrich's aperçu: "Modernes Dichten ist entromantisierte Romantik."[34]

FOOTNOTES

[1] In the 216th Fragment in the second part of the first volume of the magazine *Athenaeum*, which he and his brother August Wilhelm edited in Berlin.

[2] Schlegel had no idea of Fichte's contribution to modern scientific thought. "It is precisely this characteristic of our scientific knowledge of nature which Fichte noted and singled out. . . . One cannot deduce the theories of science from the facts. Instead, the logic of deduction in scientific method runs in the opposite direction. One deduces the facts from the theory; retaining the theory if its deductive consequences are confirmed by fact, rejecting it if they are not." F. S. C. Northrop, *The Meeting of East and West. An Inquiry Concerning World Understanding*. New York: Macmillan, 1952, p. 204f. A grasp of the fundamentals of German Idealistic Philosophy is essential to the understanding and appreciation of romanticism; I know of no more compact and lucid exposition than Northrop's chapter on Kant, Fichte, and Hegel.

[3] For an extended analysis see Raymond Immerwahr's "Friedrich Schlegel's Essay 'On Goethe's *Meister*'," *Monatshefte*, 49 (Jan. 1957), 1–21.

[4] "On the Discrimination of Romanticisms," *PMLA*, 29 (1924), 229–53; also "The Meaning of Romanticism for the Historian of Ideas," *Journal of the History of Ideas*, 2 (1941), 257–78, and "The Meaning of 'Romantic' in Early German Romanticism," *Essays in the History of Ideas*, Baltimore: Johns Hopkins Press, 1948, 190–206.

[5] P. 129 "The Concept of Romanticism in Literary History" in *Concepts of Criticism*, New Haven: Yale University Press, 1964, 128–98 and "Romanticism Re-examined," ibid. 199–221.

[6] In his summary he puts it slightly differently: "they (recent critics of romanticism) all see the implication of imagination, symbol, myth, and organic nature, and see it as part of the great endeavor to overcome the split between subject and object, the self and the world, the conscious and the unconscious," p. 220. See also Morse Peckham's proposed reconciliation of opposing views: ". . . the revolution in the European mind against thinking in terms of static mechanism and the redirection of the mind to thinking in terms of dynamic organicism." "Toward a Theory of Romanticism," *PMLA*, 66 (March 1951), 5–23.

[7] *Werke*, Jubiläumsausgabe, 38, p. 283.

[8] "une crise de la conscience européene" P. van Tieghem, *Le romantisme dans la littérature européenne*. Paris: A. Michel, 1948, p. 247; a "shift of consciousness" that "cracked the backbone of European thought" Isaiah Berlin, *Some Sources of Romanticism* (1966) quoted by L. R. Furst, p. 27, see below.

[9] Lilian R. Furst, *Romanticism in Perspective*. New York: St. Martin's Press, 1969, p. 286.

[10] by A. W. Schlegel (1798); 17 plays were translated by Schlegel, the rest by Dorothea Tieck (6) and by Count Baudissin (16).

[11] Fichte's *Wissenschaftslehre* (1794); Friedrich Wilhelm Schelling, *Ideen zu einer Philosophie der Natur* (1797); Friedrich Schleiermacher, *Reden über die Religion an die Gebildeten unter ihren Verächtern* (*Addresses on Religion for the Educated Despisers of Religion*, 1799).

[12] The published version, *Athenaeum*, second part of Vol. 3, 1800, printed as prose all but

the rhymed lines (in the fourth and fifth hymns, and all of number six). The manuscript version of the end of this first hymn is somewhat less erotic than the quoted passage.

[13] Ralph Tymms, *German Romantic Literature*. London: Methuen, p. 206.

[14] Although no woman in Germany achieved the prominence of Madame de Staël or George Sand, a number of them played an important role in German romanticism. Mention has already been made of Tieck's daughter who with A. W. Schlegel and Count Baudissin gave us the most famous and successful translation of Shakespeare's plays. In this venture Schlegel was inspired and assisted by his wife Karoline (1763–1809) whose nonconformist life was another of the signs of woman's liberation; she had been arrested as a friend of the dangerous liberal J. G. Forster (world traveler and world citizen); she later divorced Schlegel and married Schelling. Her forthright letters are a valuable source of information on the cultural and social life of the time. Dorothea Schlegel (1763–1839), though less talented, led an equally emancipated life. She was the daughter of the Jewish rationalist philosopher Moses Mendelssohn, was separated from her first husband, a banker, lived with Friedrich Schlegel some time before the marriage in 1804, and was officially converted to Catholicism with him in 1808. She published a translation of M. de Staël's novel *Corinne* and a novel of her own. One of the most influential salons of the time was presided over by Rahel Levin von Varnhagen (1771–1833) in Berlin where the young Heine was introduced to and received by a social and intellectual elite the like of which he was never to experience again.

[15] See E. K. Bennett, *A History of the German Novelle from Goethe to Thomas Mann*. Cambridge: University Press, 1938, and (ed.) B. v. Wiese, *Die deutsche Novelle von Goethe bis Kafka. Interpretationen*. Düsseldorf: A. Bagel, 1959.

[16]

No animal's too small,
Good Lord, on earth for Thee;
They're Thine, each one and all,
Thou mad'st them here to be.
 Thee they entreat,
 Both man and beast.
 The birds give Thee song,
 The fish to Thee throng,
 The bees give Thee hum,
 The lady bugs strum.
 The littlest mouse's voice is raised:
 Good Lord! Thy name be praised!
Protect us from the trap's jaws
And from the poison's kiss.
Protect us from the cat's paws
That never never miss!
 Thee they entreat . . .

—K. S. Weimar, Trans.

[17] "In Germany in a wild part of the woods there lived a little old man and his name was Gockel. Gockel had a wife and her name was Hinkel. Gockel and Hinkel had a little daughter and her name was Gackeleia. They lived in an old castle; they had no fault to find in it because there wasn't anything in it, but much could be found that needed to be put in it, like doors and windows and gates . . ."

[18] Gockel von Hanau (rooster from cock-brook; an inversion of *Auerhahn*, a kind of wild

fowl), Hinkel von Hennegau (henny from henland), Gackeleia (*gackeln*, to cackle; *Ei*, egg), Alektryo (classical allusion; a sentry who was turned into a cock for failing to warn Mars—he was entertaining a lady-friend—of the coming of dawn), King Eifrassius (*Ei*, egg; *fressen*, to eat like an animal), Queen Eilegia (egg-layer), Prince Kronovus (crown-egg); the last three royal personages live in Kastellovo; etc.

[19] A somewhat later version has recently been published and lends some support to this possibility, for the boatman that Lore Lay sees is the bishop coming with cross and standard, and the song is sung by a priest (*C. Brentanos Werke*, ed. W. Frühwald, B. Gajek, and F. Kemp. München: Hanser Verlag, 1968. Vol. I, pp. 115–18 and p. 1052). One of the persistent themes in Brentano's work is the agonizing conflict of sensuality and spirituality, particularly manifest in such poems as "Die Welt war mir zuwider" and "Ich träumte hinab in das dunkle Tal" with its cruel closing spoken by the faithless girl (Truelove) whom the poet has pursued:

> Truelove is poet's fantasy
> And I am your whore.
> Truelove, Truelove is lost forever!

[20]
> Hark, the mournful flute implores us,
> And the chilly fountains glisten.
> Golden notes are wafted towards us:
> Silently, come let us listen.
> Gentle longing, supplication,
> Moves the heart seductively.
> Through the night's soft radiation
> Luminous sounds appear to me.

—K. S. Weimar, Trans.

[21] The refrain of this song is another bit of phonic virtuousity that resists any translation:

> Es sauset und brauset
> Das Tamburin.
> Es rasseln und prasseln
> Die Schellen darin,
> Die Becken hell flimmern
> Von tönenden Schimmern,
> Um Sing und um Sang,
> Um Kling und um Klang
> Schweifen die Pfeifen und greifen ans Herz
> Mit Freud und mit Schmerz.

[22] Callot was a seventeenth century French engraver whose works, especially the grotesque illustrations of commedia dell'arte characters, combine realism and romantic originality.

[23] Ralph Tymms, op. cit. p. 361.

[24] For a detailed examination of this myth, see Kenneth Negus, *E. T. A. Hoffmann's Other World. The Romantic Author and his "New Mythology."* Philadelphia: University of Pennsylvania Press, 1965, pp. 53–66.

[25] Ingrid Strohschneider-Kohrs, "Zur Poetik der deutschen Romantik II: Die romantische Ironie" in *Die Deutsche Romantik*, ed. Hans Steffen: Göttingen: Vandenhoeck & Ruprecht, 1967, p. 80 and 91.

[26] From another perspective Cardillac is seen as a megalomaniac avenging angel correcting the vices of the world, obsessed with demonic virtue; Scudery is the maternal

figure. See Ellis, J. M., "E. T. A. Hoffmann'. 'Das Fräulein von Scuderi'," *Modern Language Review,* 64 (April 1969), 340–50.

[27]
> Moonlit magic night,
> Casting spells beneath your veil;
> Wondrous world of fairy tale,
> Return in all your ancient might!

—K. S. Weimar, Trans.

[28] For a closer look, see D. W. Schumann, "Eichendorff's *Taugenichts* and Romanticism," *German Quarterly,* (November 1936), 141–53.

[29]
> Whom God will grant His special favor
> He sends into the world to roam;
> He lets him of His wonders savor
> In forests, fields, and mountains far from home.

—K. S. Weimar, Trans.

[30]
> Lead on! I do not care to ask
> The journey's final destination.

—K. S. Weimar, Trans.

[31]
> In forest writ in clarity
> A still and sober word:
> to do the right in charity,
> and what is man's true worth.

—K. S. Weimar, Trans.

[32] For an interesting explication, see Ulrich Baumgartner, *Adelbert von Chamissos Peter Schlemihl.* Frauenfeld/Leipzig: Huber & Co., 1944.

[33] L. R. Furst, *Romanticism in Perspective.* New York: St. Martin's Press, 1969, p. 289.

[34] Hugo Friedrich, *Die Struktur der modernen Lyrik.* Hamburg: Rowohlt, 1956, p. 22.

BIBLIOGRAPHY

General

FURST, LILIAN R., *Romanticism in Perspective. A Comparative Study of Aspects of the Romantic Movements in England, France and Germany.* New York: St. Martin's Press, 1969. Illuminating study of "family likenesses" (individualism, imagination, feeling) and divergences (due to different cultural frameworks).

PRAWER, SIEGBERT (ed.), *The Romantic Period in Germany.* New York: Schocken, 1970. Essays on the historical and social background, the word *romantisch*, the novel, the *Märchen*, the *Novelle*, the lyric, the drama, the aphorism, romanticism and the German language, German romanticism and the visual arts, romantic music, and some aspects of German philosophy in the romantic period; especially perceptive and well written are essays on music (Ronald Taylor), the visual arts (W. D. Robson-Scott), the *Märchen* (James Trainer), the novel (Hans Eichner); Prawer's introduction is an exemplary précis.

SCHENK, H. G., *The Mind of the European Romantics. An Essay in Cultural History.* London: Constable, 1966. An ambitious, skillfully devised approach to the comprehensive view; provocative.

STEFFEN, HANS, (ed.), *Die deutsche Romantik.* Göttingen: Vandenhoeck & Ruprecht, 1967. Useful collection of essays on writers (Hölderlin, Tieck, Novalis, Kleist, Brentano, Hoffmann, Eichendorff) and themes (irony, Märchen).

TYMMS, RALPH, *German Romantic Literature.* London: Methuen, 1955. Penetrating and critical; full of felicities; probably the best single examination of German romanticism.

WALZEL, OSKAR, *Deutsche Romantik.* Leipzig: Teubner, 1923. Authoritative, comprehensive, profound, and a bit dated; accents the philosophical and theoretical.

————, *German Romanticism,* trans. Alma E. Lussky. Rather heavy-handed translation, faithful to a fault.

Individual Writers

NOVALIS

HAYWOOD, BRUCE, *Novalis: The Veil of Imagery.* Cambridge: Harvard University Press, 1959.

RITTER, HEINZ, *Der Unbekannte Novalis.* Göttingen: Sachse & Pohl, 1967. Complementary works: Ritter illuminates the biography mirrored by the works; Haywood undertakes a sober hermeneutic interpretation of the poetic works.

BRENTANO

HOFFMANN, WERNER, *Clemens Brentano. Leben und Werk.* Bern: Francke, 1966. A detailed study, with the accent on the man.

E. T. A. HOFFMANN

HEWETT-THAYER, HARVEY, *Hoffmann: Author of the Tales.* Princeton: Princeton University Press, 1948. An excellent introduction; more biography than interpretation.

TIECK

ZEYDEL, EDWIN H., *Ludwig Tieck, The German Romanticist.* Princeton: Princeton University Press, 1935. Thorough, critical examination of individual works.

EICHENDORFF

SEIDLIN, OSKAR, *Versuche über Eichendorff.* Göttingen: Vandenhoeck & Ruprecht, 1965. Nine essays with perceptive analysis of individual works, themes, and techniques.

Wanted! Georg Büchner. 1835.

2493. **Steckbrief.**

Der hierunter signalisirte Georg Büchner, Student der Medizin aus Darmstadt, hat sich der gerichtlichen Untersuchun* seiner indicirten Theilnahme an staatsverrätherischen Handlungen durch die Entfernung aus dem Vaterlande entzogen. Man ersucht deßhalb die öffentlichen Behörden des In= und Auslandes, denselben im Betretungsfalle festnehmen und wohlverwahrt an die unterzeichnete Stelle abliefern zu lassen.

Darmstadt, den 13. Juni 1835.

Der von Großh. Hess. Hofgericht der Provinz Oberhessen bestellte Untersuchungs=Richter, Hofgerichtsrath

Georgi.

Personal=Beschreibung.

Alter: 21 Jahre,
Größe: 6 Schuh, 9 Zoll neuen Hessischen Maaßes,
Haare: blond,
Stirne: sehr gewölbt,
Augenbraunen: blond,
Augen: grau,
Nase: stark,
Mund: klein,
Bart: blond,
Kinn: rund,
Angesicht: oval,
Gesichtsfarbe: frisch,
Statur: kräftig, schlank,
Besondere Kennzeichen: Kurzsichtigkeit.

German Literature in the Age of European Realism

J. P. STERN

University of Cambridge

The present chapter aims at offering a critical account of the period 1830–70. It has seemed proper to extend the ground so as to include the work of Theodor Fontane, the only major European realist on the German scene, and to conclude with an account of Nietzsche's *Die Geburt der Tragödie*, which should throw some light both on Nietzsche's own age and the age to come. I have thought it convenient to consider this literature not chronologically but according to its three major genres—the drama, poetry, and that most characteristic of nineteenth-century literary modes, the narrative prose of novels and *Novellen*. Attempting to give some balance to the chapter as a whole, I am conscious of unwarranted brevities (the fiction and poetry of Theodor Storm);

J. P. Stern took his M. A. and Ph. D. at the University of Cambridge, where he teaches German. He has been a Visiting Professor at the City College of New York, the University of California at Berkeley, the University of Göttingen, the State University of New York at Buffalo and the University of Virginia at Charlottesville. He is a Fellow and tutor of St. John's College, Cambridge, and has held the Cassell and Fulbright awards. He has published articles on such different topics as *The Good Soldier Schweik* and life in the West German Army, and the following books: *Ernst Jünger: a Writer of Our Time*, Cambridge and Yale, 1952; *G. C. Lichtenberg: a Doctrine of Scattered Occasions*, Indiana, 1959, and London, 1964; *Re-Interpretations: Seven Studies in Nineteenth-Century Literature*, London and New York, 1964; *Thomas Mann*, in Columbia Essays on Modern Writers, New York, 1947. He has edited *Arthur Schnitzler: Three Works*, Cambridge, 1966, and translated poems from the Czech and books on Leibnitz and Rilke. Parts of this chapter have appeared in an extended form in *Idylls and Realities*, New York (Frederick Unger) 1971.

of several major omissions (the fiction of Wilhelm Raabe is the most obvious); and of ignoring a great many minor writers whose works raise a number of highly interesting formal and historical problems. Concentrating on the major literary achievements of the time, I have had to abandon any claim to comprehensiveness, encyclopedic or otherwise. The claims of literary history are not at odds with those of literary criticism—indeed, I do not believe that either can do without the other. Nevertheless, it may be well to confess at the outset that my emphasis throughout this chapter has been critical.

The literature of this period is only loosely and at best indirectly related to the major events and crosscurrents of contemporary German history. Nor is this surprising, seeing that it is a literature written by middle-class authors and determined by middle-class values and aspirations, yet written in a political climate in which the middle classes were virtually powerless when it came to ordering any of the large-scale aspects of their lives. Occasionally protests are registered against this state of affairs—in Büchner and Heine, and in the ephemeral writings of *Jung Deutschland*—yet no coherent alternative ethos is formulated.

The early part of the era is dominated by the oppressive regime of Metternich's police state and its imitations among the smaller principalities of what had until recently been parts of the Holy Roman Empire. The opposition to this oppression, articulated by the national-liberal intellectuals, reaches its climax and quick defeat in the Frankfurt Parliament of 1848—a defeat whose shadow lies over the next seventy years of German history. The era ends with the founding of the Second Reich in the Salle de Guerre at Versailles in 1871—the triumph of that improbable combination of three incompatibles: the anachronistic idea of the medieval imperium and Romantic notion of *das Volk*, Prussian bureaucracy, and industrialism.

In terms of economic history (which Karl Marx in 1845 declared to be the only real kind of history) the period under discussion sees the belated beginning and momentous acceleration of the process of industrialization; it is here that the Protestant states of Germany take the lead. Among the circumstances favorable to this development are: a uniquely efficient system of higher technological education; an astute competition modified by state aid, protective tariffs, and cartels; and the lessons learned from the notorious English *Manchesterismus*. The powerful will to catch up with the West manifest in this development is confined to industry and commerce. Political thinking, on the other hand, fails to keep pace. Outmoded institutions must appeal for their sanction either to outmoded values or to coercion of various kinds. Gradual enfranchisement, parliamentary debating chambers, and constitutions, are wrung from the reluctant ruling princelings and heads of states, but these concessions are used lamely and ineffectually; it is in the higher echelons of the civil service that major political and economic decisions are made. The

German *Bürgertum* is exposed to a complex tug of war of ideologies which leaves it paralyzed; the several pressures which the English and French middle classes were able to accommodate over a period of centuries, one after another, the *Bürgertum* has to face all at once. From the right they have to contend with the hostility of a rigidly exclusive aristocracy, to which belongs the higher executive of the civil service. They have to cover their left flank against a proletariat that is growing in numbers by leaps and bounds. Behind them is the sad débâcle of 1848; before them, industrial expansion and economic progress—power to be wielded concretely, in the factory yard and counting house, not through sham parliaments. In this predicament the conception of nationhood emerges as the only point of positive contact with the State. During the Wars of Liberation the German intelligentsia had been strengthened in its patriotism by the example of France, its enemy. The tension between the democratic ideas of the French revolution and German nationalism remains unresolved throughout the subsequent era. In Germany the sequence of French and English—but also of Russian and Austrian—history is reversed; the Reich is founded as a political derivative of "the Nation," itself based upon a common language and literature, not upon a common political past, which is why the Reich has constantly to be defined, why it cannot be taken for granted.

And now the characteristically German situation develops: politics come to be regarded as an unworthy pursuit, undeserving of the attention of intellectuals, whereas literature, and the arts generally, are seen to offer an alternative to political engagement. All this suits the aspiring politician well enough, as is shown in one of Bismarck's early speeches (1867):

> Für Deutschland kann es niemals zweifelhaft sein, dass das, was uns zusammenhält, nicht die äussere polizeiliche Einrichtung ist, sondern die unaufhaltsame und unabsperrbare Gemeinschaft, die sich zwischen allen deutschen Ländern ausgebildet hat in der Wissenschaft, in der Kunst, in der Dichtkunst.[1]

As a definition of what, twenty years before, Karl Marx had called "*die deutsche Misere*," Bismarck's observation could hardly be more accurate. The combination of *Kultur* and police state provides the setting for that most enduring of all the characters on the German political stage, the nonpolitical, that is conservative, *Bürger*.

FRANZ GRILLPARZER

If the political life of Germany, at all events up to the middle of the century, was under the shadow of the defunct Empire, the literary life of the era was no less dominated by the august cultural heritage of Weimar, which Goethe and Schiller had bequeathed to the subsequent generation. Of the three major dramatists of the era—Grillparzer, Hebbel, Büchner—the first thus found himself trammeled by a high poetic convention of verse-drama to which his own Viennese parlance rose awkwardly and with frequent signs of strain. His first play, *Die Ahnfrau* (1817) belongs to the school of "fate tragedies" in the wake of Schiller's *Braut von Messina*; in *Sappho* (1817), which treats of the conflict between the poetess' vatic calling and her sensuous humanity, he follows closely in the footsteps of Goethe's *Torquato Tasso*. But gradually the influence of Weimar wanes, and the alienation to which the characters of Grillparzer's dramas are exposed becomes more radical than anything we find in German classical drama. The trilogy *Das Goldene Vliess* (1821) concentrates in the third part on the fate of Jason's wife, Medea, who is brought to Greece from her native island of Colchis; betrayed by her husband, she reasserts her "barbaric" origins in a monstrous act of infanticide. *König Ottokars Glück und Ende* (1825) draws on the early history of Bohemia (as does *Libussa*, 1848); in the figure of the ruthless and ambitious Bohemian king (reminiscent of Richard III) the themes of personal and political *hubris* are powerfully linked, whereas the peace-loving Rudolf I, founder of the House of Habsburg, offers a not wholly adequate antagonist. In *Ein treuer Diener seines Herrn* (1828) Bancbanus, the Hungarian king's deputy, is involved in a series of intrigues, in the course of which he loses his young wife; this figure of the utterly loyal but ineffectual servant of the state embodies one of Grillparzer's favorite themes, the dilemma between spirituality and worldliness. *Des Meeres und der Liebe Wellen* (1831) reinterprets the Greek tale of Hero and Leander, and again the dramatic interest lies in the fact that Hero is by nature unsuited to her priestly calling (as Medea was to the culture of Greece, and Bancbanus to political office). *Der Traum ein Leben* (1834, based on Calderón's *La Vida es Sueño*), represents a dramatically successful combination of realism and fairytale magic. As in *Ottokar*, the hero is driven by overweening ambition beyond the confines of the life allotted to him; but when disaster threatens, all his adventures are seen to have been but a dream. The comedy *Weh dem, der lügt* (1838), a resounding failure at the Vienna Burgtheater, is the last of Grillparzer's plays to be published in his lifetime; its serious moral theme—"every lie, even the smallest, assails the foundation of the entire human condition"—is not easily accommodated in the play's central comic figure, the scullion-boy Leon. Grillparzer's last three plays were published posthumously in 1872. In the weakest of them, *Die Jüdin von Toledo* (begun in 1824), the young and inexperienced Spanish king neglects the affairs of state, and his frigid English wife, for the young Jewess Rahel; the nobles solve his dilemma by murdering her, and the play closes as the king, beneficiary of his ministers' crime, departs on a holy crusade, leaving the regency in the queen's hands.

Ein Bruderzwist in Habsburg (begun in 1827, all but completed in 1848) mirrors Grillparzer's disillusionment with the popular cause of the Revolution of 1848.

The action centers on the Habsburg Emperor Rudolf II, his brother and successor to the throne, Matthias, and the religious and political turmoil preceding the Thirty Years' War; in addition, the lawlessness of the age is brought home to Rudolf through the misdeeds of his natural son, Don Caesar. From this complex plot the preoccupations of a lifetime emerge with startling clarity. Questions of personal devoutness apart, Grillparzer is an eminently Catholic writer: he sees the world as part of a cosmic order in which man has a fixed station with its divinely predetermined rights and duties; this is the Emperor Rudolf's vision. Ottokar exceeds his rights, Rudolf II falls short of his duties. With this static view of society informing his every action, Rudolf is bound to regard every change—indeed time itself—as disruptive of that order of which he is the appointed guardian. But, being too sensitive and scrupulous to engage in purposeful political action, Rudolf not only fails to come to terms with the new revolutionary demands for religious toleration and for middle-class rights, but also fails to protect and hand over to posterity the old order of things; the chaos that ensues on his brother's accession (Matthias is merely the puppet of his ambitious chancellor, Klesl) marks the total dissolution of the old order. In Grillparzer's last play, *Libussa* (1841), the unwritten matriarchal order of a pastoral community is challenged by men clamoring for the rule of written laws. The new order, symbolized in the foundation of Prague, makes possible a more highly organized civilization; but Libussa, upholder of the old, becomes victim of the change. The tenor is elegiac and prophetic, but the play lacks the tension which makes of *Ein Bruderzwist* one of the few great political tragedies in German.

Grillparzer's dramatic talent is not well served by the iambic pentameters or the high poetic imagery and didactic sententiousness of classical Weimar. His acute sense of the theatre is manifest not in the language of his verse but in a rich and apt use of stage effects, in powerful characterization, and in superb scenic groupings; he thinks not in words, even less in ideas, but in conflicts of characters. The alien influence of Weimar gives way to an indigenous tradition—that of the Viennese baroque drama with its emphasis on concrete, even spectacular stage effects, although the stable Catholic morality of that drama (a morality of stark black-and-white contrasts) is no longer available to him. He too, like his contemporary German dramatists and philosophers, possesses an acute historical consciousness. However, history is for him not a storehouse of wisdom, let alone a "progressive self-realization of Spirit" (as it was for his contemporary Hegel). History is a stage, a setting for changes, and each change is for the worse: a betrayal of ancient pieties, fealties, and pledges, for the sake (again and again) of self-assertion which leads to anarchy. The God-given cosmic order according to which rights and duties are apportioned is always either threatened or already destroyed, and the task of reestablishing that "order" against the anarchy of "time" is both imperative and hopeless. "Change there must be, but woe to him from whom change cometh" might well stand as a motto of most of his plays. Grillparzer's greatness as a dramatist derives from the dignity he is able to bestow on his characters in this predicament, and hence in the compassion their fall evokes in us.

FRIEDRICH HEBBEL

The nineteenth century has been called the Age of Ideologies. The ideological monoliths that dominate Europe are German in origin, obsessively systematic, pessimistic, and antinomian—that is, concerned with a reinterpretation and revaluation of the tenets of traditional morality. This description fits the philosophies of Fichte, Hegel and Schopenhauer, and the drama of Friedrich Hebbel (1813–63). The exact extent of Hebbel's indebtedness to Hegel may be impossible to determine, yet there is some evidence to suggest that he owes to Hegel the overall scheme within which his plays are located and their plots resolved. The personalities that dominate Hebbel's plays—unbending and stern, often inner-directed—are the sort of men that make up the world of Schopenhauer's philosophy; they belong to a world viewed as a product and objectivization of "the Will." Of these embattled tyrants of the Protestant parlor more will be said when we consider their role in contemporary prose fiction. In Hebbel's dramas they are the rulers and thus in a sense the creators of their world. They form the rigid, immovable part of a dialectic of development, and this dialectic is for Hebbel the essence of human history. Their function is to assert themselves and thus the status quo they represent. The protagonists of his plays are inevitably doomed, yet in their suffering and death they become (or at least are said to become) the heralds of a new order. This relentless and fully determined process is what Hebbel has in mind when (in the abstruse and often obscure commentaries on his plays) he speaks of "the Universal Law" and "the Idea" as the sole concern of the great tragedies of all times; when, with a contempt reminiscent of Hegel's, he brushes aside all humbler and less cosmic themes as trivial and arbitrary. Only a cosmically determined "necessity" is tragedy's proper concern, he argues. Now it is true that the requirement of a "necessary" connection between the different parts of tragedy had been important throughout the history of European drama. However, Hebbel's notion of "necessity"—inevitable assertion on one side and inevitable doom on the other—is postulated with a deterministic rigor it has never possessed before.

Obviously, in such an aprioristic scheme there is little room for the display of human freedom. The interests of plot and characterization too are limited, since both are above all the means to a predetermined end. The complex interplay of human motives, the nuances and disharmonies—rather than head-on collisions—of different temperaments are present in these plays as concessions to *vraisemblance* rather than as centers of dramatic interest. The traditional notions of good and evil are revalued in terms of that which does, and that which does not, further the great "historical" process of development. Yet with characters so single-mindedly bent on destroying or being destroyed, that revaluation is apt to seem too easily accomplished.

The quasi-religious, unconditioned nature of this grandiose scheme should now be obvious. The conclusion is at hand that in his dramas Hebbel is struggling with an impossibility: his ultimate aim is to represent "the Absolute" on the stage, no less. His greatest success as a dramatist lies where he is content to intimate the Absolute in a psychological light, presenting it as the object of a character's beliefs. Where he sets out on the impossible task of representing that Absolute in some more direct way, as a transcendental necessity, there rhetoric takes over from drama, and strange incoherences ensue. To say all this is to admit the adventitious nature of the metaphysics, and to suggest that the dramatist gains where the philosopher ceases to press his scheme on him.

But this is not the whole story. We notice in Hebbel's plays an interesting pattern which is only loosely connected with his doubtful cosmic theories. The static part of the dialectic, representing the status quo, is almost invariably played by men, whereas the victims of the process of "historical change" are almost invariably women. This being so, a Freudian interpretation would argue for the derivative and compensatory origin of Hebbel's metaphysical beliefs, and see them as a rationalization of a more fundamental experience, the war of the sexes. And it is in terms of such an interpretation that Hebbel's first play, *Judith* (1842), yields its fullest sense.

The play follows the apocryphal story of Judith and Holofernes fairly closely, but adds a historical meaning and psychological motivation of its own. Its protagonists become the representatives of Jewish monotheism and paganism respectively. In seeking out, yielding to, and eventually killing Holofernes, Judith believes herself to be carrying out God's plan for the Jews—she is freeing His own people from the arbitrary rule of a foreign heathen tyrant. (In this sense the play illustrates what Hebbel regards as one of the "turning points" in the history of mankind.) Judith believes herself to be the vessel of God's will because she alone among all the citizens of Bethulia has the strength of purpose and mind for the task of liberation. She is surrounded by cowards; with Holofernes' forces outside the city gates (Act III, scene xi), the atmosphere of panic among the Jews is comparable, for sheer intensity, with the chorus scenes of ancient tragedy. She alone is the worthy opponent of a Holofernes who, intended as a representative of absolute might, ends up as a caricature of bathos and grandiloquence. (Johann Nestroy, Hebbel's Austrian contemporary, wrote a splendid parody of the play.)

Why then, in carrying out God's will, does Judith fail—what makes the play "a tragedy"? Hebbel's intention, disclosed after the murder of Holofernes in Judith's dialogue with Mirza, her confidante, is clear enough. Not the divine command was her motive (she tells Mirza), not the desire to free her people from the threat of extinction, but personal revenge—". . . *nichts trieb mich, als der Gedanke an mich selbst.*" She has taken revenge (she confesses) for the violation of her womanhood and individuality, to which she submitted from Holofernes before she did the bloody deed. This, in her own view, makes her guilty of *hubris*, even though the Jews acclaim her as their saviour. And in this personally motivated excess she appears to be fulfilling Hebbel's scheme for tragedy: her strength is the cause of both her election and her undoing, yet through her undoing an example is set and a historic change accomplished.

However, another motive runs through the play, making it at once more interesting and more opaque. Judith is introduced to us as a widow, but one whose marriage was not consummated. The words in which she describes the fiasco of her wedding night to Mirza are free from the exclamatoriness which mars most of her other speeches:

> Manasses rief: ich sehe dich so deutlich, wie am Tage, und kam auf mich zu. Auf einmal blieb er stehen; es war, als ob die schwarze Erde eine Hand ausgestreckt und ihn von unten damit gepackt hätte. Mir wards unheimlich; komm, komm, rief ich, und schämte mich gar nicht, dass ichs tat. Ich kann ja nicht, antwortete er dumpf und bleiern, ich kann nicht! . . .[2]

Just as there is no one in the Jewish camp who dares face Holofernes, so there is no one who can assuage her sexual passion; Ephraim, who woos her, is as cowardly as the rest. Her virgin-widowhood is related to her courage and spiritual strength, through it she becomes the vessel of the divine will. And the imagery in which she speaks of Holofernes—

> Ragt ein Riese mit seinem Haupt so hoch in die Wolken hinein, dass ihr ihn nicht erreichen könnt, ei, so werft ihm einen Edelstein vor die Füsse; er wird sich bücken, um ihn aufzuheben, und dann überwältigt ihr ihn leicht.[3]

makes it fairly clear that, consciously or not, she sees in him the means for fulfilling her unassuaged passion. Her encounter with Holofernes (we must conclude) brings her the consummation she failed to find among her own kind. Thus her confession to Mirza is incomplete. To the motive of a divine mission betrayed by personal revenge must now be added her realization that her people's enemy was her lover—and only with this realization is the full complexity and the full tragedy of her situation encompassed.

However, much of this must remain conjecture. Hebbel introduces the erotic motive, he does something to maintain it (Judith speaks of Holofernes in a language that intimates it), but in the moment of disclosure in Act V it remains unexpressed. (Our expectation of an erotic motivation is rather more than fulfilled in Georg Kaiser's *Die jüdische Witwe* [1904–11] where it replaces all other interests.) Did Hebbel fail to see how deeply he had committed the character of his heroine to this motive of erotic fulfillment? Did he think it incompatible with his grand cosmic scheme? We have no means of telling.

Agnes Bernauer (1851) displays more clearly than any other play Hebbel's strange notion of cosmic "morality"—more clearly and more chillingly. Its central conflict involves the complete annihilation of personal interests in the name of political expediency, and the resulting historical "turning point" involves a recasting of traditional morality. The time of the action is the early fifteenth century, the tragic heroine is the daughter of the barber-surgeon of Würzburg. Her only transgression is that, of middle-class origin and "excessively" beautiful, she is married to Albrecht, only son and heir of the ruling Duke of Bavaria, and refuses to agree to the dissolution of her marriage. When the prospect of Albrecht's succession threatens to disrupt the state by civil war, the Duke orders her judicial murder. In the final scene the disrupted "moral" equilibrium is restored by the old Duke who, by abdicating and placing the symbol of reign in his son's hands, forces Albrecht to assent to Agnes's death in the name of a superior *raison d'état*. Thesis (the feudal status quo), antithesis (Agnes's unwitting challenge of the existing order), synthesis (Albrecht's new sense of political responsibility)—all are here set out in a dramatic calculation remarkable above all for its cold inhumanity.

The theme of the war of the sexes yields no valid interpretation of the play. If we think of tragedy as a genre that evokes pity in the spectator (it is hardly a very restrictive definition), then clearly Hebbel's drama is only marginally tragic; his very insistence on the "necessity" of the events leading to Agnes's death impairs this kind of tragic effect. He endows Agnes not only with an absolute devotion to her husband but also with a heedless pride in her sacrifice. This pride of the victim in being chosen by fate for annihilation the philosopher F. W. J. Schelling had singled out as the chief element in modern tragedy. It is an idea of tragedy all too readily available to drama written in German—a language which in the single word *Opfer* obliterates the distinction between "victim" and "sacrifice."

It is as an all but unresisting victim that Agnes faces the conspiracy that will smother her life, and in her passivity there is even an insinuation of compliance with the dastardly act. This passivity is met on the other side of the dramatic equation by a good deal of cold-blooded casuistry, of which the abstruse language of Duke Ernst is typical, as when he describes Agnes as "the purest victim (*das reinste Opfer*) claimed by Necessity in all centuries." And when, finally, he explains this "necessity" to his chancellor, who undertook to arrange the deed—

> Es gibt Dinge, die man wie im Schlaf tun muss. Dies gehört dazu. Das grosse
> Rad ging über sie weg—nun ist sie bei dem, der's dreht.[4]

we seem to be watching an ideological charade.

The deed too easily done; the alternatives too easily disposed of; the reasons too neatly arrayed; the expiation too readily available and consciences too easily cleared—these are the flaws of *Agnes Bernauer*. There is here little occasion for that simple and undivided feeling that tragedies evoke on both sides of the footlights, the feeling of "What a fall was there!"

Maria Magdalene (1843) affords the pleasure of reporting on a masterpiece. It is a play that belongs integrally to the tradition of domestic tragedy— *bürgerliches Trauerspiel*—from Lessing to Gerhart Hauptmann; it enriches this tradition by single-mindedly exploiting the social world to which it is confined. (The play, incidentally, is ill served by its author's theoretical introduction, in which excellent insights are buried under an extravagant syntax.)

The major flaws of Hebbel's dramas, we have seen, can be traced back to his ever-repeated attempts at conveying "the Absolute" on the stage. This he hopes to achieve by invoking historical and hence dramatic "necessity." The practice of establishing necessary (rather than arbitrary) connections between the individual parts of a play has its origin in Aristotle. Drama, for Aristotle, is the purposeful imitation of an action, and necessity is one of the means of making the imitation convincing. In Hebbel's more rigorous scheme it leads to excessively calculated dramatic structures, occasionally to melodrama and lifelessness—to a feeling in the spectator that the dramatic ends are so much more than achieved. Now, this necessity is certainly present in *Maria Magdalene*; indeed, the play owes to it its taut structure and economy of dramatic means. But, unlike elsewhere in Hebbel's large dramatic *oeuvre*, the social and personal determinism which motivates the action is not imposed from the outside. It does not take its origin in a cosmic ideology, nor do its conclusions appear to contribute to it—necessity is in the very air surrounding the characters. It is an objective social condition, yet implanted (as Hegel would say) in the most intimate subjectivity of their souls. Thus the setting of the play merges with story, form with content, social pressure with moral responsibility, yet not completely: there is no "synthesis," facile or otherwise.

The play's setting and theme is that "terrible constriction in one-sidedness" and social bigotry characteristic of life among the petite bourgeoisie of mid-nineteenth century Europe. From this constriction, and the social conformity it exacts, no one is wholly free—it informs the characters and impels the action of all the protagonists. This is the concrete social circumstance in which their imaginations are imprisoned and their lives all but completely determined; it merges with and dominates their moral qualities. For all we know from the Preface to the play, this lethal constriction and conformism may well be the "Universal Law" under its temporal aspect, "the very age and body of the Time his form and pressure." However that may be, to the drama itself the invoking of an Eternal Law behind the social conflict is irrelevant; the Absolute is mercifully inessential where the temporal is not.

Seduction and the dread of illegitimacy are the traditional motifs of German middle-class drama; here they are set in a small-town environment, at once narrow, inward-turned, and ferocious. The coffin-maker Meister Anton, tyrannical father of Klara (the seduced girl), is the representative of this ethos of conformity and moral uprightness. As a tradesman he is rigidly honest, as a citizen he is unbendingly class-conscious, as an artisan he sees in hard work (but not, incidentally, in money, the product of work) the only hallmark of morality. And the severity and self-determination of the man are at their most patent in his relationship with his daughter, whose dishonor he suspects long before it is confirmed. Hounded from scornful seducer to reluctant childhood friend, Klara anticipates by her own death Meister Anton's threat of suicide. Yet what makes the conflict between them so poignant is that it is based on a sense of values common to both.

Nineteenth-century German literature is not rich in the variety of women it depicts. Klara belongs to its most characteristic type, the Gretchen figure. The only escape she knows from the world that encompasses her is the escape into death. Her journey leads from fear to despair and ends in frenzy, and her various attempts to avoid her fate constitute the main line of the action. Yet her fate is in no sense imposed from the outside. Each step, including the initial seduction, is taken in strict accordance with her character, and her character is that of a dutiful daughter who must expiate her single lapse from virtue. She is incapable of a life outside the family circle and its taboos. Much the same is true of her childhood friend, who, in the crucial moment when he is faced with the fact of her pregnancy, falls back on the conventional judgment. When, a short while later, he recovers his love for her, it is too late: his brief moment of hesitation proves fatal. The strength he has gained leads him to revenge her death by killing her seducer, but it leads to no new life. Only Klara's brother, suspected of theft, pilloried, and at last proved innocent, makes an escape of sorts.

Obloquy is the hostile deity that rules this world. The morality that informs Meister Anton's every reaction is not "inner-directed." Nor is his attitude determined by care for his family. These are certainly important motifs in the play, but both his moral righteousness and his family relationship are subordinated to his anxious concern for a good name. Nor is this a genuinely social care—he cares for the collective only in order to protect himself against it: the foundation of his tyranny, like the foundation of his pew-renter's piety, is fear.

Meister Anton's is a hybrid morality. To his family he applies judgments derived from the small-town social collective (he judges his son guilty and suspects his daughter's loss of innocence on the strength of rumors and suspicion only). Yet the morality by which the collective is ruled is as arbitrary and subjective as the morality of any *paterfamilias* of Kafka's stories. This is the German *bürgerlich* ethos as Karl Marx and Engels depicted it in

The German Ideology of 1844–45: Hebbel's *Maria Magdalene* is its finest dramatic emblem.

JOHANN NESTROY

Are those sad monoliths *à la* Meister Anton a sport of the dour Protestant North? It is a curious fact that Austrian literature has few if any of them. The Austrian experience does not seem to include this character type, or at all events to take him seriously. Parody and farce are an essential part of the repertoire of the Viennese popular theatre—the only popular stage in all Europe with an unbroken tradition of three centuries, from the Baroque to the end of the Austrian Empire.

But then, parody is built into the linguistic situation of Austrian literature, which is what makes it so unsuitable for export. We must leave aside the vexed question of whether the Austrians are or are not Germans, the answer to which has in the recent past depended on unemployment statistics and the state of the Austrian currency rather than on high cultural considerations. Do they have a language of their own? It is difficult to think of another body of literature anywhere in Europe that is able to derive most of its comic effects from nothing more sophisticated than plain quotations of the "correct" speech habits of its mighty neighbor. Yet when a character in a Viennese comedy is to be shown in an apparently inescapable predicament, he need only employ a few abstract nouns ending in "*–keit*," "*–heit*" and the like, lace his syntax with a few subsidiary clauses, place the verbs in the proper position and get his pronominal case-endings right—and he has brought the house down, leaving the foreign critic in despair. Take scene v of act II from the comedy *Der Zerrissene*, (*Tattered and Torn*, 1835) by Johann Nestroy (1801–62). Herr von Lips, a millionaire who doesn't know what to do with his money or his life, thinks he has drowned a jealous locksmith (who in turn thinks he has drowned the hapless Herr von Lips), and flees to one of his own farms in fear of the police, disguised as a laborer. There he is recognized, and given breakfast by his god-child:

> *Lips:* O du liebe Kathi, du kommst mir allweil lieber vor! (*Will sie ans Herz drücken.*)
> *Kathi:* Aber, Göd—
> *Lips:* Gleich a Milich drauf, das kühlt. (*Frühstückt gierig und spricht währenddem weiter.*) Was mir ausserdem is, das kannst du gar nicht beurteilen. Nicht wahr, du hast noch niemanden umgebracht?
> *Kathi:* Was fällt Ihnen nicht noch ein!
> *Lips:* Na, wenn sich zum Beispiel einer aus Lieb' zu dir was angetan hätt', wärst du seine indirekte Mörderin, Todgeberin par distance.

Kathi: Gott sei Dank, so eine grimmige Schönheit bin ich nicht.

Lips: O Kathi! Du weisst gar nicht, was du für eine liebe Kathi bist! (*Umfasst sie.*)

Kathi (*sich losmachend*): O, gehn S' doch—

Lips: Gleich wieder a Milich drauf! (*Trinkt.*) So, jetzt bin ich wieder ein braves Bubi. —Dass ich dir also sag', ich hab' Visionen.

Kathi: Die Krankheit kennen wir nich auf'n Land.

Lips: Das sind Phantasiegespinste, in den Hohlgängen des Gehirns erzeugt, die manchmal heraustreten aus uns, sich krampusartig aufstellen auf dem Niklomarkt der Einsamkeit—erloschne Augen rollen, leblose Zähne fletschen und mit drohender Knochenhand aufreiben zu modrigen Grabesohrfeigen, das is Vision.

Kathi: Nein, was die Stadtleut' für Zustand' haben—

Lips: Wenn's finster wird, seh' ich weisse Gestalten—

Kathi: Wie is das möglich? Bei der Nacht sind ja alle Küh' schwarz.

Lips: Und 's is eigentlich eine Ochserei von mir, hab' ich ihn denn absichtlich ertränkt? Nein! Und doch allweil der schneeweisse Schlossergeist! —Du machst dir keine Vorstellung, wie schauerlich ein weisser Schlosser is.

Kathi: So was müssen S' Ihnen aus 'n Sinn schlagen.

Lips: Selbst diese Milch erinnert mich—wenn s' nur a bisserl kaffeebraun wär'—aber weiss is mein Abscheu.[5]

The farcical action turns, as so often in this theatrical tradition, on the curse of money, the double-dealings of false friends, and the rescue from adversity by the poor-but-faithful lover. In many of Nestroy's comedies these stock situations are embellished by the wagers and temptations of fairies and interfering goddesses; the ambience is familiar from Johann Emmanuel Schikaneder's libretto to Mozart's *Magic Flute* (1791). In Ferdinand Raimund's *Der Bauer als Millionär* (*The Peasant as Millionaire*, 1826) a plot of this kind has affinities with the story of *Everyman*, and is used as a vehicle for a simple and (alas) serious moral lesson.

Nestroy's aim, in *Der Zerrissene*, is more sophisticated. The figure of Lips is a spoof on the *Weltschmerz*, boredom and insouciance of the late Romantic hero; his very circumstances (Lips has money but no grammar) offer a farcical comment on the noble station of a Leonce. The passage I have quoted is a parody, too, on the graveyard inanities of the contemporary fate tragedies. But the real source of Nestroy's greatness—he was one of the very few actor-managers of German drama—lies neither in the plots nor even in the complex and highly effective theatrical devices of his comedies. It lies in his characterizations or, more precisely, in his astonishing verbal inventiveness and virtuosity. His famous "Couplets"—doggerel or ballad songs, sometimes improvised before the show—are a unique mixture of the topical and the perennial, full of hidden allusions to avoid the absurd censorship of Metternich's police. They are built from puns, popular sayings turned inside out, and parodies of archness and sententiousness. In them and in the fast repartees of his characters, the German (or rather Austrian) language is exploited for a *changeant*, silver-and-dross quality it had never displayed before.[6] Comparing these verbal cascades with the homely utterances of Raimund's characters, one is not surprised at his despairing remark on seeing one of Nestroy's comedies, "*Das kann i nit. Da is gar mit meine Stuck.*"[7]

Above all it is the pun—the second look at a molecule of speech, leading to the brilliant illumination of a familiar mental landscape in an unfamiliar light—which Nestroy presses into the service of his abundant theatrical talent. Nestroy's puns, like those of Karl Kraus, his greatest admirer, raise an interesting paradox in the ethics of language.[8] Only one who is deeply, perhaps intuitively, familiar with a language (and thus with the ethos of its speakers) will know where to dig below its smooth colloquial surface in order to bring up an illuminating pun; but only moments of alienation from the common concerns and "colloquialisms" of those speakers will enable him to perform the act.

GEORG BÜCHNER

Georg Büchner (1813–37), the third major dramatist of the age, is a discovery of the early twentieth century. In spite of the efforts of his friends Gutzkow and Franzos in the decades following his death, his work remained unknown to a wider public. Yet the passionate, feverish intensity that informs the twenty-three years of his life endows it with a symbolical quality. He belongs to the revolutionary generation of the 1830's, which in Germany was silenced by violent police measures and long drawn-out oppression—a combination remarkably effective for its time. But his literary genius, and the pace with which he absorbs and abandons the ideological attitudes of his contemporaries, distinguish him from all of them except Heine.

He was in no obvious sense a literary man. Born near Darmstadt, the son of a medical doctor who, as a field surgeon, had served in Napoleon's Old Guard, Georg Büchner intended to follow in his father's profession. He studied medicine at the Universities of Strasbourg and Giessen, graduating as a physiologist at Zürich where, in the last year of his life, he was appointed *Privatdozent* on the strength of his work on the nervous system of fish. In the summer of 1834 he was involved in subversive political activities in the Principality of Hesse. These culminated in the clandestine publication of a revolutionary pamphlet and its distribution among the wholly unresponsive peasantry; the pamphlet is clearly pre-Marxist in its argument, its Biblical trimmings were added by a clerical fellow-conspirator. The complete fiasco of these activities, ending with the denunciation of the conspiratorial group, probably by one of its student members, led to the disillusionment with political activism which is reflected in Büchner's first major play, *Dantons Tod*; the play was written in the first five weeks of 1835, in constant fear of arrest by the authorities and of detection by his hostile father. Büchner fled to Strasbourg in March 1835, where he resumed contact with the family of Minna Jaeglé, to whom he had become secretly engaged during his first stay there in November 1831. (A warrant for his arrest was issued in June 1835, but no extradition from France seems to have been requested.) That summer he translated two of Victor Hugo's plays and wrote *Lenz*, his only *Novelle*, based on a memoir of the life of the poet J. M. R. Lenz (1751–92), which was made available to Büchner through Pastor Jaeglé. In the late spring of 1836 he wrote his only extant comedy, *Leonce und Lena*, which failed to win a competition set by Cotta, the Weimar publishers. At this time too he wrote three papers, in French, on the nervous system of the barbel, and a number of letters to his parents and friends, which contain brief but important observations on his aims as a dramatist. In October 1836 he moved from Strasbourg to Zürich where, towards the end of that year, he wrote *Woyzeck*. At Christmas he received a letter (*à la* "more in sorrow than in anger") from his father, the first since his flight. He died in Zürich of typhoid fever on February 19, 1837, after an illness lasting seventeen days. We are told by the wife of a liberal deserter from the Hessian Army with whom he lodged that his last words were, "We do not suffer too much pain but too little, for through pain we enter the Kingdom of God." Certainly the first part of the sentence may stand as a motto to Georg Büchner's extant writings.

The elements of Büchner's life cohere in our minds into a strange yet familiar picture. Its ambience is one of hectic intellectual exertion through philosophical studies and of political enlightenment through radical pamphlets; his arrogance and aloofness accompany a capacity for intense friendship; his conspiratorial activities and utopian plans go hand in hand with naïvety in practical matters and an annihilating sense of disillusionment; suicidal moods follow on early attacks of meningitis; the medical student's shock tactics and youthful cynicism deepen into a sustained rejection of accepted bourgeois values; the consolations of conventional religion and of enlightened teleology alike are sarcastically rejected; the somewhat unreal, certainly tortuous love affair fails to sustain him at the crucial moments; never abandoning his work in physiology, he hopes to repair the shattered fabric of experience with the aid of a scientifically based philosophy of nature; and the final intervention of disease and death comes suddenly yet not unexpectedly in a life pitted throughout against a father's inescapable authority—in brief, it is as one of the anarchist or "nihilist" characters from a Dostoevski novel that the young man stands before us. What distinguishes him from such a character is his literary achievement. But to his contemporaries, and especially to his father, only the ruins of his life were discernible, not the brief triumphs of his art.

In several important senses Büchner's work is fragmentary, exploring questions rather than offering answers. It could hardly be otherwise, seeing that the theme on which it centers is that of suffering. The rudimentary and episodic movement that informs his plays is never explicitly stated. It constitutes not a system (cosmic or otherwise) at all, but it is simply a retracing in dramatic and (in *Lenz*) narrative form of his experience of life. The poles of this movement are boredom and apathy on the one hand, and the conquest of these by feeling on the other. It is a movement from unreality, intimated as the region of solipsism, unfeeling, and isolation, to reality, which is experienced above all as encroachment, violation, and ravage of the self by another. The grim fact of pain is seen initially as "the bedrock of atheism," the irrefutable proof that a just and loving and omnipotent God does not exist: "But I, if I were almighty [says the poet Lenz, on the verge of insanity, to his host, Pastor Oberlin], you know, if I were almighty, I could not tolerate suffering—I would save, save . . ." Yet the recognition that "the least twinge of pain, if it stirs only an atom, rends creation from top to bottom" (Thomas Paine in *Dantons Tod*, III, i) does not lead Büchner to the Hobbesian view that a man should put himself in a position where he may avoid pain, or to the Schopenhauerian view that he should regard it as illusory. On the contrary: in Büchner's plays a man's capacity for suffering is his bedrock of reality, his one and only proof that he *is* and that the world *is*. Thus Büchner's antihero is like a man waking from an anesthetic or a condition of total shock: the life and feeling that flow back into his limbs and flood his consciousness are the life and feeling of pain: "the sentient vein is the same in almost all men—only the hull through which it must break varies in its thickness" (*Lenz*). The breaking of this hull is men's only ontological proof, yet it is also more than they can endure: a man's proof of existence is also his undoing. Even the laconic detachment and ribald humor of Büchner the medical student contributes to this vision of men as specimens which are being "prepared"—their every spasm is watched—by a demiurge whose intentions remain hidden in sinister obscurity. The dialectic into which Büchner's "heroes" are pinned is thus not between good and evil, or hatred and love, or fate and will, but between feeling and unfeeling. Existence is manifest not yet in positive action but in sentient endurance, not yet in pleasure but in pain. This far Büchner's writings take us, but no further. The "not yet" belongs to our logic, not to his vision.

Mardi. Rien. Existé.

—*Jean-Paul Sartre*

A play on *Pietro Aretino*, possibly completed, was destroyed by Büchner's fiancé. *Leonce und Lena*, his only extant comedy, is concerned with the first half of the dialectic. The hero, prince of an imaginary kingdom à *la* de Musset, is one of those "who are incurably unhappy merely because they are" (II, ii).

His escape from a well-nigh suicidal boredom is effected by a fairy tale device of coincidences. So long as they know each other as the world knows them, Prince and Princess frustrate the silly King's matchmaking: intended for him by a royal Polonius (whose mind is filled with Kantian maxims), Ophelia is the object of Hamlet's scorn. But once they don the masks of the marionettes they "really" are, thus becoming ignorant of each other's identity, Prince and Princess fall in love and marry. The curtain comes down on a happy Lena and a caustic Leonce wryly reconciled to their union.

Büchner is writing out the experience of the post-Byronic, post-Napoleonic generation in Europe everywhere:

> *Leonce:* Komm, Leonce, halte mir einen Monolog, ich will zuhören. Mein Leben gähnt mich an wie ein grosser weisser Bogen Papier, den ich vollschreiben soll, aber ich bringe keinen Buchstaben heraus. Mein Kopf ist ein leerer Tanzsaal, einige verwelkte Rosen und zerknitterte Bänder auf dem Boden, geborstene Violinen in der Ecke, die letzten Tänzer haben die Masken abgenommen und sehen mit todmüden Augen einander an. Ich stülpe mich jeden Tag vierundzwanzigmal herum wie einen Handschuh. O, ich kenne mich, ich weiss, was ich in einer Viertelstunde, was ich in acht Tagen, was ich in einem Jahre denken und träumen werde. Gott, was habe ich denn verbrochen, dass du mich wie einen Schulbuben meine Lektion so oft hersagen lässt? . . .[9]

In what follows, the Prince's anguish ("merely because he is") is only stifled, not assuaged.

> *Dans les salons d'Arras, un jeune avocat froid et minaudier porte sa tête sous son bras parce qu'il est feu Robespierre, cette tête degoutte de sang mais ne tache pas le tapis; pas un des convives ne la remarque et nous ne voyons qu'elle . . .*
>
> —Jean-Paul Sartre

In *Dantons Tod* the encompassing emotions are substantially similar. But their proximate causes are fully intimated, and the dramatic situation is much more commensurate with their intensity than it was in Büchner's romantic comedy. The drama opens on March 24, 1794; Danton has reached the point of complete disillusionment with the cause and development of the Revolution. He now knows the trivial concerns, the greed and corruptness of "the People" on whose behalf he conducted the September massacres. He also knows the cynicism and the hypocrisy (so strong as to be self-delusive) of his fellow-revolutionaries, chief among them St.-Just and Robespierre. He has all but exhausted the round of physical pleasures—his occasional obscenities in the early part of the play are a desolate echo of past excesses. He is like a man imprisoned in a maze, who knows the mechanism of every lock and of every guard's mind, yet who also knows that unlocking the next door and outwitting the next guard is not worth the effort since it will only take him into another part of the same maze. His knowledge of his own, and of the Revolution's, predicament is as complete as it is paralyzing. This determinism is reflected in an almost suicidal *nausea vitae*, but it is also projected on to a wide historical plane: almost every second scene in the play presents some aspect of the "revolutionary" mood of "*la canaille*"—all its actions are either wholly arbitrary, or else fearful, self-seeking, and corrupt. In this initial situation Danton is incapable of any meaningful contact:

> Wir wissen wenig voneinander. Wir sind Dickhäuter, wir strecken die Hände nacheinander aus, aber es ist vergebliche Mühe, wir reiben nur das grobe Leder aneinander ab, —wir sind sehr einsam . . . Einander kennen? Wir müssten uns die Schädeldecken aufbrechen und die Gedanken einander aus den Hirnfasern zerren.[10]

The play is divided into four acts of between six and ten episodic scenes each. Seeing that Danton's and his friends' executions are, from fairly early on, a foregone conclusion, the interest of the play does not lie in the overt action but in the dialectic of emotions which the action throws into relief. Thus Danton's brilliant rhetorical defense before the Revolutionary Tribunal (III, iv) serves not to avert or even delay his fate, but to demonstrate its arbitrariness: all rational argument and all personal and political action appear overshadowed by the irrational imperative of history—"*das Muss*"—from which there is no escape. The moment Danton recognizes his own guilt in the September massacres (II, v) he recognizes that Robespierre, his puritanical adversary, is, like himself, merely another link in the chain of historical causes. When St.-Just asserts that the Revolution is governed by natural laws as strict as the laws governing physical actions (II, vii), he merely echoes Danton's own recognition that "the Revolution devours its own children" (I, v). And when Danton recognizes that his own flagrant immorality has "been turned into a political crime" (I, iii), and that all moral considerations too have thus become subject to the rule of political success, which in turn is subject to historical inevitability, it becomes clear that the area of meaningful *action* the playwright leaves to his characters is severely restricted. Once Robespierre and St.-Just have succeeded in branding Danton and his friends as traitors to the popular cause, the way to the guillotine is clear; and Danton's contempt for his rivals, coupled with his fatalism ("they will not dare," is his repeated answer to the warnings of his friends) makes Robespierre's brief victory easy. This is essentially epic theatre, though not in the sense intended by Bert Brecht, its theoretician and practitioner.

Its greatness, it seems to me, springs from two sources. The first, remarkable in a literature singularly poor in political themes, is Büchner's exploration of a variety of revolutionary attitudes. Of course, all political action in the play is *eventually* shown up as predetermined and meaningless. But this conclusion is not allowed to foreshorten the detailed exploring: a whole spectrum of reactions to the rule of terror, among the rulers and the ruled, among the temporary victors and victims, is presented before the devastating conclusions are drawn. Thus Danton's great defense speech before the Tribunal: we know it is bound to fail. But its reception has been carefully prepared by a discussion of his prospects (III, ii), its splendid rhetoric is fully reproduced (III, iv), and so are its effects (v and vi). (Like several others, these scenes are partly based on contemporary transcripts.) *Coriolanus* is not less of a political play because Shakespeare shows up tribunes and plebs as governed by self-seeking, corruption, and vacillation; nor is *Dantons Tod*, because Büchner shows up the Revolution as a juggernaut. But each turning of its lethal wheels is the result of a calculated action, and each calculation is dramatically conveyed.

At the same time *Dantons Tod* (like *Coriolanus*) is also a personal drama, the episodic portrayal of Büchner's dialectic of pain. The first two acts present a hero who is wholly heedless of his fate, who is so disillusioned that he refuses to fight for his life. The climax of the personal drama lies very near the climax of the political, but it does not quite coincide with it. It is reached at the point (III, vii) where the "vein of feeling" breaks through Danton's apathy. And the end comes upon a Danton who, having become conscious of the irreducible reality of his own existence, feels the fear of death and cares for his friends and looks for peace not in Nothingness but in the sacrificial love of his wife.

The climactic scene of the personal drama takes place in the Conciergerie, before Danton's second and final address to the Revolutionary Tribunal. He has fought his rhetorical battle well, but his friends protest that now it is too late—what is there to hope for? *Danton:* "Peace." *Philipeau:* "Peace is in God." *Danton:* "In Nothing. Immerse yourself in something more peaceful than Nothing, and if the greatest peace is God, then isn't Nothing God?" This is the credo, the ontological argument of nihilism. And Danton demolishes it in the next breath: "But I am an atheist." Here is no statement of fact but a cry of despair: a piece of irrefutable logic *and* a violent assertion of the truth of his experience—and thus the sentence implies the opposite of its overt lexical meaning. He goes on:

> Der verfluchte Satz: Etwas kann nicht zu nichts werden! Und ich bin etwas, das ist der Jammer!—Die Schöpfung hat sich so breit gemacht, da ist nichts leer, alles voll Gewimmels. Das Nichts hat sich ermordet, die Schöpfung ist seine Wunde, wir sind seine Blutstropfen, die Welt ist das Grab, worin es fault.[11]

All of which, as Danton adds, "sounds mad." Yet what has here been asserted is the opposite of that nihilism with which Danton began: it is the irreducible reality of existence. Now, this irreducible Being is nothing positive. On the contrary, it is Being filled out with pain, sensate and throbbing with painful life, but it *is*. Danton comes back to the argument (IV, v): of course peace (= Nothing) would be desirable enough: "Das Nichts ist der zu gebärende Weltgott": "Nothingness—*that* is the world's god that should be born." But (he now knows) peace *is* not, has no place in Creation. Consequently (here again the astonishing combination of cold logic and hot passion) absolute solitude too does not exist, solitude is always breached by another. Danton's love for Julie is love in the face of death (as Woyzeck's love for Marie is sealed by murder)—an emotion as irreducible as was the assertion of existence:

> O Julie! Wenn ich allein ginge! Wenn sie mich einsam liesse!—Und wenn
> ich ganz zerfiele, mich ganz auflöste; ich wäre eine Handvoll gemarterten
> Staubes, jedes meiner Atome könnte nur Ruhe finden bei ihr.[12]

It is this changed Danton that goes to the guillotine. His last words are addressed to the executioner who tries to separate him from Hérault, his last remaining friend: "Will you be more cruel than death itself? Can you prevent our heads kissing each other in the bottom of the basket?" Danton's old bravado is in these words, and his newly-found loving care.

> . . . *pitié, au secours, au secours donc j'existe.*
>
> —Jean-Paul Sartre

From *Dantons Tod* through *Lenz* to *Woyzeck* Büchner is attempting to come ever closer to the central experience of his life. Progressively discarding all that, from *its* vantage point, appears contingent, he is intent upon grasping the dialectic of feeling in its barest form. The complex political and personal circumstances in which Danton was involved are discarded in *Woyzeck*. Instead of Danton's highly articulate consciousness we are presented with a central character who is victim pure and simple—victim of his own birth and circumstances, of society, and of his own dark nature. Or rather, Woyzeck is as nearly a mere victim as it is possible (that is, dramatically convincing) for a living man to be: perhaps the greatest of the dramatist's achievements is that he gives us the imaginative measure of that state. Once again Büchner bases himself on documentary evidence (the legal and psychiatric reports on the trial for murder, in 1823–24, of a wig maker of that name; the case seems to have been the first at which psychiatric evidence supporting a plea of diminished responsibility was admitted by a German court of law). Yet in creating Woyzeck as the embodiment of a ne plus infra of the human condition Büchner is wholly original. For the figure of this downtrodden simple soldier there are no literary precedents anywhere, not even in Shakespeare, whose influence upon many details in the rhetoric of *Dantons Tod* is obvious, and once or twice overpowering. The Shakespearean parallels are here too—in Poor Tom, in Private Feeble's "I'll ne'er bear a base mind: an't be my destiny, so; an't be not, so" (*Henry IV*, ii; III, ii). But these, for Shakespeare, remain minor and peripheral figures, whereas Büchner, in moving Woyzeck into the center of the stage, makes him the protagonist of a whole vision of life.

Woyzeck is as solitary as any man can be in our world. The people around him rise up from the cracks in the earth's thin crust (an image which Büchner employs in all his works) as in a dream or delirium. They stand in certain simple social relations to the "hero," yet they involve him in nothing like a substantial plot. He earns the barest of livings as a private soldier, officer's orderly, and military barber. He has a mistress, Marie, and a child—it is for them he works and endures the humiliation of his service. The Captain (a sketch of hypocrisy and defective sympathy) taunts him with accusations of immorality and rumors of Marie's unfaithfulness. The Doctor (a harsh satire on inhuman scientific curiosity, perhaps on Büchner's father) rewards Woyzeck with a pittance for experimenting with his digestive system in order to observe his mental reactions. And the Drum Major, all virile sexuality and brute strength, seduces Marie. Yet these three, outlined in the briefest possible way and with unparalleled dramatic energy, are not Woyzeck's antagonists so much as the inescapable and, since he is defenseless, necessarily hostile facts of his existence.

Woyzeck is the very a priori of man: not, that is, a philosophical abstraction but the embodiment of Lear's anguished cry to Poor Tom, "Is man no more than this . . . Thou art the thing itself. Unaccommodated man is no more but such a poor, bare, forked animal."

Does love belong to the irreducible being of such a man? Marie, a victim of degrading indigence but also of her deprived eros, is not so much the object of Woyzeck's love as rather the one hold he has on existence: the only thing, in the threatening void outside his tormented mind, that tells him that he *is*. Hardening her heart against him, Marie returns the Drum Major's embraces; and Woyzeck, a good man and a good father to their child, murders her. The deed is done in a passion of jealousy, yet its true source lies even deeper, at the barest level of self-assertion. It is the act of a man who must "make a bruise or break an exit for his life"; who must carve a notch upon the tree of experience before he is himself crucified on it; who must do *this* deed since no other, more positive, lies within his power.

Although Woyzeck is presented in a state of all but complete deprivation, he is an individual, sharply outlined against all others, not so much by virtue of a distinct consciousness as by the capacity for suffering that echoes through his wayward, somnambulistic consciousness. Even more succinctly but also more powerfully than in *Dantons Tod*, Büchner again conveys his feeling for the fragmentariness and discontinuity of experience by resorting to episodic scenes. In both plays (but more successfully in *Woyzeck*) these scenes are made up of strange mosaics of words arranged in contrasting imageries of grays and violent crimsons, which trace out his antihero's movement towards the reality of pain. Apathy and boredom are presented by an imagery, sometimes obscene, related to the physical functions (the digestion and sex). The repetitious tedium of the daily chore of dressing-eating-sleeping, the "symbols of exhaustion"—discarded clothes, mechanical dolls and marionettes, frozen ground and arid wastes and the smell of the grave, ashen skies and marshy landscapes— these are the images that give poetic form and dramatic substance to one side of the dialectic:

> *Woyzeck:* Ich geh. Es is viel möglich. Der Mensch! Es is viel möglich.
> —Wir haben schön Wetter, Herr Hauptmann. Sehn Sie, so ein schöner, fester, grauer Himmel; man könnte Lust bekommen, ein' Kloben hineinzuschlagen und sich daran zu hängen, nur wegen des Gedankenstrichels zwischen Ja und wieder Ja—und Nein. Herr Hauptmann, Ja und Nein? Ist das Nein am Ja oder das Ja am Nein schuld? Ich will drüber nachdenken.[13]

In intense dramatic contrast with this is the language of flesh and blood, of suffering and of the Crucifixion, the language of violence:

> Das Messer? Wo is das Messer? Ich hab es da gelassen. Es verrät mich! Näher, noch näher! Was is das für ein Platz? Was hör ich? Es rührt sich was. Still.—Da in der Nähe. Marie? Ha, Marie! Still. Alles still! Was bist du so bleich, Marie? Was hast du eine rote Schnur um den Hals? Bei wem hast du das Halsband verdient mit deinen Sünden? Du warst schwarz davon, schwarz! Hab ich dich gebleicht? Was hängen deine Haare so wild? Hast du deine Zöpfe heut nicht geflochten? . . . —Das Messer, das Messer! Hab ich's? So![14]

Words, everywhere in Büchner's writings, are such strange, isolated objects: now like gaudy phials of poison, now again like knives quivering in the target; now like scalpels dissecting limbs, now like gory wounds, now again like muffling gags of cotton wool. Woyzeck speaks without expectation of being understood or hope of being spared. Yet his all but incoherent language, rent by doubts, sign of his utter isolation, is also the hallmark of Woyzeck's authenticity. In contrast to this, all coherent speeches in the play are satirical diatribes on the hypocrisy of the hostile world that engulfs him. The Doctor's learned disquisitions on Woyzeck's physical reactions to his Pavlovian experiments, the Boothkeeper's exhibition of a calculating horse—

> Ja, das ist kein viehdummes Individuum, das ist ein Person, ein Mensch, ein tierischer Mensch—, und doch ein Vieh, ein Bête. (*Das Pferd führt sich ungebührlich auf.*)[15]

or the parody of a teleological sermon Büchner had heard, put into the mouth of a drunken journeyman:

Warum ist der Mensch? Warum ist der Mensch?—Aber wahrlich, ich sage euch: Von was hätten der Landmann, der Weissbinder, der Schuster, der Arzt leben sollen, wenn Gott den Menschen nicht geschaffen hätte?[16]

(which strikingly resembles Lucky's monologue in *Waiting for Godot*)—all these quite coherent speeches contain not an ounce of truth or sympathy or insight: they are wordy lies against Woyzeck's inchoate truth. Their very rhetoric— the world's coherent discourse itself—is the harbinger of chaos, pain, and death. A number of figures pass hurriedly before our eyes: Andres, his fellow-soldier, a mere human vegetable, who provides a contrast to Woyzeck's sentient soul; Marie, whose last words before she succumbs to the Drum Major are words of dead indifference; the Grandmother, with her fairy tale about the earth void of life, the moon a piece of rotten wood, and the stars "that were little golden gnats stuck on pins just as the shrike sticks them on blackthorns"; the Jew who sells Woyzeck the fateful knife; the Policeman who sums up Woyzeck's passion, "A good murder, a good honest murder, a lovely case. As nice a case as you could wish to see"—they are all but shadows in that icy void which Woyzeck must somehow breach, even if with a deed of violence.

Insisting on the proletarian status of Woyzeck and on the indigence of his circumstances, Marxist criticism offers a useful corrective to the disembodied assertions of existential metaphysics, to its egregious contempt for social fact. But that criticism is wrong in suggesting that material deprivation is the sole source of Woyzeck's anguish, and that therefore his condition is remediable. What if his circumstances were different . . . ? They are not detachable. One only has to ask the question to see its absurdity. Woyzeck is what he is: "the thing itself," the very a priori of man. "The poor you have always with you" is not a statement in defense of the capitalist system.

HEINRICH HEINE

Where all is rotten it is a man's work to cry stinking fish.

—*F. H. Bradley*

Evaluations of Heinrich Heine's writings have been bedeviled by comparisons with Goethe's. In such comparisons his lyrical poetry has inevitably been brand-ed as shallow and derivative, his emotions as insincere and divided. He himself, it may be said, invites the comparison. Almost to the end of his life he writes poetry which, consciously or instinctively, alludes to the tradition of the *Volkslied* that Goethe had all but initiated and immeasurably enriched. In verse-forms, range of images, and sentiments alike these allusions span Heine's creative life, from *Junge Leiden* (*Early Sorrows*, 1817) and the immensely popular *Das Buch der Lieder* (*Book of Songs*, 1827, published when Heine was thirty) to the *Letzte Gedichte* (*Last Poems*, 1852) and the posthumously published verses of his Paris exile. To speak of Heine as a *German* poet is to speak of one who continues the tradition of the *Volkslied* into the post-Romantic age, and completely modifies it to accommodate a new, un-Goethean kind of consciousness.

Leaving aside the question of ultimate stature, the comparison with Goethe is justified when we consider the sheer variety and range of Heine's poetic *oeuvre*. Both were, emphatically, all-purpose poets. They saw in poetry not a sacerdotal activity, not an aesthetic rite or a mode of utterance reserved for high occasions and deepest feelings only, but something like their natural language, suitable for Sundays and weekdays alike. They are both blessedly prolific and generously unfussy, sometimes undiscriminating, in their productions. Their creativeness takes many and varied forms, it readily moves from poetry to easy versification and hence to prose. Their lives are devoted to their poetic and literary *métier*, but this devotion is in no sense exclusive and solemn. Theirs is a poetic existence in the sense that they are instinctively driven to give meaning to all their experiences through their poetry, to *use* them in and for their art. In this respect as in several others Heine's self-consciousness is more fully developed, certainly more fully and unsparingly expressed, than Goethe's; and it is in several ways a different, less harmonious self. There is no equivalent, in Heine, to the persona of savant, elder statesman, and "sage of Weimar" which Goethe so often assumed in the last three decades of his life. Heine's highly developed sense not only of irony but of humor saw to it that whatever attitude he struck he was never pompous. But underlying these differences is their confidence that the self and all its most private joys and sorrows, its loves and hates, its trusts and betrayals and its changing beliefs, are worthy of being made the subject of poetry—that their self is *interesting* to contemporary and future generations. In this confidence, combined with the not unimportant fact that it is justified, lies their greatness.

Furthermore, neither of them is an intellectual. Instead, they are possessed of a bright, worldly intelligence; they use ideas but are hardly ever interested in them for their own sake. "I have never thought about thinking," Goethe writes in one of his epigrams; Heine sums up his "Doktrin" as follows:

> Schlage die Trommel und fürchte dich nicht,
> Und küsse die Marketenderin!
> Das ist die ganze Wissenschaft,
> Das ist der Bücher tiefster Sinn.
>
> Trommle die Leute aus dem Schlaf,
> Trommle Reveille mit Jugendkraft,

Marschiere trommelnd immer voran,
Das ist die ganze Wissenschaft.

Das ist die Hegelsche Philosophie,
Das ist der Bücher tiefster Sinn!
Ich hab sie begriffen, weil ich gescheit,
Und weil ich ein guter Tambour bin.[17]

Both were critical, sometimes scathingly so, of the overwhelmingly intellectual and philosophically informed culture of their times. Goethe made a few concessions to it, which take the form of a high moral seriousness and occasional sententiousness; in this respect Heine learns much but concedes nothing—his critical response to the *furor philosophicus* ranges all the way from banter and jokes to cutting sarcasm. Unlike Goethe he is interested in finding out the historical and social causes behind the philosophical passion, which he sees as an integral part of Germany's past and present—a present to which he does not attempt to set up a rival cultural kingdom as Goethe had done in Weimar. The coherent and even to some extent autonomous *Geist der Goethezeit* has no equivalent in Heine's age. The direction of his creative intelligence is incomparably more social and political.

Time and again Heine's detractors (they are many and they come from very diverse quarters) have denied him the highest title in the German cultural vocabulary, that of *Dichter*, calling him a superior journalist. What is certain is that the prose he wrote is (as Nietzsche acknowledged) an unparalleled liberation. His eye for the telling metaphor, his quick wit and sharp tongue, his regard for the limpid phrase and variations of pace, for sheer readability, have few if any precedents in German prose, and make him the grandfather of German journalism. He does not, when an argument bores him, go on to bore the reader with it, but is only too pleased to drop it. He has, more than any German author before him, an eye on his public. Occasionally he curries favor with his public at the very point where he is tearing that public to shreds. Nothing, almost nothing is sacred to him, certainly not his own lyrical poetry, a levity which many German critics have found unforgivable. He wrote for the day— so runs the hostile argument—and his writings have perished with the day, except for a few deeply-felt lyrical poems in the Goethean tradition . . . . (Such judgments are like solemn skids on slippery ground; von Hofmannsthal's lugubrious vindication of Heine is a case in point.) It seems that precisely the opposite is true. Where it is serious and "deep," consciously "perennial," Heine's poetry hardly ever speaks to us in the authentic voice of uncontentious lyricism; there indeed his ease of utterance is apt to become fatal. Some of his early poems, even some of the confessionary poems of his last years, unrelieved by irony, strike a note of bathos. And it may as well be admitted that he has occasionally perpetrated some of the ghastliest rhymes in the language, which no appeal to irony, parody or spoof can salvage. His unique and permanent achievement lies where his writing is fully committed, or rather exposed, to the modes and concerns of his day, where any hankering after poetic immortality is made an issue of and ironically encompassed. The anecdotal extravaganzas and mock rhetoric; the romanticism of "deep" moods alternating with easy colloquialisms; the double-take and the joke (sometimes a little off, occasionally obscene); and the multi-leveled sententiousness—rarely serious, mostly ironical, ribald, sarcastic, using pastiche, persiflage, and shock effects—these are the devices of his greatest poetry, whether its themes be social or personal, or a characteristic mixture of both. His unique achievement lies where his poetry, filtered through a rich and divided self-consciousness and irony, reaches truth and depth and Germany, and where the poetic forms bequeathed to him by Goethe and the Romantics are no longer explored but exploded. A superior journalist? His poetry *was* written for his day, and the more fully it encompassed it the more it lives in ours. His immense vulnerability is his finest inspiration. What divides him from the journalist is his fatal inability to forget the evil and misery in the world. Many are the political and philosophical ideas he short-circuits by means of a joke. The feelings of his outraged humanity, on the other hand, are never appeased. As he grew older he, like Marx, certainly did not grow more tolerant.

Parody, Thomas Mann once observed, is the expression of love for a form that is no longer viable. Some of the greatest poems in Heine's first collection, *Das Buch der Lieder*, are parodistic in this sense, being informed by a tension between the traditional form and the divided self. The third in the group "Die Heimkehr" calls up, conventionally enough, the German countryside in the month of May, with its river and busy mill; a boy is fishing from a boat; girls are dancing on the lawn and bleaching the linen; "and oxen and meadows and woods" are all included in this charming landscape that Caspar David Friedrich might have painted. The idyllic and fairy tale quality of the scene is underlined as it is surveyed by the poet from some far-off old ramparts; the shapes he sees are "friendly" and "tiny, full of color." Why then does the poem begin, "My heart, my heart is heavy . . ."? This too is a traditional opening: it raises in the reader the expectation of a contrast between the happy idyllic scene and a tale of unrequited or betrayed love. This is the contrast by means of which Heine achieved some of those effects that thrill us a good deal less than they did his contemporary public. But here the expectation of the obvious is disappointed, the reader is in for a grotesque surprise. The penultimate stanza still belongs to the landscape idyll:

> Am alten grauen Turme
> Ein Schilderhäuschen steht;
> Ein rotgeröckter Bursche
> Dort auf und nieder geht.[18]

But in the last stanza the idyll is shattered:

> Er spielt mit seiner Flinte,
> Die funkelt im Sonnenrot,
> Er präsentiert und schultert—
> Ich wollt, er schösse mich tot.[19]

No word of explanation or expatiation follows. It is pure caprice, that last line, yet it is also a stark omen of violence, and thus meaningful. The alienation of a traditional form has come to express the chasm that opens up between the poet and a landscape that was, and is suddenly no longer, idyllic and harmless. It may well be that not many of his contemporaries appreciated the full effect of these poetic shock tactics. At all events, it is ironical that so good a reader and sympathetic a critic as Theodor Fontane (writing in 1892), while praising much of Heine's poetry for its realism, singled out this poem as a regrettable Romantic aberration.

I have spoken of the close rapport, attested by the huge profits pocketed by his Hamburg publisher, that existed between Heine and his public. Certainly this rapport extended to his ironies, even if perhaps not to the more violent ones—his admirers included such sophisticated political enemies as Metternich and his secretary, Gentz. There is a good deal of the licensed clown, the court Jew, in his attitude to the German Philistines whom Heine so deeply and consistently despised, in his contempt for their "sated virtues" and "cash-on-the-spot morality." Much has been written on the harmful, trivializing effect all this had on his art. But what this rapport vouchsafed him—not as a man but as an artist—was the substance of his freedom and insight.

He had his first dose of German anti-Semitism as a little boy, it was with him throughout his turbulent life, it followed him fifty years later into his slow death in the "mattress grave" in Paris; he never bore his Jewishness meekly, but vaunted it like a yellow star on his coat or again clattered it along like a dog with an empty tin tied to his tail. (Among his own tribe he fared hardly better, as may be seen from his observation about Baruch Spinoza, who "was solemnly expelled from the community of Israel and declared unworthy henceforth to bear the name of a Jew. His Christian enemies were magnanimous enough to leave him that name.") He knew sordid poverty, and from his millionaire uncle he experienced the very opposite of that solidarity and charity which is supposed to be characteristic of Jewish family life. Money or rather the prospect of money made him fawn on its possessors, including the fabulous Rothschilds, turned him into an informer, cost him untold hours of fruitless bargaining with skinflint publishers. Baptised into the Lutheran Church, he anticipated by self-mockery the public derision and the futility of the act. He hated his fatherland with the fervor of a betrayed lover and (like James Joyce, like Karl Kraus) neither his emotions nor his thinking ever moved beyond its innermost concerns. He was the first of that long line of spiritual exiles who have consoled themselves for the reality of life in Germany by hypostatizing the German language and making of it their very own unassailable citadel. He railed against the Jewish and Christian God, and in his *Letzte Gedichte* cursed his fate and enemies more terribly than any German poet since J. C. Günther. Yet that collection, too, contains a poem, "Ich war, o Lamm, als Hirt bestellt," of surpassing tenderness and (nothing came harder to him) Christian humility; it is among the most moving in the German language. He wrote of love: of its happiness and enchantments, more often of its betrayals and bondage, rehearsing in his poems its every color and hue; if anyone after Goethe could have significantly added to that theme, it was he. And when death came, after eight years of progressive paralysis, he certainly did not "go gentle into that good night" but retained his poetic creativeness and bright intelligence to the end.

Yet where, in all this, are there signs of freedom and insight? Not in the travails of the man but in the products of the creative mind. The circumstances of his life are the vital substance from which he gained his freedom, his writings are the realm in which that freedom and insight are manifest. There is, after all, a strange truthfulness about his work. The man who suffers is *not* healed in the mind that creates. It is a divided self—his *Zerrissenheit*—that speaks to us from his pages. The struggle never ceases: the strife between love and hate, trust and betrayal, beauty of art and the ugly truth of life, between Germany and France, between the aristocrat and the rabble-rouser, is never appeased. It is Heine's creative self-consciousness, his ability not to smother or assuage but to express these many conflicts, which makes for the delight of his poetry. His self-consciousness is vast but rarely excessive and unnerving, for it almost always finds an adequate image or fiction to contain it; when it fails, he can turn even a comment on the failure into a wry story. His overt political sympathies apart, he was the least democratic of poets, quickly bored with expatiation, caring nothing for smooth transitions. A surprisingly large number of his poems end abruptly, inadvertently, their arguments left hanging in midair. These laconic endings are signs not of a creative flaw, not of a gnostic fragmentariness, but of an aristocratic impatience. They express a sudden contempt for that rapport from which the poem has been fed. But the capriciousness is made meaningful because in the abrupt ending he still retains his firm hold on the reader's sensibility; only now the poet's rapport with the reader is no longer accommodating but critical, even derisive. Heine's imagination could not function in those aerial spaces of unconditioned freedom towards which the German Romantics had aspired; it worked at its finest when fully enmeshed in, even enslaved by, social and personal circumstances, in the *données* of the real world. He was, in this sense, the first and the greatest German realist of the nineteenth century. Yet much of his work, taking the form of romances and extravaganzas and fairy tales, is quite unlike the realism of Balzac or Dickens or Tolstoy. But so is the reality he describes, the substance from which he frees himself. No one understood better than he that yearning for the aerial spaces of "pure spirit," for the freedom from the actual and humiliating circumstances of German life, which informs the poetry as well as the political and philosophical writings of the German Romantics. Heine wrote not in their tradition but about it: he wrote its history, he ridiculed its hold on the contemporary scene, he warned of its future transformation:

> The German revolution will not be any the gentler or milder for having been preceded by Kant's Critique and Fichte's transcendental idealism, let alone by the *Naturphilosophie* of our age. By means of these doctrines revolutionary forces have evolved which are only waiting for the day when they can break out and fill the world with horror and amazement. Kantians will come forward who will treat the phenomenal world without piety, and will rage with sword and claymore through the very foundations of our European life, extirpating its last roots in the past. Fichteans will appear on the scene, armed in their self-willed fanaticism, knowing neither fear nor self-interest; for they live in the spirit and defy the material world, like the first Christians who were similarly not to be overcome either by physical torture or physical temptation. But more terrifying than any of these will be the "*Natur*"-philosopher . . . for he will be in league with the primæval forces of Nature, conjuring up the dæmonic powers of the old Germanic pantheism, and because in him that lust for battle will reawaken which is known to us from the Germans of ancient times, which does not fight to destroy, nor to conquer, but simply for the sake of fighting. It is the finest merit of Christianity that it has somewhat tamed that brutal German lust for battle, though without destroying it completely. And on the day when that potent talisman, the Cross, breaks, the savagery of the old warriors will flare up again, and the mindless Berserker's fury of which the Nordic bards have sung. That talisman is rotten, and the day will come when it will fall to pieces altogether. Then the old gods of stone will rise up from the ancient ruins and will rub the dust of a thousand years from their eyes, and Thor with his giant hammer will leap up at last and shatter the Gothic cathedrals. . . .

Be warned, you people across the border, you Frenchmen, and don't interfere with what is going on at home in Germany. . . .

Don't laugh at these fantastical visionaries who are expecting that the realm of appearances will be shaken by the same revolution as that which shook the realm of the spirit. The idea comes before the deed, as lightning comes before thunder. Now, the German thunder, like the German himself, is not very subtle and a little slow in coming. But come it will. And when at last you hear such an explosion as you have never heard in all history, then you will know that the hour has struck. And when they hear this gigantic noise, the eagles will drop dead from the air, and the lions in the distant deserts of Africa will hide in their regal caves, their tails between their legs.[20]

Some sophisticated Marxist critics have treated Heine's work by standing Freud on his head. Heine's love poems (they have suggested), especially those in which the loved one is indicted of cold caprice and betrayal, in which her beauty and physical charms are contrasted with her crude, or frivolous, or deceitful mind, are not "really" about women at all but about Germany, or at any rate about the contemporary world. This method of interpretation is more helpful than its bare summary suggests. Clearly it cannot be applied to much of his early poetry. Few of the poems in *Lyrisches Intermezzo* for instance, too well known to need even listing, can reasonably be seen in this way. But from the time Heine settled in Paris (1831), more especially from *Neue Gedichte* (1844) onwards, the poetic traffic between eros and the world—the world of politics and of culture, philosophy and religion, as well as of Germany—comes more and more to dominate his poems, until, in his last poems, the correspondence between eros and world becomes the characteristic mode of his unsolemn muse. In terms of his creative self-consciousness, the ironical division within the poet's mind is now perceived as a reality in the contemporary world at large.

The story of Heine's political opinions is no less unsettling than any other aspect of his life and writings. The general drift of his sympathies after 1830 is attested in an exchange of letters (and perhaps a meeting) with Karl Marx in 1844–45; and it is clear that even before the fiasco of 1848 he had been moving towards the left, from republicanism to communism. The remarkable document which testifies to his allegiance is the 1855 *Vorwort* to a collection of articles he had written in the years 1840 to 1843 for a German newspaper. It is no exaggeration to say that this preface contains the classical defense of the literary man's allegiance to the communist cause, that in the hundred years which follow few if any ideas have been added to that much discussed topic. However, here too (it is well to recall) he writes not as a doctrinaire intellectual but as a poet and a brightly intelligent contemporary; not, certainly, as a party man but as a political freelance. But has not recent history taught us that the position of the freelance more than almost any other is incompatible with the communist ideology? This, precisely, is what the *Vorwort* of 1855 is about (hence my claim that little has been added to the debate it initiates).

The poet in him (he tells us) looks forward "with dread and fear to the time when these sinister iconoclasts [the communists] will seize power and with their brutal fists destroy all the marble images of my beloved world of art," when "the lilies of the field which toil not nor spin and yet are arrayed as beautifully as King Solomon, will be ripped out of the soil of society," and when "alas! the grocers will be making paper bags out of my *Book of Songs* and will wrap in them the coffee or snuff of the old women of the future. Alas, all this I foresee, and an inexpressible sadness fills me when I think of the decline with which communism threatens my poems and the entire old order of the world. And yet, I confess it freely, this very communism works like a charm on my mind, a charm I cannot resist." Not because he is a trimmer, but because logic and emotion alike make it irresistible: logic, which is based on the premise "that all men have the right to eat," and which he feels compelled to follow even if *fiat justitia pereat mundus* (and not only the world of art . . .). We can see that, like Brecht the author of *Die Massnahme*, Heine would have made a disconcerting party member. But the second, the emotional reason is even more powerful than the first. It is hatred—and Heine was a magnificent hater—

> . . . the hatred that I bestow on our common enemy, who forms the sharpest contrast to communism . . . —I speak of the party of the self-styled representatives of nationalism in Germany, of those false patriots whose love of country consists in nothing but an imbecile dislike of everything foreign and especially of the neighboring countries . . . the remnants or successors of the Teutonomanes of 1815. . . . And now that the sword slips from the dying man's hand he is revived by the conviction that communism will assuredly dispatch them, not with a blow, no, with a mere kick, as one squashes a toad, even so will the giant squash them. It is because I hate the nationalists that I would fain love the communists.[21]

This then is the fullest expression we have of the general direction of Heine's political sympathies. Its value as prophecy is too obvious to need stressing. Its value to the Party, in his own time and subsequently, is less easily determined, seeing that the partisanship it expresses (in both the "logical" and the emotional parts of the argument) is so vividly qualified that in the end it hardly comes to more than "the devil we don't know is better than the devil we know." The divided mind is still there, the strife between beauty and the world is unresolved; and one would dearly like to hear Heine's comment on his bronze statue in East Berlin, described by a recent critic as a socialist-realist fantasia displaying the communist shirt of the Free German Youth draped round the massive shoulders of a miner.

There *are* points in Heine's later work where the divided self is united, where the irony lets up: in the depiction of the devil he knows he is quite single-minded. No poem of his contains an affirmation of the communist cause. The contemporary world yielded him no substance for such a poem, and the future he saw was bereft of poetry. It is in his great songs of hate that the division is resolved, in the depiction of what outraged the sense of compassion of the man and the "intemperate susceptibility" of the poet (as Matthew Arnold called it: above all in *Die schlesischen Weber* (*The Silesian Weavers*, 1845), perhaps the greatest poem written on behalf of the proletarian cause.

Inspired by their abortive revolt of June of that year, the poem does not set out to render the feelings of the starving weavers in a direct, mimetic way; it is, emphatically, not a naturalistic poem (and it is about as close to "socialist realism" as a scene from the *Inferno*). Instead, it is informed by the highest rhetoric. Uninterrupted by picturesque asides, unalleviated by irony or joke, unburdened by any personal or poetic self-consciousness and unabridged by a contemptuous ending, it is an image of deprivation and a paean of hate in the same way as so many of Goethe's poems are paeans of happiness and joy. Its central image, raised from concrete circumstance into a rhetorical fortissimo, is the image of the loom and the winding sheet which the weavers are weaving—

> Deutschland, wir weben dein Leichentuch,
> Wir weben hinein den dreifachen Fluch
> —Wir weben, wir weben![22]

There is a classical, exemplary quality about the poem which makes it unnecessary to elaborate the critical obvious: its argument is entirely encompassed by the central image (for example, "the shuttle flies in the creaking loom/All day and all night we weave thy doom") and in the emotions of the weavers; the rhythm, related to the rhythm of work, is heightened into the monotonous beat of a choral refrain that is both poignant (never melancholy) and threatening; the weavers' threefold indictment of "God, King, and Fatherland"; the superb craftsmanship of the poem's five stanzas, each of five lines, containing two pairs of four-foot iambics with alternating feminine and masculine rhymes and the overriding iambic refrain; and its structure, which frames the three stanzas of the indictment in a single opening stanza whose third line is heightened from "Deutschland, wir weben dein Leichentuch," to the chilling and momentous "Altdeutschland, wir weben dein Leichentuch," of the last stanza—it is this classical quality that makes of *Die schlesischen Weber* one of the greatest poems in a language most of whose articulate speakers have been only too ready to scorn "A nasty song, fie, a political song!" and to look on the poem and its author with a jaundiced eye.

Close analyses of Heine's poetry (of the kind favored by the ancient "New Criticism") tend not only to elaborate the obvious, they can also be peculiarly misleading. Words to him are not mysterious, let alone mystical verbal icons. Like Schiller—only more successfully—he is above all a rhetorical poet. (Like Schiller's, too, his libertarian sympathies are those of an aristocrat.) Heine's aim as a poet is not the conveying of an idea, the solving of a problem, or the creation of a "heterocosmic" world of feeling or of the imagination; his aim is not even the conveying of an intimate personal experience—he is not primarily "*ein Erlebnisdichter*." On occasion he can do all these things in his poetry, but its real aim is the inducement of moral feelings in the reader and their forthright, autocratic manipulation—I mean feelings which belong to the totality of our persons, including our public and social self. Hence his rhetoric cannot be dismissed as a defection from lyricism—it is not an empty gesture. It is an essential means of his poetic undertaking.

It would be misleading to end with *Die schlesischen Weber*. Heine wrote no more than three or four poems of this kind, none as accomplished. The division of mind and muse goes on, all the way to the end. His great Judaic fling ends as wryly as the rest, the creative energy never ebbs, there is no death-bed conversion, he hurtles his imprecations into the dark night. I have stressed the antinaturalistic, rhetorical mode of *Die schlesischen Weber* as I have stressed the antinaive, *sentimentalisch* mode of the best of his earlier love poetry. The language of art—of masks and carnivals, of music, sculpture, and painting, of poetry within poetry, of emblems and mementos—came to him naturally, and Nature herself enters his poetry only in terms of its human significance, as a pathetic fallacy. All these elements are present in that poem which many regard as his last, *An die Mouche* (1856), dedicated to Elise Krinitz, a young German woman living in Paris who, in the last year of Heine's life, fell under the spell of his personality and who enticed him, paralyzed and blind and suffering almost constant pain, for a last time into that ambience of intelligent eros which was the ruling passion of his life.

The poem recounts a dream of death. Its central artifice is a renaissance marble sarcophagus, whose bas-relief portrays all the emblems, the archetypes —*Fabelzeitfiguren*—of man's history and creative imagination: the shameless heathen gods next to Adam and Eve "each in the figleaf apron chastely clad," Paris and Helena next to Moses and Aaron, Phoebus Apollo, Frau Venus and Balaam's ass as well as Lot "who with his daughters drank and merry made," Mount Sinai and young Jesus in the temple. The round of archetypes is also a list of the poet's themes: he is the dead man in the coffin; as in several earlier poems, the divided mind is bodied forth in the eerie *Doppelgänger* theme. A similar division runs through the images assembled in the bas-relief. The Greek figures are sharply—*grell*—contrasted with the Judaic ones, the spiritual with the natural, the pagan with the Christian, the harmony of the marble composition hides a strife of contrasts. A yellow-and-mauve passionflower— the loved one—inclines over the poet's grave, each detail of its blossom expressing (as in the legend) an aspect of the passion of Christ. An inconsolable silence reigns in the moonlit night. Then a conversation begins between the poet and the loved one, but it too is silent, beyond the indication of human language . . . . No imagery could be "higher," more luscious—this surely, we feel, is artifice carried beyond the point of poetic redemption . . .

It is a bewildering poem, bewildering above all in the variety of its themes. Death and a highly peculiar resurrection, *musée imaginaire* and cultural history, eros and the passion of Christ, Dionysus and Apollo, all are held together—but how precariously!—by an allegorical first person tale. And as for the central image, that sarcophagus, we feel, belongs to the nineteenth-century Baroque of Père Lachaise rather than the Renaissance; it is an imitation of an imitation. Here, we feel, is contemporaneity with a vengeance! If in the first fifteen stanzas (the "cultural history") the statuary is relieved by a few touches of humor, the next fourteen (the passionflower and its communion with the poet) are cast almost entirely in the language of high pathos and deep feeling. But this is the language which (as we have seen) Heine can wield only in the space of a short poem; he is unable to sustain the note of uncontentious lyricism (as Goethe does in *Marienbader Elegie*), and one wishes he didn't try. The bathos is redeemed, at least partly, by what follows. Towards the end of that second section (stanza 29), where the wordiness of that wordless communion begins to pall, Death is apostrophized as the only source of eros ("Nur du kannst uns die beste Wollust geben"), it is contrasted with the restlessness of "stupid, brutal life," and then:

> Doch wehe mir! Es schwand die Seligkeit,
> Als draussen plötzlich sich ein Lärm erhoben:
> Es war ein scheltend, stampfend wüster Streit,
> Ach, meine Blum verscheuchte dieses wüste Toben![23]

(The Marxist critics may note that "*la Mouche*," Elise Krinitz, disclaimed any identification with the flower: it was, she said, Heine's way of conveying his communion with his "*patrie lointaine*.") The break comes not a moment too soon. The images on the bas-relief begin a violent quarrel, the frantic call of Pan vies with the anathemas of Moses, the Barbarians berate the Greeks, the old battle between Truth and Beauty is resumed, there is no quietus even beyond the grave. Instead, the hideous braying of Balaam's ass drowns the contending voices of gods and saints and heroes. Is it the voice of bigotry and stupidity that wakes the dead man from his grave, the poet from his nightmare? But then, the braying of his ass made Balaam turn his curses into blessings, it saved the people of Israel and put Balaam, at least for a while, on the path of righteousness. Is simple, asinine piety the answer to it all? And is the poet's awakening to the wretched sound of heehaw a resurrection, as some have declared? On the contrary: it is the intimation of the eternal recurrence of all that Heine regarded as vulgar and opinionated in his age. "Once I saw both naked, the greatest of men and the least—all-too-like one another they were, all-too-human even the greatest!—this was my disgust of man," wrote Heine's most perceptive admirer three decades later.[24]

The poem ends with invective and bitter sarcasm—not even in his grave (it tells us) is the poet safe from the hideous strife. But there is a fuller reading of those last stanzas. Does he *want* to be safe from that strife? For Heine, to be safe would be to be dead. Beyond their sarcasm the last lines and the whole poem convey an unabating care, a concern with the fractious world even in the hour of death. Many are the indulgences Heine allowed himself, but the cultivation of an exclusive, private feeling was not among them.

And so the divisions of a lifetime are unhealed, the battle is unfinished:

> Woran liegt die Schuld? Ist etwa
> Unser Herr nicht ganz allmächtig?
> Oder treibt er selbst den Unfug?
> Ach, das wäre niederträchtig.
> Also fragen wir beständig,
> Bis man uns mit einer Handvoll
> Erde endlich stopft die Mäuler—
> Aber ist das eine Antwort?[25]

Heine wrote in one of his last poems, on *Lazarus*; and another in that group ends:

> Ohnmächtige Flüche! Dein schlimmster Fluch
> Wird keine Fliege töten.
> Ertrage die Schickung, und versuch,
> Gelinde zu flennen, zu beten.[26]

EDUARD MÖRIKE

. . . like a Greek bowl: inwardness that has sprung open, the weight of existence lightened in the created thing.

—*Romano Guardini*

The area of experience charted by the lyrical poetry of Eduard Mörike (1804–75) is not difficult to delimit. Its settings are rural, provincial, uncontaminated by contact with the great world. At its most memorable it is concerned with intimate personal encounters and their evanescence. Its tranquility and its deep emotions are those of a solitary soul, only the ineluctable passage of time, not faction and strife, intimates the common lot of man. It excels at showing man in contact with the natural world; Nature often acts as a consoler, a giver of meaning to human relations, sometimes she underlines man's essential solitude. Those readers in Germany and abroad who, until a generation ago, saw the finest achievement of nineteenth-century German literature in its lyrical poetry, justly recognized in Mörike its finest representative. But even if one suspects that this view has now become something of a cliché, his achievement remains assured. In the word *Erinnerung* the German language underlines the inwardness of memory, of recollection, its re-creative inward intimation, and German critics have often pointed to the special place that lyrical poetry has in this inward re-creation of the past. In this sense Mörike is a German lyrical poet par excellence. What makes him into a modern European poet is the fact that in many of his poems such a re-creation no longer takes the form of a story or fable but of an extended image. The freshness and apparent simplicity of his poetic utterance give one the impression that several decades of aesthetic debate and Romantic theorizing have left no trace in his verses, that idealism, industrialism, and the social movements of his time have passed him by, unconsidered. Thus the poem "Verborgenheit" (Hidden Sorrow," 1832) expresses a gentle resignation, a contentment with that which the heart has already experienced, and a renunciation and apprehension of further turbulent emotions; yet its first and last stanzas begin with the line "Lass, o Welt, o lass mich sein!," and it is as a renunciation of the world that this poem has commonly been read. We know, from Mörike's correspondence with writers fully involved in contemporary controversies, that he knew that world—vicariously perhaps, but well enough. But we also know from some of his prose writings that he firmly exercised his choice as a poet, and consciously resisted being drawn into the arena. In this as in most other ways he was the opposite of Heine.

Such a consciousness of withdrawal, it is clear, is hardly compatible with that simplicity of diction for which Mörike is often praised. He is not the "naive" poet of Schiller's definition. But the consciousness that enters his poetry is confined to personal feelings. It expresses not so much a deliberate withdrawal from the issues of the contemporary world as an apprehension of and a withdrawal from the things around him, from the données of private experience. The themes of parting and solitude predominate. The apparent simplicity of his finest poems is a measure of his success in conveying the consciousness of loss by converting it fully into poetic story and image—the result, it may be, of a complex creative process. As to that, we have no means of telling, the process of transformation leaves little or no trace in the poems. They do not readily lend themselves to a reconstruction of his inner biography. Therefore, instead of attempting to establish his, or their Entwicklungsgeschichte, I shall confine myself to a discussion of two of his poems, leaving out his ballads, narratives and miniature epics.

Mörike began writing in the age of Goethe and in the heyday of German Romanticism. Yet he was a contemporary of Baudelaire, and his last poems overlap the poetry of Verlaine and the Symbolists. His work intimates some awareness of the changes that lyrical poetry underwent during his lifetime; it does so more clearly than his retired existence in a Swabian backwater would suggest. Implicitly challenging the traditional notion of poetry as an Aufeinander (which Lessing had contrasted with the Nebeneinander of painting), Mörike's poetry turns from story to meaningful image for its most characteristic effects. He wrote no theoretical statement of his aims, and only a reader who saw his work through anachronistic preconceptions could persuade himself that Mörike wrote poems about the writing of poems. (Such a reader is hard put to it not to see all poetry in this light.) He has extended the area of German poetry, but his discoveries seem to have been largely intuitive. The consciousness that informs his poems has as its object not poetry but the human emotions. As for his art, he might have repeated his fellow-countryman Albrecht Dürer's modest paradox, "Was aber die Schönheit sei, das weiss ich nit." ("As for what Beauty may be, I wot not.")

The tradition in German literature which recent criticism has dwelt on contains no traces of Mörike's serenity. Fragmentariness, visions of the extremes of the human condition, exposure to the demonic forces of being, and an unnerving search for the roots of that being accompanied by dread and *Angst*, a longing for the unconditioned and a lack of accommodation in the real world—these make up our current image of German poets. Having few if any of these traits, Mörike's poetry is unfashionable; accustomed to seeing depth always as the depth of despair, we are apt to find his affirmations shallow. But he has considered the dark side of the world, he too knows that the world of the unhappy man is different from the world of the happy. Yet his creativeness bears him on, all the way to the completed form, to the point where discord is transmuted into the harmony beyond. Yet again, this is no aestheticism, no triumph of perfect form over base, irredeemable matter. On the contrary, underlying his poetry and rarely made explicit is a belief in the connectedness of the human and the divine. Art for him is not an expression of the ineffable but of the world, or at least of a small, intimate part of the world, as a creation of God, "pulcher horologium Dei."

Only occasionally—once or twice in his poetry, more often, though not always successfully, in his prose—he allows desolateness itself to speak. The cycle of his five short *Peregrina* poems (1824) relates to the most painful of his love affairs, to a girl, half vagrant half *dévote*, he met during his years as a student at Tübingen. This cycle contains, if anything in Mörike, a direct evocation of the demonic, destructive forces of love.

From Wilhelm Meister's Mignon and Eduard's Ottilie to Peregrina (first conceived by Mörike in the context of a *Bildungsroman*), and to Stifter's "*braunes Mädchen*," even perhaps to Hans Castorp's Clavdia Chauchat and Josef K.'s Leni, there runs a line of mysterious girlish figures who disrupt by their untoward appearance the placid, often staid lives of their lovers or would-be protectors. Whence they come and whither they go we are not told. The threat they represent to the virtues of the *biedermeier* or *bürgerlich* world in which they alight is symbolized in the erotic challenge they offer (this theme is isolated in the orgiastic Lulu figures of Frank Wedekind's plays). But the erotic is only one aspect (and often a deeply hidden one) of their powerful instinctual lives. They are free from qualms of conscience, even from ordinary consciousness itself. They seem to lead an existence beyond good and evil, to which those who briefly harbor them respond with bewilderment and anguish.

The Peregrina of Mörike's poems, that "anima naturaliter pagana," knows nothing of the Pauline "It is better to marry than to burn," nothing of the fire of conscience that consumes her lover. The poet calls her "an unknowing child," smilingly she hands him the "death in the cup of sin." (We must wait for the third section to allay our suspicion that this line is mere bathos.) The second poem contains the attempted accommodation. It describes the solemn wedding and the graceful, airy bower in which it takes place, the garden, faintly echoing the noise and music of the feast, in which they spend their night of love. But even now, in the fervor of his embraces, the union is not complete. The accommodation, in *this* setting and under *this* solemn dispensation, would have to be entirely on the lover's terms. The lack of sexual fulfillment ("too soon for my desire, tired too soon/ the lovely head lay lightly in my lap") is but part of a strangeness that lies beyond all possible appropriation: it is a butterfly, not a lover, not a wife, that he holds in his arms. And when he wakes her, it is into "*his* house" that he takes "the wondrous child."

Never again will desolation speak so directly in Mörike's verses as it does in the third poem of this elegy of passion. The word that opens these lines, "*Ein Irrsal . . .*," so much more than "A madness . . .," has the full force of tragic conflict behind it. What else than a thing of unreason can he call his discovery of her "long-standing betrayal"? What else is there left for him to do than, "with weeping eyes but cruel," send her away forever? The discovery of her betrayal side by side with the sure knowledge of her love, the silence with which she accepts his verdict and leaves, the sickness of heart and the unappeasable longing to which her departure condemns him—these are the simple emotive elements from which this scene is created, they yield a poignancy that may be compared to Troilus's discovery of Cressida's betrayal, or to Dante's Paolo and Francesca episode. The aesthetic effect of all such scenes in literature (they are among the greatest it can yield) derives alike from a full expression of the horror of the betrayal or transgression committed, *and* a full expression of the beauty of the passion now so absolutely condemned. The poet's horror at the "madness" and his harsh judgment would be mere moralizing were it not contrasted with, and thus given living substance by, the beauty it must destroy. Must? The ordinance is that of a simple Christian morality. He obeys it, but his heart learns no consolation.

The final two poems are given over to the unabating sorrow that follows her departure. This cycle is an early work—the bare, direct invocations of grief exceed, once or twice, Mörike's poetic gifts, and issue in a *poésie larmoyante* (in the life of poets, does their expressiveness sharpen or their capacity for suffering blunt?). Again and again his imagination returns to the beloved figure of the "unknowing child," but each of the scenes it conjures up ends in the recollection of the betrayal. Nor can the imagination encroach upon reality: the last poem, a sonnet, ends on a note of despair.

Into this narrative line are woven three scenes which have the static quality of pictures. The first is that of the wedding bower, a tented garden folly with serpentine pillars and latticed roof; this curious and elaborate design seems to suggest the unreality of the solemn ritual that will take place in it (Mörike will return to this image in a later poem). It contrasts strongly with the second picture, which is directly inspired by the girl, Maria Meyer, who was found unconscious and destitute in the streets of Tübingen some days before Mörike met her, and who later turned up under similar circumstances in Heidelberg, begging for his help. The third poem of the cycle ends:

> —Wie? wenn ich eines Tags auf meiner Schwelle
> Sie sitzen fände, wie einst, im Morgen-Zwielicht,
> Das Wanderbündel neben ihr,
> Und ihr Auge, treuherzig zu mir aufschauend,
> Sagte, da bin ich wieder
> Hergekommen aus weiter Welt!

This image is repeated in the final sonnet,

> Die Liebe, sagt man, steht am Pfahl gebunden,
> Geht endlich arm, zerrüttet, unbeschuht;

And third, there is the scene

> Ach, gestern in den hellen Kindersaal,
> Beim Flimmer zierlich aufgesteckter Kerzen . . .[27]

when Peregrina appears before him, "tormented image, piteous and beautiful," ("Bildnis mitleid-schöner Qual"). Each of these scenes contributes to the action of the cycle, yet each is also reminiscent of the *Genrebilder* of the Romantic school of painting.

The few flaws of the *Peregrina* poem are obvious. The emotion that informs it is expressed with a rawness, a directness which, once or twice, exceeds Mörike's poetic means and turns into bathos. Significantly, it is in pictures—moments of rest in the flow of recollected experience—that he instinctively seeks an "objective correlative" for his feelings. But they in turn tend to alienate the action, for they live on another plane.

Mörike's *Auf eine Lampe* (1846) has been more often interpreted than any other poem of his because it seems to anticipate the Rilkean *Dinggedicht*; because the perfection it achieves is peculiarly accessible to us; because it is enigmatic and is said to contain a major "poetic ambiguity"; because we feel that it has, and speaks of, the sort of timelessness that we are apt to identify with immortality—the only kind of immortality we contemplate without too much strain on our credence.

Yet the greatness of the poem is in no way diminished by the suggestion that it is very much of its own time. The time, I mean, when Karl Marx wrote of the alienation of the products of labor into profit-making commodities of the capitalist market economy, evaluated not in relation to their use but as "fetish objects," that is, status symbols; the time when Stifter wrote in celebration of "Geräthe," of the well-made things of yesteryear, products of devoted labor which his contemporary world passed by heedlessly; when Mörike's friend Theodor Vischer wrote that exquisitely boring, maniacal, humorous novel, *Auch Einer* (1879), concerned wholly with the conspiracy of objects against man, their maker and victim. The object, or rather its recollection, its *Er-innerung*, now comes to serve as a symbol of arrest in the ineluctable flux of events. As objects-of-use the heavy secretaires, the antimacassars and mullion windows of the age proclaim respectability and moral probity; as objects-of-art its historical paintings and allegorizing statuary express a longing for the values of a bygone era. Among such objects belongs "the beautiful lamp" which Mörike re-creates and apostrophizes in the poem "Auf eine Lampe":

> Noch unverrückt, o schöne Lampe, schmückest du,
> An leichten Ketten zierlich aufgehangen hier,
> Die Decke des nun fast vergessnen Lustgemachs.
> Auf deiner weissen Marmorschale, deren Rand
> Der Efeukranz von goldengrünem Erz umflicht,
> Schlingt fröhlich eine Kinderschar den Ringelreihn.
> Wie reizend alles! lachend, und ein sanfter Geist
> Des Ernstes doch ergossen um die ganze Form—
> Ein Kunstgebild der echten Art. Wer achtet sein?
> Was aber schön ist, selig scheint es in ihm selbst.[28]

The poem opens on a nostalgic, almost defensive note: the festive room, recalling that *Freudensaal* in which Peregrina's wedding was celebrated, lies now abandoned; the lamp that once illuminated and now seems only to adorn it may soon be moved. It lives its own life, heeded by none but—the poet? He is not named, it is as though the spirit of creative art itself were speaking through the silent beholder, all vestige of story has disappeared. Yet the nostalgia is not all-pervading, it provides a framework in which the poem's dominant argument is set. For it *is* an argument which the poem develops—not in the least abstruse or abstract (as perhaps all interpretations of the poem are apt unhelpfully to suggest), but filled out by the image and the emotions and reflections it engenders.

The beautiful object-of-use is the object-of-art of today. This process, with which we are only too familiar from the higher reaches of the souvenir trade, is not dwelt on in the poem. The object has become and is now a work of art, and the poem is concerned to show that this process has not resulted in an impoverishment. The lamp is not, we can see, a creation of classical times but rather (like the vision of *An einem Wintermorgen*) a work of classicism. (Just so the title of the poem, "Auf eine Lampe," is reminiscent of the many poems from *The Greek Anthology* from which Mörike copiously translated, poems dedicated to objects of sacred or emotional value.) The figures of the composition are expressive of laughter and joy. The "gentle spirit of gravity" is distinct from the spirit of gaiety, allegorized (as in Keats *Ode on a Grecian Urn*) in the "leaf-fringed legend" of the bronze relief; this "gravity . . . suffuses the entire form." The lamp is a manmade thing, a repository and emblem of human endeavor, and thus possessed of a *pesanteur* all its own. It is "a wrought thing of art of the *genuine order*"—"der *echten* Art" a word we find hard to take in any poetic context (the German is not much easier) because it has become a cliché, and in this context because it has a connotation of the defensive about it. Yet what the word sums up is no more than what has already been intimated. The combination, in the finely-wrought thing, of joy, charm, and gentle seriousness—the integrity of the work-of-art—is what makes it "genuine"; not unique—and only today isolated—but part of an order, "supremely fine of its own kind" (as Aristotle would say).

The lamp is no longer an object-of-use: the light it now sheds is therefore of a different kind. The illumination it offers is that of a work of art, which "shines, full of bliss, within itself."[29] If the harmony inherent in the object displays the "consonantia" of St. Thomas' threefold definition of a work of art, then the last line shows forth its inward, self-contained luminosity, its "claritas," while its "integritas" is intimated in "the gentle spirit of gravity" that "suffuses the entire form." It is this "sanfter Geist des Ernstes" which presents our greatest interpretative difficulty, because it attributes to the work of art a quality we rarely associate with it. It is by virtue of this quality that King Solomon's raiments in all their glory are different from the lilies of the field, the man-made is different from the natural. The poem does not speak of this contrast, it is only concerned with one side of it. It tells us that the world pays no heed to a work of "the genuine order." We may the more easily understand this order if we bear in mind that for Mörike's contemporaries—including the major authors of his age except Heine—the weightiness and seriousness of man's endeavor, of the products of his work—indicated a *moral* quality; that "*Ernst*" was the hallmark of the moral, in a sense the religious, worth of labor.[30] Sometimes this seriousness has disconcerting results—hence Schopenhauer's invective against German "ponderousness" (*Schwerfälligkeit*), "manifest in the way they walk, in their conversation, in their language, in everything they do." Mörike seems aware of this danger—he speaks of the "*gentle* spirit . . . ."

This notion of gravity as the integrating mode of a work of art is, as I have said, alien to us. We must not confuse it with Rilke's images of "weighty inwardness." In Mörike's poem it intimates above all a moral quality. The "integritas" of "the whole form [which this gentle spirit] suffuses" is not designed to exclude us. It is not an hermetic or "aestheticist" self-containedness, but a perfection that manifests at once a moral and an aesthetic value; and through the moral it is connected with the rest of man's world, or at least with those who will heed it. The more the object—the lamp: the poem—achieves its own perfection, the more meaningful it is to us. The more serenely it shines forth within itself, the more perfectly it illumines the world of which it is a part. "Beauty is truth, truth beauty" has ceased to be a vexing paradox. The beautiful object-of-use, we have said, is no more. The unity of the true and the beautiful is now in the beautiful, in the work-of-art—at least, for the few who will pay heed; at least, for a little while longer: "Noch unverrückt, o schöne Lampe, schmückest du . . . ."

ADALBERT STIFTER

> . . . and that we could have pure beauty, unadulterated by anything that is beautiful.
>
> —L. Wittgenstein

Between the poetry of Eduard Mörike and the prose writings of his exact contemporary Adalbert Stifter there are several thematic affinities. Both confine their work to the private sphere of experience; the settings they choose are rural and natural; the values they praise are those inherent in intimate human relations and in the soul of the solitary man. The notion of man as a political animal is largely alien to them (to Stifter after 1848 it is increasingly distasteful); it is certainly never a positive inspiration of their muse. In Mörike's work none of this is a source of friction. In the lyrical poetry he wrote the limitation of themes could remain intuitive. Stifter wrote almost exclusively narrative prose —a form, or rather a variety of forms, which is less easily accommodated to such a range of themes. There are two main reasons for this difficulty.

The writing of verse implies a number of obvious formal restrictions unknown to prose. But it also implies a certain freedom—the poet's freedom to choose his own restriction. Of course, the choice is not unlimited; Mörike *is* a poet of his times. But in a distinct sense his chosen form is his world—at least in the sense that the form will dictate his inclusions and omissions, his scale of what is or is not important and appropriate. And only then will the relevance of the poem to our world become apparent—or it may even then remain hidden and opaque. Similarly, the language he uses will be related to the language of the market place in a variety of ways, but it will not be simply identical with it. "The cause of the people," Hazlitt observes ruefully, "is indeed but little calculated as a subject for poetry." Prose, on the other hand—narrative prose no less than expository—is the social and democratic form par excellence. It is uniquely involved in the historical and social circumstances, the living customs and moral standards of its readers who are also its speakers; and nineteenth-century realistic prose is a singularly direct expression of this involvement. Therefore, the less compatible their preoccupations and standards are with the artist's conscience, the more problematic will be his attitude towards the whole enterprise of conveying "to his readers also," and "in *their* language," *his* vision of what the world is and what it ought to be. Stifter is among the first of that long line of German writers who have experienced and been unsettled by this quandary well before it disturbed English or even French writers. Where the social condition of man is seen as derivative and their common everyday world as somehow provisional, the prose writer will be faced with problems of composition quite different from those of the realistic tradition of nineteenth-century Europe.

The other difficulty I have in mind relates more directly to the comparison with which I began. We have seen something of the predominance, in Mörike's poetry, of image over story, and took it to be a characteristic trait of his work. The same is true of Stifter, only the shift occurs in genres in which we do not expect it, and it is more radical. Stifter wrote two long novels and some thirty *Novellen*. Are these then stories without a story? Not quite. Certainly his early work, into the early 1840's, is full of palpable events and adventures, sometimes of a weird and wonderful kind, often inspired by Jean Paul. But even these early stories have not much by way of plot, the chief carrier of story in narrative prose. "You can only create if you care," George Orwell wrote about Dickens. Care—what about? Dickens cared about Mr. Dombey in his counting house; Stifter about the wanderer in the green forest. To invest creative energy in plot and story is to accept as meaningful, to care for, the social sphere in which alone the convolutions and proliferations of a plot are enacted. It is to accept the actual world, which is the world of men's social experience first and foremost, as a reality, hard or otherwise. It is to see "the world" as capable of yielding the profoundest interests, spiritual and moral as well as aesthetic. It is to acknowledge it as a creation not wholly alienated from its Creator. Stifter seems to have had few of these certainties when he began writing, and none when, thirty years later, he ended his labors and his life.

Adalbert Stifter was born in 1805, the son of a smallholder in the village of Oberplan near the sources of the Vltava, Bohemia's main river, in a region that contains the last remaining virgin forest of Europe. He died in 1867 as a retired inspector of schools, little known among a wider public, in Linz on the Danube, the capital of Upper Austria. A distance of some forty miles separates the two places. A few episodic stills may help us to identify the man: the penniless student, employed as a tutor to the children of the upper bourgeoisie and aristocracy of Vienna (including the Metternichs), standing in the courtyard of a patrician house, his best suit spattered by mud from the wheels of a starting carriage; the prematurely aging school-inspector yearning for a journey to Italy, pottering among cacti, keeping an exact record of the havanas he smokes and the sweet wines he drinks; the elderly recluse writing letters of high moral seriousness and aesthetic import to a publisher who exploits him, and letters of loving homage to an ignorant, shrewish wife; the man who, seeing in his childless marriage a judgment of God, adopts three girls and loses all of them through early death; the writer who hardly ever mentions so indelicate a matter as money, speculates in dubious shares, totters from one financial crisis to the next, puts all his hopes in the state lottery (like a character from the Viennese comedies he despised as immoral); and finally, the invalid who, tormented for years by colics and abdominal spasms, in a last moment of unbearable pain from cirrhosis of the liver, takes his own life. What deprivations, what narrowness of worldly experience, what need for solace and enrichment through Nature and Mind are manifest in this life, contemporary French and English writers would have difficulty in imagining. Yet its tenor is not exceptional. In its narrowness and resignation as well as in its absence of dramatic turning-points, this life is fully representative of the lives of most nineteenth-century German poets. Paris, London, the Empire overseas . . .: the words have an exotic, adventurous sound to German ears. They speak of vice and splendor, of *worldliness*, of an established and richly varied social order as well as of a freedom beyond the German experience. A country-house party in Meredith—lords and ladies of dubious descent and rich genteel bankers, all stripped of their finery by the shrewd pen of a tailor's son—seems to take place on another planet; but the same applies to Stephen Blackpool's bitter conversation with Mr. Gradgrind; and to the funeral of Poor Jo.

Stifter's work never moves far away from the cares his life inflicted on him, his creative imagination remains fettered to them, but the facts are idealized and carefully veiled in his stories. In examining the fabric of his writings it is relevant to know that their purpose to him was that of a beautiful veil. However, what it hides is the pettiness of his circumstances, not the tragic nature of his life. Simple existence is not necessarily the same as the good life; the image that shines through the beautiful veil is something quite other than a harmless village idyll.

Stifter published his first *Novelle*, *Condor*, in 1840, and the following collections of his stories and novels appeared in his life time: *Die Mappe meines Urgrossvaters* (1841, continued 1845, its third version was left uncompleted at his death); *Studien* (I and II, 1844; III and IV, 1847; V and VI, 1850); his most famous collection, a series of six stories, each taking its title from a semi-precious stone found in the mountainous regions of his homeland, *Bunte Steine* (1853, 1863); his novel *Der Nachsommer* (1857, 1865); and *Witiko*, an historical novel of epic dimensions (I, 1865; II, 1866; III, 1867), planned as the first part of an immense chronicle of a twelfth-century noble Bohemian family. Most of his *Novellen* were heavily revised for the collections I have mentioned; recent reprints of the stories as originally published (in periodicals) show that the revisions tend to replace dramatic and even melodramatic effects by that complex and heavily circumstantial style which we have come to regard as characteristically his own. (The revisions are thus comparable to those that Henry James made for the New York edition of his works.) The *Novelle* we shall examine here in its final version, *Der beschriebene Tännling* (*The Inscribed Firtree*, 1846), belongs to the second volume of *Studien*.

The story and overt message of *Der beschriebene Tännling* have the naïveté of a tale found in a village almanac. The bare retelling of it makes a modern reader blush with embarrassment (unless he puts on his Great Literature face, when he becomes impervious to anything). The tale, set in the early eighteenth century, concerns a poor and beautiful girl, Hanna, who lives with her old mother in a solitary mountain cottage near a well consecrated to the Holy Virgin; a hot-tempered lumberman, Hanns, is in love with the girl and uses his hard-earned wages to buy her precious gifts. An elaborate deer hunt is arranged in the region for the entertainment of the feudal prince and of his vast entourage of lords and ladies, among them Guido, who falls in love with Hanna; Hanns is determined to take his revenge on Guido, but in a dream a vision of the Virgin Mary saves him from committing the murder he had planned; the two men never meet. Hanna leaves with Guido for the great city and marries him, and the story closes with Hanna's visit to her native region a great many years later: "She had a dark velvet cloak wrapped round her body and was leaning back in the carriage. Her face was finely drawn and pale, ... Hanns, his face deeply lined, stood by the wayside." She does not recognize him. The last paragraph underlines the message of the tale. Both had prayed to the Virgin of the Well; Hanna (according to ancient custom) on the day of her first confession had asked for a fine silken dress embroidered with gold and silver; what Hanns prayed for while contemplating the murder of Guido we do not know. When the village girls, after hearing of Hanna's wedding, recall that Hanna's wish was granted, the old smith replies: "She received the Virgin's curse, not her grace—the Virgin's wisdom, grace and miracle were granted to quite another person."

This tale could be told (and in a sense *is* told) in a very few pages. If we add up the passages in which this action is described, the very few lines of terse dialogue, the few paragraphs containing simple and unprobing character-descriptions, we shall find that most of the story's thirty-odd closely printed pages are devoted to its natural setting, to recitals of the various customs associated with the places of the action, and to a description of the hunt. Thus the girl, Hanna, is introduced only after more than six pages have been devoted to a detailed account of the mountainous landscape not far from the south-western border of Bohemia and Upper Austria, an account which ranges widely over the whole region. The narrator begins as one who is finding his place on a detailed map of the region. He pinpoints the fir tree of the title, its trunk covered with mementos carved once in the sapling but now scarred and gnarled through many decades of the tree's vigorous growth. He moves to a hill—but it is not yet the one on which stands the bare little house in which

Hanna will live with her mother—moves on to another neighboring forest and meadow; contemplates the effect of clouds and morning air on the color of the distant Alps; alights near two solitary houses; moves to the little church nearby, dedicated to the Virgin of the Blessed Well in which Hanns will bathe his eyes and face, moves on to the village of Oberplan to tell the full story of the first miracle that happened at the well, and finally describes the house in which Hanna is brought up near the church. Why does he linger so? We feel that he would much rather not tell the story at all, not disrupt the natural setting—which is no longer a "setting" but the center of his attention, the very substance and core of his tale. It is as if he were unwilling to turn to the tale of passion, betrayal, and desolation. We notice that the story is divided into four sections, entitled "The Grey Bush," "The Clearing of Many Colors" (Hanns's place of work), "The Green Forest" (containing the description of the hunt), and "The Dark Tree" (in which Hanns, waiting for Guido, has the saving vision). And again, this division is more meaningful in terms of the changing landscapes than it is in terms of the stages of the action to which it roughly corresponds. The greyish-green hill; the clearing in the forest gleaming with the brilliant scarlet of wild strawberries and the mauve of raspberries, with the golden brown of singed bracken and the heavy black of bare earth; the sharply bounded lethal area of the dark-green forest (*"Jagdraum"*) into which the wild animals are driven for massacre; the skyscapes—pristine blue, watery grey, dappled with baroque Bohemian cloud, hidden behind whitish mists— are not all these more important than the figures in the landscape? Certainly it is they rather than the figures that are the bearers of existence, they *are*. And what (the bewildered reader will ask) does *that* mean, what could it possibly mean?

The hunt, not the turning of a human fate, is the story's true climax. We recognize it as the symbol of Hanna's transition, or rather abrupt movement, from one order to the other. This movement has been prepared for—even as a girl she was shown to be susceptible to the fine clothes and jewels that Guido's world promises. Yet it comes suddenly and silently, only a single brief comment from the author describes her feelings. As for Guido's feelings, they are conveyed by static images: a confusion, a deep blush, a distant picture of him kneeling before Hanna, that is all. While two pages are given to the festive meal after the first meet, Hanna and Guido exchange not a single word. Hanns, we read, "knew nothing of all this"; then "he learned all"; and his night of agony, prayer, and deliverance is conveyed, not through his emotions but solely through the simple things he does, the places he goes to. These characterizations could not be more bare or more effective, nor could the contrast between them and their "settings" be more marked. Just as the descriptions of the countryside were so much more than a setting of the story, or the symbols of human peace, so the description of the hunt is so much more than a symbol of a single human fate. The hunt is elaborately planned by the prince's servants

and organized with the help of some of the villagers. And yet its actual description—among the most powerful in Stifter's writings—does not give one
the impression of a human action at all. It begins with a piece of music ("*eine
rauschende Waldmusik*") played on wind instruments, echoing back from the
forest in "notes of terror and sudden calls of fear, for the ears of the forest knew
only the sounds of thunder and storm, not the terrible sounds of music." There
follows the sound of a single hunting horn. Dogs are let loose into an area of
the forest which has been roped all round by impenetrable nets. A shot is
heard. An anguished stag throws itself against the canvas, a wild cat springs up
a tree. Guns discharge their loads, bullets hit, explosions flash, white smoke
fills the lethal area. But there are no people. The narrative voice is mainly passive, once or twice "one saw . . . one heard . . . ," for the rest it is the objects
and animals themselves that seem to perform this rite of death; only when it is
over do the servants move in, to gather the corpses.

There are no elaborate verbal simplicities in this passage, it is full of strife
where the earlier scenes were full of peace. But once more we have the impression that something other than a human agency is at work, something other
than the wills of individual men. Is it not again existence in and by itself, this
time bearing death and destruction, that is invoked? It becomes clear that
even the conflict, between a countryside at peace and "the world" bearing
terror and discord and desolation, is not the fullest statement of the story's
theme. What the story intimates is this, this almost unstatable conflict between
two modes of existence, one positive the other negative, in which men are
involved but which reaches beyond, behind them.

In Stifter's stories and in his great novel a most delicate balance is struck
between the barest of actions, the simplest psychology, and a high ontological
aim. He does not suggest that man, the issue of individuation, is (as Sartre would
put it) *in the way*—not quite. Whenever he has occasion for an explicit statement, he affirms that man is able to attain to existence, and live in harmony
with its order. *To be*, in that region, however, to melt into its dark-green forests
and bare grey rocks and blueish-white glaciers, is no longer to be quite recognizable in ours.

GOTTFRIED KELLER

> . . . *the embedding of random persons and events in the general course of con-
> temporary history, the fluid historical background* . . .
>
> —*Erich Auerbach*

It may now be salutary to descend from the ontological altitudes of the
Bohemian Forest to the less exacting region of Swiss democracy. The works
of German prose in the age of European realism fall into place on a scale whose

least realistic—that is, most characteristically German—point is marked by the writings of Stifter; the work of Theodor Fontane lies at the other end of that scale. The fiction of Gottfried Keller (1819–90) lies close to Fontane's, yet it does not commit itself to the *données* of the contemporary social world with Fontane's singlemindedness. *Der grüne Heinrich* (*Green Henry*) is the last major work in German to stand under the direct impact of the Goethean tradition. It is a *Bildungsroman*, a novel of development and initiation. Yet at the same time it represents something of a compromise between the Goethean notion of "becoming," which is a display of the human potentialities for growth and refinement, and the claims of realism, which insists on subordinating those potentialities to the prosy responsibilities of social life.

In its first version (1854) Keller's novel was such a flop that his sister used the unsold copies as winter fuel. The second version (1879) differs from the first in presenting the hero's life in the first person, and it ends on a positive note (rather than with his somewhat unconvincing death). "The final version," it has been said, "asserts the vitality of social life and makes the individual, even in his eccentric course, a representative man."[31] It remains to be seen just how strong is this vitality of the social world as presented in the novel.

It describes the boyhood, adolescence, and early manhood of Heinrich Lee, known from his manner of dressing, and also from a certain callowness, as "Green Henry." Through pride, affectation, and fortuitous circumstances the boy comes to think of his minor talent for drawing and painting as a great artistic gift. He leaves his native Swiss town and the village in which he spent some of his boyhood to study painting in Munich, the artistic center of the Germany of that time. There he abysmally fails to make even a modest living from his art. And he finally returns, via some very unconvincing romantic detours, to a modest post in the civil administration of his home town. Heinrich's widowed mother, his rustic relations, schoolfriends, several art teachers, two girl friends, the companions of his bohemian life in Munich, and an aristocratic protector who turns out to have watched the young man's fortunes with a benevolent eye—these are the main background figures against which Heinrich's development is traced.

The book is remarkable above all for its refreshing honesty and unpretentiousness. Keller's narrative manner, for three-quarters of the way, is determined by a lively and clear-sighted impartiality. He consistently refuses to sentimentalize his hero's self-imposed predicament or to extenuate his failings. The accuracy of Keller's psychological insights, especially in the early chapters, is matched by forthright moral indictments which have hardly a trace of the didactic about them; they are ensconced in scenes in which the circumstances of Heinrich Lee's life are pared away, one by one, until the effects of his self-absorption or indulgence emerge with startling clarity. At these points the road on which he has been traveling becomes so narrow that he can no longer avert his eye from the havoc he has wrought.

We recognize the device of the *Bildungsroman*, from Wieland's *Agathon* (1766; 1798) through Goethe's *Wilhelm Meister* (1795f.), Novalis' *Heinrich von Ofterdingen* (1800; 1802), Mörike's *Maler Nolten* (1832) to Stifter's *Der Nachsommer* (1857) and Keller's novel as a distinct genre of German literature. It is a description of a journey, from inexperience, egotism, and emotional self-absorption into "life." It is always a story of initiation and preparation—a story of provisional states of mind all pointing toward a goal. But this goal is either not quite reached or else only perfunctorily described. The journey is incomparably more absorbing than its end. If the hero's emotional entanglements and social encounters have something incomplete and provisional about them, this is precisely because all that happens to him is made meaningful not in its own terms but as part of a development, of a *Bildung* of character and heart. As for those who accompany him a little of the way, they are merely means to his end. The matter is neatly summed up by Clavdia Chauchat, the heroine of one of the last great *Bildungsromane*, Thomas Mann's *Der Zauberberg* (*Magic Mountain*, 1924), in a conversation with the hero, Hans Castorp: "To be passionate—that means to live for the sake of living. But one knows that you [Germans] all live for the sake of experience. Passion, that's forgetting yourself. But what you all want is self-enrichment—*c'est ça.*"

These are some of the *données* of the "novel of initiation," which any practitioner of the genre is bound to take issue with. Keller places his hero in a fairly well-defined social context that is governed by a simple and unprobing *bürgerlich* morality. His task is to adjust the predetermining aspects of the genre with the claims of realism. More specifically, the question arises how he will set about accommodating the morality of means-to-an-end, a kind of *moralité par provision*, to a less flexible morality of good and evil. The episode of Heinrich's dealings with one of his art teachers, a man called Römer, is one of several instances which point up the novelist's task.

Römer is presented as that which Heinrich Lee is not, a genuine artist. He has come to Heinrich's native town (Zürich) after many failures, accompanied by sinister rumors concerning his past life. Heinrich lends him some of his mother's money. At a crucial point in Römer's haunted life, in a pique of vanity and self-righteousness, Heinrich asks for the return of the money, in a letter that is little short of blackmail. Römer instantly pays up and leaves, and is never seen again. In a subsequent venomous letter from Paris, addressed to "my dear young friend," Römer makes it abundantly clear that Heinrich's action was the *coup de grâce* which has thrown him into abject poverty and moral disintegration. Sometime later Heinrich confesses his perfidy to Judith, the more mature of the two girls to whom he is attached. He does so contritely, adding that "the story will be a warning to me"; his self-reproaches, he feels, as good as atone for the misdeed. Judith indignantly repudiates the suggestion: atonement is not so easily come by, Heinrich has done enough to reproach himself for the rest of his life: "'and this bread is good for you [she adds], and

I'll certainly not spread the butter of forgiveness on it!' Then she stood still, looked at me, and said, 'Why Heinrich, do you really know that you now have a life on your green conscience?'"

In such forthright statements of the irretrievable nature of past experience, of the finality of wrong-doing, Keller's novel presents an advance on Goethe's *Wilhelm Meister*. For there the genre itself, with its underlying view of experience as a series of experiments, had run counter to the making of such clear-cut moral judgments. However, in the next few lines the philosophy of the genre reasserts itself. Heinrich does not reply to Judith's accusation. But in his own mind he finds it only too easy to assimilate the experience, "because, after all, it belongs to my person, to my story, to my nature, otherwise it wouldn't have happened!" The objective aspect of the deed recedes behind its subjective meaning. The Goethean view of character development is extended, but the genre catches up with the advance.

Keller's engaging honesty consists quite simply in his refusal to do what every other author of a *Künstlerroman* has done—to make Heinrich into a great artist who is misunderstood. He is ready to show that what Heinrich is abandoning when he decides to give up his artistic ambitions is no more than a mediocre dilettantism, that at this point all is gain and nothing sacrifice. Keller exposes this dilettantism in detailed stages, unsparingly revealing the process at work in all inauthentic displays of talent. Thus Heinrich's failure to get a beech tree on to his drawing paper is a failure in straightforward representational terms due to inadequate draftsmanship. Heinrich then tries to compensate by concentrating on the grotesque in natural shapes and exaggerating them into lurid caricature. Finally, in Munich, he abandons all ideas of representation and lapses into surrealistic doodles, which Keller is old-fashioned enough to regard as a piece of self-indulgence.

The dilemma Keller exposes is known to every man who has applied himself to a creative task for which he is inadequately equipped by nature, and which he has chosen for wrong reasons, mainly of vanity. All this is antiromantic and honest, but also, alas, somewhat undramatic. Bad art is equated with irresponsibility, which may come as something of a relief to readers saturated with literature about the "amoralism" or "demonism" of art. But Keller seems unaware of slipping into the opposite (and equally egregious) attitude—I mean into the philistinism, writ large by the later "socialist realists," which equates good art with social responsibility. A possible conflict between the social and the aesthetic is not explored—perhaps Keller felt the theme had been done too often before. Long novels, E. M. Forster once observed, are apt to need winding up. When no other major conflict takes its place the book begins to flag and well before the end all but collapses; similarly Keller's "bread-and-butter" style with its sensible, *petit-bourgeois* metaphors drops from agreeable sobriety to flatness. The message Heinrich discovers is the simple "This way is no way." If the paean in praise of adult social responsibility on which the novel closes is unexciting, not to say insipid, then here again the genre asserts itself: the journey is always so much more absorbing than its goal. And as for the journey's relevance to the goal—the prospect of a lifetime's loyal service as a municipal pen-pusher—the reader remains less than fully convinced.

What has gone wrong? Once more we find the philosophy of the *Bildungsroman* encroaching on Keller's realistic intention: the heritage of Goethe is hard to escape. The genre answers to the feeling we have for the fleetingness of experience, for the promise of fulfillment just around the corner and always in the moment to come. It takes the sting of finality out of experience and replaces it not only (as we have seen) by the notion of development but also by a *plan*. Wieland's, Goethe's, and Stifter's heroes all discover that their progress has been benevolently watched over—not by Providence but by a philosopher, a club of freemasons, a wise old man or (in Heinrich Lee's case) a rich count. It is a halfhearted solution, which pays lip service to realism by employing a human agency, and at the same time disrupts it by showing once again that it was pointless to be apprehensive about the hero's acrobatics in the world when all the while there was a safety net spread out under him. (Thomas Mann in the *Joseph* novels, 1933–43, will go all the way and show a hero who even *knows* that he can come to no harm). What is it that prevents Keller (as it prevented his predecessors) from launching his hero wholeheartedly on the stormy seas of the real world? A brief comparison with, say, *Le Rouge et le Noir* helps to clarify what is characteristic of the whole German tradition which Keller's realism challenges but which he cannot wholly shake off.

The social inertia, the *resistance* which the world offers to Julien Sorel's ambitions is magnificently powerful. The measure of these forces is not so much that they lead to his violent end but that each, hero and world, gives as good as it gets. Leaving his father's sawmill, Julien enters a world depicted with such assurance, such singlemindedness of reference, such relevant circumstantiality, as is displayed in no German novel of the nineteenth century before Fontane. To compare the political cabal in which Julien gets involved in Paris with the lengthy discussions on road planning and civic duties which teach Heinrich Lee how to become a responsible member of the Helvetic Confederation is like moving from a city forest of predatory animals to alpine pastures. It is to recall the narrowness of the German—or, for that matter the Swiss—social and hence literary scene, and Keller's acquiescence in it. The irony with which Stendhal reports on Julien's progress has none of Keller's gentleness and bemused detachment. Its wryness implies a supreme narrative confidence, a perfect *rapport* between author and public—and this again has no equivalent in the German literature of the age outside the pages of Heine. The *Bildungsroman* makes of the hero's entry into the world something of a problem—shall he, shan't he?—as though he could somehow avoid it. For Stendhal the idea that world and society are anything but the firm *données* of the hero's situation does not arise. The idea that society will in some mysterious way yield before the hero's *weaknesses*—which is what it does in Keller's novel —is quite alien to Stendhal's scheme of things; and, it may not be irrelevant to add, to life as we know it. (Little wonder that Nietzsche, surrounded by conflicts of troubled inwardness, fell in love with the Will to Power.) Whatever Sorel wants he must fight for. The passion displayed in the course of that fight gives Stendhal's novel a dimension that is lacking in Keller's. Hence, the scheme of moral values challenged through Julien's actions is consistently more important. Heinrich is engaged in a protracted tussle with his art and his conscience, in a conflict with selfishness, heartlessness, irresponsibility; yet all these are *his* qualities: once he has sorted them out, the world offers no challenge. The problems he has to face intimate much more than a mere "aesthetic" concern, for his "art" manifests a defective moral sensibility. Yet in this way too the circle of the self is merely widened, never breached; the world is not exactly unreal but malleable.

Not all of Keller's narrative difficulties in *Der grüne Heinrich* were solved when he decided to give his novel a first-person narrator. Even in the final version several of its chapters are apt to turn into self-contained stories, into *Novellen*, and this tendency becomes even more marked in his later work, especially in *Martin Salander* (1886). We may see in this tendency a certain lack of narrative strength, of that energy to "go through to the end" with an extended story which is the hallmark of the great novelist; the matter is put quite simply in a recent deprecation of the short-story writer: "Anyone can be good for a week, but who can be good for a year, or two, or three?"[32] But there is another way of looking at this issue of the *petit genre*. Attacking Wagner's grandiose conception of the *Gesamtkunstwerk* (the "total work of art"), Nietzsche writes: "Nowadays it is only the small thing that can be truly well made. Only in that is integrity still possible.[33] And when Nietzsche goes on to praise the excellence of Keller's prose,[34] he has in mind not the novelist but the author of a group of *Novellen* whose very form turns to good account one of the compositional weaknesses of *Der grüne Heinrich*.

Moreover, in the course of exploring that smaller genre Keller achieves in *Die Leute von Seldwyla* the cohesion of theme that had occasionally eluded him in the novel. The ten stories assembled in the two volumes of that collection (I, 1856; II, 1874) seem at first sight to be only loosely connected. They are all set in "Seldwyla," an imaginary little Swiss town which, in its slothful and foolish ways, owes something to the "Abdera" of Aristophanes and Wieland. Yet for all their variety of mood, narrative manner, and sophistication, these *Novellen* have a unity beyond that of their common setting. Each of them is built around a mania, a single *idée fixe*, the staple of satirical comedy, and the narrative manner of each story is determined by the kind of *idée fixe* of which it treats. Thus the first, a cautionary tale of a cure for the sulks, is told in the tone of a child's story—not of a fairy tale but of a curious anecdote about the real world as it might be told to a child. Sometimes the characters move jerkily, like marionettes; the charm of such stories lies in their lifelike artifice. From wit, lighthearted irony, farce, burlesque, and caricature, through oblique and direct social criticism, all the way to the tragic manner, harsh satire, and the grotesque—Keller's stylistic range is remarkably wide. Among these, caricature is the most frequent device, because it is the most direct expression of that "terrible constriction of life in one-sidedness" (the phrase is Hebbel's), of those life-denying manias which are Keller's main theme.

All this is crowded into Seldwyla, an imaginary yet realistic nineteenth-century small-town setting and its environs. And now, because Keller takes issue with the *petit-bourgeois* constriction—because he no longer acquiesces in it—the taint of provincialism is gone. Nowhere is this more patent than in *Romeo und Julia auf dem Dorfe*, in the way he alters the grand Shakespearean theme to fit a totally different social situation. We witness the deterioration of two fathers from proud, patriarchal figures to litigious maniacs; we watch their quarrel over a stony piece of land intensifying, and see the two families abandon their farmsteads and move into the squalid quarters of the Seldwyler *Lumpenproletariat*; we see how, for all their innocent tenderness, all the love they bear each other, the two children-lovers are held and ultimately crushed by the world of their parents which is the only world they know. Now we understand that the Seldwyla setting is no fortuitous or fanciful framework but the precise and fitting condition of their lives: what is enacted in the Swiss backwater is a European theme.

At the same time we remain aware that the term "social realism," which we readily apply to Balzac or Dickens, does not quite fit. The atmosphere of a cautionary tale, complete with a moral message, informs each of these stories. Since even the most serious of them retains a fairy tale element, their psychology is unsearching. There is a polarity of good and evil; it is not rigid, education and good will enable some of the Seldwylers to mend their ways, but the processes of moral improvement or deterioration are based on the simplest motives and issue in the simplest ends. In *Frau Regel Amrain und ihr Jüngster* a spendthrift father has returned after years of fortune hunting in America, to find that his wife and son have saved the family business he left on the verge of bankruptcy, and are unwilling to let him take over its management:

Und er zog einige Wechselbriefe hervor sowie einen mit Gold angefüllten Gurt, was er alles auf den Tisch warf, und es waren allerdings einige tausend Gulden oder Taler. Allein er hatte sie nicht nach und nach erworben und verschwieg weislich, dass er diese Habe auf einmal durch irgendeinen Glücksfall erwischt, nachdem er sich lange genug ärmlich herumgetrieben in allen nordamerikanischen Staaten.... So ging er in die Stube, die man ihm eingeräumt; dort warf der alternde Mann seine Barschaft unmutig in einen Winkel, setzte sich rittlings auf einen Stuhl, senkte den grossen betrübten Kopf auf die Lehne und fing ganz bitterlich zu weinen an. Da trat seine Frau herein, sah, dass er sich elend fühlte, und musste sein Elend achten. Sowie sie aber wieder etwas an ihm achten konnte, kehrte ihre Liebe augenblicklich zurück.[35]

We note the beautifully rendered detail of the chair, the telling image of the childlike old man. But we also note the curiously unprobing account of the husband's and wife's reactions, and the absence of any comment on the *petit-bourgeois* scheme of values that underlies these reactions. Clearly, money is not everything in their ethos; or rather, there seem to be two kinds of money, and only one—that acquired by hard work—has any value in their eyes. And in Keller's too? He does not tell us.

Keller is at his best where he shows that trivial baseness is not really trivial, that the mood of *Gemütlichkeit* may on occasion stand in a terrifying alliance with depravity and cruelty; where he understands how close and powerful the alliance is, and how it is bound up with the stifling setting of the *petite bourgeoisie*; in fine, where he explores the social facts of his world. What gives his work a European quality and relevance is the fact that this provincial milieu and its inbred morality are a European phenomenon. In the stories of Gogol, Dostoevski, and Jan Neruda the satirical vein of Keller's Seldwyla is continued and intensified, the *petit-bourgeois* mentality dissected, the *idée fixe* which informs it shown up in all its harshness and, ultimately, its demonic obsessiveness. Keller's *Novellen* explore not the radical conclusions of one of the major themes of European realism but its less strenuous approaches. Occasionally his stories open towards tragedy or purposeful satire; more often their temper is that of idyll or fairy tale.

THEODOR FONTANE

With Theodor Fontane (1819–98) nineteenth-century German literature fully enters the tradition of European realism, not a moment too soon. His major novels are written at a time when that tradition is about to be superseded by the experimental schools of French and German naturalism, in whose prose works the focus shifts from integrated scenes of social life to blowups of discrete, often discontinuous details.

The son of a Gascon Huguenot father and a Cévenoise mother, Fontane was born and bred on the North Sea coast of Prussia. No writer ever took the grades to Parnassus more circumspectly and with more deliberation. In 1850, aged thirty, Fontane gave up both a reasonably good job as pharmaceutical dispenser and his liberal opinions, and accepted a job in the Press Office of the Prussian government, taking over its shortlived London correspondence in 1855, and resigning his agency in 1858. There now followed a checkered career of journalistic, literary, and educational ventures. As correspondent of various, mainly reactionary, Berlin papers, including the notorious *Kreuzzeit-*

ung, Fontane made a name for himself with reports from the War of Schleswig-Holstein of 1864, the Austrian Campaign of 1866, and the Franco-Prussian War (in the course of which he was arrested as a spy and spent a short time as prisoner of war on the Ile d'Oléron). Throughout the '50s and '60s he had received various government grants for work on historical studies in Mark Brandenburg, and in 1876 he accepted the secretaryship of the Prussian Royal Academy of Arts. The promised sinecure turned out to be an imposition and, against strong protests from wife and family, he again resigned. By this time he had published two war books, four volumes of travels in Mark Brandenburg full of picturesque local history, a slim volume of ballads inspired by Sir Walter Scott, and a volume of impressions of London (the outcome of three long visits as a correspondent). There is a good deal of charm and humor in these books, some fine descriptive writing but, like Dickens' *American Notes* and Henry James's *A Little Tour of France*, they are approaches to literature rather than the thing itself.

And now, at the age of fifty-six—the lateness is without parallel among great writers—he took the last step towards his art. A whole life, varied and not unadventurous, fell into place: commercial experience, service in the army and in the Prussian bureaucracy, landed *Junkers* and ironical generals, small shopkeepers, Protestant parsons and Catholic *dévots*, conservative *von und zu's* and progressive schoolmasters; a few dogs and elegant Englishmen and picturesque Austrians in the margin; marriages and divorces, bankruptcies and get-rich-quick schemes, duels and illnesses and the gentle sloping of life towards death—he "knew it all inside out," it was all merely waiting for him to set it down. At his death, twenty-two years later, he could look back on a harvest of seventeen novels and *Novellen* (and a number of short stories), at least half of them major achievements, and confess that he had "accomplished what I had been destined for from the beginning." And when a friend wrote that "perhaps he could have achieved more if [he] hadn't been kept back by perpetual 'hard struggling,'" Fontane replied, "All that business about 'struggling' is superficially true. But even if I'd had to struggle less [*wenn ich weniger gestruggelt hätte*], I wouldn't have achieved more. The little that was in me came out in that way too. I've no complaint against my fate." The understatement is characteristic of Fontane; one cannot (alas) think of another German writer, past or present, who would have made it as unaffectedly.

For of course Fontane *is* a German novelist. Intellectual bad manners, especially nationalistic ones, have a tenacious life. Among some German academic critics of the older generation Fontane is still regarded as something of an alien intruder (see his family background); his favorite genre, the *Gesellschaftsroman*, the novel of high society, is in their eyes too frivolous and worldly, too "French," to deserve serious scholarly attention; and his achievement is seen as the end product of a spent tradition. These disparagements throw more light into the oubliettes of the arbiters of yesterday than they do on a writer whose achievement is only now being made available to an English-speaking public by a faithful and sympathetic translator.[36] Fontane may be a late comer in European terms, in German literature he is above all an innovator. His narrative work contains strands of a specifically German literary tradition, but these are integrated into an overall conception of the historical and social novel which is cosmopolitan in its outlook, and in its very structure indifferent to national jealousies. He has learned a great deal from Sir Walter Scott, Thackeray, and Dickens; from Balzac, and probably also from Flaubert; he is fully alive to his contemporaries Ibsen and Zola—he is, in other words, a European novelist. And as such he creates a locale as unmistakable as Dickens' London, Flaubert's Paris, Tolstoi's Moscow, Jan Neruda's Prague or Eça de Queiroz's Lisbon: he is *the* novelist of the Berlin, Prussia, and Germany of the Second Reich "as it really happened." The notion that these twin aspects of Fontane's art—its international connection and its stable local setting—are somehow incompatible could occur only to those who believed that the Wilhelminians lived on the moon or in Never-Never Land (as some of his and our contemporaries appear to do). The whole scale of milieux from the lower middle class to the *Junkers* and the courtly entourage of Berlin—the working classes are on the whole outside Fontane's range—has such a fascination for him that occasionally he contents himself with presenting milieu almost as the substance of a story, as a five-finger exercise on an instrument which he plays with an unparalleled virtuosity and assurance. One such story offers him an occasion for a brief observation on that complicated relationship between Germany and "the West" to which, twenty-odd years later, his heir Thomas Mann devoted a long and far from exhilarating book[37]—an observation, incidentally, which sums up many of the arguments of the present chapter:

> Wer was hat, nun ja, der kann das Leben so nehmen, wie's wirklich ist, der kann das sein, was sie jetzt einen Realisten nennen, wer aber nichts hat, wer immer in einer Wüste Sahara lebt, der kann ohne Fata Morgana mit Palmen und Odelisken und all dergleichen gar nicht existieren.[38]

There are not many such detachable passages in Fontane, partly because his fiction is unself-conscious, partly because it dissolves all crystallized opinion in the medium of extended conversations—and the wealth and variety of his kinds of conversation has only recently been fully appreciated.[39] The tolerantly ironical yet incisive tone of the passage, on the other hand, is fully characteristic of his art.

But is the statement true of the Germany of his day? Are we not quoting out of context, which (in this story) is the impoverishment and decline of a minor aristocratic family? After all, what Fontane depicts is the Germany of the heirs of Bismarck, of the *Junkertum* and "*Kaiser Willem der Zwote*," of the "*Pickelhaube*" and "*Reichsadler*" and the Prussian civil service; lobster and

Vouvray at Kempinski's; the Krupps and Ballins and the rayon factories of Elberfeld-Barmen; a nascent colonial empire with aspirations in Africa, China, and the Middle East—who is there, in this rich and assertive society, who "has nothing, [and] . . . has to live in a Sahara desert"?

It is Thomas Mann's *Buddenbrooks* (1901) that explicitly takes issue with the apparent contradiction characteristic of the German *fin de siècle*, the contradiction between a growing material enrichment and a growing spiritual discontent and alienation from the materialistic civilization of the age. Mann resolves it, with narrative means of a radically ironic kind, by placing the contradiction firmly in the center of his stage. Fontane's irony is much gentler, more tolerant, his novels are structured less antithetically. He senses and intimates the velleities of his contemporary world, but he is too deeply involved in that world, he cares for it too much and too directly, to become a "good" prophet of the bad. In their métier at all events, the great realistic novelists are on the whole indifferent prophets. The prophesies of doom they must leave to the philosophers. For prophesy implies the possibility of an alternative interpretation of experience, and thus a detachment from the encompassing reality of the world; whereas realism is founded in a creative acknowledgment of social reality, an assent, however critical, to the world not as an interpretation at all but as the one and only bedrock certainty there is. The philosopher, interested as he is in the interpretability of the world, offers alternative points of view. No sooner does Nietzsche praise "our present delight in the Real" (the basis of Fontane's work), welcoming it as a reaction against "our old delight in the Unreal, which we have indulged in for so long and to excess," than he proceeds to question "our problematic lack of discrimination and finesse" in respect of that Real.[40] What Nietzsche criticizes is not an inadequate moral (let alone ethical) discrimination, but an epistemological and existential attitude. Moving further and further away from proposals for a reform of existing contemporary reality, Nietzsche is increasingly committed to another, a new kind of reality altogether: a realm (passionately invoked but speculative for all that) which the realistic *romanciers* may not enter.

Fontane too is critical of contemporary vulgarities, material and spiritual alike. But the alternative values he intimates are as firmly embedded in the encompassing "Real" as are the vulgarities of fanaticism, intolerance, and bad taste he shows up. He has a congenital sympathy for those who "can't exist without a fata morgana with palms and odalisques and all that sort of thing." Those of his characters who experience this need—they are varied and come from all the walks of life he presents—tend to live on the ineffectual margins of society. But they are not the "alienated outsiders" of existentialist literature. Their morality is in several ways different from the morality of the people nearer the center of society, their lives are above all more private. But, after all, that inner circle too, with its notoriously cold and often inhuman ethos of the Prussian imperative, is upheld by living people—that is, by people full of private doubts and mental reservations under their self-imposed discipline. The center itself, the center of power where "historic" decisions are made, Fontane does not depict (nor does he construct a theory that offers an alternative account of the course of history, as Tolstoi did in the last chapters of *War and Peace*). But the people near the center of power as Fontane presents them are not without a secret sympathy with those whom it is their role to govern and generally keep on a short rein—the fata morganists of all kinds.

Fontane has been accused of snobbery in the choice of his milieux; of siding with the aristocracy against the common people; and of depicting the latter only in their comic or sentimental aspect. It is certainly true that he has no eye for the economic plight of the proletariat, for what the Naturalists called "the Social Problem." As to the lower middle classes, their representatives tend to become comic when they move out of their proper sphere, into the ambience of political radicals and rabble-rousing reformers. Yet the heroine of *Irrungen, Wirrungen* (*Trials and Tribulations*, 1888), a working girl living in the most modest circumstances, possesses an honesty and intensity of emotion which are not matched by her aristocratic lover. The strength and beauty of her character lie in her capacity not to allow the inevitable parting to impair the quality of the love that precedes it. Lene's renunciation of Botho involves suffering but no disillusionment, because it has been anticipated and accepted throughout the affair. Her acknowledgment of the ways of the world implies no conformism on Fontane's part. His judgment on Botho, the dashing young officer who dutifully marries into "family" and money, is as subtle and un-emphatic as is the rest of the story.

Lene marries one Gideon Franke, a somewhat solemn foreman in a metal factory (visiting in top hat, black gloves, and all) and a lay preacher of the Pietist persuasion. A figure of fun? Not quite. In an interview with Botho, whom he has come to question about Lene, Franke turns out to be a man of the utmost tolerance, honesty, seriousness, and loving concern. The comic aspect of the man is not hidden ("Ja, Herr Baron, auf die Proppertät kommt es an und auf die Honnetität kommt es an, und auf die Reelität"[41]); nor is the fact that he has gone a long way for his convictions: "I was over in the States for a good while. And even though not everything over there is pure gold, no more than here, *one* thing *is* true: you learn to look at things differently, not always through the same spectacles." It is not Gideon Franke who is the fool at this interview.

Fontane knows that the "high society" from which his novels are drawn is, if not doomed, yet certainly ill-equipped for survival. He knows that its notion of a man's "proper place in life" is upheld by an outdated ethos, and that social changes, involving the demise of the old families, are in the air; "I'm becoming more and more democratic [he writes in 1894] and the real nobility is just about the only class left that I can still appreciate. All that lies in betwixt and between—*Spiessbürger, bourgeois*, officials, the so-called 'cultured' classes—gives me little joy." His fastidious dislike of ostentation and pretentiousness goes hand in hand with a very special affection for the paternal benevolence, frugality, and quixotic innocence of the *Junkers* of the old, that is Frederician, school. They are to him quite the most picturesque and absorbing figures on the social scene, and thus the proper objects of his creative attention. Twenty years before he sets out on his literary career, Fontane confesses to a friend (in a letter from London, 25-iv. 1856) that "my preoccupation with politics is, after all, only literary," yet in the same breath he criticizes "our habit of overestimating *art* at the expense of *life*." Scornful of the self-importance of the politicking *littérateur*, he at the same time questions the ethos of *l'art pour l'art*: the remark is characteristic of his freedom from every fanaticism, political or aesthetic. I have quoted it to offer reassurance to our democratic sensibilities: more important than Fontane's partisanship of the landed gentry is his informed and critical *interest* in their reactions to the process of social change.

Fontane depicts the reality that is, and its antecedents in the recent past, not the utopia that might or should be. His love of anecdote, in the service of that past, makes him occasionally err on the side of prolixity. His narrative mode is social, which means that in his treatment of intimate situations he preserves an unprobing decorum. An adulterous affair is in progress but the lovers' meetings are not described.[42] Or again: An elderly man, Privy Councillor Ladalinski, has entered a village church, to view the body of his only son, killed in a futile sortie. Only an old sexton is his guide in the darkening church: "At first it seemed as if the candles would go out, but then they started to burn properly. Taking up the cloth that covered the bier and placing it on the altar steps, the old man said quietly: 'Well, the Lord be with you, my dear sir.' Count Ladalinski had risen and stood at the narrow end of the bier. 'Am I at his head or at his feet?' he asked. 'At his head.' 'I think I'd rather stand at his feet.' After this they changed places and lifted the lid, the old Privy Councillor keeping his eyes firmly shut. Only then did he look at his son, steadily and for a long time, and to his own surprise he found that his heart was beating calmly."[43]

What strengthens Fontane's realism is a spirit of sympathetic but far from undiscriminating tolerance, and a decorum which encompasses but does not intrude on men's deepest feelings. It is this twin quality of his style which, in a time such as ours when the literary shocks of sex and violence are two-a-penny, makes for the value and interest of his work.

Fontane's *Vor dem Sturm* (*Before the Storm*, 1878), his first work of fiction, is his and German literature's masterpiece in the genre of the historical novel. It derives many of its settings from Fontane's early volumes of travels in the Prussian province of Brandenburg (1862–82), through which he first became known to a wider public. Like *War and Peace* (1869), it is a panorama of life in the Napoleonic era, presenting the intertwining fortunes of a number of families and private persons in the shadow of a warlike action, though it is cast on an altogether smaller scale. Its events and complex plot span the time between Christmas Eve 1812 and early spring 1813; the locale is delimited by the triangle Berlin–Küstrin–Frankfurt an der Oder, and the countryside in between. This concentration in time and space is abandoned only where Fontane's episodic vein takes us into the histories of the families depicted, or where the Spanish War of Succession, Borodino, or Napoleon's Russian campaign are discussed by the leading characters of the novel. The uniqueness and distinction of *Vor dem Sturm* seems to me to lie in the political conflict into which other strands, sentimental attachments, and literary activities are subtly laced. This conflict demands moral decisions, involves a full range of nationalistic attitudes, and raises questions fundamental to the whole social edifice of the Prussian state. It is argued out step by step, and it is acted out in life and death. In taking up this major political theme and bringing it to its conclusion undistracted by promptings from a "higher sphere",[44] the novel achieves a distinction unique in German fiction.

In *Unwiederbringlich* (*Beyond Recall*, 1891), his crowning achievement, Fontane unites the European tradition of social realism with a characteristically German theme. The novel has been compared with *Madame Bovary*, but the parallel will not take us further than the fact that the act of adultery (central to both) is partly founded in the contrast between the boredom of provincial life and the exciting social whirl of the city; the two heroines—Emma Bovary and Christine Holk—are made of very different stuff, and their conflicts are of a very different order.

The chosen settings of the action—Schloss Holkenäs on the North Sea coast of Schleswig-Holstein; the Danish capital with its rococo residence, Tivoli Gardens, and minuscule royal court; and Schloss Friedrichsburg, the Princess Royal's favorite castle—are described with that eye for architectural detail which is one of the delights of Fontane's narrative manner. Buildings, interiors, and the niceties of social intercourse are all firmly related to the story, yet there is none of that emphasis on the symbolizing nature of the objects that make up the milieu which we find in the early work of Thomas Mann, Fontane's only great disciple. The story concerns a marital incompatibility between Count Helmuth von Holk and his wife Christine. It begins with the abandoning of the old castle of Holkenäs; the building of a new one, indicative of Holk's restlessness, fills Christine with forebodings. (One is reminded of a similar episode in *Buddenbrooks*, where it marks the first step of "the Firm's" decline.) Holk, an attractive and not unintelligent nobleman "in the prime of life," has the virtues and weaknesses of his comfortable character. He is neither thoughtless of his family nor consistently frivolous; easygoing yet with a sense of decorum and even self-importance; pleasure seeking yet with occasional qualms of conscience. There is about him a certain suggestibility which waits for the occasion but does not determine it, and his self-knowledge too is at best limited to the occasion in hand. He has all the qualities of Eduard, the hero of Goethe's *Die Wahlverwandtschaften* (*Elective Affinities*), short of Eduard's generous impetuosity; in terms of Schopenhauer's characterology Holk is nearly all "empirical self," and has only mutability for his immutable substance. His wife Christine, on the other hand, is all that Holk is not: brought up on the strict religious principles of pietist Herrnhut, she is by nature melancholy, severe, and inclined to censoriousness. She is determined to guide their children in the path of righteousness, and has the strength of convictions firmly held and uncompromisingly practiced. Yet she is not simply religious for in adversity it is her injured pride that comes uppermost. In her rigidness she approaches the condition of that "intelligible self" (for Schoperhouer, the foundation of human character) which is increasingly scornful of all the "empirical" world offers. Unlike Ottilie, the young heroine of *Die Wahlverwandtschaften,* Christine undergoes no dramatic development. But she resembles the Ottilie of the last part of Goethe's novel in the severity of her withdrawal and in the impenetrable solitude of her end.

Fontane's novel contains no such abridged summary of the two characters as I have presented. The story opens on a fairly harmonious and happy relationship. Each conversation between Holk and Christine, and with other members of the family, household, and neighborhood of Holkenäs, serves to underline the contrast and growing conflict, each event widens the gulf. In several novels Fontane voices his conviction that marriage based on the principle of "complementaries," on a union of opposite characters, will not work: Holk and Christine bring out the worst in each other.

It is Holk "from whom scandal cometh." Called to do his stint as the Princess's gentleman-in-waiting in Copenhagen, he finds himself stimulated by life in the capital; he flirts with the married daughter of his landlady; falls in love with Ebba von Rosenfeld, a lady-in-waiting whom he saves from a conflagration at Schloss Friedrichsburg, which dramatically ends their only night of love; and insists on a separation from Christine, only to find himself rejected by Ebba. Yet in all this Holk is moved by no passion, no clear intention even, but by each occasion as it presents itself to his yielding character. Christine too is not without blame. In her distaste for the frivolous court life she lets Holk go alone to Copenhagen, in her severity and pride she taunts him with his weaknesses and impairs the chance of a reconciliation even before the adultery has occurred, and before he has taken his unfortunate (and, in the event, ridiculous) decision. She thus offers the occasions which he is only too glad to convert into causes. Fontane apportions no guilt and pronounces no judgment; the story is the working out of an incompatibility which no good intention on either side can alter, since all intentions are worsted by the fixed "intelligible" character of one and the unsteady "empirical" character of the other.

The novel is built from the dominant contrast between the somewhat somber and simple north German life at Holkenäs and the "Parisian" life of an aged Princess whose social graces are not free from cynicism and whose love of intrigue is not without a touch of evil. It is the Princess who arranges for Ebba and Holk to be lodged in the same outlying tower of Schloss Friedrichsburg. A subtler intimation of her delight in seeing the intrigue grow occurs during the sledging expedition that ends Chapter 25. Ebba and Holk have left the company and are skating down a frozen waterway that issues into Lake Arre and beyond it into the open sea. As they speed towards the narrow belt of ice, the disposition of three wills (Ebba's and Holk's, but also the absent Princess') in the strategy of the affair is firmly established:

> Their eyes met and seemed to be asking: "Shall we?" And the answer was, at least, not a refusal; but just as they were about to pass a line of small firs marking the final limit of safety, Holk suddenly swung towards the right, pulling Ebba with him. "We've reached the limit, Ebba. Shall we go beyond it?" Ebba drove the points of her skates into the ice and said: "If you are thinking of going back, that means that you want to, and that's good enough for me. In any case, Erichsen and Schimmelmann [two members of the party] will be expecting us, though perhaps not the Princess."[45]

Some of the contrast between Holkenäs and Copenhagen rubs off on Holk. To his wife he is bound to appear at his most frivolous and worldly, whereas at court he is apt to cut the somewhat awkward figure of a country nobleman; in fact he is not quite at home in either place. An example of what Ebba will ridicule as Holk's "misplaced solemnity" recalls to us the strong sense, in this novel of emotional conflict too, of Fontane's social realism. During one of his first meetings with her, Holk airs his somewhat pompous knowledge of genealogy by informing Ebba that his own greatuncle's second wife was a Rosenberg, that "all the Rosenbergs descended from the brother of the Archbishop of Prague," and other sundry matters of consuming interest of which Ebba confesses herself ignorant:

> "From which I should deduce [Holk continues] that you probably belong to the Lipinsky and not to the Gruszczinsky branch of the family."
> "To my great regret, not even that. True, if I'm allowed to put Lipeson instead of Lipinsky, a boldness which that illustrious family will, I trust, forgive, then perhaps I might claim a link between myself and that family by using that form of the name. You see, I'm a Rosenberg-Meyer or more correctly a Meyer-Rosenberg, granddaughter of the Meyer-Rosenberg who was well known in Swedish history as King Gustav III's personal pet Jew."[46]

Well may the relentless genealogist wince.

After this we are hardly surprised that it is Ebba who, first in a conversation with the Princess, then in the course of her scathing rejection of Holk's suit, gives us the fullest explicit insight into his character. Meeting her for the first time after the Friedrichsburg escapade, he has come to press his claim on her, but he does not get beyond telling her that he has left his wife. Instantly and without the slightest compunction she rebuts his advances:

> My dear friend, you're quite incorrigible. I remember telling you at the very beginning of our acquaintance and later on as well, in any case, more than once, that you were on the wrong track. Nor will I take anything back, on the contrary. All those things that I used to mention merely to tease you and irritate you a little when I was feeling impertinent, I shall now repeat in deadly earnest and even as an accusation. You try to be a courtier and a man of the world and you are neither one nor the other. You're half-hearted in both and you're always sinning against the most elementary rules of the game—particularly at the present moment. How can anyone, where a lady is concerned, refer to words that she was foolish enough—or perhaps kind enough—to utter in an unguarded moment? All that remains now is for you to mention certain *happenings* and you'll be the perfect gentleman. Don't try to interrupt, I've worse things to say to you yet. Except for the small matter of constancy, Mother Nature has endowed you with everything needed to make a good husband and you should have been content with that. In any neighboring territory, you're completely at a loss and you only go from one blunder to another.[47]

It is entirely characteristic of the tolerant realist that the truth about his hero should come not from Christine who takes a pride in her righteousness, but from Ebba who is certainly no better than she should be; truth, for Fontane, is not the prerogative of the truthful.

The structure of *Unwiederbringlich* (*Beyond Recall*) is very nearly flawless, but not quite. After Holk's slightly ridiculous suit ("*ein Korb . . . einer der rundesten . . .*") has been rejected, he spends eighteen months on aimless travels (in a somewhat similar situation Eduard, the hero of Goethe's novel, departs for the wars). At the end of this time we find Holk looking down on a fashionable square near Hyde Park and poring over the announcement of Ebba's marriage in the society column of the London *Times*. Negotiations between husband and wife are taken up by Christine's brother, Arne, and Schwarzkoppen, the family parson, and at last a reconciliation is effected. As in *Effi Briest* so here too there is something of a hiatus. Between climax and final disaster the novelist is playing for time. For two brief chapters he accompanies Holk on his travels, has him kept informed of events at home, but leaves Christine's solitude unexplored. The reconciliation is strengthened by a reconsecration of their marriage; Chapter 33 begins, "However, the feeling of sadness that had dominated the moving ceremony appeared to be unjustified, and 'the happiness of Holkenäs' seemed really to be returning." But while Holk has little difficulty in resuming the relationship as if nothing had happened, Christine is unable to forget the tort. There are no more reproaches; on the contrary, Holk is conscious of Christine's "desire to forget," but her "empirical self" is fighting an unequal battle. One by one Christine sheds her ties. The children have no more need of her, her feeling towards Holk is dominated by resignation, even her old confidante, Fräulein Julie von Dobschütz, is excluded from her intimacy, until at last her solitude becomes absolute. This is Fontane's return to the old German theme, to that condition of isolation, at once implanted by fate and self-imposed by the will, in which Goethe's Ottilie too ends her life. In abandoning Christine after the climax, he allows himself no room in which to give a full image of her solitary soul, no room to show at all fully how the ties break under the weight of her melancholy and severity. Once again Fontane's decorum prevails, but here it curtails a legitimate interest. He does not, after all, care for too much intimacy; he prefers to suggest causes through their effects. It is well for a novelist to curb his psychological curiosity, to leave intact the enigmatic charm at the center of his character; perhaps Fontane applies the curb a little too soon.

A simple little ballad about the happiness of days beyond recall is sung by one of the children; it ends with the lines, "Doch die mir die liebsten gewesen sind,/Ich wünsche sie nicht zurück."[48] This is the last word on Christine's life; under this motto she sets out on her last journey. Through her suicide no divine retribution is exacted, as it is through Anna Karenina's; nor is she driven to it by a round of trivial contingencies, as is Emma Bovary. We hear of a brief moment of hesitation but of no last anguished confusion (however, we have only "dear Dobschütz's" letter to go by): Christine's decision is still illuminated by her immutable will. Once wounded, "the intelligible self" can never heal again.

Christine's spirituality as Fontane portrays it—the spirituality of "*geschlossene Persönlichkeit*"—is hostile to the one value to which, in his novels, all values are related. This value is not happiness—to set up happiness as essential to human life would have seemed unrealistic to a man who had not too much experience of it in his own life. It is neither justice nor truthfulness nor integrity—all of which splendid virtues he is apt to depict at precisely the points at which they cease to be virtues and become excuses for fanaticism or self-assertion. The central value that emerges from his novels is involved, though none too securely, in all these. It is tolerance—a value, it may be relevant to add, with which neither his world nor ours is over-endowed.

STORIES OF CHARISMA AND FATE

From Goethe's *Werther* (1774) and *Die Wahlverwandtschaften* (*Elective Affinities*, 1809) through Rilke's *Die Aufzeichnungen des Malte Laurids Brigge* (*Notebooks of Malte Laurids Brigge*, 1910) to Thomas Mann's *Doktor Faustus* (1947) the twin themes of solitude and isolation have formed a major aspect of German narrative prose; it is not too much to say that in the explorations of solitary experience lies its major contribution to world literature. Some of the formal problems to which these explorations gave rise in the age of realism have been mentioned. The characteristic solution, as we find it in the stories of Adalbert Stifter, combines a parochial setting with existential depth.

Rilke's artist as a young man is absolutely alone, the hostile city that surrounds Malte is a world not of people but of things, his only company are his childhood memories. Where solitude falls short of such radical alienation, as it does in nineteenth-century stories, there the simplest and least extended social organizations will serve best to set out the theme. Thus the society that Stifter presents is insistently paternalistic. He confines his stories to the master-servant, father-son, old man-youth, husband-wife relationships; and even in *Witiko*, his last novel, the attempt to present the wider canvas of a warlike situation recedes behind pedagogic intentions realized within a feudal nexus, where fealty to the lord and king is still based on a pattern of familial values.

In the stories of Theodor Storm (1817–88) the themes of solitude and isolation form a dominant dialectic of guilt and punishment. Solitude as a "natural," that is initially given, disposition of mind is no longer the ground of personal value (as it was with Stifter), but the isolation and inconsolable loneliness to which it leads are experienced as a punishment. The guilt of the solitary man, in Storm's early stories, is not a moral failing but a predicament of individual fate. Sometimes (as in *Immensee*, 1852) it is manifest in an inability to divulge and conquer the deprivation; at other times (*Viola Tricolor*, 1874) love and sympathy in the face of mortal danger succeed in bridging the gulf; then again (*Aquis Submersus*, 1877) moral guilt is added to the fated predicament. In *Carsten Curator* (1878) and several other stories the brief happiness by which an elderly man's marriage is attended leaves him, on his bereavement, overwhelmed with responsibilities and an unabating sense of loss. In his last (and perhaps greatest) *Novelle*, *Der Schimmelreiter* (*The White Horseman*, 1888), Storm embodies the deprivation in a charismatic figure. Hauke Haien's life's work, the building of a dyke in his Frisian village, is achieved at the price of his increasing isolation from the community whose safety and survival his work serves, but it is this same heroic alienation that leads to his doom.

In 1825 the political scientist Adam Müller had coined the term *geschlossene Persönlichkeit* (an enclosed, or rather embattled, personality); in fiction this is a character whose contacts with the outside world are narrowed down to the assertion of his purposeful and uncompromising will to power. In a century at whose beginning stands the figure of Napoleon this conception of human character becomes dominant. It is embodied in Melville's Captain Ahab and Dickens' Mr. Dombey, in Storm's Hauke Haien and in the father-figure of Otto Ludwig's *Zwischen Himmel und Erde* (*Between Heaven and Earth*, 1856).[49] These men are, in a metaphorical sense, the creators of the worlds they command; at the moment when his immovable will collapses, "Mr. Dombey's

World" (this is Dickens' own chapter heading) dissolves also. Arthur Schopenhauer, the philosopher of "the embattled personality," builds his system by
taking the metaphor seriously.

The charismatic leader-figure in his essential isolation is also central to the
prose-work of the Swiss Conrad Ferdinand Meyer (1825–98), whose historical
novels and *Novellen* have worn less well than his poetry. Highly charged contrasts of moods and colors, which in the stories make for melodrama, are
perfectly contained and balanced in short lyrical poems intimating the entice-
ment of tranquillity and death. Dark surfaces and landscapes are briefly illuminated by sharp streaks of color ("Auf dem Canal Grande"; "Erntegewitter"),
moods of sultry repose ("Schwüle"), or melancholy ("Eingelegte Ruder")
issue in moments of clarity and insight. A sonnet-like impression of a nocturnal
journey on the lake of Zürich ("Im Spätboot") hides in its core a moment of
mystery, and again the poem ends on a note at once melancholy and enticing:
"Schmerz und Lust erleiden sanften Tod" ("Pain and joy endure a gentle
death"). Meyer's poems point the way from *fin de siècle* decadence to that near-
identity of thing, word and experience of imagism, more especially to the
Dinggedichte (object poems) of Rilke's *Neue Gedichte* (1907) and to the Paris of
Malte Laurids Brigge. In the poem "Schwarzschattende Kastanie" the firmly
evoked sense-impression of a chestnut tree on the lake shore is briefly contrasted with a merry group of bathing children; but the group is not wholly dominated by the central image, it retains a life of its own. Such poems as "Zwei
Segel" ("Two Sails") and "Der römische Brunnen" ("Roman Fountain"), on the
other hand, are wholly confined to the evocation of objects of the outer world;
their contours are made meaningful both as parts of reality *and* as discrete
symbols of a reality in which explicitly human elements are no longer mentioned: twentieth-century imagism has its ancestry in these poems.

In Meyer's stories elements of "poison, passion, putrefaction" are handled
all too freely. His great "renaissance" personalities may be fantasy compensations
for his own psychological inadequacies; to us their "amoral" greatness seems
suspect. The novel *Jürg Jenatsch, eine Bündnergeschichte* (1874) tells of the high
adventures and gory death of a Lutheran buccaneering parson of the early
seventeenth century, whose heroic life is divided between Swiss patriotism,
anti-Habsburg guerilla warfare, and amorous intrigues. In a scene before the
altar of a Venetian church are assembled all the most perishable ingredients of
historical romance: a group of youthful warriors under a picture by "Maestro
Titiano," a pack of elegant greyhounds, searing amorous glances behind veils
of black lace. Actually, what Meyer's tableaux recall is not Titian but Hans
Makart (1840–84), whose luxuriant costume canvases and stage decors (much
admired by A. Hitler) were all the rage in the Second German Empire. The prose
is not free from theatricalities, a riot of verbs of violent motion and emotion
gives it an effect of breathlessness, though occasionally (especially in *Der Schuss
von der Kanzel, A Shot from the Pulpit,* 1883) it is relieved by touches of humor and

ironical characterization. Meyer's attempts at exploring a spiritual conflict in his charismatic heroes leave one disappointed. Of the several interpretations the life of St. Thomas à Becket has received, *Der Heilige* (*The Saint*, 1879) is certainly the most surprising. Like T. S. Eliot and Jean Anouilh, Meyer is fascinated by the central enigma of Becket's character—the conversion of the power-loving courtier and superb diplomat into a passionate defender of the Christian Church. Unlike the playwrights, the *Novelle* writer finds it necessary to heighten the conflict between Archbishop and King by introducing a revenge motive. Thomas the Chancellor is given a daughter[50] who is seduced by Henry and inadvertently killed on her flight from "Engelland" to France. That the abduction and death of his daughter should rankle with Thomas is hardly surprising. But Meyer's narrative intention is more ambitious. The revenge for Grace's death is meant to *contribute* to and be a part of Becket's ascetic and Christian spirituality ("*er wurde immer christlicher*"), a spirituality which leads to the conflict with his sovereign and his eventual death in martyrdom. The story ("*Rahmenerzählung*") uses the device of a worldly narrator, a jolly crossbowman, who does not pretend to understand the logic behind this egregious spirituality; the present writer has fared no better.

With Annette von Droste-Hülshoff's *Novelle*, *Die Judenbuche* (*Jew's Beech*, 1845) we return to the localized setting (Westphalia); here a strong fate element, superstitions, peasant avarice, and those deep prejudices which are exacerbated by poverty and rural isolation, combine into a detective story whose mystery is solved by the workings of retributive justice. Similar ingredients go into the *Novelle*, *Die Schwarze Spinne* (*The Black Spider*, 1842–46) by the Swiss parson Jeremias Gotthelf (1797–1854). In his patriarchal ethos, simple psychology, as well as in that distrust of urban life which is endemic to the writers of the age, Gotthelf shows affinities with Stifter; however, the interest of his immense romans-fleuve is not (so it seems to me) easily discernible to readers who are unwilling to equate highmindedness and didacticism with literary values.

FRIEDRICH WILHELM NIETZSCHE

On the borderline live the strangest of creatures.

—G. C. *Lichtenberg*

The German student-soldiers of the First World War, who are reported to have carried Goethe's and Mörike's poems in one pocket of their knapsacks and Nietzsche's *Zarathustra* in the other, belong to a generation that never recovered from the conflict of divided allegiances.

This conflict, in which the main themes and issues of the literature under review are involved, is at the center of Nietzsche's passionate thinking. Yet

Nietzsche, for all his partisanship, was anything but a Nietzschean, the connection between his writings and its ideological "message" is hardly more than adventitious. He is the first, and remains the greatest, antisystematic philosopher of modern Europe. The true history of his ideas is simple enough; it is summed up by Vauvenargue's reflection, "Great men, while teaching little men to think, have set them on the path of error." His thinking and writing at its best displays a vital, passionate commitment to an uncompromising truthfulness, of which his lack of discursiveness and his aphoristic style are the hallmarks; whereas, as F. H. Bradley observed, "Our live experiences, fixed in aphorisms, stiffen into cold epigram" or, in the case of the Nietzscheans, into lifeless and life-destroying ideology. His finest insights have been turned into a ragbag of -isms: vitalism, racialism, social Darwinism, and anti-Semitism, and they became a main part of the superstructure of fascism. His writings, and especially the notebooks published posthumously by his sister under the title *Der Wille zur Macht* (*The Will to Power*, 1902 f.), contain elements of all these doctrines; they also contain thoughts scathingly hostile to all these -isms. It is the glory as it is the curse of those least restrictive forms he increasingly chose—aphorism, question-and-answer paragraph, brief or extended reflection—that they are able to accommodate and give expression to an unnerving speculative freedom. What saves the greater part of his work from chaotic contradictoriness (and we shall see that not all his contradictions lead to chaos), what the "Nietzscheans" were bound to ignore, is the style and temper of his thinking. And if an excuse be needed for including a sketch of at least one of Nietzsche's books in a history of German literature, it lies in the fact that an original style of thinking and writing is deployed in the service not of an ideology, not of a novel system of values even, but of a new style of life.

Whatever other intellectual vices Nietzsche may display, he never allows himself the comfort of an easy way out. He is the most energetic and strenuous of thinkers, who comes to see a major value in the personal and "existential" (the term is Kierkegaard's, not his) commitment of a man to his thinking, and who judges ideas primarily by a man's existential right to them. It was Nietzsche (not Sartre) who first saw man as the creator of his values, and who demanded that our thinking "and hypothesizing shall reach no further than [our] creative will."[51] This demand for a harmony between a man's vital powers on one hand and his reflective and cognitive capacities on the other Nietzsche does not always restrict to high philosophical matters: "Worthy did this man seem to me, and ripe for the meaning of the earth. But when I beheld his wife, the earth seemed to me like a dwelling-place of the senseless."[52] Again and again, in Nietzsche's observations on the thinkers and men of action of the past, it is not their detached opinions that matter to him but the quantity of personal being involved in their opinions or beliefs *together with* the quality of that being: "God is an hypothesis. But who is there that could drink all the bitter torment of that hypothesis without dying." Moreover, this unity of a man's thinking and doing, enjoined from Nietzsche's earliest books to his last jottings, is not a matter of exhortation only. The aspiration toward it forms a major aspect of his manner of philosophizing, of his several literary styles, and imposes a coherence on the seemingly absolute speculative license.

Friedrich Nietzsche was born in 1844 in Röcken, a small town not far from Leipzig, into a family which on both sides came from Lutheran clerical stock. The background is characteristic; from Handel through Lessing and Wieland to Hermann Hesse, German culture owes to the Lutheran parsonage a special debt which, as often as not, takes the form of a reaction against its spiritual ethos. His father died when Nietzsche was five years old, probably of a mental malady; at all events, the boy's attacks of migraine were taken to be hereditary. At the age of fourteen Nietzsche became a pupil at the famous school of Pforta (where Klopstock, Lessing, and Fichte had been students), destined by his mother for a clerical career; at Pforta he discovered the poetry of Hölderlin, at that time almost unknown. At the University of Bonn, which he entered in 1864, he attended lectures in classical archaeology and philology, and history of art. His later criticisms of the one-sidedness of the German educational ethos must not obscure the fact that to the German universities of his time we owe the finest achievements and most important discoveries of modern classical scholarship—achievements, moreover, to which he contributed and for which he retained an ambivalent admiration. A year later Nietzsche followed his teacher F. Ritschl to Leipzig. His studies were interrupted by a few months' service as a stretcher-bearer in an artillery regiment at Naumburg, from which he was discharged after an injury. In February 1869, even before he had submitted his doctoral dissertation, he was called to the University of Basle where, in the following year, he was given the chair of classical philology. Volunteering as a medical orderly in the Franco-Prussian war of 1870, he was discharged after a month's service with grave gastric troubles. On his return to Basle severe attacks of migraine increasingly affected his eyesight; he resigned his teaching post after prolonged leaves of absence some six years later. From 1877 to the end of his conscious life in 1888 he lived, mainly on a small university pension, in various parts of Switzerland, Northern Italy, and Southern France, his threatened energies entirely devoted to his philosophical undertaking; only occasionally—in the course of his friendship and break with Richard Wagner, whom he first met in 1868—did he engage in polemical encounter.

Nietzsche's life is like an image of the life of the intellectual refugee of the 1930's. With a small case of books and a paraffin stove he moved from Alpine boardinghouses to modest rooms in Nice, Venice, and Genoa, restless and entirely solitary. Hardly any friendships endured the strain of his exacting personality for long; again and again his relations founder on his refusal of compromise with those from whom he demanded absolute allegiance, regarding them at the same time as intellectually inferior. From this charge perhaps only his Basle colleague, the historian Jakob Burckhardt for whom he retained an admiration tinged with irony, is ultimately exempt.[53] Burckhardt, he felt, had chosen to remain within the comforting precincts of scholarship—a refuge Nietzsche himself had rejected; but for all that it was Burckhardt who knew the full extent of his philosophical venture and who understood what forces had determined Nietzsche's choice.

The all-but-absolute solitude of Nietzsche's creative life is the setting as it is a major determining factor of his all-but-absolute individualism. For whom did he write? For the best among his contemporaries? For the future? The changes of tone, the varieties of rhetorical devices, all issue from soliloquy. His most "popular" work, *Zarathustra*, its style leaning on Luther's Bible but also on Heine's *Atta Troll* (without any of Heine's humor), is dedicated "to None and All," meaning presumably a public of his own creation. In due course that public came into being—but its qualities horrified him.

The writings Nietzsche himself published span the astonishingly short period of sixteen years. Beginning with *Die Geburt der Tragödie aus dem Geiste der Musik* (*The Birth of Tragedy*) of 1872 and ending with the autobiographical *Ecce Homo* of 1888, he wrote some fourteen major works, which are followed by a convolute of more than a thousand notes intended for a final systematic résumé of his life's work. The heroic quality of this achievement in the face of increasing odds is surely without parallel; only rarely (in *Morgenröte*, *Aurora* of 1881, his own favorite book, and its sequel, *Die fröhliche Wissenschaft*, *The Gay Science* of 1882) is the intellectual pace of his writing anything but the most exacting.

Early in January 1889, in a street in Turin, he suffered a physical and mental collapse from which he never recovered. His disease, general paralysis of the insane, is thought to have been syphilitic in origin. He endured it, with intermittent periods of sanity, in the hideous care of his sister. Surrounded by the "Nietzsche-Archiv" through which this self-important lady was cashing in on his growing fame, he died at Weimar in 1900.

. . . schauen zu müssen und zugleich über das Schauen hinaus sich zu sehnen . . .[54]

In his second work, *Unzeitgemässe Betrachtungen* (*Thoughts out of Season*, 1873–76), in the section entitled "Vom Nutzen und Nachteil der Historie für das Leben" ("On the Uses and Abuses of History in Life," 1874), Nietzsche assails the "disinterested" study of the past, and the untrammeled pursuit of knowledge generally. Such pursuits, he writes, are a subterfuge of those who are morally and existentially incapable of fulfilling, let alone determining, the demands of their own age. His first work, *Die Geburt der Tragödie aus dem Geiste der Musik* (*The Birth of Tragedy from the Spirit of Music*), on which I shall here concentrate, is the brilliant masterpiece of his classical apprenticeship. His manner of exposition implicitly refutes the time-honored distinction between creative and learned prose—he convinces as much by telling anecdote and story as he does by discursive argument. In his account of the history of Greek drama and thought there is no difference of status between "was" and "was believed to be." Like most nineteenth-century writers he sees the origin of Greek drama in the chorus, and the chorus is for him, quite literally, the train of Dionysus on his drunken revels in the forest. In their ecstasy ("*Rausch*") and in their dirge his followers are one with their god. What they express in their music and song is the oneness of all things, the absence of individuation in their world. (This idea points back to Schopenhauer's world of the Cosmic Will, and forward to Freud's "oceanic feeling" as well as to Heidegger's "*Angst.*") Intuitively, as yet unbeknown to them (for to know would be to be distinct and separate from the object of knowledge), their song expresses the desolateness of all things and of life itself. This desolateness is for Nietzsche the fundamental disposition of man ("*das menschliche Urgefühl*"). According to legend, King Midas hunts Silenus in vain; and when he traps him at last, it is to ask him the meaning of life. This myth Nietzsche uses to illustrate (perhaps explain) the onset of self-consciousness and tragic apprehension. "You want to know what life is about?" (Silenus asks Midas) "The best is out of your reach, for the best of all things is not to have been born, not to be, to be nothing." In this knowledge men become sober and reflective, they are no longer at one with themselves (we think of Schiller's "*sentimentalisch*" poet, but also of the fourth elegy of Rilke's *Duineser Elegien*). The task of the Dionysian troupe is now to hide this terrible knowledge from themselves and, eventually, from those who watch their revels. This they do by making an image of it, an ecstatic show, a story, an action. It is of the essence of that story that it should *both* preserve the tragic nature of the knowledge they now possess *and* make it bearable. And the god who helps them to fashion this story, who helps them to organize this knowledge in a bearable, that is beautiful, form, is the image-making god Apollo.

At this point we have reached the two fundamental modes of knowledge-and-life which encompass Nietzsche's view of tragedy (and a good deal more besides): its Dionysian foundation ("*Urgrund*") and the Apolline order superimposed upon it. The distinction has its roots in Schopenhauer's dichotomy of the world as Will and Idea; it is related to Heine's distinction between "Nazarene" and "Hellenic" art; it comprehends but goes beyond Aristotle's distinction of matter and form; above all, it belongs among the three or four memorable arguments in the history of modern European aesthetics. When the Dionysian element predominates, ecstatic chaos threatens; when the Apolline predominates, the tragic feeling recedes. Of the two, the Dionysian remains the fundamental, but the balance in the great works of tragic art is of the subtlest and most precarious. It is achieved in Aeschylus, reaches its finest form in Sophocles; and where—as in the work of Euripides—the Dionysian is attenuated and finally suppressed, there tragedy dies and the thwarted god (in *The Bacchae*) takes his revenge.

The predominance of the Dionysian in Greek tragedy at its finest indicates intuition and ecstasy as the only authentic mode of artistic creation; it implies, more specifically, an unreflective belief in the germinal myths (Aristotle's stories of "the great families") from which tragedy is fashioned, a belief the poet shares with his public. What these myths represent is not a mimetic *action* but a *mood*, "*eine Grundstimmung*," which we have called a style of life. This conception of a "mood" is, throughout Nietzsche's writings, more fundamental than rational argument. The decline of tragedy begins where creative ecstasy gives way to cold calculation: now the old myths become objects of analysis, and the gods are judged according to the prosy maxims of reasoned justice. Man's unreflective exposure to the tragic spectacle Nietzsche had identified with aesthetic delight; now tragedy is expected to yield a didactic, moral message. Thought takes over from art, the reign of Socrates begins. Socrates is the ugly, inartistic man par excellence. His emphasis on conviction through cleverness in rational argument is the refuge of one who has no understanding of the ecstatic mystery of art, no fervor of belief in the gods.

The death of tragedy in the new reign of rationalism is followed by the emergence of new genres—the Aesopian fable and the Platonic dialogue. The latter especially is a debasement of the ancient form, its essential aim is the destruction of the ancient myths and natural pieties. Tragic man is superseded by rational, scientific man, the creative pessimism of Silenus' mystery gives way to the flat optimism of the Socratic paradox (which Nietzsche presents not as a paradox but as the basic dogma of Socratic morality—in other words, he does to the Socratic paradox what the Nietzscheans did to *his* paradoxes). In the identification of knowledge with virtue, of the clever and well-informed man with the good, Nietzsche sees the crowning folly of Socrates' impious conviction that reason and science can reach to the ground of man's being. There is perhaps no need to belabor the obvious: Nietzsche's account of the death of tragedy and his critique of Socratic rationality is a critique of contemporary (nineteenth-century) scientism and *its* shallow optimism.

What we have followed up to this point is, roughly, the historical and critical argument of *Die Geburt der Tragödie* (*Birth of Tragedy*). Before turning to its constructive part it may be useful to consider three main objections that are likely to arise in the reader's mind. First, and most obviously, scholars are likely to impugn many of his sources, especially in the polemic against Socrates, as suspect in their authenticity; it takes no great classical learning to see that some of these sources are hardly more than time-hallowed gossip. There is, secondly, Nietzsche's peculiarly mixed manner of seeking to convince: a compound of rhetoric, anecdotes, sorties into "straight" scholarship, appeals to the authorities of Kant and (in the passages on music) Schopenhauer, and, imposed on these, penetrating psychological insights and inferences.[55] And there are, thirdly, occasional distortions, or at least suppressions of evidence pointing to different conclusions. Some or all of these objections, it may be added, are likely to be raised against his later works also. All one can do is point to the profound insights into the modern mind that the essay affords, and to ask what other work that sails under the flag of "classical scholarship" offers a comparable illumination. Again and again we are faced with the paradox of impatient exaggerations (=untruths) leading to astonishing revelations (=truths).

What Nietzsche has undertaken is not primarily a piece of scholarship but a critique of the modern mind in its exaltation of reason over music and art, of rational morality against myth. Moreover (we now move into the "constructive" part of the argument), the essay aspires to being not only a critique but a contribution to the new myth of which modern Europe—or rather Germany—is in such dire need. Once we have accepted the account of the decline of Greek drama as caused by the demise of life-giving myths, it follows that a rebirth of tragedy and of the arts, indeed of the *tragic sense of life*, can only come about through the birth of new myths. Music is not only the source of tragedy, it is also (here Nietzsche takes over Schopenhauer's argument in Book 3 of *Die Welt als Wille und Vorstellung* [*The World as Will and Idea*] the one art above all others which encompasses and most directly retraces the whole world of man, "its weal and woe"; it does this in a medium to which considerations of morality, utility, and survival itself are irrelevant. "Only as an aesthetic phenomenon"—as music or as a tragic spectacle—"is the being of man justified": three times the thought is repeated in Nietzsche's essay, each time its ostensible aim is to free the aesthetic from importuning moral considerations, from rationality itself. Yet behind this ostensible aim lies the belief with which Nietzsche's historical account began. Ultimately the function of music and of tragedy is not so much to justify the world as rather to make it bearable. And—this is Nietzsche's grand finale—it is in the music of Richard Wagner, in the third act of *Tristan und Isolde*, that the new German myth is born.

Why Wagner, why Germany? We might also ask, why "the Superman," why the paradox of "the Eternal Recurrence"? The questions take us back to the "style" of Nietzsche's philosophical venture, to the fact that he never reconciled himself to its being "merely" a philosophical and reflective undertaking. The very violence of his notorious metaphors, especially in *Zarathustra*, points to dissatisfaction with his role as a thinker; so do some of Nietzsche's poems; so do his various rhetorical styles and parables and his mixing of literary genres. A philosopher of life? To Nietzsche this was a contradiction in terms, for "life" as he saw it was the *ground* of all thought[56] and could therefore not be defined, let alone determined, by thought. He counters the dogmas of rationalism by subordinating thought to "life," "nature," "instinct," "fact," "good taste," and other such professedly nonrational criteria; and in so doing rebuts all rational criticism *ex hypothesi*. From this contradiction springs the breathtaking energy of his thinking, and his ever-present need for concreteness, for a *grounding* of his thought in the world. In *Die Geburt der Tragödie* "Wagner" and "Germany" fulfill, or seem to fulfill, this need. But this early work already fore-shadows the way Nietzsche's ethical program—to create a new, finer style of life—will merge with his epistemological program—to close the gap between world and interpreted world.

The fantastic racial notions of Nietzsche's later work and some of his remarks about national character, which bring the blush of embarrassment to his reader's cheek, derive from his brief and superficial acquaintance with the contemporary biological sciences; so do the "Superman's" most repellent qualities. Science, in the early 1880's, seems to him to offer the firm ground he seeks for his philosophy. The doctrine of the "Eternal Recurrence," that proving stone of the Superman's worth, is a part of this search. "To be com-pelled to look and at the same time to yearn beyond the looking": the doctrine is to supply man's need for a metaphysic, but this metaphysic is to be concrete and "immanent" since in it life, *this* life, is to be made eternal:

> I shall return [Zarathustra proclaims] with this sun, with this earth, with this eagle, with this snake—*not* to a new life, or a better life, or a similar life:
> —I shall return always to this self-same life, in the greatest and in the smallest things, that I may again teach the recurrence of all things,
> —that I may speak again the Word of the great noon of earth and of men, that I may again herald the Superman to all men.[57]

And to this recurrence the Superman is to give his absolute assent. So great is to be his love of life that even when life is to be perpetuated in all its greatness and triviality ad infinitum and ad nauseam, without change or added meaning, he should assent to it. Then indeed he has proved himself, then he has fully exposed himself to the merciless rays of the midday sun, the sun that sheds its harsh light into every nook and cranny of experience, leaving no comfort in the dark caves and picturesque grottoes of ancient comforts and religions. This is the most difficult faith—likely to make our vital powers shrivel up in horror—that the Superman's creator has devised for him: this, ultimately, is to be the new myth that Wagner had failed to supply, that should raise us and our culture to the level of ancient, pre-Socratic Grece.

One of Friedrich Hölderlin's early poems is entitled "Mein Eigentum." In it he evokes the necessaries of a man's life: orchard and field, vineyard, house and hearth:

> Es leuchtet über festem Boden
> Schöner dem sicheren Mann sein Himmel.[58]

Without these things a man's body and soul are dispossessed and unaccom-modated. So much so, Rilke takes up the thought (1912), that

> und die findigen Tiere merken es schon,

dass wir nicht sehr verlässlich zu Haus sind
in der gedeuteten Welt.[59]

The poet (Hölderlin continues) has no such possessions, yet he too needs a sheet anchor in the world,

dass . . . heimathlos meine Seele mir nicht
Über das Leben hinweg sich sehne
Sei du, Gesang! mein freundlich Asyl! . . .[60]

The poet-philosopher Nietzsche faces a predicament at once similar and more radical. The man *he* finds is not "safe," but gross and comfortable; his "possessions" are contemptible; gone is heaven's beautiful gleam, a dark wintery sky broods over him. And the philosopher's "song"—where shall he find substance for it? Another of Hölderlin's poems takes up the central question of Nietzsche's philosophy:

Weh mir, wo nehm' ich, wenn
Es Winter ist, die Blumen, und wo
Den Sonnenschein
Und Schatten der Erde?[61]

FOOTNOTES*

[1] As for Germany, there can be no doubt that what holds us together is not that external institution, the police, but the community between all German lands that has evolved in the sciences, in the arts and in literature—a community whose development cannot be arrested.

[2] Manasses called: I see you as clear as daylight, and he came towards me. Suddenly he stopped. It was as if the black earth had stretched out her hand and were holding him from below. A ghostly feeling seized me. Come, come, I called, and I was not ashamed. I cannot, his answer came dark and leaden, I cannot . . . .

[3] If a giant's head points so high into the sky that you cannot reach it, why then, throw a jewel at his feet—he will stoop to pick it up, and then you will easily overpower him.

[4] There are things that must be done as in one's sleep. This is one of them. The great wheel passed over her, now she is with him who turns it.

[5] *Lips*: Oh my dear Kitty, I get fonder of you every moment. (*Makes to embrace her.*)
Kitty: But godfather . . .
Lips: Quickly, a glass of milk to cool me down. (*Breakfasts greedily, talking all the time.*) You just don't know all the other things I feel. Tell me, you've never done anybody in?
Kitty: How can you think such a thing!

* All uncredited translations in the footnotes are translations by J. P. Stern.

Lips: Well, if for instance a man did himself harm for love of you, that would make you into his indirect murderess, death-dealer par distance.

Kitty: Thank heavens, I'm no such cruel beauty.

Lips: Oh Kitty! You don't know what a dear Kitty you are! (*Embraces her.*)

Kitty (freeing herself): Now, go away . . .

Lips: Quick, another glass of milk! (*Drinks.*) There now, I'm a good little boy again. —I must tell you, I have visions.

Kitty: That's an illness we don't know in the country.

Lips: Phantasms they are, created in the hollow ducts of the brain, which sometimes step out from within us and place themselves, Mephistopheles-wise, on the Santa Claus Market of our solitude—extinguished eyes rolling, dead teeth gnashing—and with a threatening skeleton hand they incite to a moldy funereal box-on-the-ear. That's a vision.

Kitty: Why, I never knew what things people from the city go through . . .

Lips: When it gets dark I see white figures . . .

Kitty: How can that be? At night all the cows are black.

Lips: And I'm really an ox. Did I drown him deliberately? No. And yet, all the time I see this snow-white ghost of a locksmith before me! You've no idea how gruesome a white locksmith is.

Kitty: But you must put him out of your mind.

Lips: Even this milk reminds me of him—if only it had a dash of coffee-color in it—I'm horrified of white.

6 At least, not on the stage; in prose the earlier master of this mode is his fellow-Viennese Abraham a Santa Clara (1644–1709).

7 "That's beyond my powers. That's put paid to my plays." Raimund (1790–1836) committed suicide a few days later.

8 This will be considered more fully below; see p. 295

9 *Leonce:* Come, Leonce, let's have a monologue, and I will listen. My life yawns at me like a big white sheet of paper that I should fill with writing, but I can't produce a single letter. My head is an empty ballroom, a few withered roses and crumpled ribbons on the floor, broken violins in the corner, the last dancers have taken off their masks and are looking at each other with eyes weary to death. I turn myself inside out like a glove twenty-four times a day. Oh, I know myself, I know what I shall be thinking and dreaming in a quarter of an hour, in a week's, a year's time. God, what have I done that you should make me recite my lesson over and over again, like a schoolboy? . . . (I, iii)

10 We know little of each other [he says to Julie, his wife]. We are thick-skinned creatures, we stretch out our hands to each other but it is wasted effort, we are only rubbing our coarse hides together—we are very solitary . . . Know each other? We should have to break open each other's skulls and drag the thoughts out of each other's brain-coils. (I, i)

11 Oh, that accursed sentence: "Something cannot become Nothing!" And I am that something, that's the pity of it! Creation has spread itself everywhere, nothing is empty, everything is crawling with it. Nothingness has murdered itself. Creation is its wound, we are the drops of its blood, the world is the grave where it lies rotting.

12 O Julie, if I were to go alone! If she were to leave me solitary! And even if I were to fall asunder utterly, dissolve entirely—yet would I be a handful of tormented dust, and every atom of me could find peace only in her.

13 *Woyzeck* [when taunted with Marie's unfaithfulness]: I must go. Many things are pos-

sible. A human being! Many things are possible.—Fine weather we're having, Captain, Sir, Look you now, such a fine sky, all gray and hard. It almost makes you want to knock a hook in it and hang yourself on it, just because of the little dash between Yes and again Yes—and No.—Well, Captain, Sir: Yes and No? Is the No to blame for the Yes, or the Yes for the No? I will think about that.

14 [Woyzeck (after the murder), alone on the edge of the forest, near the pond]: The knife? Where is the knife? This is where I left it. It will hang me! Closer, still closer! What— What's that noise? Something moved. Sh! . . . close at hand. Marie? Ha, Marie. Hush. It's so quiet. Why are you so pale, Marie? Why have you got that red cord round your neck? Who paid you with that necklace for your sins? You were black with sins, black! Have I made you white now? Why does your hair hang down so wild? Didn't you plait it this morning? . . . The knife, the knife! Have I got it? There now. People! I hear them coming—there!

15 Yes indeed, ladies and gentlemen, here's no stupid beast, here is a person, a human being, an animal human being—and yet [*the horse misbehaves, as Woyzeck had done earlier*] an animal, a beast . . .

16 Why is man? Ah, why is man? Verily, verily I say unto you: what should the ploughman live on, the plasterer, the cobbler and the physician, if God had not created man?

17
> Beat the drum and be not afraid.
> And kiss the *cantinière*!
> That is the sum of all sciences,
> That's what all books are about!
>
> Wake all people from their sleep with your drum.
> Drum their reveille with youthful might,
> March with your drum at their head.
> That is the sum of all sciences.
>
> That is old Hegel's philosophy.
> That's what all books are about!
> I've grasped its meaning because I am clever
> And because I can drum so well.
>
> .   .   .

18
> Beside the old grey tower
> There stands a sentry box;
> A lad in a bright red tunic
> Is marching to and fro.

19
> He is playing with his musket,
> The sun makes it shine red,
> Presenting arms and shouldering,
> I wish he would shoot me dead.

20 C. P. Magill, ed., *Zur Geschichte der Religion und Philosophie in Deutschland*, (London: Duckworth, London 1947), p. 174f.

21 Did Karl Kraus know this Preface when, at Rosa Luxemburg's death, he wrote:
    Communism is in reality nothing but the antithesis of a particular ideology that is both thoroughly harmful and corrosive. Thank God for the fact that Communism springs from a clean and clear ideal, which preserves its idealistic purpose even though, as an antidote, it is inclined to be somewhat harsh. To hell with its practical import: but

may God at least preserve it for us as a never-ending menace to those people who own big estates and who, in order to hang on to them, are prepared to dispatch humanity into battle, to abandon it to starvation for the sake of patriotic honor. May God preserve Communism so that the evil brood of its enemies may be prevented from becoming more barefaced still, so that the gang of profiteers . . . shall have their sleep disturbed by at least a few pangs of anxiety. If they must preach morality to their victims and amuse themselves with their suffering, at least let some of the pleasure be spoilt!

        —*Die Fackel*, XXII, 554 (November, 1920), p. 8.

[22] Germany, here we sit weaving thy shroud, weaving into it the threefold curse—we weave, we weave!

[23]
> Ah, woe is me! A tumult rose without,
> And chased all calm and happiness away.
> I heard them arguing with stamp and shout,
> My gentle flower drooped with sore dismay.

[24] Friedrich Nietzsche, "Der Genesende," in *Also sprach Zarathustra*, Part III.

[25]
> What's to blame? Is it perchance
> That our Lord's not quite almighty?
> Or himself plays all those tricks?
> Ah, *that* would be base indeed.
>
> So we go on, asking questions,
> Till at last they stuff a handful
> Of solid earth down our throats—
> But is that an answer?

[26]
> Impotent curses! The worst of them
> Will not kill a single fly.
> Bear your fate and try
> To cry a bit, to pray.

[27]
> What if one day I found her sitting
> Upon my threshold in early dawn, as once she did,
> The wanderer's bundle by her side,
> Her eyes trustingly looking up to me,
> Saying, Here I am again
> I am come back again, back from the world!
>
>   .   .   .
>
> At the cruel stake, they tell us, love stands bound,
> Ends barefoot and deranged, in tatters dressed. . .
>
>   .   .   .
>
> Yesterday, in the children's room
> By the bright flicker of their pretty candles. . .

[28]
Yet undisturbed, O beautiful lamp, you still adorn,
On fine-wrought chains suspended gracefully,
The ceiling of this near-forgotten festal room.
On your white marble bowl, about whose rim
Entwines an ivy garland of gold-green bronze
A ring of children dances gaily hand in hand.
What charm is in all this! Laughter, yet a gentle spirit
Of gravity suffuses the entire form.

> Wrought from the genuine order is this art. Who pays heed to it?
> But what is beautiful shines blissfully within itself.

My translation owes much to N. K. Cruickshank's; see Eduard Mörike, *Poems of Mörike*, trans. N. K. Cruickshank and G. F. Cunningham (London: Methuen 1959), p. 76.

29 The last line, "Was aber schön ist, selig scheint es in ihm selbst," has been the subject of a learned controversy between the literary historian, Professor E. Staiger, and the philosopher, Martin Heidegger. The former offers the interpretation that "that which is beautiful *seems* blissful (i.e., has the semblance of bliss) in itself," while the latter reads, "that which is beautiful *shines* blissfully within itself." Characteristically, neither interpreter gives a thought to the actual social and historical circumstances to which the poem belongs and from which it issues. They confine their placing of the poem to evidence from the aesthetic arguments of Mörike's contemporaries: Staiger quotes Theodor Vischer in support of *"videtur,"* Heidegger Hegel in support of *"lucet"*; the linguistic difficulty of (Swabian?) *"ihm,"* where *"sich"* would have been expected, remains in both cases. I have accepted Heidegger's reading, because I know of no poem of Mörike's containing the antithesis "art–reality" which Staiger's reading would imply, but above all because Heidegger's *"lucet"* is relevant to the central image of the lamp and thus to the integrity of the poem, whereas Staiger's *"videtur"* is not. (Cf. Emil Staiger, *Die Kunst der Interpretation* [Zürich: Atlantis, 1955], p. 24f.

30 This identification of weightiness of person and work with value is present in the anti-Semitism of Gustav Freytag's *Soll und Haben* (1854), (the Germans have *"Ernst,"* the Jews do not); in the central figures of Theodor Storm's later *Novellen*; in the father figure and in the fraternal conflict of Otto Ludwig's *Zwischen Himmel und Erde* (1856); it takes a comic form in Wilhelm Raabe's *Der Stopfkuchen* (1891); we shall see it in Keller, even more clearly in Stifter. Heine does not share this ethos but knows it intimately, for example, in the contrasts he draws between Germany and Paris.

31 Roy Pascal, *The German Novel* (Manchester: University Press, 1957), p. 35.

32 Norman Mailer, *The Short Fiction of Norman Mailer* (New York: Dell Publishing Company, 1967), p. 10.

33 *Der Fall Wagner*, Kröner ed., V (Leipzig, 1930), p. 42.

34 *Menschliches, Allzumenschliches*, ed. cit., II, 227.

35 He brought out a few bills of exchange and a belt full of gold, threw it all on the table— and indeed, it came to several thousand florins or dollars. However, he had not amassed this fortune gradually, and wisely omitted to mention that he had got hold of it at one swoop through some stroke of luck, having tramped around all the North American States for a long time in poverty . . . He went into the room they had given him. There the ageing man threw all his money into a corner, sat down astraddle on a chair, placed his sad large head on its back, and began to weep bitterly. His wife came in, saw that he felt miserable, and she had to respect his misery. Now, as soon as she could respect something in him, her love instantly returned.

36 See *Beyond Recall* (i.e., *Unwiederbringlich*), (Oxford: Oxford University Press, 1964), and *Effi Briest* (Harmondsworth: Penguin Books, 1967), introduced and translated by Douglas Parmée.

37 *Betrachtungen eines Unpolitischen*, 1914–19.

38 If a man *has* something—well of course, he can take life as it really is, he can be what nowadays they call a realist. But if a man has nothing, if he always has to live in a Sahara

desert—why then, he simply can't exist without a fata morgana with palms and odalisques and all that sort of thing.

—*Die Poggenpuhls* (1896), Chap. iv.

39 See Mary E. Gilbert, *Das Gespräch in Fontanes Gesellschaftsromanen* (Leipzig: Palaestra 174 [Mayer and Müller] 1930); and Peter Demetz, *Formen des Realismus: Theodor Fontane* (München: Hanser Verlag, 1964).

40 *Morgenröte* (1886), IV, par. 244.

41 You see, sir, what really matters is decency and honesty, sir, and reliability!

42 *Effi Briest* (1895), Chaps. xix-xxi.

43 *Vor dem Sturm*, Chap. lxxix.

44 As unfortunately happens in the only other major German novel dealing with nationalism, Franz Werfel's *Die vierzig Tage des Musa Dagh* (1933), which is impaired in just this way.

45 *Ed. cit.*, trans. by Douglas Parmée, p. 222f.

46 *Ibid.*, p. 113.

47 *Ibid.*, p. 169f.

48 But those days that were dearest to me, I do not wish them back.

49 The role of this character in Hebbel's dramas has already been discussed; see above p. [288]

50 For good symbolical measure, and heedless of anachronism, she is called Grace. On the other hand, in order presumably to evoke a twelfth-century atmosphere, the prose abounds with "*gen's*", prepositional "*ob's*," noninterrogative "*wann's*", and warlike vocabulary like "*Rüdengeheul und Pferdegestampf.*"

51 *Also sprach Zarathustra*, II, Chap. ii.

52 *Ibid.*, I, Chap. xx.

53 See Erich Heller, "Burckhardt and Nietzsche," in *The Disinherited Mind* (New York: Farrar, Straus and Cudahy, 1957).

54 . . . to be compelled to look and at the same time to yearn beyond the looking . . . .

—*Die Geburt der Tragödie*, Section 24

55 Nietzsche himself raises these objections in the dithyrambic "Versuch einer Selbstkritik" of 1886.

56 See above, p. [290]

57 *Also sprach Zarathustra*, III, Chap. xiii.

58   Above firm ground his heaven gleams
        More beautifully to the safe man.

59   even the canny animals notice
        that we are not very reliably at home
        in the interpreted world.

—*Duineser Elegien*, I

60   lest homeless my soul should yearn
        on and beyond life,
        be you, song, my friendly refuge.

61   But oh, where shall I find
        When winter comes, the flowers, and where
        The sunshine
        And shade of the earth?

                            —"Hälfte des Lebens,"
                            Michael Hamburger, trans.

BIBLIOGRAPHY

History

New Cambridge Modern History, The, vol. 10, *The Zenith of European Power*, 1830–70, ed. J.P.T. Bury; see especially chapter vii, "Imaginative Literature" by Erich Heller. New York: Cambridge University Press, 1960.

SCHNABEL, FRANZ, *Deutsche Geschichte im neunzehnten Jahrhundert*. Freiburg: Herder, 4 vols., 1948–55.

TAYLOR, A. J. P., *Bismarck, the Man and the Statesman*. London: Hamish Hamilton, 1955.

Social and Intellectual History

BRAMSTED, ERNEST KOHN, *Aristocracy and the Middle Classes in Germany; Social Types in German Literature, 1830–1900*. Chicago: University of Chicago Press, 1964.

DAHRENDORF, RALF, *Gesellschaft und Demokratie in Deutschland*. München: R. Riper, 1965.

KOHN, HANS, *The Mind of Germany; the Education of a Nation*. New York: Charles Scribner's Sons, 1960.

Realism and Nineteenth-Century German Literature

AUERBACH, ERICH, *Mimesis; the Representation of Reality in Western Literature*. trans. W. R. Trask. Princeton: Princeton University Press, 1953.

BENNETT, E. K., *A History of the German Novelle from Goethe to Thomas Mann*, 2nd ed., Revised by H. M. Waidson. New York: Cambridge University Press, 1961.

BRINKMANN, RICHARD, *Wirklichkeit und Illusion; Studien über Gehalt und Grenzen des Begriffs Realismus für die erzählende Dichtung des 19. Jahrhunderts*. Tübingen: M. Niemeyer, 1966.

HELLER, ERICH, *The Artist's Journey into the Interior, and Other Essays*. New York: Random House, Inc., 1965.

LEVIN, HARRY, "A Symposium on Realism," arranged by Harry Levin in *Comparative Literature*, III/3, Oregon, 1951.

LUKACS, GEORG, *Deutsche Realisten des neunzehnten Jahrhunderts*. Bern: Francke, 1951.

MARTINI, FRITZ, *Deutsche Literatur im bürgerlichen Realismus 1848–1898*. Stuttgart: Metzler, 2nd ed., 1964.

MAYER, HANS, *Von Lessing bis Thomas Mann. Wandlungen der bürgerlichen Literatur in Deutschland*. Pfullingen: Neske, 1959.

SILZ, WALTER, *Realism and Reality; Studies in the German Novelle of Poetic Realism*. Chapel Hill: University of North Carolina Press, 1954.

STERN, J. P., *Re-Interpretations; Seven Studies in Nineteenth-Century German Literature*. New York: Basic Books, 1964.

WEIGEL, HANS, *Flucht vor der Grösse; Beitrag zur Erkenntnis und Selbsterkenntnis Österreichs*. Wien: Wollzeilen Verlag, 1960. (Essays on Grillparzer, Nestroy, Stifter.)

Grillparzer

BAUMANN, GERHART, *Franz Grillparzer. Sein Werk und das österreichische Wesen*. Wien: Herder, 1954.

FÜLLEBORN, ULRICH, *Das dramatische Geschehen im Werk Franz Grillparzers*. München: W. Fink, 1966.

MÜLLER, JOACHIM, *Franz Grillparzer*. Stuttgart: Metzler, 1963. (ed. Metzlers Realienbücher für Germanisten.)

YATES, DOUGLAS, *Franz Grillparzer, A Critical Biography*. Oxford: B. Blackwell, vol. i (the only vol. published), 1946.

Nestroy

KRAUS, KARL, *Nestroy und die Nachwelt. Zum 50. Todestage gesprochen*. . . . Wien: Herder, 1912.

ROMMEL, OTTO, *Johann Nestroy: der Satiriker auf der Altwiener Komödienbühne*. Wien: Herder, 1948.

Hebbel

MEETZ, ANNI, *Friedrich Hebbel*. Stuttgart: Metzler, 1962. (ed. Metzlers Realienbücher . . .)

PURDIE, EDNA, *Friedrich Hebbel, A Study of His Life and Work*. London: Oxford University Press, 1932.

Büchner

KNIGHT, A. H. J., *Georg Büchner*. Oxford, B. Blackwell, 1951.

MAYER, HANS, *Georg Büchner und seine Zeit*. Wiesbaden: Limes, 2nd ed., 1960.

VIETOR, KARL, *Georg Büchner: Politik, Dichtung, Wissenschaft*. Bern: Francke, 1949.

Heine

BUTLER, E. M., *Heinrich Heine; A Biography*. London: The Hogarth Press, 1956.

FAIRLEY, BARKER, *Heinrich Heine, An Interpretation*. New York: Oxford University Press, 1954.

GALLEY, EBERHARD, *Heinrich Heine*. Stuttgart: Metzler, 1963. (ed. Metzlers Realienbücher . . .)

PRAWER, S. S., *Heine, The Tragic Satirist; A Study of His Later Poetry, 1827–1856*. New York: Cambridge University Press, 1961.

SAMMONS, JEFFREY L., *Heinrich Heine, The Elusive Poet*. New Haven: Yale University Press, 1969.

Mörike

MARE, M. L., *Eduard Mörike, The Man and the Poet*. London: Methuen, 1957.

MEYER, HERBERT, *Eduard Mörike*. Stuttgart: Metzler, 1961. (ed. Metzlers Realienbücher . . .)

WIESE, BENNO VON, *Eduard Mörike*. Tübingen: Rainer Wunderlich, 1950.

Stifter

BLACKALL, E. A., *Adalbert Stifter, A Critical Study*. New York: Cambridge University Press, 1948.

LUNDING, E. P., *Adalbert Stifter. Mit einem Anhang über Kierkegaard und die existentielle Literaturwissenschaft*. Kjøbenhavn: Nyt Nordisk Forlag, 1946.

STAIGER, EMIL, *Adalbert Stifter als Dichter der Ehrfurcht*. Zürich: Arche, 1952.

Keller

FRÄNKEL, JONAS, *Gottfried Kellers politische Sendung*. Zürich: Oprecht, 1939.

LUKACS, GEORG, *Gottfried Keller*, Berlin: Aufbau, 1947.

Meyer

HENEL, HEINRICH, *The Poetry of Conrad Ferdinand Meyer*. Madison: University of Wisconsin Press, 1954.

Storm

BERND, CLIFFORD A., *Theodor Storm's Craft of Fiction; the Torment of a Narrator*. Chapel Hill: University of North Carolina Press, 2nd ed., 1966.

McCORMICK, E. A., *Theodor Storm's Novellen: Essays on Literary Technique*. Chapel Hill: University of North Carolina Press, 1964.

ROGERS, T. J., *Techniques of Solipsism: a Study of Theodor Storm's Narrative Fiction*. The Modern Humanities Research Association: Cambridge, 1970.

Fontane

DEMETZ, PETER, *Formen des Realismus; Theodor Fontane*. München: C. Hanser, 1964.

MANN, THOMAS, "Der alte Fontane," in *Adel des Geistes*, Stockholm: Bermann-Fischer, 1945, pp. 543–573.

Schopenhauer

COPLESTON, F. C., *Arthur Schopenhauer, Philosopher of Pessimism*. London: Burns, Oates & Washbourne, 1946.

Nietzsche

HEIDEGGER, MARTIN, *Nietzsche*. Pfullingen: Neske, 1961.

KNIGHT, A. H. J., *Some Aspects of the Life and Work of Nietzsche*. New York: Cambridge University Press, 1933.

WOLFF, H. M., *Friedrich Nietzsche, der Weg zum Nichts*. Bern: Francke, 1956.

From the manuscript of Rilke's
Sonette an Orpheus.

I

Da stieg ein Baum. O reine Übersteigung!
O Orpheus singt! O hoher Baum im Ohr!
Und alles schwieg. Doch selbst in der Verschweigung
ging neuer Anfang, Wink und Wandlung vor.

Tiere aus Stille drangen aus dem klaren
gelösten Wald von Lager und Genist;
und da ergab sich, daß sie nicht aus List
und nicht aus Angst in sich so leise waren,

sondern aus Hören. Brüllen, Schrei, Geröhr
schien klein in ihren Herzen. Und wo eben
kaum eine Hütte war, dies zu empfangen,

ein Unterschlupf aus dunkelstem Verlangen
mit einem Zugang, dessen Pfosten beben, —
da schufst du ihnen Tempel im Gehör.

Modern German Literature 1900–1966

ADOLF D. KLARMANN

University of Pennsylvania

Centuries never stop with a zero nor do they start with a zero. When we speak of intellectual periods, of literary movements, of schools of philosophy, of directions in art, we quickly find out that the zero is a very accidental figure and that the periods which we are considering either begin earlier or later. The period that we are trying to consider here, namely the period of contemporary German literature, begins either a decade or so before or possibly a decade after the turn of the century. One ought to keep in mind that the nineteenth century was not really spent until the First World War (1914 or 1918). However, to set the frame properly it might be advisable to review the important steps in the world of literature immediately before the century point.

As far as the "acceptable" literature around 1870 was concerned, the general trend was in the direction of either neo-Schillerian imitation of the historical play, the "professorial" novel, again preoccupied with historical subjects though not necessarily German, and a poetry which in its top figures, viz., Eduard

Adolf D. Klarmann received his B. A. and M. A. from New York University, his Ph.D. from the University of Pennsylvania, and his Litt. D. from Lebanon Valley College. He taught at New York University, the University of Rochester, and the University of Pennsylvania, and was Visiting Professor, at the Universities of California at Los Angeles and Berkeley, at the Johns Hopkins University, and at the University of Colorado. He has been a Jusserand, Fulbright, and Guggenheim Fellow and is the editor of the literary estate of Franz Werfel. Eight volumes of Werfel's works have appeared so far under his editorship. He has published extensively in scholarly journals both here and abroad, and has contributed to encyclopedias and anthologies of essays.

Mörike (1804–75) and Conrad Ferdinand Meyer (1825–98), reached a pinnacle of perfection in contrast to the other genres and which in its kind remains unexcelled. It is noteworthy that their contemporaries paid little attention to the best dramatists and novelists. Franz Grillparzer, Christian Dietrich Grabbe, Georg Büchner, (Christian) Friedrich Hebbel, and Ludwig Anzengruber are among the neglected, as are Gottfried Keller, Conrad Ferdinand Meyer, Theodor Fontane, and Wilhelm Raabe. We must remember that the mid-nineteenth century is a moment in history of rapidly shifting values and concepts. It is the early pinnacle of the triumphant bourgeois and the burgeoning capitalist, it is the self-assured time of pragmatism and positivism with its built-in supreme optimism concerning man's future in the sciences. It is the moment of the proletarization of the previously self-sufficient peasant as he moves to mushrooming urban centers, creating slums and misery in his flight from the soil. It is the exploitation of a much too rapidly growing industrialism and, above all, it is the newly-won glory of a rejuvenated fatherland which, in good Wagnerian fashion, was acquiring the strength and the arrogance of a young Siegfried in the brand new German Empire and its nationalistic militarism. The generation born around 1860 rebelled against the chauvinism of the Wilhelminian period and identified itself largely with the lot of the poor which they wished to improve by a neorationalistic kind of social democracy. At the same time, one must keep in mind a different kind of rebellion against the bourgeois values, derived from Schopenhauer and especially from Nietzsche, that led to a type of literature which, though contemporary with nationalism, showed concern only for artistic problems. In striking contrast to other European countries both camps were dedicated to nationalism, though in varying degree and accent.

One customarily starts the consideration of contemporary German literature with the rise of German naturalism or, to be specific, with the first performance of Gerhart Hauptmann's (1862–1946) *Vor Sonnenaufgang* (*Before Sunrise*) in 1889 by the so-called *Freie Bühne* (Free Theatre) in Berlin. To be sure, naturalism is not indigenous to Germany. Its primary inspirations came from France, Scandinavia, and Russia. It is difficult to talk about the naturalist movement without at least paying brief respect to its great writers outside of Germany: In France, men like Balzac, Flaubert, the brothers Goncourt, and, especially, Zola, with their antimetaphysical attitude and their detached, detailed descriptions; in Norway, above all Ibsen, the father of the modern and psychological drama with his focus on marital problems and bourgeois hypocrisy, diagnosed but left unresolved; and the two great Russians, Tolstoi and Dostoevsky, chroniclers of masses of human beings and of the low levels of society. Different as they may be from each other, still they have in common the theme of man's search for emancipation in a world which is subject to laws not of his making.

In Germany, in contrast to the French example of Zola which actually sparked the German movement, the most successful attempts are made not in prose but in the drama. The prose, such as it is, tends at first to follow the social reportage of a Dickens rather than Zola. The first name coming to mind is that of Max Kretzer (1854–1941), an early specialist of the Berlin underworld whom, oddly enough, early critics considered the German Zola but whose productive genius very quickly collapsed. The person who stands out as a master of the naturalistic novel in content and form is a woman, Clara Viebig (1860–1952), who is particularly interesting because in her we see a blending of two aspects of modern literature. One is social empathy and the other is a skillful adaptation of the traditional *Heimat-Roman*, the provincial novel, to the modern norm. In works such as *Kinder der Eifel* (*Children of the Eifel*, 1897) and *Das Schlafende Heer* (*The Sleeping Army*, 1904) she uses the vernacular and dialect, thereby linking directly with Arno Holz (1863–1929), the father of the *Konsequente Naturalismus* (consistent naturalism).

Holz starts as a great admirer of Zola only to turn away from him quickly because he thought that Zola applied the universal laws of heredity and environment too mechanically. Life cannot be equated with science and human fate cannot be analyzed by scientific experimentation as if it were a chemical solution. Dispensing heredity and environment empirically is not the answer for Arno Holz. He substitutes for Zola's definition of art as a piece of nature seen through the temperament of the artist his own conception, according to which art has the tendency to become again nature and does so commensurate to the methods used, the means employed, and the relative talent of the artist. In applying his theories to literature, he establishes the two most important concepts of naturalism, namely *Rhythmus der Persönlichkeit* (rhythm of personality) and *Sekundenstil* (second style).

The rhythm of personality is the exact reproduction of an individual's speech habits. The second style is a conscious attempt on the part of the writer to reproduce nature as it reveals itself to him in one second. This means, for instance, that upon entering a room, the writer concentrates upon one spot and minutely and objectively reproduces all sensory impressions without involving himself at all. There is no psychologizing, nor any indication as to what goes on inside the characters. The most successful attempt of this kind is made by Arno Holz with his early collaborator Johannes Schlaf (1862–1941) in the famous collection of sketches *Papa Hamlet* published in 1889 under the pseudonym Bjarne P. Holmsen (a tribute to the prestige of Ibsen and to Scandinavian writers in general).

The impact of Arno Holz' early writings upon his immediate contemporaries was tremendous. Gerhart Hauptmann dedicated his first play, the aforementioned *Vor Sonnenaufgang*, to the same Holmsen.

One would expect a naturalist movement to be primarily concerned with social conditions. To a certain degree that is the case. However, upon closer scrutiny one finds that beneath the surface of social concern the emphasis shifts from the general situation to the specific impact on the problems of the individual. Thus Hauptmann's first play takes place among Silesian peasants under whose meager acres suddenly coal was found. Their total degradation, not as a result of poverty but of sudden abundance, is an important ingredient of the drama. To be sure, young Gerhart Hauptmann is still very much captivated by the idea of heredity and environment and he carries it to incredible lengths in this play.

Another important element for Hauptmann and German naturalism is introduced here: the missionary, the self-appointed redeemer, the young man with a call, the incorruptible mind who rises above his own class and its prejudices, and who feels called upon to shed the light of truth, cost what it may (shades of Ibsen's *Wild Duck*). Like so many of Hauptmann's weak heroes, he only causes havoc.

Hauptmann's fame lies primarily in his so-called social dramas, *Die Weber* (*The Weavers*, 1892) and *Hanneles Himmelfahrt* (*Hannele's Ascension*, 1894), a comedy *Der Biberpelz* (*The Beaver Coat*, 1893), and the tragedies *Fuhrmann Henschel* (*Drayman Henschel*, 1899), *Rose Bernd* (1903), and *Die Ratten* (*The Rats*, 1911). Social concern is only one aspect of the poet's deep sympathy with suffering and the individual's futile attempts to escape the clutches of fate. Very early, however, two inexorably connected problems appear which are not only inherently those of Hauptmann but also are symptomatic for his contemporaries as, for instance, Hermann Sudermann (1857–1928): the tragedy that arises from the artist's intellectual insufficiency and his fatal course between two types of women, the domestic and intellectually inferior and the dynamic intellectual. This problem is an old one and was extensively treated by Ibsen. Hauptmann's *Einsame Menschen* (*Lonely People*, 1891), *Kollege Crampton* (1892), *Michael Kramer* (1900), *Die Versunkene Glocke* (*The Sunken Bell*, 1896), and the historical tragedy *Florian Gever* (1896) bear witness to his deep personal concern with these problems. The older Hauptmann becomes more and more involved in symbolical and mystical themes. Following in Goethe's footsteps, though not always with outstanding success, he experiments with a number of variations on Goethian themes as Mignon, Iphigenia, and the autobiographical *Buch der Leidenschaft* (*Book of Passian*, 1929) and *Abenteur meiner Jugend* (Adventure of My Youth, 1937).

In his early naturalist days Hauptmann wrote what to this day remains an exemplary *novella* in the naturalistic technique, *Bahnwärter Thiel* (*Switch Watchman Thiel*, 1888). His *Der Ketzer von Soana* (*The Heretic of Soana*, 1918), another *novella*, is a passionate avowal of the heathen hedonism as distilled from the then all-pervasive Nietzsche mania. Perhaps his most remarkable bit of prose writing is the long novel *Der Narr in Christo Emanuel Quint* (*The Fool in Christ. Emanuel Quint*, 1910) in which in the figure of a simple Silesian worker, he re-enacts the possible return of Christ, conscientiously maintaining for himself the position of an objective reporter. His *Die Insel der grossen Mutter* (*The Island of the Great Mother,* 1924) is a rather interesting version of the utopian novel on the theme of an Amazon state.

The uniquely German seeker and dreamer who populates so many novels of the first two decades of the century struggles with these problems of his insufficiency and of love and either succumbs or escapes from the demands of life into one sort of mystical detachment or another. Many works of Hauptmann's fellow Silesian and friend Hermann Stehr (1864–1940), as *Der begrabene Gott* (*The Buried God,* 1905), *Drei Nächte* (*Three Nights,* 1909), and *Der Heiligenhof* (*The Saints' Farm,* 1917), etc., fall into this category, as do largely the psychologically ambitious novels of Jakob Wassermann (1873–1934), *Die Geschichte der jungen Renate Fuchs* (*The Story of Young Renate Fuchs,* 1900), *Caspar Hauser* (1908), *Das Gänsemännchen* (*The Goose Man,* 1915), and *Christian Wahnschaffe* (1919). The early Hermann Hesse (1877–1962) in *Peter Camenzind* (1904) shares these problems and his later prose works extend and deepen his analytical scrutiny of the lonely soul, torn between its many base and noble components, possibly finding peace in an Eastern renunciation or in service to humanity: *Demian* (1919), *Siddhartha* (1922), *Der Steppenwolf* (1927), *Narziss und Goldmund* (1930), and *Das Glasperlenspiel* (*Magister Ludi,* 1943). His poetry and short stories and novels are a strange and often uneven admixture of romanticism, psychoanalysis, and Eastern and Western philosophy. He was awarded the Nobel Prize in 1946. Hesse is enjoying at present a great popularity among young Americans, a popularity which is not shared by young people in other countries, least of all in Germany. This present fad is difficult to explain and the only thing that could be gleaned from numerous conversations with young students is that in Hesse the young American seeks a romantic refuge from the harsh realities of the present and a welcome release from the oppressive visions of an unfeeling world, as represented for them for instance in Kafka or Sartre.

Besides the deterministic ideas and the triumphal progress of the sciences toward a socially and scientifically well-ordered positivistic paradise, at least three other forces helped form the profile of the new century: Schopenhauer's Eastern-directed spirit of pessimism and resignation, Nietzsche's epochal discovery of the all-powerful unchartered drive which he associates with the god Dionysus, and, putting a scientific and empirical foundation under it, Sigmund Freud's penetration into the subconscious. From personal experience and artistic choice, they loom large in the entire *oeuvre* of Hermann Hesse. On the other hand, these latter forces are also largely responsible for the rise of a literature which, in spite of its several common denominators with naturalism, namely the moral relativism arising from the attempt to comprehend motivation of human actions, is also antithetical to naturalism.

Whereas naturalism aspires toward the highest possible objectivity by total exclusion of the writer's personality and its submergence in speech and gestures of the characters, the concurrent movements of impressionism and neoromanticism tend to stress the subjective note, both in expression and characterization.

Also the concern with the aesthetic aspects of art becomes dominant to the point where art no longer serves any other purpose but itself, art for art's sake. It seems self-evident that the poem, which rather languished in the more restricted naturalistic climate, flourishes in this different setting. Interestingly enough, it is Arno Holz himself who must be counted among the most important liberators of modern German poetry, primarily because of his fantastic geometrically constructed epic effusion *Phantasus*. In this work, moving at random from present to past, historical or paleoanthological, from place in space to outer space, from mood to mood, his lines vary from a long sentence to a single word or letter and gyrate dizzily around the imaginary middle axis, as he calls it. It is a poetic achievement of great impact upon the younger generation of German poets, comparable to that of Walt Whitman's surging verse and Baudelaire's sensuous symbolism.

While it cannot be denied that there is something resembling a worker's poetry at that time, it is much more the poem of a Detlev von Liliencron (1844–1909) which indicates a new style to his younger contemporaries. Liliencron is a keen observer but not so much of nature as one might expect as of people, situations, and mores. In more or less quick and onomatopoetic impressions, he catches the sounds, the smells, the glitter, and the rhythm of a hot-blooded life. His themes are rather limited, war, love, and death, but at its best his poetry has a special rhythmic quality, a concreteness and compactness, and a vivid suggestiveness, as in *Siegesfest*:

> Flatternde Fahnen
> Und frohes Gedränge.
> Fliegende Kränze
> Und Siegesgesänge.
>
> Schweigende Gräber,
> Verödung und Grauen.
> Welkende Kränze,
> Verlassene Frauen.
>
> Heisses Umarmen
> Nach schmerzlichen Sehnen.
> Brechende Herzen,
> Erstorbene Tränen.[1]

Much indebted to Nietzsche in spirit and form is Richard Dehmel (1863–1920) whom some of his contemporary critics viewed as Germany's greatest poet since Goethe. This reputation, though very much reduced in more recent considerations, is largely based on his great facility with words and his rather too-fervent treatment of life and love. Not to be overlooked are his attempts at weaving balladesque features into a historical or contemporary situation and his unhackneyed presentation of the human rather than the social plight of the worker. Different in style and idea as his ballads may be from the more conventional concept, they place him among the small group of modern balladists as Börries von Münchhausen (1874–1945), Agnes Miegel (b. 1879), and Ina Seidel (b. 1885).

Nietzsche's rediscovery of the inexorable vitality of instincts and hidden drives within man in his *Die Geburt der Tragödie aus dem Geiste der Musik* (*The Birth of Tragedy from the Spirit of Music*, 1871), and his vision of the Zarathustran superman; the conscious, highest possible artistic refinement of the depths of human experience in the symbolism of the poetry of Baudelaire, Verlaine, Rimbaud, Mallarmé, and others; the prose of a Gabriele D'Annunzio; the reconsideration of the Renaissance by Jakob Burckhardt; the matriarchal mysteries of Bachofen—all of these gave rise to an artistic tendency for which Heinrich Mann created the term *Renaissancism.* By it he meant the reaffirmation of the proud, self-centered, uncompromising spirit beyond good and evil of the Machiavellian Renaissance man and his devotion to life, beauty, and art as an inseparable oneness of existence. Mann himself celebrates this spirit in his novel triology *Göttinnen* (*The Goddesses*, 1903). The flourishing form- and beauty-conscious drama of the neo-romanticists yields to this spirit with abandon and vies in the artistic presentation of total surrender with the Dionysian in such form-perfect creations as Ernst Hardt's *Tantris der Narr* (*Tantris the Fool*, 1907), Herbert Eulenberg's (1876–1949) *Anna Walewska* (1899), and even Hugo von Hofmannsthal's (1874–1927) *Elektra* (1903), where perversion, cruelty hysteria, and madness overpower with their dreadful and beautiful presence.

The precocious talent of the latter poet was discovered early by Stefan George (1868–1933) with whom German poetry, for the first time in some decades, entered into the stream of the great European poetic tradition of a classical and symbolical provenance, as practiced by the great French poets. George's early poetry divorces itself completely from any concerns or problems of the day and rises to the status of a high, self-celebrating cult which tolerates nothing else in its company. Art is the highest purpose of art and serves no one but itself. With Hofmannsthal and a few others, George publishes the most esoteric *Blätter für die Kunst* (*Journal for Art*, 1892–98) which, ignoring the average reader, is addressed like the poetry of George exclusively to the few initiates and the anointed. George's *Algabal* (1892) is probably the most telling example. The beauty of form, the very image of the poem, the type of print, the alphabet and punctuation—all become of prime importance, compared to which the content loses essential meaning:

> Becher am boden;
> Lose geschmeide.
> Frauen dirnen
> Schlanke schenken

Müde sich senken;
Ledig die lende
Busen und hüfte;
Um die stirnen
Der kränze rest.[2]

In a neoheathen spirit, the poets of the group which Hofmannsthal had left early dedicate themselves to aesthetic orgies of exploring the world of decadence and evil. In this frenzy of Dionysian indulgence they envision the new Boy God whom George celebrates in his deeply moving *Maximin* verses of *Der siebente Ring* (*The Seventh Ring*, 1906). In Maximin Christianity and heathendom are reconciled in the corporeal manifestation of the divinity and in the deification of the human body. George soon comes to play the role of the seer among his followers and, not unlike Nietzsche, almost becomes a myth during his lifetime. In searing visions and retrospections he tells of the horrors of the war and its consequences in *Der Krieg* (*The War*, 1917) and *Das neue Reich* (*The New Empire*, 1928): "Kein Triumph wird sein/ Nur viele Untergänge ohne Würde," ("There will be no triumphs, only downfall without dignity"). In his late years he envisions a new humanity and a new Germany, which has been tragically misconstrued by some as his endorsement of the German millenium. Nothing could have been further from the poet's intention in his profound contempt for the *plebs vulga* than an identification with the faceless but entrenched petit bourgeois: "Weit minder wundert es, dass so viel sterben/ Als das so viel zu leben wagt," ("It is less surprising that so many die, than that so many dare survive."): and so he willed to be buried in Swiss soil.

Hofmannsthal and his older friend Arthur Schnitzler (1862–1931) are the most important representatives of impressionism of the Viennese variety, unmistakably unique regardless of individual differences. Schnitzler's first plays, *Liebelei* (*Love Affair*, 1895), *Freiwild* (*Open Game*, 1896), *Das Vermächtnis* (*The Bequest*, 1897), etc., might be considered Viennese attempts at being naturalistic. The difference quickly becomes obvious. Nowhere is there any consideration of the typical social problems, nowhere does the action take place in a proletarian milieu. The protagonists are almost always members of the upper bourgeois or nobility, their involvements with the lower classes are strictly personal and, as likely as not, amatory. In the final analysis the victims, such as they are, are victims of prejudices or misunderstandings. Schnitzler is the first to introduce a specifically Viennese type, the *charmeur* and narcissistic egotist. An outstanding example of the latter category is Anatol, the less-than-hero of the seven episodes of the same name (1889–90). Contrary to prevailing contemporary criticism, Schnitzler by no means idealizes nostalgically the frivolity and *fin de siècle* elegance of a dying Austria but rather in the constant duping of Anatol, in his final loneliness, indeed ridiculousness, the moralist Schnitzler sits in objective judgment over his city and age. The vain self-seekers in the end must face alone their own failures and their lonely deaths. Though psychology in its romantic as well as clinical implication plays a major role in the writings at the turn of the century, only since Schnitzler can one speak of a truly searching, probing in depth of the human soul, wherein he even anticipates the first published findings of Sigmund Freud. In plays and *novellas* on a variety of problems, the common denominator is man's intrinsically tragic struggle with forces within himself and his attempts at self-deception in illusions, play acting, and dreams. *Der grüne Kakadu* (*The Green Cockatoo*, 1899), *Paracelsus* (1899), *Der einsame Weg* (*The Lonely Road*, 1904), and *Der Ruf des Lebens* (*The Call of Life*, 1906) are some of the important stations. Schnitzler is an unsurpassed master of the shorter form, the *novella* and the one-acter. In a remarkable variety of themes he treats of man's games of life and love which he almost always sets in Imperial Austria, in the twilight of a world as Werfel called it.

The seventeen-year old Hugo von Hofmannsthal's poetic prologue to *Anatol* with all the beautiful sadness of a deceptively bright autumn day in the dying glory of eighteenth century Vienna sets the tone for this world of glistening make believe. In *Der Tor und der Tod* (*Death and the Fool*, 1893) the teen-age Hofmannsthal introduces in the face of death the realization of a life wasted in the empty pursuit of beauty and egotistic evasion of human compassion and responsibility (or what he calls "pre-existence"). Hofmannsthal's poetry is of a transcending beauty, full of the melancholy music and the knowledge of death, as in "Ballade des äusseren Lebens" (1895):

> Und Kinder wachsen auf mit tiefen Augen,
> die von nichts wissen, wachsen auf und sterben
> und alle Menschen gehen ihre Wege.
>
> Und süsse Früchte werden aus den herben
> und fallen nachts wie tote Vögel nieder
> und liegen wenig Tage und verderben.
>
> Und immer weht der Wind und immer wieder
> vernehmen wir und reden viele Worte
> und spüren Lust und Müdigkeit der Glieder.
>
> Und Strassen laufen durch das Gras, und Orte
> sind da und dort, voll Flacken, Bäumen, Teichen
> und drohende, und totenhaft verdorrte ...
>
> Wozu sind diese aufgebaut? und gleichen
> einander nie? und sind unzählig viele?
> Was wechselt Lachen, Weinen, und Erbleichen?
>
> Was frommt das alles uns und diese Spiele,
> die wir doch gross und ewig einsam sind
> und wandernd nimmer suchen irgend Ziele?

Was frommt's, dergleichen viel gesehen haben? . . .
Und dennoch sagt der viel, der "Abend" sagt,
ein Wort, daraus Tiefsinn und Trauer rinnt

wie schwerer Honig aus den hohlen Waben.[3]

At the same time the consciousness of being a link in the unbreakable chain of generations in an eternity and of the oneness of the entire cosmos finds its articulation in the poet's visions. The poem is thus a justification and affirmation of the world and the poet; for him his art is no longer its own fulfillment. In assuming the great responsibility of service he humbly becomes the voice and the conscience of a mute world. In his comedy *Der Schwierige* (*The Difficult Man*, 1921) the futility of evading commitments is demonstrated. In his *Jedermann* (1911), inspired by the English Everyman, and in his *Das grosse Salzburger Welttheater* (*The Great Salzburger World Theatre*, 1921), adapted from Calderon's play, he recreates in a modern revival of the medieval mystery the profoundly religious drama of submission to and acceptance of the divine will. In the gripping final version of his drama *Der Turm* (*The Tower*, 1920–26), taken from Calderon's *La Vida es sueño* (*Life is a Dream*), he warns in vain of the impending age of the new barbarians and laments the futile return of redeemers to a world that refuses to recognize and accept them. This play is Hofmannsthal's last will. His and Richard Strauss' modern opera successfully aspires to a new union of poetry, drama, and music: *Elektra* (1903), *Rosenkavalier* (1911), *Ariadne auf Naxos* (1912), etc.

The neoromantic spirit and its Dionysian fascination with the irrational, the deviate, the morbid, its dedication to death as a life force, its rediscovery of the dark side of human motivation, has undergone many mutations and has invested some of the best in contemporary German writing. Having said as much, we must quickly add the obvious lest it be overlooked: a great writer can never be compartmentalized nor forced into a preconceived mold. To be sure, writers of note pass through contemporary styles but they remain, above all else, themselves. Thus the connection of a Hesse, of a Hauptmann, and even more so of a Thomas Mann, with any one movement must of necessity remain tangential.

We have mentioned Hesse in passing once before when speaking of the novel of the seekers and the dreamers. Even then we alluded to his interest in the hidden drives within man's soul, of which the once very popular *Steppenwolf* (1927) is an example. Hesse's neoromantic hero possesses at times almost magic powers of communicating with the natural and the supernatural; he is driven on the one hand by a never-satisfied search for the new and adventurous or, on the other hand he retires into the solitude of monastic contemplative life (*Narziss und Goldmund*, 1930); again he follows the irrepressible call of the chosen to a *Morgenlandfahrt* (*Journey to the Orient*, 1932), a journey of the soul to the Orient or, finally, he devotes himself to pure intellectual pursuit only to realize its sterility and to return to life, service, and death in *Das Glasper-lenspiel* (*Magister Ludi*, 1943). Hesse's neoromanticism has regained much of the essence of old romanticism. Its sometimes too-sweet scent has alienated the writers of the youngest generation.

None of this sweetness is present in Thomas Mann (1875–1955). From the outset his debt to romanticism lies primarily in his personal version of romantic irony. We encounter it first with minor emphasis in *Buddenbrooks* (1901). This novel to all outward appearances follows a traditional German pattern of the nineteenth century, namely that of the family novel. Mann, however, writes it with reversed denominators, for instead of the rise we are treated to the story of decline. Instead of the naturalistic deterioration of a Zola family, here the cause is rather the increasing refinements by which the robust stock is gradually depleted until the last member of the family, an artistically gifted boy, dies an ugly death before he comes to grips with life. It is as if raw life were taking vengeance on its deprecators. Two of several very important Mannian moments are introduced here for the first time: the inherent danger that art represents in the regulated and orderly existence of society, and the conflict of art and life or, better, of the artist and the bourgeois, In *Tonio Kröger* (1903) this clash is fully developed. On the one hand the artist, as the one who is different from the rest and whose ecstasies and depressions are suspect to the tolerant, good-looking average bourgeois, feels keenly his isolation and remoteness and therefore cannot help but envy the ordinary man and long to be like him. On the other hand he feels a sense of contempt for the well-groomed ordinary man who cannot understand—nor does he care to understand—what agonies and joys the artist experiences. Hence Thomas Mann's artist is doomed to alienation in his environment as well as in his art. Depending on the point of view from which the story is written, the artist is tragic (*Der Tod in Venedig*, *Death in Venice*, 1913), tragicomic (*Tristan*, 1903), or in the extreme a charlatan (*Felix Krull*, 1954).

Ever since *Buddenbrooks*, Mann's fascination with sickness and death—another true romantic heritage—is an ever more dominant note, its important stations *Der Tod in Venedig*, *Der Zauberberg* (*The Magic Mountain*, 1924), and *Doktor Faustus* (1947). The reason for it is obvious: sickness and death possess the power of granting the distinction of exclusiveness and isolation. They are the two moments which are essential to the totality of life and only against the background of their ubiquity do the games of life assume their true mean-ing. Yet devotion to the dark forces is dangerous and leads to self-destructive emotions. Hence the call of life which Hans Castorp hears in the famous chapter "Snow" in *The Magic Mountain* as he is about to succumb to the lures of death: "For the sake of goodness and love, man shall not concede to death the mastery over his thoughts." This encyclopedic novel presents in the herme-tic insularity of the mountain a total view of European culture before 1914 and unfolds in its microcosm the forces in the outside world which fight symbolically for the mind and soul of man and inevitably lead to the cataclysm of the war. Castorp is last seen marching off to battle in the field grey anonymity of the group.

Myth and history, archetype and individual uniqueness of personality and its mythic repetition through eons, Bergsonian speculation on time are the strata of the Joseph tetralogy, *Joseph und seine Brüder* (*Joseph and His Brethren*, 1933–44). Ironical playing with the very structure of the language reaches here a high point which borders on mannerism. This temptation the mature Mann finds difficult to resist.

Mann's increasingly intense dedication to humanism experiences a serious jolt with the coming of National Socialism. He realizes that intellectual indulgence, forbearance, and blindness which forgo the obligation of furthering the cause of humanity literally deliver it to the forces of evil, of the devil. Assuming his share of the total guilt Mann, Zeitblohm, all of Germany, can only join in the prayer: "God have mercy on your poor soul, my friend, my Fatherland," in *Doktor Faustus*:

> Deutschland, die Wangen hektisch gerötet,
> taumelte dazumal auf der Höhe wüster
> Triumphe, im Begriffe, die Welt zu gewinnen
> Kraft des einen Vertrages, den es zu halten
> gesonnen war, und den es mit seinem
> Blute gezeichnet hatte. Heute stürzt es, von
> Dämonen umschlungen, über einem Auge die
> Hand und mit dem andern ins Grauen
> starrend, hinab von Verzweiflung zu
> Verzweiflung. Wann wird es des
> Schlundes Grund erreichen? Wann wird
> aus letzter Hoffnungslosigkeit, ein Wunder,
> das über den Glauben geht, das Licht der
> Hoffnung tagen? Ein einsamer Mann
> faltet seine Hände und spricht: "Gott sei
> Eurer armen Seele gnädig, mein Freund,
> mein Vaterland."[4]

The romantic tradition is the keynote in the first publications of Ricarda Huch (1864–1947) where the Dionysian life force dominates, as in *Erinnerungen von Ludolf Ursleu dem Jüngeren* (*Recollections of Ludolf Ursleu the Younger*, 1892), *Vita Somnium Breve* (later *Michael Unger*, 1903), and *Aus der Triumphgasse* (*From Triumph Street*, 1902). The greatest testimonial to her devotion to romanticism is her excellent, extensive, and authoritative study on the romantic movement. Her ideas of the heroic man of action and his glories and the dangers to society which he presents are the core of a two-volume work on *Garibaldi* (1907), her *Leben des Grafen Federigo Confalonieri* (*Life of Count Federigo Confalonieri*, 1910), and, finally, *Wallenstein* (1915), in which no longer the spectacular hero but the anonymous little sufferer from the heroic games of the great absorbs the reader's sympathy and attention. Not unlike Thomas Mann, a fascination with the problems of romanticism and the tragic sense of the heavy German guilt characterize her life and work.

A degree of moral relativism, in one way or another, is a trait which both naturalism and aestheticism have in common, though for different reasons. To the naturalist and the early impressionist, man's faults are the results of the workings of inner and outer forces which are beyond his immediate control; therefore, the understanding of them precludes the total condemnation of them. On the other hand, the aesthete is by determination beyond good and evil and lives according to a subjective personal law. It is the noteworthy contribution of Paul Ernst (1866–1933), *Der Weg zur Form* (1906), and a small school of neo-classicists (W. von Scholz, b. 1874; Samuel Lublinski, 1868–1910) to have reintroduced the concept of the absolute good into literature and thereby to have anticipated one important aspect of expressionism. This new moral note is coupled with a sense of responsibility to form and language.

Form and beauty arising from the intense identification with the classical and Christian world are also the common denominators of the two *poetae docti*, Rudolf Borchardt (1870–1945) and Rudolf Alexander Schröder (1878–1962).

Also Rainer Maria Rilke's (1875–1926) beginning moves in sensitive neo-romantic musical form-conscious imagery. One is occasionally reminded of young Hofmannsthal with whom Rilke shares his Austrian baroque heritage, although Rilke is unmistakably the product of the beautiful and mysterious city of Prague, which was also the home town of Kafka and Werfel. Here three cultures have lived side by side for centuries: German, Czech, and Jewish; here the spirit of the gothic and the baroque blend. Out of Rilke's openness to the Slavic world, especially to that of Russia, grows his dialogue between God and the Russian monk in *Das Stundenbuch* (*The Book of Hours*, 1906), in which Rilke's essentially metaphysical nature becomes revealed, as are indications of a religiosity without God. Under the direct impact of the great French sculptor Auguste Rodin, whose secretary Rilke was for a time, the subject of a poem turns into an artistic self-statement of mysterious penetration under its surface, as for instance in *"Der Hund"* from Rilke's *Neue Gedichte* (1907, 1908):

> Da oben wird das Bild von einer Welt
> aus Blicken immerfort erneut und gilt.
> Nur manchmal, heimlich, kommt ein Ding und stellt
> sich neben ihn, wenn er durch dieses Bild
>
> sich drängt, ganz unten, anders, wie er ist;
> nicht ausgestossen und nicht eingereiht
> und wie im Zweifel seine Wirklichkeit
> weggebend an das Bild, das er vergisst,

um dennoch immer wieder sein Gesicht
hineinzuhalten, fast mit einem Flehen,
beinah begreifend, nah am Einverstehen
und doch verzichtend: denn er wäre nicht.[5]

Whereas originally love meant romantic love and death a heroic death, now love becomes the great transmuter of things and people and is born from the desire of sacrifice—of things so that they may rise from being objects of observation to a total transformation into their own nature; of people in renunciation, nonfulfillment, and nonpossession of the beloved. Death now shows his other face, that of sickness, ugliness, wretchedness, as Malte Laurids Brigge witnesses it in Paris in the novel *Die Aufzeichnungen des Malte Laurids Brigge* (*The Notes of Malte Laurids Brigge*, 1910). Yet life, in spite of existential anguish, is its own glory, its own highest purpose, and man the one chosen to experience all its heights and depths. In *Duineser Elegien* (*Duino Elegies*, 1923), those inexhaustible ten poems for the coming of which Rilke had been waiting long and painful years and which then overwhelmed him in one ecstatic splurge, and in *Sonette an Orpheus* (*Sonnets to Orpheus*, 1922), all fifty-five of which he dashed off in three weeks, the plaint of man's life and its transitoriness finally rises to a praise and a glorious affirmation. Let us listen to the breathtaking music of the first Elegy which introduces the angels, those higher beings, neither human nor yet divine, in whom perception is heightened to a point beyond human endurance:

Wer, wenn ich schriee, hörte mich denn aus der Engel
Ordnungen? und gesetzt selbst, es nähme
einer mich plötzlich ans Herz: ich verginge von seinem
stärkeren Dasein. Denn das Schöne ist nichts
als des Schrecklichen Anfang, den wir noch grade ertragen,
und wir bewundern es so, weil es gelassen verschmäht,
uns zu zerstören.[6]

Rilke's poems, in contrast to George's sculptural perfection, breathe an air of music with an emotional sweep which anticipates and outdoes the *suada* of the expressionist poets.

Expressionism, apart from the romanticism of the early eighteen hundreds, is the one movement which is specifically German and which has spread from Germany to other countries. Like so many literary schools, it derives from art and is first of all a movement of protest. It is the old story, the clash of generations accentuated now by the conviction that the world of the fathers—the rising bourgeois sociologically speaking, the realists and aesthetes artistically speaking—is totally corrupt and beyond repair, and (shades of Ibsen) must therefore be destroyed so that a new world can be born. The artist, whether painter like Kandinsky (1866–1944) or poet like Paul Kornfeld (1899–1942) exists by his very negation of all materialistic values. This spirituality and all-embracing self-denial of love and his total identification with the world's sorrow permeate his every thought. The agnosticism or hypocrisy of the elders is blamed for the distance that separates man from man and fosters indifference, exploitation, and cruelty. The time is ripe for a new redemption, for a return of the Messiah. A tremendous, profoundly religious yearning for a new brotherhood under the one Father seizes the young poets, as each in his own way tries to re-establish God's Kingdom, some like the touchingly sweet Reinhard Johannes Sorge (1892–1916) by the poet's personal assumption of the messianic mission, others like Franz Werfel (1890–1945) devoutly resigning themselves to being the voice, the vessel, the pen of the divine will. In their cosmic love they include the entire universe; in their redemptive urge they reach even to God, a God whom Werfel pictures as having exhausted all persuasions and who, finally, having sacrificed his own Son, needs redemption through the love of man.

It is self-evident that this great store of love will address itself to suffering mankind whose material pains cry out for alleviation. From the outset this movement of youths (most of them were born around 1890) has a strong social note, which need not necessarily be confused with socialism. As a matter of fact, about 1910 when the movement is still young, the predominant note is anarchistic and metaphysically optimistic.

The outbreak of the First World War (1914–18) is at first a traumatic disappointment. The waves of hatred seem to warp and consume all the hope and charisma these young men cherished. In an apocalyptic fury they cry out against the dreadfulness of their time and their fellow men, heaping abuse on the liars and demagogues and learning to despise the very language in which they are flaying themselves, for the word is anybody's slave and will serve any cause. But soon there arises a new, a burning ray of hope for a better world; the very carnage that devours hecatombs will also destroy the systems that make such conditions possible; just as the Apocalypse is an end and a beginning so now, too, with the rise of the new man, the new Golden Age will dawn.

In the course of the war developments become discernible which indicate a bifurcation of the movement into two main tendencies: one that remains primarily metaphysical and sceptical of all material panaceas, as in Franz Werfel and Georg Kaiser (1878–1945), and the other which assumes a strong activistic political accent and early identifies itself with the Communist party. Their leader, Kurt Hiller (b. 1885), though not a Communist, sees the obligation of a writer strictly in active participation in the settling of the burning problems of the day, rather than in metaphysical dreams. Its most important convert to the cause Johannes R. Becher (1891–1958), the late poet laureate of East Germany and author of the National Hymn of the German Democratic Republic, demands that the writer prepare himself to lead the revolution in "Eingang" from *An Europa* (1916):

Der Dichter meidet strahlende Akkorde.
Er stösst durch Tuben, peitscht die Trommel schrill.
Er reisst das Volk auf mit gehackten Sätzen. . . .

Der neue, der Heilige Staat
Sei gepredigt, dem Blut der Völker, Blut von ihrem Blut, eingeimpft.
Restlos sei er gestaltet.
Paradies setzt ein.
—Lasst uns die Schlagwetter-Atmosphäre verbreiten!—
Lernt! Vorbereitet! Übt euch![7]

A movement as revolutionary as expressionism must of necessity cause a total upheaval. In its re-evaluation of all values it takes nothing for granted, neither in society nor in family—patricides, intended or actual, abound in it— nor in the very idiom that it uses. It is as much a linguistic as an ideological revolution. The poet's heart is so full of pent-up emotions that it literally bursts and scatters the traditional shackles of sentence, logic, and grammatical structure. In varying degrees the poems, especially those written in the wrath of the war, explode in ejaculatory lines, dropping articles, inventing a punctuation of emotions, converting all description into action. It is very significantly the verb and the verbal form that practically eliminate the normal descriptive adjective. This explosive type of writing finds its tersest condensation in the staccato lines of August Stramm (1874–1915), a Ph. D. in economics, who wrote a dissertation on the International Postal Union in 1909. An officer with reserve rank of captain, Stramm fell on the Russian front. Here is an example, *Patrouille* (1915):

Die Steine feinden
Fenster grinst Verrat
Äste würgen
Berge Sträucher blättern raschlig
gellen
Tod[8]

Two further and more radical steps toward the abandonment of the meaning of a statement are the adoption of the montage pattern as in Dada (Kurt Schwitters, 1887–1948; Hugo Ball, 1886–1927; the sculptor Jean [Hans] Arp, 1887–1966) and a poetry carried ad absurdum in the substitution of mere sounds for words (Rudolf Blümner, 1873–1945). Besides the above-mentioned explosiveness, especially before the outbreak of the war, another stylistic tendency becomes evident which patterns itself on the effusive, long, enumerative, musical line of the Psalms, of a Walt Whitman, and also of Arno Holz' *Phantasus*. Here we encounter again a kinship with Rilke who gives to and receives from the movement a great deal. The best representative of this genre is Franz Werfel in whom his generation quickly recognizes its foreordained voice. His so-called "O Mensch" poetry with its childlike love for all and his touching hope and desire of partaking in all suffering is the purest Easter voice of the time's aspirations.

Expressionism abounds in countless avant-garde journals and anthologies. Historically by far the most important are *Die Aktion* and *Der Sturm* and Kurt Pinthus' anthology of poetry *Menschheitsdämmerung* (*Dawn of Humanity*, 1919).

Like all young movements, expressionism had its precursors—in poetry Rilke, Ernst Däubler, and Else Lasker-Schüler, in drama Frank Wedekind and August Strindberg, and in the novel Heinrich Mann (1870–1950).

We have already dealt briefly with Rilke's intenseness of love and his redemptive yearnings; we might refer specifically again to his mastery and handling of language and form, the best examples of which, the *Duino Elegies*, were written during and after the flourishing of expressionism.

Däubler's (1876–1934) cosmogonic dreams of his long epic poem *Das Nordlicht* (*The Northern Light*, 1910), while retaining the classical mold, glitter in ecstatic visions of bold imagery so dear to the expressionists.

Else Lasker-Schüler (1876–1945) is not a political revolutionary nor a social reformer. Her poems are pure poetry, distinguished by remarkable fancy and creativity. Her close personal relations with many of the younger poets, even more than her writing, made her impact felt on her time. Her *Hebräische Balladen* (*Hebrew Ballads*, 1913) have the strength and simplicity of the Old Testament. Her world is above all a world of love, her sorrows are the sorrows of love expressed with fervor and devout religiosity.

It is appalling how grim a harvest the war had reaped among the young writers. After an early beginning in the footsteps of George and Hofmannsthal, the Alsatian Ernst Stadler (1883–1914), who died at the age of thirty, published in 1913 a volume of poetry *Aufbruch* (*The Rise*), the very title of which is an expressionistic manifesto. The poet breaks with the tradition of formal beauty which he now considers as a self-indulgence. In long, rhythmic, flowing lines, he seeks also for a *Mitmenschentum* (fellowship of humanity) in the sordid worlds of the slum, the insane asylums, the sickrooms, taking in, in Rilkian empathy, the full measure of dread and filth. George Heym (1887–1912) raises these worlds to a monomaniacal obsession. Ugliness loses its repulsiveness and becomes as in painting a subject of poetic concentration and even transfiguration. This note, in all expressionist writers, grows in intensity. In some, as in Werfel, it is an indication of the artist's redemptive urge.

What in Stadler's poetry we encountered as fascination with the city becomes with Georg Heym a moloch and a nightmare. In visions which in their metaphoric images vie with the exquisite tortures of a Bosch's *Last Judgment* and the fright of the world in Alfred Kubin's (1877–1959) graphic work, he conjures up all the visitations of hell in a fiendish conspiracy against a helpless, wincing, pitiful, groveling heap of humanity. In wide-eyed, bloodcurdling prophecies, he anticipates the agonies of the war, the outbreak of which he does not live to see. He drowned while ice-skating at the age of twenty-four.

Contrary to the generally optimistic spirit among the young poets, one can call Heym's expressionism apocalyptic though even here under all the ashes of a final cataclysm there seems to smoulder a weak spark of the possibility of a rebirth. Heym's world is inhabited by unheard-of gods and spirits of a mythology all his own. This mythogenic spirit is shared by many expressionists. In a grotesque variation of black humor we encounter it in Heym's Berlin friend of the *Neuer Klub*, Jakob van Hoddis (1887–1942) whose poem *Weltende* (*World's End*) published in 1911 inaugurates this type of poetry—*Dem Bürger fliegt vom spitzen Kopf der Hut* (*The Hat Flies Off the Burgher's Pointed Head*), etc., or in Alfred Lichtenstein's (1889–1914) *Die Dämmerung* (*Dawn*).

It is noteworthy that the three expressionist poets whom present day criticism brackets as greatest, namely Heym, Trakl, and Benn, in one way or another are apocalyptic. The reason for the critics' preference lies not only in an artistic judgment but perhaps even more in the close analogy of the poet's prevailing mood and the existential despair of the present. A generation that has gone through another war and had to fight without illusion or idealism, except for finishing a dirty business, only to lose the peace again, would naturally be drawn to a world view whose pessimism and, indeed, nihilism speak to the despair of modern man.

Georg Trakl (1887–1914), like Heym, lives in a world dominated by vengeful gods and tormenting spirits who wreak punishment on individuals, cities, and states in an annihilating wrath of retribution. In Trakl, however, this is a reflection of his own terrible awareness of an inexpiable guilt. The poet stands in the midst of the cataclysm and bears the responsibility for its eruptions. In lines of the sublime melody of an Hölderlin ode, Trakl transforms his world in intricate symbols that defy a definitive interpretation. Like so much of poetry since Rilke, the poem is an indissoluble entity that must not be broken. Certain figures and colors are repeated with a regularity that ascribes the poetic purpose of a *chiffre* to them: the shepherd, the pond, the black horse, etc. Trakl's poetry is profoundly a personal poetry and as such it is not typically expressionistic, though in its form expressionism reaches heights of perfection.

Nor is Gottfried Benn (1886–1956) typical, for the poetry of the young physician who knows life from the ugliest, most hopeless, inexorable encounter with naked humanity on the marble slab of the morgue, has no ideals or illusions or hopes or faith left. He knows what wretched misery is, he knows the cause, and he knows that there is no answer. What he sees is beyond sympathy and calls forth only cynicism and a nihilistic resignation. The poet and his poem have no obligation, no mission. Benn is one of the very few expressionists to have lived to a ripe age and to have seen himself in historical perspective. After a silence of many years he returns in 1948 to what he calls "Phase Number Two" of expressionistic style in which he runs the full gamut, returning in his

Statische Gedichte (*Static Poems*) to an avowal of form as the only counter-
balance to a nihilistic world. Art as creative joy in and of form assumes the
transcendence that religion lost in "Ein Wort":

> Ein Wort, ein Satz—: aus Chiffern steigen
> erkanntes Leben, jäher Sinn,
> die Sonne steht, die Sphären schweigen,
> und alles ballt sich zu ihm hin.
>
> Ein Wort—ein Glanz, ein Flug, ein Feuer,
> ein Flammenwurf, ein Sternenstrich—
> und wieder Dunkel ungeheuer
> im leeren Raum um Welt und Ich.[9]

It is this kind of poetry which in a world of disillusionment with all traditional
values seems temporarily to be a guidepost to the homeless spirit of the young
poets of the fifties in Germany and abroad and which seems to link them to
Ezra Pound and T. S. Eliot.

As was briefly alluded to above, the pure antithesis to all this despair and
detachment is the poetry of Franz Werfel (1890–1945). The very titles of his
first volumes clearly indicate the total involvement in the life and fate of his
fellow man here and in the beyond: *Der Weltfreund* (*The Friend of the World*),
Wir Sind (*We Are*), and *Einander* (*Each Other*). In verses which either retain
the traditional form and transform it to a totally new concept or pour forth
in long lines gratefully learned from Whitman, the poet literally sings of
the joy of existence. This to him is proof of divine grace of selection from
nothing to being. He evokes the melancholy nostalgia of memories of childhood common to all. He pleads with all who suffer to allow him a share of
their pain. In "Warum, mein Gott" from *Einander* (1915) he communicates his
happy knowledge that God *is* and above all he proclaims his persuasive certainty that love is the only answer to the vicissitudes and visitations of life:

> Was schufst du mich, mein Herr und Gott,
> Der ich aufging, unwissend Kerzenlicht,
> Und flackre jetzt im Winde meiner Schuld,
> Was schufst du mich, mein Herr und Gott,
> Zur Eitelkeit des Worts,
> Und daß ich dies füge,
> Und trage vermessenen Stolz,
> Und in der Ferne meiner selbst
> Die Einsamkeit?!
> Was schufst du mich zu dem, mein Herr und Gott?
>
> Warum, warum nicht gabst du mir
> Zwei Hände voll Hilfe,
> Und Augen waltend Doppelgestirn des Trostes?

Und eine Stimme, regnend Musik der Güte,
Und Stirne überhangen
Von sanfter Lampe der Demut?
Und einen Schritt durch tausend Strassen,
Am Abend zu tragen alle
Glocken der Erde
Ins Herz, ins Herze des Leidens ewiglich?!

Siehe es fiebern
So viele Kinder jetzt im Abendbett,
Und Niobe ist Stein und kann nicht weinen.
Und dunkler Sünder starrt
In seines Himmels Ausgemessenheit
Und jede Seele fällt zur Nacht
Vom Baum, ein Blatt im Herbst des Traumes
Und alle drängen sich um eine Wärme,
Weil Winter ist
Und warme Schmerzenszeit.

Warum, mein Herr und Gott, schufst du mich nicht
Zu deinem Seraph, goldigen, wilkommenen,
Der Hände Kristall auf Fieber zu legen,
Zu gehn durch Türenseufzer ein und aus,
Gegrüsst und geheissen:
Schlaf, Träne, Stube, Kuss, Gemeinschaft, Kindheit, mütterlich?!
Und da ich raste auf den Ofenbänken,
Und Zuspruch bin, und Balsam deines Hauses,
Nur Flug und Botengang und mein nichts weiss,
Und im Gelock den Frühtau deines Angesichts![10]

Werfel's poems have a transcendental mission—"*Sie reden in mancherlei Gestalten nur von Einem, von dem permanenten Existenzbewusstsein, das ist Frömmigkeit,*" ("They speak in manifold guises but of one thing, namely the permanent consciousness of being, and that is devoutness"). The outbreak of the First World War shattered temporarily this idyllic messianism. The very next volume of poetry *Der Gerichtstag* (*Judgment Day*, 1919) finishes the mysterious sentence that is formed by the titles of his books: *We are for each other Judgment Day*. The poem temporarily disintegrates into raving accusations, its form is splintered into expressionistic screams and ejaculations, the poet's word itself is impugned. Yet throughout and above this despair there shines the confidence that there is a higher purpose to it all and that a metaphysical fate asserts itself and, above all, that the poet is not a messiah but only an articulation of the divine voice, the pen with which God chooses to write. This last secure conviction Werfel retains throughout the rest of his life, long after the buffeting waves of expressionistic ecstasies and agonies have passed. In all his ensuing work, be it poem or drama or novel or essay, in many forms of realistic allegory he proclaims his unswerving certainty of the metaphysical verities.

In his "magic triology" *Spiegelmensch* (*The Mirror Man*, 1920), inspired by *Faust* and *Peer Gynt* and yet entirely different in its almost operatic form, Werfel depicts in a new kind of Pilgrim's Progress the development of the young man Thamal from the vanity of a false renunciation of the world in the struggle with his base *alter ego* to a genuine renunciation in patient waiting for the coming of the Saviour, a covenant which is eternally renewed in every expectant mother. In the play *Bocksgesang* (*Goat Song*, 1921), the mystery of the ineradicable evil in creation is presented in an historical setting. It is this dramatic form which Werfel favors from now on; thus his *Juarez und Maximilian* (1924) and *Paulus unter den Juden* (*Paul Among the Jews*, 1926) which dramatizes the great moment in the history of salvation when St. Paul leaves the Jews to preach to the gentiles. He treats a related theme in the play *Das Reich Gottes in Böhmen* (*God's Kingdom in Bohemia*, 1930) in which the schism between the Catholics and the Hussites remains unhealed. Even his most contemporary play *Jacobowsky und der Oberst* (*Jacobowsky and the Colonel*, 1945) is an allegory on the parallelism of the paths of the Christian (in Werfel's language identical with Catholic) and the Jew. His *novellas* and especially his novels present the external metaphysical verities skillfully obfuscated in an exciting realistic story. *Barbara oder die Frömmigkeit* (*The Pure in Heart*, 1929), a *roman à clef* of Viennese society at the collapse of the monarchy, indicates the futility of intellectual panaceas. *Die Geschwister von Neapel* (*The Pascarella Family*, 1931) presents in a striking combination two symbolisms, the sun and the planets, and the redemption of God the Father through the Son. *Die vierzig Tage des Musa Dagh* (*The Forty Days of Musa Dagh*, 1933) re-enacts in a frightening anticipation of the Nazi terror, the story of the flight into the promised land in the historical struggle of the Armenians against the genocidal brutalities of the Turks during World War I. *Höret die Stimme* (*Harken Unto the Voice*, 1937) deals with the ever renewed mystery of the choice of the divine voice. After his miraculous escape from the Nazis, Werfel writes his moving *Das Lied von Bernadette* (*The Song of Bernadette*, 1941). What in the opinion of this writer is one of the greatest books of the first half of this century, *Der Stern der Ungeborenen* (*The Star of the Unborn*, 1946), appeared posthumously. In it in a wonderful blending of the *Divine Comedy* and Jonathan Swift, Werfel, with an exquisite and benign sense of irony, projects the new perfect world a hundred thousand years hence which is doomed to destruction as is everything that is built solely on material values.

Let us now return to our consideration of expressionism. Expressionism considers as its primary function the communication of a message; therefore, it stands to reason that its most obvious vehicles are the poem and the stage. The origins of the new drama go, if anything, further back than those of the poetry. Practically at the very threshold of naturalism Frank Wedekind (1864–1918) brought out his *Frühlings Erwachen* (*Spring's Awakening*, 1889) in which form, style, content, tendency, and message defy everything that the early naturalists believed in. No attempt is made to present on the stage a reality in the spirit of a Zola or an Ibsen. This play is a touching dirge on the sorrows of puberty, an accusation against the adults for evading their responsibilities toward the young, a melancholy statement of the loneliness and the inner torment of insecurity and ignorance. The characters are all intentionally overstated so that on the one hand the young people in their emotional genuineness and purity are superdimensional, while on the other hand the adults, especially the teachers, become caricatures. The purpose of the latter is clear. Wedekind is among the first in modern literature to attack and ridicule the bourgeois for his hypocrisy, mendaciousness, egomania, and ruthlessness. The romantic writers, as well as Heine, Grabbe, and Büchner, are Wedekind's ancestors. The attack on the bourgeois, the *épater le bourgeois*, has become a well established tradition ever since. There are other antitraditional elements in the play, which twenty years later become the accepted norm with the expressionists. The play is split up into a great many partially disconnected scenes (not unlike the plays by the Stormer and Stresser, Lenz) encouraging the later station drama of ex- ressionism. It is also practiced by Strindberg at about the same time as Wedekind experiments with it. Like him, Wedekind has a message to deliver on the human condition, though both recommend different panaceas and both preach their brand of morality. The language is almost a sober lyricism (it changes to a dryly mordant tone in Wedekind's later plays). There is little if any attempt to maintain a verisimilitude with daily life or the speech of the average man. Wedekind does not hesitate to introduce on the stage a suicide carrying his head under his arm. The dead high school student attempts to lure the hero away from life to the bliss of death, only to be stopped by the appearance of a *vermummter Herr*, a veiled gentleman, the symbol of life, who pulls the youth back again with the call to explore the unknown life.

Wedekind's total disregard for the accepted tradition of the stage and his daring experimentations endeared him to the expressionists. His messianic penchant for preaching the new morality of the liberated flesh, of honesty in the relation of the sexes, indeed of the true sacredness of the senses, finds fervent admirers among the young as it shocks his own contemporaries. The *femme fatale* of his plays, Lulu, in *Erdgeist* (*Earth Spirit*, 1895), and *Die Büchse der Pandora* (*Pandora's Box*, 1901) is the scourge of men, not as in Strindberg because of any inherent evil, but because in the final analysis she is only what man made of her. Symbolically every one of her men calls her by a different name. The note of the bizarre and utterly grotesque is very significant and becomes intensified as again and again he demonstrates the vengeance of the senses on their dis- torters or suppressors (*Schloss Wetterstein*, 1910; *Simson*, 1914, etc.).

His own role as the ever-misunderstood and exploited moralist is attested to by his touching verse play *König Nicolo* (*King Nicolo*, 1901), the grotesque play *Karl Hetmann der Zwergriese* (*Karl Hetmann, the Dwarf Giant*, 1904), and finally his theodicee *Die Zensur* (*Censorship*, 1908), with its defense of sensual love as the natural ally of religion. The picaresque theme of the modern adventurer, *Marquis von Keith* (1900), finds repeated variations right up to our own time.

The modern stage as a vehicle for new and old drama undergoes a revolution and a liberation from conventional norm as a result of the plays of Wedekind and Strindberg, the full impact of which becomes evident only with the coming of expressionism.

Following in the footsteps of Wedekind, Carl Sternheim (1878–1942) in his series of twelve comedies *Aus dem bürgerlichen Heldenleben* (*From the Burgher's Heroic Life*) continues the unmasking of the bourgeois by presenting in concentrated form and an uniquely personal expressionistic speech, situations as they exist and are tolerated in the venal aristocracy, the capitalist bourgeois, and the proletarian protestor. The result? There are no heroes, no heroic causes. In his *Bürger Schippel* (*Burgher Schippel*, 1912), the social outcast Schippel rises to total acceptance in the bourgeois world because of his incomparable tenor voice which is needed in the quartet to win the coveted wreath and because he marries the bourgeois daughter after her one flight into enchantment with the prince. The loss of Mrs. Maske's undergarment as she stretches to see the emperor and his sons go by lays the foundation for the phenomenal rise to fortune and aristocracy of her son: *Die Hose* (*The Undergarment*, 1911); *Der Snob* (1914), and *1913* (1915). In *Tabula Rasa* (1916) the Socialist party boss is feathering his own nest. In recent years Sternheim's comedies more than the dramas of any other expressionist have staged a remarkable and telling comeback.

The beginnings of Georg Kaiser (1878–1945) are also in the tradition of Wedekind. His comedies, however, contain a touch of the tragic as the downfall of the naive protagonist is brought about by his taking the bourgeois at face value. Wedekind's concern with sensual freedom also finds an echo in Kaiser's comedies, *Die jüdische Witwe* (*The Jewish Widow*, 1911), *Europa* (1915), etc. At first hardly noticeable in his work, an all-pervading question may be detected, the constant permutation of which earned him the scornful appellation of *Denkspieler* (thought juggler), a reproach which Kaiser encouraged by defining the purpose of the drama as the thinking of a thought to its logical conclusion and by considering Plato's *Dialogues* as his greatest inspiration. The question alluded to is an old one: Man's search for his place. In the pursuit of an answer, Kaiser establishes a variety of situations to which all answers but one are invariably disappointing. In his *Von Morgens bis Mitternachts* (*From Morn to Midnight*, 1916) the cashier's realization of the emptiness of his life in his pursuit of thrills and happiness ends in death. In the trilogy *Die Koralle* (*The Coral*, 1917), *Gas I* (1918), and *Gas II* (1920), the several ways of establishing a happy society by escapism and materialistic means collapse and the denouement is world conflagration. The subtlest answer is adumbrated in his *Die Bürger von Calais* (1914), inspired by the same historical incident that gave rise to Rodin's famous group: the new man who joyfully takes upon himself the mission of self-sacrifice for humanity. The blind father of Eustache de Saint-Pierre announces his birth as he accompanies the body of his son who has taken his own life lest he deprive one of the six burghers of the grace of sacrifice:

> Schreitet hinaus—in das Licht—aus dieser Nacht. Die hohe Helle ist angebrochen—das Dunkel ist verstreut. Von allem Tiefen schliesst das siebenmal silberne Leuchten—der ungeheure Tag der Tage ist draussen!— Er kündigte von ihm—und pries von ihm—und harrte mit frohem Übermute der Glocke, die zu einem Fest schwang—dann hob er den Becher mit seinen sicheren Händen vom Tisch und trank an ruhigen Lippen den Saft, der ihn verbrannte. Ich komme aus dieser Nacht—und gehe in keine Nacht mehr. Meine Augen sind offen—ich schliesse sie nicht mehr. Meine blinden Augen sind gut, um es nicht zu verlieren: ich habe den neuen Menschen gesehen-in dieser Nacht ist er geboren!—Was ist es noch schwer—hinzugehen? Braust nicht schon neben mir der stossende Strom der Ankommenden? Wogt nicht Gewühl, das wirkt—bei mir—über mich hinaus—wo ist ein Ende? Ins schaffende Gleiten bin ich gesetzt—lebe ich —schreite ich von heute und morgen—unermüdlich in allen—unvergänglich in allen . . .[11]

Here Georg Kaiser joins the ranks of the expressionist seraphic visionaries whose voices tend to go unheard in this age of lost faith. The expressionistic form reaches its exemplary state. The station drama, the confessional drama, the soul drama, the *Ich* drama, or whatever other term one chooses, find in Kaiser and his fellow dramatists eloquent representatives. Most noteworthy is the development of expressionistic language. We have alluded to it while considering poetry and Sternheim's comedies. In Georg Kaiser the experimentation in contraction reaches algebraic terseness and occasionally even defies comprehension. The engineer, seeking to win the mass of workers over to his charge to vengeance and destruction, shouts down his pacifist rival: "Findet ihr nicht den Schrei für Verrat, der euch anspeit? Schweigt euer Schelten vor einem Antrag, der euch schächtet? Vergesst ihr den Zuruf, der stiess zu mir mit Gelöbnis?" (*Gas* II).

We encounter a similar and yet unrelated obfuscation in Fritz von Unruh's (1885–1970) stirring early plays which leave the reader breathless from an enormous overcharge of pathos and emotion: *Ein Geschlecht* (*A Clan*, 1916), and *Platz* (The Square, 1920). Unruh, like Kaiser, seeks the new man, as does the gentle Ernst Toller (1893–1939) who, though an active revolutionary, shrinks from force in *Die Wandlung* (*The Change*, 1919), *Masse Mensch* (*Man and the Masses*, 1921) and *Die Maschinenstürmer* (*The Machine Stormers*, 1923). A unique mythogenic note among the expressionist seekers is struck in Ernst Barlach's (1870–1938) naive and chthonian mysticism of a world in search of God. The same heavily expressive gesture that characterizes his sculptures is also typical of his plays and prose, as in *Der tote Tag* (*The Dead Day*, 1912), *Der arme Vetter*

(*The Poor Cousin*, 1918), *Der Findling* (*The Foundling*, 1922), *Die Sündflut* (*The Flood*, 1924), and *Der blaue Boll* (*The Blue Boll*, 1926). One might note in passing that one of the best known expressionist painters, the Austrian Oskar Kokoschka (b. 1886) is among the first expressionist dramatists with his *Mörder Hoffnung der Frauen* (*Murderer, the Hope of Women*) written in 1907. The problem of the conflict of generations which played a relatively minor role with the playwrights mentioned, except Unruh, finds strong articulation in such writers as Walter Hasenclever (1890–1940), *Der Sohn* (*The Son*, 1914); Reinhard Johannes Sorge (1892–1916), *Der Bettler* (*The Beggar*, 1912); and Franz Werfel, *Spiegelmensch* (*The Mirror Man*, 1920).

We have mentioned Heinrich Mann as a forerunner of expressionism. His inspired corrosive scorn of his contemporary society and in particular the law-abiding German citizen in *Professor Unrat* (*Professor Muck*, 1905), *Zwischen den Rassen* (*Between the Races*, 1907), *Die Kleine Stadt* (*The Small Town*, 1909), and *Der Untertan* (*The Subject*, 1918), as well as his impassioned defense of the individual against the omniscient rationalism of a pedantic state anticipate expressionism and metarealism. His great late novels on the life of *Henri Quatre* (1935–38) shine with the glow of his earlier aesthetic consciousness which he shared with D'Annunzio, while displaying an almost classical control of form and a newly won affirmation of life's reality.

Prose is not the preferred medium of expressionism, yet some outstanding individual examples come to mind, for example: Robert Walser's (1876–1956) surrealistic miniatures and novels of a dreamlike structure reminiscent of Kafka, who greatly admired him (*Geschwister Tanner* (1907), *Der Gehülfe* (1908), and *Jacob von Gunthen* (1909), Kasimir Edschmid's (1890–1966) *Die sechs Mündungen* (1915), Franz Werfel's *Nicht der Mörder der Ermordete ist schuldig* (*Not the Murderer but the Murdered is Guilty*, 1920), or Sternheim's *Chronik von des 20. Jahrhunderts Beginn* (*The Chronicles of the Beginning of the Twentieth Century*, 1918), but on the whole they are a passing phase in the writers' development. Among the major German writers only one, Alfred Döblin (1878–1957), is and remains expressionist from the outset. Already in 1913 he publishes the stories *Die Ermordung der Butterblume* (*The Murder of the Buttercup*). The same year he writes a visionary novel *Die drei Sprünge des Wang-Lun* (*The Three Leaps of Wang-Lun*, 1915) with descriptions of the religious wars of China during the Boxer Rebellion, culminating in a note of the futility of an individual's attempt to change the world. In *Wadzeks Kampf mit der Dampfturbine* (*Wadzek's Struggle with the Turbine*, 1918) and the later *Berge Meere und Giganten* (*Mountains, Oceans, and Giants*, 1924), technology and nature are the relentless masters. Stylistically and humanly Döblin's masterpiece is *Berlin—Alexanderplatz* (1929), the story of the little man Franz Biberkopff who tries to go straight but stumbles from crime to crime. This novel uses a collage technique. The staccato course of the epic is interrupted by repeated intrusions of headlines and statistical reports, thereby rounding out a totality of the metropolis of Berlin as complete as no amount of epic detail could ever accomplish. The novel also most successfully makes use of the inner monologue of the Joycean type. The author, who in his earlier works resisted an inherent metaphysical urge, converts to Catholicism after Hitler's rise to power. In retrospect it becomes clear, however, that Döblin's characters, though they may be resigned to being reduced to mass fates, still nourish a lost hope of getting more from life than just bread.

In *Berlin—Alexanderplatz* we encounter a world in which the chiliastic dreams of the early expressionists have yielded to the disillusioned reality of defeated Germany, a bleak land of unemployment, inflation, and doom. The art of survival, of winning the daily battle against odds, obsesses the little man and his chronicler the author. A new sense of factual realism replaces the exclamatory panaceas of bright futures. Hans Fallada's (1893–1947) *Kleiner Mann, was nun?* (*Little Man, What Now?* 1932) tells in simple sober language of the losing fight of a decent young couple. The earthy aspects of this new realism are represented in the theatre of Carl Zuckmayer (b. 1896) in *Der fröhliche Weinberg* (*The Merry Vineyard*, 1925) and *Der Hauptmann von Köpenick* (*The Captain of Köpenick*, 1930). Arnold Zweig probes reality with psychoanalytical means in *Der Streit um den Sergeanten Grischa* (*The Case of Sergeant Grischa*, 1927). Franz Werfel continues to present in realistic guise his allegories of religious mysteries. Hans Carossa (1878–1956) adds a new touch of an idealization of humanity in his largely autobiographical writings, *Das Rümanische Tagebuch* (*Rumanian Diary*, 1924), *Der Artz Gion* (*Doctor Gion*, 1931), etc. In Ernst Wiechert's (1887–1950) *Der Wald* (*The Forest*, 1922), *Die Magd des Jürgen Doskocil* (*The Maid of Jurgen Doskocil*, 1932), and *Der Totenwald* (*The Forest of the Dead*, 1945) reality again becomes imbued with mysticism and symbolism, while in Richard Billinger's (b. 1893) folk plays ghosts and heathen cults are in full sway again (*Rauhnacht*, 1931). New realism has become the fetish of the Third Reich in the *Blut und Boden* (blood and soil) literature as has the glorification of the German: (Friedrich Griese, b. 1890; Hans Blunck, 1888–1951; Edwin Erich Dwinger, b. 1898; Hanns Johst, b. 1890; Hans Grimm, 1878–1959.) In Erwin Guido Kolbenheyer's (1878–1962) *Paracelsus* (1917–26) and Ernst Jünger's (b. 1895) *In Stahlgewittern* (*In Tempest of Steel*, 1920) nationalistic literature achieves a certain artistic and philosophical level. Jünger's *Auf den Marmorklippen* (*On the Marble Cliffs*, 1939) and the novel *Heliopolis* (1949) are written in highly perfected sterile German and represent his disenchantment with the Nationalist Socialist Party.

One island of resistance from within against chauvinism is the new Catholic wave consisting to a large degree of converts. Gertrud von LeFort (1878–1971) probes divine grace and the mystery of selection in her best known *novella Die Letzte am Schafott* (1931), adapted by Georges Bernanos as *Dialogues des Carmelites*. Elisabeth Langgässer (1899–1950), the "half-Jewess," considers nature in its "panic forces" as unredeemed in the Christian meaning. In her best known, complex, symbolical novel *Das unauslöschliche Siegel* (*The Inextinguish-*

able Seal, 1946) baptism and grace are the main themes. In a definitely "experimental style" harking back to medieval mysteries, God and Satan are the contesting actors. Early in the Hitler era, the Baltic Werner Bergengrün (1892–1964) raises the question of the conflict between power and justice in his novel *Der Grosstyrann und das Gericht* (The Grand Tyrant and the Court, 1935). In his novel *Im Himmel wie auf Erden* (*In Heaven as on Earth*, 1940), the nihilism of the present is revealed in a sixteenth century story.

Tangentially related to these yet completely a lone figure is Hanns Henny Jahnn (1894–1959) whose daring plays and involved novels deal largely with man's struggle to discover himself in a theology without God. At the basis of his endless conflicts that defy solution lie the physical and mystical manifestation of sex. (Plays: *Pastor Ephraim Magnus*, 1919; *Medea*, 1924; *Thomas Chatterton*, 1955. Novels: *Perrudja*, 1929; the trilogy *Fluss ohne Ufer*, *River Without Banks*, 1949–50.) Still another protesting voice is that of Hermann Kasack (1896–1966) who was forbidden to write after 1933. In his novel *Die Stadt hinter dem Strom* (*The City behind the River*), started in 1942, he depicts in visions of a Kafkian nightmare the horrors of a ghost town under the corruptive forces of a soulless totalitarianism. Surreal escapists from a world gone mad with power and materialism are Ernst Kreuder (b. 1903), *Die Gesellschaft vom Dachboden* (*The Attic Company*, 1946) and Arno Schmidt (b. 1910) with his deeply pessimistic satire *Leviathan* (1949).

One author who, chronologically speaking, starts writing at the very outset of expressionism remained so far unmentioned because his true and lasting impact on world literature became evident only with the second World War: Franz Kafka (1883–1924). Like Rilke and Werfel he was born in Prague and cannot be comprehended without the specific mystic, Slavic background of that city. Though his major novels had been published shortly after his death by his friend Max Brod (b. 1884), only a small circle was aware of their importance. Soon National Socialism closed Germany to him and not until the French existentialists discovered in him the great artistic articulation of modern man's dilemma, did postwar Germany and the rest of the world realize his great importance. There is hardly a writer about whom ever since so many and so divergent books and theories have been written. Kafka's basic concerns are few but fundamental. His figures live in a cosmos which conspires against them and denies them a haven and a justification for their existence; therefore, they are doomed to live in fear and trembling before forces they do not know but which they know exist, to whose unlistening ears they must explain themselves constantly. This Kafkian world which, in contrast to the prevailing fashion of expressionism, is expressed in a classical clear language, is a world of unrelieved nightmare; Kafka uses with almost scientific accuracy the technique of the dream in which everything follows an inexorable logic and not the disrelated spinning of fantasy. In this dream existence there is no escape from the fate of utter loneliness, try as the character may on his headlong course to find a surcease. Moreover, Kafka's traumatic relation to his strong-willed father must be borne in mind—his hundred-page letter to his father which was never sent is an eloquent testimonial—when reading works like *Die Verwandlung* (*Metamorphosis*, 1912); the futile wooing for toleration and acceptance throbs coldly in *Der Prozess* (*The Trial*, 1925) and *Das Schloss* (*The Castle*, 1925). In both of these latter novels, the main character is suddenly summoned, in the first to a trial without an accusation, in the second to a castle and its surrounding community into which he is finally allowed as he dies. In both novels tragic irony and futility are overwhelming. To attempt to establish definitive answers to Kafka's work is a hopeless task. One can but muse and wonder: What is Josef K's transgression in *Der Prozess*? Is it his noninvolvement? And why is K. refused entrance in *Das Schloss*? Is it because he seeks it so fervently with the desire of escaping from himself? Who would dare to answer.

Generally speaking, the principal purpose of the novel is to tell a story, at least this seems to be the tradition of the nineteenth century in England, France, and Russia, and partially also in Germany. The German novel at the turn of the century follows that definition fairly closely, but within the second decade of the twentieth century a new type of novel begins to appear in Europe in which the story, such as it is, is a frame within which the author in a more or less discursive way expostulates on ideas more or less vaguely connected with the epic thread. The term "essayistic novels" seems appropriate. Some important examples have already been mentioned, as Thomas Mann's *Der Zauberberg*, or Hermann Hesse's *Das Glasperlenspiel*. To the latter's utopian theme might be added Alfred Döblin's *Die Babylonische Wanderung* (*Babylonian Migration*, 1934), Ernst Jünger's *Heliopolis*, and as perhaps the finest example of the utopian statement, Franz Werfel's posthumous novel *Der Stern der Ungeborenen* (*The Star of the Unborn*, 1946).

However, the new essayistic novel or antinovel has become a well-established tradition and bears its most successful fruit in the Viennese novelists, Robert Musil (1880–1942), Hermann Broch (1886–1951), Albert Paris Gütersloh (b. 1887), and Heimito von Doderer (1896–1966). With Thomas Mann they give strength and hope to a new literature in the German language after the total collapse of all values and illusions in 1945. They are a revelation to the defeated German nation and to an uprooted youth.

Musil's great Torso, *Der Mann ohne Eigenschaften* (*The Man Without Qualities*), remained unfinished at his death in Swiss exile in 1942. The first volume had come out in 1930, a second in 1932, a third was edited by his widow in 1943, but the world took little cognizance until a by now famous lead article in the *London Times Supplement* of October 28, 1949, called enthusiastic attention to the greatness of the author. Since then many further rudimentary chapters have been published and have had their authenticity questioned. Not unlike Thomas Mann's *Der Zauberberg*, it is an encyclopedic novel while the story is of very secondary importance; Musil tries to encompass all of life, the world, the illusions, the false realities, the escapisms of modern man, his attempts at giving importance and meaning to his illusory games, and the frantic gyrations at pretending that his voids are filled. In general, in an exquisite form of irony in attitude and even more so in language, Musil while never aiming for the mannerisms of a Thomas Mann observes as a scientist the world about him and sits in judgment of himself, his time, his nation, indeed the whole world. Ulrich, the man without qualities, the intellect uncommitted to anybody or anything, is the perfect catalyst for a madly whirling world, dizzily galloping toward its own destruction in the First World War and equally giddily losing itself in inconsequential cares which, however, create the conviction of a solid reality. The very concrete basis for the happenings in the first part of the novel, the so-called parallel action, demonstrates the absence of any sense of a genuine reality, namely the preparations for the celebration of the seventieth anniversary of the ascension to the Austrian throne of the Emperor Franz Joseph I. (The Prussians are planning a similar national commemoration for William II's thirtieth anniversary.) What could better demonstrate the illusoriness and blindness of an age? In the latter part, as Ulrich proceeds to seek tenable values for what he calls "the other existence" in a disenchanted world, Musil's essayistic tendency increases. Here, as in the works of Joyce in England, Proust and Gide in France, Pirandello in Italy, and Unamuno in Spain, to mention but a few great names of the age, experimentation with the concept of reality and the idea of time which had already variously preoccupied Thomas Mann, is the main intellectual as well as spiritual concern.

This is also the common denominator in Hermann Broch's *oeuvre*. Already in his triology *Die Schlafwandler* (*The Sleepwalkers*, 1931–32), in which he treats three phases of contemporary German development, 1913 to 1933, the reality of action is permeated by a search for a totality of experience. With a fatal fascination, the mathematically and philosophically competent writer observes and analyzes the disintegration and departmentalization of the oneness of all positive values and the resulting alienation in specialization. He thus establishes the *hubris* of rationality which in its coldness plunges man into the faceless irrationality of a mass community. Out of this fate in the end, only selflessness and love can save mankind; it is the mission of the writer to lead the way.

Presenting this search for a totality of experience on the levels of history, morality, and metaphysics, Broch's work begins to assume aspects of surrealism. This tendency is even more evident in *Die Schuldlosen* (*The Guiltless*, 1950)—the title is meant ironically—in which the figures are drawn with an abstract anonymity bordering on the allegorical. In his best known novel, *Der Tod des Vergil* (*The Death of Vergil*, 1945), his poetic accomplishment and stylistic experimentation are at their peak. His great admiration for James Joyce is evident in the masterful and original handling of the interior monologue. In contrast to Joyce, however, there is an elegiac lyrical sweep in it as Broch presents in one unending monologue the last eighteen hours of the dying poet Vergil, the last reckoning of his life and his art, his realization of its futility and emptiness and his decision to destroy the *Aeneid*, which he finds wanting in moral values. The yielding to Augustus' remonstrations Broch justifies as a final victory over the poet, as an act of self-sacrifice. The whole is projected against a canvas of history, not too dissimilar from ours, in which the death throes of a disintegrating world are clearly recognizable. Again we recognize reality and time as very relative concepts, neither of which stays on empirical levels.

Striving for totality or better, universality, in the Goethian sense, and a devotion to reality by no means identical with realism are also the characteristics of Albert Paris Gütersloh in whom the Austrian baroque celebrates a joyous revival. With gargantuan sentences within monumental paragraphs he tries in his nonnovel *Sonne und Mond* (*Sun and Moon*, 1965) to penetrate in a constantly changing kaleidoscopic mutation of metaphors, the bland world of reality. In this fascinating net of divergent speculations the epic thread is lost but not missed and then picked up again. In a striking example of romantic irony, the serious and constant concern with the soul according to strict Catholic doctrine is skillfully and almost indiscernibly woven in.

Heimito von Doderer is Gütersloh's most enthusiastic disciple and admirer. Their paths, however, pursue different courses from the outset. While in a baroque romantic way Gütersloh allows his imagination unbounded freedom and avoids following a set and preconceived structure, Doderer's seemingly rambling telling of a story is carefully plotted and laid out with the exactness of an architect. Nevertheless, he achieves the impression of total casualness. For both Gütersloh and Doderer the almost sacred idea of Imperial Austria is the soil in which their work grows. In contrast to Gütersloh, Doderer hardly ever leaves its historic reality which, on the whole, encompasses in its span of time the generations from just before the end of the empire to the hectic agonies of the recent past. Less interested in philosophizing than his fellow Viennese, he nevertheless is interested in presenting the *Menschwerdung* and in depicting a reality that *is*, instead of one that *should be*. The tendency to strike out in search for the nonexistent, the illusory, *die zweite Wirklichkeit*, the second reality as he calls it, upsets the equilibrium of his many characters who form the imposing gallery of Viennese types. Few Austrians, succeeded as well as Doderer in giving the total image of Vienna with its scurrilous humor and its big and small tragedies. His most famous novel, *Die Strudelhofstiege* (1951) and *Die Dämonen* (1956) concentrate on the fate of Vienna up to the downfall of the First Republic in 1927.

Out of the safe and arrested island within a turbulent world, Switzerland, come two odd novels by Max Frisch (b. 1911). *Stiller* (I'm not Stiller, 1954) is the story of a lost identity, in the tradition of Pirandello. Once more it raises the question of experiencing reality as actually lived and as observed by the outsider. *Homo Faber* (1957) relates the complex fate and adventures of the engineer Faber who, in his quest for the causality of his life, refuses to allow for the existence of any higher forces that do not yield to a mathematical analysis.

The collapse in 1945 left a complete physical and spiritual vacuum in Germany. As noted above, the new and experimental novel, especially as practiced by the Austrian fantastic realists or, better yet, metarealists, from Kafka to Doderer, the stylistic experiments of the Americans, Hemingway, Dos Passos, and Faulkner, as well as the French existentialists, excite the curiosity of young German writers who are desperately trying to establish new values in order to combat the inner chaos. It was primarily the vision of Hans Werner Richter that was responsible for the creation of *Gruppe 47*, a group of conscionable young writers dedicated to salvaging and maintaining positive values in German literature. This group in the beginning at least was anticlerical and filled with social consciousness. Very soon, however, it changed to a loosely-knit society of writers, primarily interested in the quality and originality of their writings. Though their status is unofficial, there rose from their numbers the best known writers of a new Germany, some of the group's prize winners being Günter Eich (b. 1907), Heinrich Böll (b. 1917), Ilse Aichinger (b. 1921), Ingeborg Bachmann (b. 1926), Martin Walser (b. 1927), Günter Grass (b. 1927), Johannes Bobrowski (1917–1965), and among their members are Alfred Andersch (b. 1914), Hans Magnus Enzensberger (b. 1929), Wolfgang Hildesheimer (b. 1916), Uwe Johnson (b. 1934), Siegfried Lenz (b. 1926), Jakov Lind (b. 1927), and Peter Weiss (b. 1916), to mention only a few of the best known. All have been widely translated. It is impossible to find a common denominator for them all. Their engagements vary widely, especially with their years, for they were born anywhere from the beginning of the century to the downfall of the Third Reich. Yet, divergent as their tendencies may be, in one way or another they continue to experiment within the frame of a realism which is distinguished from that practiced by the eminent realists of the nineteenth century by being primarily metarealistic. Their reality, though on the surface an objective reportage of a facet of the outside world, is crystalline in its nature, thereby by its transparency allowing a refracted view behind each apparent front. As with the American writers, the result of this rendition of realism is one more form of nonmetaphorical treatment of factual moments in reality, the sum total of which adds up to a specific and sought-after-individual impression. Thus we find, for instance, that Heinrich Böll in his best known novels *Wo warst du, Adam?* (*Where Were You, Adam?*, 1951), *Billiard um Halb Zehn* (*Billiards at Nine-Thirty*, 1959), or *Ansichten eines Clowns* (*Opinions of a Clown*, 1963) maintains a realism which is fraught with his hatred of war and destruction and his profound misgivings of the new materialism of the *Wirtschaftswunder* (economic miracle). He became president of the International PEN-Club and was awarded the Nobel Prize in 1972.

Uwe Johnson attempts in his novels *Mutmassungen über Jakob* (*Speculations About Jacob*, 1959) and *Das dritte Buch über Achim* (*The Third Book About Achim*,

1961) to present the tragedy of a divided Germany with its different and contradictory values, mores, and psychology. In a daring stylistic experiment he fuses the simultaneousness of experiences on either side of the political demarcation line by a collage of corresponding impressions, accentuated by special type and personal punctuation. Though less productive and less publicized than Günter Grass, he is considered by many serious critics the most important and constructive innovator. In his experience of reality as recorded by the characters in his books, the relativity and many-leveled structure of reality become evident and the previously omniscient author turns, in Johnson, into a conscientious reporter, groping for truth in a maze of complex and incomprehensible factors. Johnson himself emigrated from East to West in 1959.

The city of Danzig, the birthplace of Günter Grass, is the ever-returning locale of his novels. All three, Die Blechtrommel (The Tin Drum, 1959), Katz und Maus (Cat and Mouse, 1961), and Hundejahre (Dog Years, 1963), are in a way variations on the locale of Danzig and on the theme of the German which, in contrast to Hans Erich Nossack's (b. 1901) style of restrained, bitter eyewitness reportage in his Der Untergang (The Downfall, 1943, published in 1948), presents the incredible reality of Germany just before, during, and after the Nazi interlude as an enormous background for the adventures and fates of altogether picaresque characters. One is reminded of the panorama of Grimmelshausen's Simplicissimus as well as of Swift's penetrating satire. Die Blechtrommel is the first German literary product that was immediately and universally acclaimed as a masterpiece and it has become new Germany's passport to a respected status in world letters. It attests the popularity of black humor and allegory and shows kinship with an international type of absurd literature. The invention of Oskar Matzerath, the self-ordained dwarf who at the age of three refuses to grow is bizarre, grotesque, baroque, and yet a fully convincing anti-Bildungsroman figure. On his tin drum (shades of Heine's LeGrand) he interprets and criticizes the bourgeois world into which he is born and which soon enough triumphantly assumes leadership in the national socialism of Germany. Grass' misgivings of the German economic miracle and the resurgence of the invincible philistine, the enthusiastic Nazi of yesterday, are genuine and bode ill for the future. Whether Grass is the great genius as he is acclaimed today or whether his boundless originality and imagination in story and style overshadow serious flaws remains to be judged by his future works. His dramatic attempts have so far failed, on the whole; his last play Die Plebeier proben den Aufstand (The Plebians Rehearse the Revolution, 1965), dealing with Brecht's passivity toward the East Berlin Workers' uprising of 1953, is an example of the documentary theatre.

Martin Walser's relation to reality, initially characterized by a Kafkian alienation of the individual and society, in Ein Flugzeug über dem Haus (An Airplane over the House, 1955) changes to a satirical compromise of "going along" in Ehen In Phillipsburg (Marriages of Phillipsburg, 1957) and to a sell-out to complete accommodation in *Halbzeit* (*Half-time*, 1960). He, too, turns to drama; in *Eiche und Angora* (1962) he treats the rise of the petit bourgeois between 1945 and 1955.

At the end of World War II, only one tragic voice was heard out of the total debacle of the German drama and this all too briefly: Wolfgang Borchert (1921–47) in *Draussen von der Tür* (*Outside in Front of the Door*, 1947) speaks of the fate of the returning soldier who seeks in vain an answer to his desperate whys. This most gifted work shows, however, inexplicable traits of expressionism which the author could hardly have known since the Nazis had outlawed this "decadent art." The dramatist of the generation, however, and for better or worse one of the most potent influences on the modern theatre is Bertolt Brecht (1898–1956), who was then writing his best plays in exile, especially in the United States. His beginnings go back to the last phase of expressionism: *Baal* (three versions: 1918, 1919, 1926), *Trommeln in der Nacht* (*Drums in the Night*, 1919; produced 1922), and *Im Dickicht der Städte* (*In the Thicket of the Cities*, 1921; produced 1924). They show, however, none of the forward-looking, expressionistic new man; on the contrary, they are full of uncommitted nihilism with the typically Brechtian accent on the art of survival against odds and principles. This philosophy, though never explicitly stated (protestations to the contrary notwithstanding), in the end seems to be the human and poetic creed of Brecht for, alas, a dead hero no matter how heroic his death is dead and does no one any good. Unhappy the land that needs a hero, his Galileo wryly observes. The heroic gesture may be admirable but it remains but a gesture while life and living must go on. No matter how the theoretical goals in his best plays may have been intended, the reality and, indeed, the tragedy of them all, as in *Das Leben des Galilei* (*The Life of Galileo*, three versions: 1938–39, 1945–46, 1955), *Mutter Courage* (*Mother Courage*, 1939; produced 1941), *Der Kaukasische Kreidekreis* (*The Caucasian Chalk Circle*, first produced at Carleton College, Minnesota, 1948), and *Der gute Mensch von Sezuan* (*The Good Woman of Setzuan*, 1938; produced 1943), is this very acceptance of the fact that life must go on if things are to get better. Brecht's great importance, besides his remarkable achievement as the creator of a new drama form and a viable, socially motivated poetry of great simplicity and clarity, especially the new singable ballad, lies in his dramaturgy. Breaking with the Aristotelian tradition of catharsis, his "epic" drama demands of the audience the reaction of alienation (*Verfremdung*) from the happenings on the stage, that is, a sense of outrage and a desire for change rather than a classical identification with and empathetic understanding of the characters. The epic theatre is intended as an outspoken contrast to the pure dramatic theatre. The action does not develop, it grows by accretion of more or less independent scenes or sketches, the total sum of which reveals the desired didactic effect. By the same token the actor must never become identified with the character that he is playing but must maintain the theatricality of his presence on the stage. Brecht accentuates this moment through interruptions of the stage business by songs and pseudo-ad libs addressed to the audience. All of these elements are common to the folk play, especially of the Viennese variety of Johann Nestroy. Brecht, however, prefers to admit the influence of the Oriental theatre. His magnificently fertile imagination brings forth an original form of the musical with a message as in his *Dreigroschenoper* (*Threepenny Opera*, 1928, with music by Kurt Weill, an adaptation of John Gay's *The Beggar's Opera*, 1728) and *Aufstieg und Fall der Stadt Mahagonny* (*The Rise and Fall of the Town of Mahagonny*, 1929) which he conceives as the modern answer to what he calls the "culinary" opera. Least successful are his numerous *Lehrstücke* (*Didactic Pieces*) in which he dryly and unimaginatively toes the Communist party line.

The most enthusiastic follower of Brecht's new form and antibourgeois line, though not of his *Weltanschauung*, is Max Frisch, especially in plays like *Die Chinesiche Mauer* (*The Chinese Wall*, 1947), and *Biedermann und die Brand-stifter* (*Biedermann and the Incendiaries*, 1956). His *Andorra* (1962), in which he returns to his concern for the question of identity and reality, suffers from sensationalism.

His fellow Swiss, Friederich Dürrenmatt (b. 1921), proceeding from expressionism, discovers in Brecht the great master and liberator of the drama but at the same time also the danger of overwhelming the theatre by making it subservient to an extraneous idea. Dürrenmatt fully accepts the challenge of reducing bourgeois truths and realities ad absurdum and he relishes in twitting the stodgy Swiss respectablity behind which he discovers avarice, selfishness, and utter lack of charity. He outdoes Brecht in his madcap command of all stage tricks and reverently invokes the caustic and critical spirit of Johann Nestroy. His drama form is the grotesque comedy for, as he maintains, our age of computerized fates no longer can give birth to a tragic hero. His humor is black humor and at his best, as in *Ein Engel kommt nach Babylon* (*An Angel Comes to Babylon*, 1954), *Die Ehe des Herrn Mississippi* (*The Marriage of Mr. Mississippi*, 1952), and, above all, *Der Besuch der alten Dame* (*The Visit of the Old Lady*, 1956), it reaches tragic dimensions.

In the Brechtian tradition also are the plays of Peter Weiss (b. 1916). His monstrously titled *Die Verfolgung und Ermordung Jean-Paul Marats dargestellt durch die Schauspielgruppe des Hospizes zu Charenton unter der Anleitung des Herrn de Sade* (*The Persecution and Assassination of Jean-Paul Marat as Performed by the Inmates of the Asylum of Charenton under the Direction of the Marquis de Sade*, 1964) has become like *Die Blechtrommel*, an international success, not so much because of its intrinsic excellence as because of its stunning originality and the great opportunities it offers the director. Here the stage is the primary force and it uses the play almost as the opera uses a libretto. In Weiss' own definition it attempts to present the conflict of extreme individualism and a political and social revolution. In his play *Die Ermittlung* (*The Investigation*, 1966), Weiss enters the popular German documentary theatre. In a literal yet spurious presentation of the Auschwitz trials in Frankfurt all traces of the traditional drama are obliterated. Aspects of the important Austrian *Kulturkritiker* Karl Kraus' (1874–1936) *Die letzten Tage der Menscheit* (*The Last Days of Mankind*, 1922) have left their imprint on it as well as on the popular documentary plays: Rolf Hochhuth, *Der Stellvertreter* (*The Deputy*, 1963); Heinar Kipphardt, *In der Sache J. Robert Oppenheimer*, (1964); Günter Grass, *Die Plebejer proben den Aufstand*, (1966); etc.

Postwar German poetry, too, rejoins avidly the world stream. The great impressions come from abroad; Ezra Pound, T. S. Eliot, the French symbolists and surrealists, Valéry, Hofmannsthal, Rilke, the Expressionists and, above all, Trakl and Benn are recognized as the source for new articulation, for a new canon in a world where "God has no face and no ears," (Borchert). The search for an inner reality, for a faith from within, for an artistic cosmic order in contradiction to surrounding chaos, the search for a nature which responds to the poet's invocations and the urge to write because the loneliness and forsakenness are unbearable in muteness—the painter Paul Klee's tragic lines in his diary, "Ich schaffe pour ne pas pleurer, das ist der letzte und erste Grund," ("I work so as not to cry, this is the last and the first reason,") express poignantly this feeling and are the core of a good deal of this poetry. On the other hand, there is the balladesque poem of Brecht which in its epic form seeks redress for social ills, not in the party line poetry of the East German laureate Johannes R. Becher (1891–1958) but in its accent on the individual and personal incident and fate. There is a great variety and experimentation among the modern poets of West and East Germany, a remarkable degree of decent and creditable writing, but one would be hard put to bestow the accolade of greatness upon any of them. Perhaps the best in the West is Paul Celan (1920–1970) who is also a translator from the French and Russian. The poets that arose after World War II have, with all their personal differences, one thing in common: the disillusionment with any sort of lyrical rendition of a reality. Though there is some renaissance of nature poetry it, too, is imbued with the feeling of being abandoned rather than with that of finding, or even hoping to find, a romantic refuge. Ever since Rilke the tendency to obscurity of an intrinsically personal and hermetic statement is all pervasive. The "concrete poetry" of writers such as Franz Mon, Eugen Gomringer and Ernst Jandl, with its emphasis on the visual aspects of letter arrangement, is reminiscent of some of the experiments of the Dadaists. The modern poet, in continuation of expressionism, is deeply conscious of the intensely musical nature of the poem. However, in contrast to its optimism he dwells in worlds of darkness and forsaken loneliness into which death comes as a welcome redeemer. This uncanny blending of intricate musical form and a melancholy renunciation is perhaps most strikingly evident in Paul Celan's "Todesfuge" in *Mohn und Gedächtnis* (1952). The "black milk of morning" is a metaphoric disguise for the lethal gas of the death chambers of the concentration camps:

SCHWARZE Milch der Frühe wir trinken sie abends
wir trinken sie mittags und morgens wir trinken sie nachts
wir trinken und trinken
wir schaufeln ein Grab in den Lüften da liegt man nicht eng
Ein Mann wohnt im Haus der spielt mit den Schlangen der schreibt
der schreibt wenn es dunkelt nach Deutschland dein goldenes Haar
    Margarete
er schreibt es und tritt vor das Haus und es blitzen die Sterne er pfeift
    seine Rüden herbei
er pfeift seine Juden hervor lässt schaufeln ein Grab in der Erde
er befiehlt uns spielt auf nun zum Tanz

Schwarze Milch der Frühe wir trinken dich nachts
wir trinken dich morgens und mittags wir trinken dich abends
wir trinken und trinken
Ein Mann wohnt im Haus und spielt mit den Schlangen der schreibt
der schreibt wenn es dunkelt nach Deutschland dein goldenes Haar
    Margarete
Dein aschenes Haar Sulamith wir schaufeln ein Grab in den Lüften da
    liegt man nicht eng
Er ruft stecht tiefer ins Erdreich ihr einen ihr andern singet und spielt
er greift nach dem Eisen im Gurt er schwingts seine Augen sind blau
stecht tiefer die Spaten ihr einen ihr andern spielt weiter zum Tanz auf

Schwarze Milch der Frühe wir trinken dich nachts
wir trinken dich mittags und morgens wir trinken dich abends
wir trinken und trinken
ein Mann wohnt im Haus dein goldenes Haar Margarete
dein aschenes Haar Sulamith er spielt mit den Schlangen
Er ruft spielt süsser den Tod der Tod ist ein Meister aus Deutschland
er ruft streicht dunkler die Geigen dann steigt ihr als Rauch in die Luft
dann habt ihr ein Grab in den Wolken da liegt man nicht eng

Schwarze Milch der Frühe wir trinken dich nachts
wir trinken dich mittags der Tod ist ein Meister aus Deutschland
wir trinken dich abends und morgens wir trinken und trinken
der Tod ist ein Meister aus Deutschland sein Auge ist blau
er trifft dich mit bleierner Kugel er trifft dich genau
ein Mann wohnt im Haus dein goldenes Haar Margarete
er hetzt seine Rüden auf uns er schenkt uns ein Grab in der Luft
er spielt mit den Schlangen und träumet der Tod ist ein Meister aus
    Deutschland
dein goldenes Haar Margaete
dein aschenes Haar Sulamith[12]

    Probably the best poet in the East is Johannes Bobrowski (1917–66). The
women rank high with Ingeborg Bachmann (b. 1926) and Marie Louise Kas-
chnitz (b. 1911). Heinz Piontek (b. 1925), Karl Krolow (b. 1915), Hans Egon

Holthusen (b. 1913), Rudolf Hagelstange (b. 1912), Hans Magnus Enzensberger (b. 1929), Günter Eich (b. 1907), and Walter Höllerer (b. 1922) are some of the names that deserve to be mentioned in ever so brief a resume. Nelly Sachs (1891–1970), the touching poetess of the Jewish sorrow, is one of the recipients of the Nobel Prize for literature for 1966.

Where does German literature go from here? Who can venture an answer? The preoccupation with the eternal problems of guilt and of purpose, of time, of life and death in the face of the well-nigh inevitable doom of a world gone mad, the quest for ideas that will create a form, we daresay, will go on as long as man's knowledge of his existence goes on, for better or worse, in Germany or anywhere else.

FOOTNOTES

[1]

Fluttering flags
and joyful throngs.
Highflying wreaths
and victory songs.

Silent somber graves.
Desolation and horror.
Withered wreaths,
Bereaved women.

Ardent embraces
dispelling sharp fears.
Breaking hearts
and dull dry tears.
—K. S. Weimar, trans.

[2]

Goblets on the ground;
Pendant adornments.
Ladies, women
Slender limbs
Wearily sinking;
Bared the breasts,
Loins and hips;
About the foreheads
Traces of wreaths.
—K. S. Waimar, trans.

[3]

And children grow up tall with searching eyes
that know of nothing, grow up to pass away,
and all the people go their ways.

And fruits once tart grow sweet one day
and fall at night like lifeless leaden birds
and lie for days until they wither away.

And still the wind does blow, again and again
we listen and utter many words
and we can feel some pleasure and some pain.

And highways run across the grass; suburbs
are here and there, with torches, trees,
and ominous, deadly, dried-up lakes.

But why have these been built? What makes
them all so unalike? So many names?
What can it mean, the sequence: weddings, wakes?

To what avail is all of this, these games,
to us whom lonely adult lives enclose,
who wander never knowing what our aims?

To what avail to be in all of this at home? . . .
And yet to say "the evening" means so much,
a word from which a sapient sadness flows

like heavy honey from the empty comb.

—K. S. Weimar, trans.

4 At that time Germany, with fever-reddened cheeks, was reeling at the height of wild
triumphs, just about to win the world by virtue of that compact which it was wont to
keep and which it had signed with blood. Today in the embrace of demons, one eye
covered, the other staring into fearful horror, it is plunging down from despair to despair. When will it reach the bottom of the abyss? When will the light of hope dawn from
out of absolute hopelessness, a miracle that surpasses faith? A lonely man folds his hands
and speaks: "May God have mercy on your poor soul, my friends, my fatherland."

5   Up there the image of a world is made
continuously of looking and it prevails.
But every now and then some thing quite unafraid
comes down to him whenever image-veils

he penetrates, down here, unlike his state:
not quite expelled and not accepted,
and half in doubt his own reality incepted
surrenders to the image-correlate,

but only to extend continuously
his face to it with almost imploration,
near to understanding, accommodation,
and yet desisting, else he would not be.

—K. S. Weimar, trans.

6 Who, if I cried out, would hear me of the orders of the Angels? and even if it were that
one would suddenly take me to his heart: I would perish of his more powerful existence.
For beauty is nothing but terror's inception which we can barely stand, and we admire
it so, because it imperturbably disdains to demolish us.

7 The poet avoids radiant sonorities.
He blows upon the tuba, pounds the drum shrill.
He whips the people up with abbreviated sentences. . .

The new, the Holy State
be proclaimed, with blood of nations, blood of their blood inoculated.
Completely let it be formed.
Paradise begins.
Let us extend this electric atmosphere!
Learn! Prepare! Practice!

8 The stones oppose
 Window grins betrayal
 Branches throttle
 Mountains bushes leaf rustley
 Shouting
 Death.
 —K. S. Weimar, trans.

9 A word, a sentence—: ciphers yield
 intelligible life, sudden sense,
 the sun stands still, mute spheres congealed,
 around the word all things condense.

 A word—a flight, a fire, and radiance,
 a flash of flame, an astral zone—
 and once again the dark immense,
 the void around the world and man alone.
 —K. S. Weimar, trans.

10 Why madest thou me, my Lord and God,
 I who rose up, unknowing candle-light,
 And now am here in the wind of my guilt;
 Why madest thou me, my Lord and God,
 For the vanity of the word,
 And that I this should join,
 And bear presumptuous pride,
 And in my own remoteness
 Loneliness?!
 Why madest thou me for this, my Lord and God?

 Why gavest thou me not, why not,
 Two hands of helpfulness,
 And eyes, a sovereign constellation of comfort?
 And a voice of April, raining friendship's music,
 And forehead decked with
 The soft sweet lamp of humbleness?
 And one long stride through countless streets,
 To bear in the evening all the
 Bells of this earth
 Into the heart, the heart of suffering for ever?!

 Behold in fever
 So many little children now in bed,
 And Niobe is stone and can not weep.
 And dark the sinner stares
 Into his heaven's vast delimits.
 And every soul at night falls from
 The tree, a leaf in dream's own fall.
 And all are pressing round some warmth,
 For winter
 And warm is sorrow's season.

 Why, my Lord and God, madest thou me not
 To be thy seraphim, of gold and well received,
 To lay the hand's cool crystal on the fever,

To pass through sobbing doorways in and out?!
How welcome! Hail and greetings:
Sleep, tears, my room, a kiss, communion, childhood, matriarchal?!
And that I sit to rest before the hearth,
A messenger, a flight, anonymous,
And in my hair the dew of thine own countenance!

—K. S, Weimar, trans.

11 Step forth—into the light—out of this night. The big brightness has dawned—darkness is dispersed. From every depth the sevenfold silvery radiance seals—the mighty day of days is without! It proclaimed of him—and sang his praise—and awaited with joyous ebullience the bell which tolled to a celebration—then he lifted the goblet from the table with sure hands and drank with deliberate lips the juice that consumed him. I come from out this night and go into no more night. My eyes are open—I close them no more. My sightless eyes are good to lose it no more: I have seen the new man—in this night he is born! Why is it still difficult to pass on? Does not the surging stream of those to come roar close by me? Does not the throng that thrives thrust by me—past me—forward? Where is there an end? I have been moved into the creative flow—I live—I step forth from today and tomorrow—indefatigible in all—imperishable in all . . .

12 COAL-BLACK milk of morning we drink it at evening
we drink it at noon and at daybreak we drink it at night
we drink and we drink
we shovel a grave in the sky there is room enough there
A man lives in the house he plays with the vipers he writes
he writes when it darkens to Germany your golden hair Marguerite
he writes it and steps out of doors and the stars are shining he whistles for his dogs to
     come
he whistles for his Jews to come out to shovel a grave in the ground
he commands us strike up a tune for the dance

COAL-BLACK milk of morning we drink you at night
we drink you at daybreak and at noon we drink you at evening
we drink and we drink
A man lives in the house and plays with the vipers he writes
he writes when it darkens Germany your golden hair Marguerite
Your ashen hair Shulamite we shovel a grave in the sky there is room enough there
He shouts dig deeper into the earth you here and you there start singing and playing
he clutches the gun in his belt he waves it his eyes are blue
dig deeper your spades you here and you there keep playing that dance tune

COAL-BLACK milk of morning we drink you at night
we drink you at noon and at daybreak we drink you at evening
we drink and we drink
a man lives in the house your golden hair Marguerite
your ashen hair Shulamite he plays with the vipers
He shouts play the death tune sweeter death is a master from Germany
he shouts strike up the fiddles more darkly you'll rise like the smoke to the sky
you'll have your own grave in the clouds there is room enough there

COAL-BLACK milk of morning we drink you at night
we drink you at noon death is a master from Germany
we drink you at evening and at daybreak we drink and we drink
death is a master from Germany his eye is blue
he hits you with bullets of lead his target is you

a man lives in the house your golden hair Marguerite
he sets his dogs after us he gives us a grave in the sky
he plays with the vipers and dreams death is a master from Germany
your golden hair Marguerite
your ashen hair Shulamite   —K. S. Weimar, trans.

BIBLIOGRAPHY

Histories of Modern German Literature and Collections of Essays:

ALKER, ERNST, *Die Deutsche Literatur im 19. Jahrhundert, 1832–1914.* Stuttgart: A. Kröner, 1962. An excellent survey.

BERTAUX, FELIX, *A Panorama of German Literature from 1871 to 1931*, transl. John J. Trounstine. New York: Whittlesey house, McGraw-Hill, 1935. Good for a quick review; somewhat superannuated.

DAVID, CLAUDE, *Von Richard Wagner zu Bertolt Brecht.* Frankfurt: Fischer Bücherei, 1964. Excellent, though very personal.

DEMETZ, PETER, *Postwar German Literature. A Critical Introduction.* New York: Western, 1970. Admirably fulfills the promise of the subtitle.

FRIEDMANN, H., and OTTO MANN (eds.), *Deutsche Literatur im 20. Jahrhundert.* 2 vols. Heidelberg: W. Rothe, 1961. I-*Strukturen*; II-*Gestalten.* Good, but uneven depending on contributor.

GRENZMANN, W., *Deutsche Dichtung der Gegenwart.* Frankfurt a. M.: M. H. F. Menck, 1955. Though a bit out of date still quite readable.

HATFIELD, HENRY, *Modern German Literature: The Major Figures in Context.* London: Edward Arnold, 1966. Very personal but well written and well documented. Good!

NATAN, ALEX (ed.), *German Men of Letters.* II. London: O. Wolff, 1963, III, 1964. On the whole very good scholarship and fine writing.

NAUMANN, HANS, *Die Deutsche Dichtung der Gegenwart, 1885–1923.* Stuttgart: J. B. Metzler, 1923. Still very good in spots—alas, tempi passati.

REICH-RANICKI, MARCEL, *Deutsche Literatur in West und Ost. Prosa seit 1945.* München: Piper, 1966. Provocative and exciting.

RITCHIE, J. M. (ed.), *Periods in German Literature.* London: O. Wolff, 1966. Good and British in its objective detachment.

WEBER, DIETRICH (ed.), *Deutsche Literatur seit 1945.* Stuttgart: Kröner, 1968.

VON WIESE, B. (ed.), *Deutsche Dichter der Moderne: Ihr Leben und Werk.* Berlin: E. Schmidt, 1969. Most contributions are excellent, a fine anthology of essays.

Genres:

NOVEL

ARNTZEN, HELMUT, *Der Moderne Deutsche Roman*. Heidelberg: W. Rothe, 1962. Five essays on five individual great novels and some general observations.

WAIDSON, H. M., *The Modern German Novel: A Mid-Twentieth Century Survey*. London and New York: Oxford Univ. Press, 1959. So far the only treatment in English. Very good on the whole.

DRAMA

GARTEN, H. F., *Modern German Drama*. New York: Grove, 1959. To be well recommended as introduction.

LYRIC

HAMBURGER, M., and C. MIDDELTON (eds.), *Modern German Poetry, 1910–1960*. New York: Grove Press, 1962. Anthology, especially recent poetry, bilingual text with an impossible introduction.

HESELHAUS, CLEMENS, *Deutsche Lyrik der Moderne, von Nietzsche bis Yvan Goll*. Düsseldorf: A. Bagel, 1961. Very good, but one-sided in its preoccupation with form.

Periods:

NATURALISM

SOERGEL, A., *Dichtung und Dichter der Zeit*, ed. Curt Hohoff. vol. 1. Düsseldorf: A. Bagel, 1961. An old war horse rejuvenated, still valuable for out of the way quotations.

IMPRESSIONISM, ETC.

BOWRA, C. M., *The Heritage of Symbolism*. London: Macmillan, 1962. Excellent, though not specifically for German literature.

EXPRESSIONISM

DENKLER, HORST, *Drama des Expressionismus*, Programm Speiltext Theater. München: Fink, 1967. Fine analysis according to most recent scholarship.

FRIEDMANN, H., and OTTO MANN (eds.), *Expressionismus: Gestalten einer literarischen Bewegung*. Heidelberg: W. Rothe, 1956. Collection of essays on individual authors, with varying excellence.

KLARMANN, ADOLF D., "Expressionism in German Literature. A Retrospect of Half a Century." MLQ, 26 (March 1965), 62–92.

MUSCHG, W., *Von Trakl zu Brecht: Dichter des Expressionismus*. München: Piper-Verlag, 1961. Highly personal; excellent, always stimulating.

ROTHE, WOLFGANG (ed.), *Expressionismus als Literatur.* Bern: Francke, 1969. Impressive overview ranging from the penetrating to the rather sketchy; seven essays on aspects of Expressionism (literary preludes, social, technological, and theological dimensions); three genre studies; studies of fourteen lyric poets, twelve dramatists, eight prose writers; four essays on the Dada postlude; with bibliographies for each contribution.

SAMUEL, RICHARD, and THOMAS R. HINTON, *Expressionism in German Life, Literature and the Theatre (1910–1924).* Cambridge: W. Heffer, 1939. An early study of the field, good, with limitation of time.

SOERGEL, A., *Dichtung und Dichter der Zeit,* ed. Curt Hohoff. vol. 2. Düsseldorf: A. Bagel, 1963.

SOKEL, WALTER H., *The Writer in Extremis: Expressionism in Twentieth-Century German Literature.* Stanford, Calif.: Stanford Univ. Press, 1959. The best book on Expressionism, tends in spots to be too personal.

WILLETT, JOHN, *Expressionism.* New York: McGraw-Hill, 1970. Copiously illustrated and documented general introduction to Expressionism in all the arts; with all the merits, and encyclopedic distractions, of the survey.

RECENT

"German Writing Today," *London Times Literary Supplement* Sept. 23, 1960, I-XX. Excellent brief survey.

FLORES, JOHN, *Poetry in East Germany.* New Haven: Yale Univ. Press, 1971. Interesting triadic thesis: adjustments (Stephen Hermlin, Franz Fühmann); visions (P. Huchel, J. Bobrowski); revisions (Kunert, Braun, Mickel, Biermann); well written and well argued.

BIBLIOGRAPHY OF INDIVIDUAL WRITERS

Gottfried Benn

LOHNER, EDGAR, *Passion und Intellekt: die Lyrik Gottfried Benns.* Neuwied: Luchterhand, 1961.

Bertolt Brecht

DEMETZ, PETER (ed.), *Brecht.* A Collection of Critical Essays. Englewood Cliffs: Prentice-Hall, 1962.

ESSLIN, MARTIN, *Brecht: A Choice of Evils.* London: Eyre & Spottiswoode, 1959.

GRAY, RONALD, *Bertolt Brecht.* New York: Grove, 1961.

GRIMM, REINHOLD, *Bertolt Brecht.* Stuttgart: Metzler, 1961.

WILLETT, JOHN, *The Theatre of Bertolt Brecht.* London: Methuen, 1959.

Hermann Broch

DURZAK, MANFRED, *Hermann Broch*. Hamburg: Rowohlt, 1966.

STRELKA, JOSEPH, *Kafka, Musil, Broch und die Entwicklung des modernen Romans*. Wien: Forum, 1959.

WEIGAND, HERMANN, "Broch's *'Death of Vergil'*: Program Notes," PMLA, 62, (June, 1947), 525–54.

ZIOLKOWSKI, THEODROE, *Hermann Broch*. New York: Columbia Univ. Press, 1964.

Friedrich Dürrenmatt

BÄNZIGER, HANS, *Frisch und Dürrenmatt*. Bern: Francke, 1962.

KLARMANN, ADOLF, D., "Friedrich Dürrenmatt and the Tragic Sense of Comedy," *Tulane Drama Review*, 4, (Summer 1960), 77–104.

Stefan George

BENNETT, E. K., *Stefan George*. Cambridge: Bowes and Bowes, 1954.

DAVID, CLAUDE, *Stefan George*. (Übertragen aus dem Französischen von Alexa Remmen und Karl Thiemer) München: Hanser, 1967.

SCHULTZ, H. STEFAN, *Studien zur Dichtung Stefan Georges*. Heidelberg: Lothar Stiehm, 1967.

Gerhart Hauptmann

BEHL, C. F. W., *Gerhart Hauptmanns Leben; Chronik und Bild*. Berlin: Suhrkamp, 1942.

GARTEN, H. F., *Gerhart Hauptmann*. New Haven: Yale Univ. Press, 1954.

Hermann Hesse

ZELLER, BERNHARD (ed.), *Hermann Hesse* in Selbstzeugnissen und Bilddokumenten. Hamburg: Rowohlt, 1963.

ZIOLKOWSKI, THEODORE, *The Novels of Hermann Hesse*. A Study in Theme and Structure. Princeton: Princeton Univ. Press, 1965.

Georg Heym

KRISPYN, EGBERT, *Georg Heym. Reluctant Rebel*. Gainesville: Univ. of Florida Press, 1968.

MAUTZ, KURT, *Mythologie und Gesellschaft im Expressionismus. Die Dichtung Georg Heyms*. Frankfurt a/M: Athenäum, 1961.

SCHNEIDER, KARL LUDWIG, *Der bildhafte Ausdruck in den Dichtungen Georg Heyms, Georg Trakls, und Ernst Stadler:* Studien zum lyrischen Sprachstil des deutschen Expressionismus. Heidelberg: Winter, 1954.

Hugo von Hofmannsthal

ALEWYN, RICHARD, *Über Hugo von Hofmannsthal*. Göttingen: Vandenhoeck & Ruprecht, 1964.

EXNER, RICHARD, *Hugo von Hofmannsthals "Lebenslied". Eine Studie*. Heidelberg: Winter, 1964.

HAMMELMANN, HANNS A., *Hugo von Hofmannsthal*. New Haven: Yale Univ. Press, 1957.

Franz Kafka

GRAY, RONALD (ed.), *Kafka. A Collection of Critical Essays*. Englewood Cliffs: Prentice-Hall, 1962.

POLITZER, HEINZ, *Franz Kafka. Parable and Paradox*. Ithaca: Cornell Univ. Press, 1962.

SOKEL, WALTER, *Franz Kafka. Tragik und Ironie: Zur Struktur seiner Kunst*. München: A. Langen, 1964.

Georg Kaiser

FRUCHTER, MOSES J., *The Social Dialectic in Georg Kaiser's Dramatic Works*. Phila. 1933.

KENWORTHY, BRIAN J., *Georg Kaiser*. Oxford: Blackwell, 1957.

PAULSEN, WOLFGANG, *Georg Kaiser. Die Perspektiven seines Werkes*. Tübingen: M. Niemeyer, 1960.

Detlev von Liliencron

SCHUMANN, DETLEV W., "Detlev von Liliencron (1844–1909). An Attempt at an Interpretation and Evaluation." *Monatshefte*, 36, (Dec. 1944/Feb. 1945), 385–408; 65–87.

Thomas Mann

BRENNAN, JOSEPH G., *Three Philosophical Novelists: James Joyce, Andre Gide, Thomas Mann*. New York: Macmillan, 1964.

CHURCH, MARGARET, *Time and Reality. Studies in Contemporary Fiction*. Chapel Hill: Univ. of North Carolina Press, 1963 (incl. Joyce, Woolf, Huxley, Faulkner, Wolfe, T. Mann, Kafka, Sartre, Proust, Bergson).

HATFIELD, HENRY (ed.), *Thomas Mann. A Collection of Critical Essays*. Englewood Cliffs: Prentice-Hall, 1964.

HELLER, ERICH, *The Ironic German, a Study of Thomas Mann*. Boston: Little, Brown, 1958.

Robert Musil

BAUMANN, GERHART, *Robert Musil*. Bern: Francke, 1965.

KAISER, ERNST and WILKINS, EITHNE, *Robert Musil. Eine Einführung in das Werk*. Stuttgart: Kohlhammer, 1962.

PIKE, BURTON, *Robert Musil. An Introduction to his Work.* Ithaca: Cornell Univ. Press, 1961.

TROMMLER, FRANK, *Roman und Wirklichkeit.* Eine Ortsbestimmung am Beispiel von Musil, Broch, Roth, Doderer und Gütersloh. Stuttgart: Kohlhammer, 1966.

Rainer Maria Rilke

BUTLER, ELIZA M., *Rainer Maria Rilke.* Cambridge: The Univ. Press, 1946.

SIMENAUER, ERICH, *Rainer Maria Rilke; Legende und Mythos.* Bern: P. Haupt, 1953.

WOOD, FRANK H., *Rainer Maria Rilke: the ring of forms.* Minneapolis: Univ. of Minnesota Press, 1958.

Georg Trakl

BASIL, OTTO, *Georg Trakl* in Selbstzeugnissen und Bilddokumenten. Hamburg: Rowohlt, 1965.

WETZEL, HEINZ, *Klang und Bild in den Dichtungen Georg Trakls.* Göttingen: Vandenhoeck & Ruprecht, 1968. (See also Schneider and anthologies of essays above.)

Franz Werfel

BRASELMANN, WERNER, *Franz Werfel.* Wuppertal: Emil Müller, 1960.

KLARMANN, A. D., *Das Reich der Mitte.* Graz: Stiasny, 1961. (Introduction)

KLARMANN, A. D., "Franz Werfel's Eschatology and Cosmogony," *MLQ,* 7, (Dec. 1946) 385–410.

PUTTKAMER, ANNEMARIE VON, *Franz Werfel. Wort und Antwort.* Würzburg:Werkbund Verlag, 1952.

SPECHT, RICHARD, *Franz Werfel.* Versuch einer Zeitspiegelung. Wien: Zsolnay, 1926.

GENERAL BIBLIOGRAPHY

Reference Works and Bibliographies

ARNOLD, ROBERT F., *Allgemeine Bücherkunde zur neueren deutschen Literaturgeschichte*. Berlin: W. de Gruyter Co., 1966. (4th ed. by Herbert Jacob). Book titles on world literature and especially on German literature in all its ramifications, on biography, bibliography, and fields (like music and philosophy) related to it.

BRAAK, IVO, *Poetik in Stichworten*. Literaturwissenschaftliche Grundbegriffe. Kiel: F. Hirt, 1969³. Excellent for quick orientation; precise definitions, copious examples, with references to pertinent literature.

EPPELSHEIMER, HANNS W., and CLEMENS KOTTELWESCH, *Bibliographie der deutschen Literaturwissenschaft. 1945—*. Frankfurt am Main: Klostermann, 1957ff. Indispensable guide to publications since the war.

GREGOR, JOSEPH, *Der Schauspielführer*, 8 vols. Stuttgart: Hiersemann, 1953ff. Handy, helpful reference; first two volumes give characterization and summaries of German plays from Middle Ages to Expressionism; volumes 7 and 8 same of plays of world literature from ca. 1920 to 1963.

HANSEL, JOHANNES, *Bücherkunde für Germanisten* (Studienausgabe). Berlin: Erich Schmidt, 1968⁵. New editions keep this valuable reference tool up to date; see especially reference to histories of German language and literature (general, acc. to eras, genres, etc.), list of pertinent magazines, etc.

HANSEL, JOHANNES, *Personalbibliographie zur deutschen Literaturgeschichte* (Studienausgabe). Berlin: Erich Schmidt, 1967. Bibliography of bibliographies for 300 authors from the Middle Ages to the present; also information on literary remains.

KAYSER, W., H. RÜDIGER, and E. KOPPEN, *Kleines literarisches Lexikon*, 3 vols. Bern: Francke, 1966[4]. Precise, accurate characterizations of authors (I and II) and definitions of literary terms, movements, etc. (III).

KÖRNER, JOSEF, *Bibliographisches Handbuch des deutschen Schrifttums*. Bern: Francke, 1949[3]. The most important single-volume bibliographical tool.

KOSCH, WILHELM, *Deutsches Literatur-Lexikon*, 4 vols. Bern: Francke, 1949–58[2], 1963ff[3]. Concise information on critical concepts, metrics, authors, scholars, titles, etc.: bibliographical information, valuable though not always absolutely accurate.

MERKER, PAUL, and WOLFGANG STAMMLER, *Reallexikon der deutschen Literaturgeschichte*, 4 vols. Berlin: W. de Gruyter Co., 1925–26, 1955ff[2]. Brief discussions (many excellent, some just adequate) of genres, literary and critical concepts, by experts in the field: bibliographies.

OLBRICH, WILHELM, *Der Romanführer*, 13 vols. Stuttgart: Hiersemann, 1950f. Judiciously brief plot summaries of German novels and novelle from the Barock to 1963 (in vols. 1–5 and 13).

Literature

GENERAL

BITHELL, JETHRO, *Germany. A Companion to German Studies*. London: Methuen, 1955[5]. Fourteen essays on language, literature, history, thought, and the arts, ranging from adequate to very good; somewhat impaired by the odd limitation that all contributors be British-born.

BOESCH, BRUNO, *Deutsche Literaturgeschichte in Grundzügen*. Bern: Francke, 1967[3]. Twelve epochs, each treated by a specialist; the Swiss view is stressed: quality is somewhat uneven.

DAEMMRICH, H. S. (ed.), *The Challenge of German Literature*. Detroit: Wayne State University, 1971. Ten essays, from courtly literature to literature since 1933; the somewhat encyclopedic coverage and introductory nature obstruct the fulfillment of the title's promise.

FRENZEL, HERBERT A., and ELISABETH, *Daten deutscher Dichtung*. I. *Von den Anfängen bis zur Romantik*. paperback München: dtv 28, 1966[3] II. *Vom Biedermeier bis zur Gegenwart*. München, dtv 54, 1966[3]. The most concise survey with useful summaries of individual works as well as of the intellectual situation of each period. (2 vols. bound in one: Köln-Berlin; Kiepenheuer Witsch, 1962.[3])

FRICKE, G., and V. KLOTZ, *Geschichte der deutschen Dichtung*. Hamburg-Lübeck: Matthiesen, 1949[1] (many editions). Very good one-volume history, including an amazing amount of information.

HAMBURGER, MICHAEL, *Contraries. Studies in German Literature*. New York: Dutton, 1970. Collection of 11 excellent studies ranging from Hölderlin and the Romantics to Nietzsche, Mann, and the Expressionists.

HELLER, ERICH, *The Disinherited Mind*. Essays in Modern German literature and thought. New York: Farrar, Strauss and Cudahy, 1957. Nine essays extending from Goethe and the Idea of Scientific Truth to The Hazard of Modern Poetry, distinguished by provocative, beautifully formulated insights.

MARTINI, FRITZ, *Deutsche Literaturgeschichte von den Anfängen bis zur Gegenwart*. Stuttgart: Kröner, 1960[10]. A handy guide, not entirely free of bias: very useful bibliographies.

ROBERTSON, JOHN G., *A History of German Literature*, rev. Edna Purdie. New York: British Book Center, 1959[4] (originally 1902). Objective presentation from an essentially nineteenth century viewpoint, updated in successive revisions.

ROSE, ERNST, *A History of German Literature*. New York: New York University Press, 1960. Stresses aesthetic criteria and presents German literature against a background of cultural history.

STAMMLER, WOLFGANG, *Deutsche Philologie im Aufriss*. Berlin: E. Schmidt. I. 1957[2]. Articles on methodolgy, language, and dialects; especially useful F. Martini on "Poetics" and E. Frenzel on "Stoff- und Motivgeschichte"; II. 1960[2]. on the various genres; III. 1962[2]. on influences on German literature, folklore, language in modern communications media (except TV!).

WILPERT, GERO VON, *Deutsche Literatur in Bildern*. Stuttgart: Kröner, 1957. Fascinating collection of portraits, photographs, manuscripts, title pages, etc.

Genres

POETRY

FRIEDRICH, HUGO, *Die Struktur der modernen Lyrik*. Von Baudelaire bis zur Gegenwart. Hamburg: Rowohlt, 1957[2]. Very important study; examination of French Symbolists and modern European poets; characteristics of the "modern": depersonalization, dissonance, dictatorial fantasy, etc.

KLEIN, JOHANNES, *Geschichte der deutschen Lyrik von Luther bis zum Ausgang des Zweiten Weltkrieges*. Wiesbaden: F. Steiner, 1957. Monumental survey; commentaries on individual texts; tends too much to facile categorizing.

PRAWER, S. S., *German Lyric Poetry;* a critical analysis of selected poems from Klopstock to Rilke. London: Routledge & Paul, 1952. Perceptive, stimulating interpretations of individual poems.

VON WIESE, B. (ed.) *Die deutsche Lyrik; Form und Geschichte*. Düsseldorf: A. Bagel, 1956. Two volumes of interpretations of more than 90 poems, from the Medieval to Brecht; varying in quality from mediocre to first-rate.

DRAMA

GUTHKE, KARL S., *Modern Tragicomedy*. An Investigation into the Nature of the Genre. N.Y.: Random, 1966. The history and theory illustrated with examples from general European literature; special consideration of Ibsen's *The Wild Duck*.

MANN, OTTO, *Geschichte des deutschen Dramas*. Stuttgart: Kröner, 1960. Best available one volume history; factual and conservative; helpful capsule bibliographies.

VON WIESE, B (ed)., *Das deutsche Drama vom Barock bis zur Gegenwart;* Interpretationen. Düsseldorf: A. Bagel, 1958. Uniformly excellent interpretations in 2 volumes; I selects 21 plays from J. Bidermann to Grillparzer; II examines 23 plays from Raimund to Dürrenmatt.

THE NOVEL

LÄMMERT, EBERHARD, *Bauformen des Erzählens*. Stuttgart: Metzler, 1955. Impressive analysis of narrative techniques: action, point of view, time and tense, dimensions of voice, etc.; pregnant bibliography.

LUKÁCS, GEORG, *Die Theorie des Romans. Ein geschichtsphilosophischer Versuch über die Formen der grossen Epik*. Neuwied: Luchterhand, 1963. Though written in 1914 and disowned even by its author, an important theoretical work; a dialectic approach based on Hegel and Kierkegaard.

PASCAL, ROY. *The German Novel, Studies*. Manchester: University Press, 1956. Good commentary on four *Bildungsromane* (*Meister, Grüner Heinrich, Nachsommer, Zauberberg*) and 5 novelists (Gotthelf, Raabe, Fontane, Kafka, Th. Mann) largely against background of the English novel.

VON WIESE (ed.), *Der deutsche Roman vom Barock bis zur Gegenwart;* Struktur und Geschichte. Düsseldorf: A. Bagel, 1963. Interpretive essays in 2 volumes: I treats 9 novels (from *Simplicissimus* to *Münchhausen*); II examines 10 novels (from Gotthelf to Musil).

THE NOVELLE

BENNETT, E. K., *A History of the German Novelle*. (revised and continued by H. M. Waidson) Cambridge: University Press, 1965. A slightly faded classic (originally: From Goethe to T. Mann, 1934) updated by addition of 2 chapters (Short Story and 20th Century scene)

KLEIN, JOHANNES, *Geschichte der deutschen Novelle, von Goethe bis zur Gegenwart*. Wiesbaden: F. Steiner, 1960[4]. Seeks to establish nature and types of *Novelle* from Goethe to Le Fort and Friedrich Georg Jünger; historical survey with hundreds of plot summaries and capsule bibliographies.

VON WIESE, B., *Die deutsche Novelle von Goethe bis Kafka*. Interpretationen. Düsseldorf: A. Bagel, 1959. Opens with concise characterization of the *Novelle*, then 17 penetrating essays on representative novelle from 1785 to 1924; with very useful bibliography.

Periodicals

Germanistik. Tübingen: M. Niemeyer. Quarterly: extremely valuable, often critical compilation of publications in the whole field.

PMLA. Wisconsin: G. Banta Co. Annual bibliography issue: selected list of useful books and articles (compiled from more than 1000 periodicals). Annually précis culled from some 150 journals are collected in the *MLA Abstracts*.

For list of journals see J. Hansel, *Bücherkunde für Germanisten (op. cit.)* Section V (Zeitschriften).

Index

Abraham a Santa Clara, 103
Ackermann (der) aus Böhmen, 91
Alexanderlied, 78
Anacreontics, 106-7
"Angelus Silesius," 101

Barlach, Ernst, 332-33
Baroque, 95-104
Beast epic, 90
Becher, Johannes R., 323-24
Benn, Gottfried, 326-27
Bergengrün, Werner, 335
Biedermeier, 211, 214-15, 259
Bildungsroman, 270-71
Bismarck, Otto von, 225
Blut und Boden, 334
Bobrowski, Johannes, 344
Bodmer, Johann Jakob, 106, 109
Böhme, Jacob, 100-101
Böll, Heinrich, 339
Boniface, Saint, 66
Borchert, Wolfgang, 341
Brant, Sebastian, 90
Brecht, Bertolt, 341-42
Breitinger, Johann Jakob, 106, 109
Brentano, Clemens, 194-204

Broch, Hermann, 336, 337-38
Brockes, Barthold Heinrich, 105
Büchner, Georg, 236-45

Carmina Burana, 72
Celan, Paul, 343-44
Cenodoxus, 100
Chamisso, Louis Charles Adelaide, 214-15
Concrete poetry, 343

Dada, 324
Däubler, Ernst, 325
Dehmel, Richard, 314-15
Döblin, Alfred, 333-34, 336
Documentary theatre, 342
Doderer, Heimito von, 336, 338
Droste-Hülshoff, Annette von, 289
Dürrenmatt, Friedrich, 342

Easter play of Muri, 87
Ecbasis captivi, 71
Eckhart, Johannes (Meister), 86
Eichendorff, Josef Freiherr von, 211-14
Ekkehard of St. Gall, 69-70
Enlightenment, 104-9
Erasmus, Desiderius, 92
Ernst, Paul, 321
Expressionism, 322-27, 329-34

Fallada, Hans, 334
Fastnachtsspiele, 87-88
Fate tragedies, 198
Faust, 154-57
Fausten, Historia von D., 89
Fichte, Johann Gottlieb, 185, 191, 216 n. 2, 251
Fischart, Johann, 94-95
Fleming, Paul, 98-99
Folksong, 88-89
Fontane, Theodor, 276-86
Frisch, Max, 338-39, 342

Gellert, Christian Fürchtegott, 107

George, Stefan, 315-16
German language
  borrowings, 55-59
  dialects, modern, 43-45
  dictionaries, 61
  East Middle German, 51-52
  Gothic, 36-38
  grammar
    ablaut, 40
    adjectives, 17
    adverbs, 20
    auxiliary verbs, 17-18
    conjunctions, 19-20
    consonants, 11-12
    determiners, 19
    infinitive clauses, 30
    infinitive phrases, 30-31
    nouns, 16
    prepositions, 19
    pronouns, 18
    question words, 20
    sentence types, 20-22
    spelling, 10, 13
    stress, 13-14
    subjunctive, 32-33
    subordinate clauses, 28-29
    umlaut, 9, 48-49, 53
    verbs, 15-16
    vowels, 8-9
    word order, 22-26
  Grimm's Law, 39-40
  Hochdeutsch, 4-6
  Hochsprache, 2-7
  Low German, 4
  Middle High German, 48-51
  Niederdeutsch, 4
  Old High German, 37, 45-49, 65-69
  Old Low German (Old Saxon), 37
  Plattdeutsch, 4
  Proto-Germanic, 37
  Schriftsprache, 2
  Standard German, 2-7
  Verner's Law, 40
Gessner, Salomon, 106
Gleim, Johann Wilhelm Ludwig, 106, 107-8
Goethe, Johann Wolfgang von, 125-28, 141-58, 160, 185-87, 189
Goths, 42-43, 65-66

Gottfried von Strasbourg, 82-83
Gottsched, Johann Christoph, 54, 106, 108-9
Götz, Nicolaus, 106
Grass, Günter, 339, 340
Grillparzer, Franz, 225-28
Grimmelshausen, Hans Christof von, 102-3
Gruppe 47, 339
Gryphius, Andreas, 99-100
Günther, Christian, 104
Gütersloh, Albert Paris, 336, 338

Hagedorn, Friedrich von, 106, 107
Haller, Albrecht, 105-6
Hardenberg, Friedrich von. *See* Novalis
Hartmann von Aue, 79-80
Hauptmann, Gerhart, 310, 311-13
Hebbel, Friedrich, 228-34
Heine, Heinrich, 188-89, 208, 211, 215, 245-57
Heinrich von Morungen, 74-75
Heinrich von Veldeke, 79
Heliand, 68
Herder, Johann Gottfried, 136-38
Hesse, Hermann, 313, 318-19
Heym, Georg, 325-26
Hildebrandslied, 67-68
Hiller, Kurt, 323
Hoddis, Jakob van, 326
Hoffmann, E. T. A., 204-8
Hofmannsthal, Hugo von, 317-18
Hofmannswaldau, Christian Hofmann von, 103
Hölderlin, Friedrich, 175-82, 296
Holz, Arno, 311, 314
Hrotsvita, 71
Huch, Ricarda, 320-21
Humanism, 90-95
Hutten, Ulrich von, 92

Jahnn, Hanns Henny, 335
Johnson, Uwe, 339-40
Jünger, Ernst, 334

Kafka, Franz, 335-36
Kaiser, Georg, 230, 331-32

Kant, Immanuel, 161-62, 166, 251
Kasack, Hermann, 335
Keller, Gottfried, 269-76
Klassik, 146-50, 151, 162-65
Kleist, Heinrich von, 165-68
Klopstock, Friedrich Gottlieb, 138-39
Kürenberg, 73

Langgässer, Elisabeth, 334-35
Lasker-Schüler, Else, 325
Le Fort, Gertrud von, 334
Leibnitz, Gottfried Wilhelm, 104
Lenz, J. M. R., 237
Lessing, Gotthold Ephraim, 131-36
Liliencron, Detlev von, 314
Lohenstein, Daniel Casper von, 103
Luther, Martin, 51-52, 92-94

Mann, Heinrich, 315, 333
Mann, Thomas, 278, 279, 319-20, 321
Marx, Karl, 225, 233-34, 252
Meier Helmbrecht, 83
Meistergesang, 88
Merseburger Zaubersprüche, 68
Meyer, Conrad Ferdinand, 288-89
Mörike, Eduard, 257-64
Moscherosch, Hans Michael, 103
Musil, Robert, 336-37
Mysticism, 86, 101

Naturalism, 310-13
Neithart von Reuental, 78
Neoclassicism, 310
Neoromanticism, 307
Nestroy, Johann, 234-36
Nibelungenlied, 83-85
Nietzsche, Friedrich Wilhelm, 289-97, 315, 316
Notker Balbulus, 86
Notker "Labeo" or "Teutonicus," 46-47, 71
Novalis, 190-94

Opitz, Martin, 97-98, 99, 101

Otfried, 69

Pauli, Johannes, 89
Pietism, 105

Realism, 223
Reformation, 90-95
Reinke de Vos, 90
Reinmar von Hagenau, 73-74
Reuchlin, Johannes, 91-92
Reuter, Christian, 103
Rilke, Rainer Maria, 321-22
Runes, 66
Ruodlieb, 70-71

Sachs, Hans, 87-88
Sachs, Nelly, 345
Scheffler, Johannes, 101
Schilda, 89
Schiller, Friedrich, 158-65
Schlegel, August Wilhelm, 188-89
Schlegel, Friedrich, 185-89
Schnitzler, Arthur, 316-17
Schopenhauer, Arthur, 288, 293-95
Schwänke, 89
Spee, Friedrich von, 101
Sprüche, 76
Stabreim, 67
Stadler, Ernst, 325
Stehr, Hermann, 313
Sternheim, Carl, 331
Stifter, Adalbert, 264-69
Storm, Theodor, 287
Stramm, August, 324
Sturm und Drang, 146-48, 159-60

"Tagelied," 74
Tatian, 45-47
Tieck, Ludwig, 208-11
Till Eulenspiegel, 89
Toller, Ernst, 332
Trakl, Georg, 326

Ulfilas, 65-66
Unruh, Fritz von, 332
Uz, Johann Peter, 106

Wagner, Richard, 295-96
Walser, Martin, 339, 340-41
Waltharius manu fortis, 69-70
Walther von der Vogelweide, 75-78, 83, 90
Wassermann, Jakob, 313
Wedekind, Frank, 329-31
Weiss, Peter, 342-43
Werfel, Franz, 323, 327-29
Wickram, Jörg, 94
Wiechert, Ernst, 334
Wieland, Christoph Martin, 139-41
Winckelmann, Johann Joachim, 128-31
Wittenweiler, 90
Wolff, Christian, 104
Wolfram von Eschenbach, 80-82

"Young Germany," 215

Zesen, Philipp von, 103
Zigler, Heinrich Anselm von, 103
Zuckmayer, Carl, 334